God's Decree and Man's Destiny

Gerald Bonner

Gerald Bonner

God's Decree and Man's Destiny

Studies on the Thought of Augustine of Hippo

VARIORUM REPRINTS
London 1987

British Library CIP data

Bonner, Gerald
God's decree and man's destiny: studies
on the thought of Augustine of Hippo. —
(Collected studies series; CS255)
1. Augustine, *Saint, Bishop of Hippo*
I. Title
270.2′092′4   BR1720.A9

ISBN 0–86078–203–4

Published in Great Britain by

Variorum Reprints
20 Pembridge Mews London W11 3EQ

Printed in Great Britain by

Galliard (Printers) Ltd
Great Yarmouth Norfolk

VARIORUM REPRINT CS255

CS255

CONTENTS

This volume contains xvi + 294 pages.

PUBLISHER'S NOTE

The articles in this volume, as in all others in the Collected Studies Series, have not been given a new, continuous pagination. In order to avoid confusion, and to facilitate their use where these same studies have been referred to elsewhere, the original pagination has been maintained wherever possible.

Each article has been given a Roman number in order of appearance, as listed in the Contents. This number is repeated on each page and quoted in the index entries.

TO THE
INSTITUTUM PATRISTICUM AUGUSTINIANUM
AND THE
COLLEGIO INTERNAZIONALE AGOSTINIANO S. MONICA
AT ROME
THESE COLLECTED PAPERS ARE
RESPECTFULLY DEDICATED
AS AN EXPRESSION OF GRATITUDE
FOR MUCH KINDNESS

PREFACE

These twelve essays were published over a period of a quarter of a century, between 1959 and 1984. Despite the length of time during which they were composed, and the fact that, in the best tradition of Augustine himself, they were largely occasional pieces, designed to answer particular requests, there is a coherence among them, in that they represent two apparently conflicting aspects of Augustine's thought: Augustine the contemplative theologian and spiritual master; and Augustine the teacher of Predestination, who holds that only a very small part of the human race will be saved, with the rest being left in the mass of perdition. The former aspect is the theme of the earlier papers, the latter of the last five. In these I have been primarily concerned with the historical circumstances of the Pelagian Controversy which led to the expression of Augustine's predestinarian theology in its final and most uncompromising form — indeed, the Augustine Lecture of 1970: *Augustine and Modern Research on Pelagianism* (No XI) attempts to provide an outline for a modern history of the Pelagian Controversy — partly because the theological aspect has been discussed in my book *St Augustine of Hippo: Life and Controversies* (London 1963; 2nd ed. Norwich 1986), but even more because the work of scholars over the past hundred years has revealed the enormous quantity of historical material available which needs to be analysed and evaluated before anything like a comprehensive history of Pelagianism can be attempted. Indeed, the publication in 1981 by Johannes Divjak of a hitherto unknown collection of Augustinian letters, two of which are discussed in No XII, is a warning against any supposition that all the evidence must by now be inevitably available.

The earlier articles are more theological. They arise, in part, from a long interest in the Eastern Orthodox Church, whose theologians have often seen Augustine as a symbol of disunity between East and West. This has led me to give particular consideration to two doctrines which are commonly alleged by the Orthodox to constitute major theological differences between Greek and Latin Christianity, namely the Double Procession of the Holy Spirit from the Father and the Son in the economy of the Trinity, of which Augustine is said to be the author; and the concept of Deification, which is sometimes asserted, in the West as well as in the East, to be peculiar to Greek theology, with the Latins preferring to speak of Justification by Faith. I have examined Augustine's teaching on the Double Procession in the essay 'St Augustine's Doctrine of the Holy Spirit' (No V) and have argued that, while Augustine certainly teaches a doctrine of double procession, he does so in a way which does not conflict with the teaching of the Greek Fathers, and avoids those theological pitfalls which are commonly alleged by the Orthodox to spring from it. The concept of Deification is mentioned in my first three papers (it is discussed at greater length in an article which is due to appear in the *Journal of Theological Studies* in October 1986[1]). Here, the evidence that Augustine does speak of deification is overwhelming, and has been available since Victorino Capánaga published his magisterial article on the subject in 1954.[2] It is, however, a fact of life in the humanities that information which is a commonplace for the specialist often takes a long time to come to the notice of scholars working in neighbouring fields. I can only hope that my reiteration of what Augustinian scholars may take for granted will be noticed by those for whom the views of Augustine are of interest as a principal representative of Western patristic theology. More than most authors Augustine has been the object of unjustified denunciation by those who have not read him.

This being said, it remains true that Augustine is a cause of offence to many who actually have read his works and do not denounce him from the strong position of dogmatic ignorance. His eventual approval of the coercion of religious schismatics, after he had previously opposed it; his gloomy teaching about human sexuality, after a youth which had fallen short of the highest standards of Christian chastity; and above all his predestinarian theology, which is for all practical purposes equivalent to Calvinism, have aroused violent reactions in readers who have nevertheless appreciated the greatness of Augustine's personality. 'Sex and sin are ... two watchwords of Augustinianism, two pillars of its temple,' wrote one critic, who could elsewhere admit that 'Augustine possessed endowments, at once intellectual and spiritual, of a kind before unknown in the West and unsurpassed even in the East.'[3] It is necessary that any serious student of Augustine should recognise, and not attempt to palliate, the harsher side of Augustine's thought.

Yet there is that other aspect of Augustine, illustrated in a study like Dr Isobelle Bochet's *Saint Augustin et le désir de Dieu* (Paris 1982), which admirably depicts the optimism and the dynamism (a

word which not infrequently appears in Dr Bochet's text) of
Augustine's notion of the human soul in its striving for the Vision of
God. It is this other aspect with which my first three articles are
concerned, and in them I have tried to bring out those qualities
which recommend Augustine as a teacher for those who are seeking
to follow the Christian way. Here I have sought to show the positive
side of Augustine's teaching, and its ecclesial exemplification in his
eucharistic theology (No VI), in which the Church, which is the
Body of Christ, is offered to the Father by Christ, the great High
Priest, of whom the human priest is but the minister; and to draw
attention to the fact that, in Augustine's view, following African
tradition, the eucharist, which is 'the sacrifice of our redemption,' is
to be offered for the departed, so that in its action the living and the
dead are both comprehended. St Monica's death-bed plea to be
remembered at the Lord's altar is one which, through her son, has
become familiar to succeeding generations.

Over the years I have become increasingly conscious of the
apparent incompatibility of the two aspects of Augustine's thought
which I have described. They are not, it is true, absolutely
incompatible. One can understand Augustine's notion of the desire
of God as a natural endowment of man ('Thou hast made us for
Thyself, and our heart is restless until it may repose in Thee') in such
as way as to believe that it is to the elect, and to the elect alone, that
Augustine's contemplative teaching applies. This may indeed have
been Augustine's own thought, if we remember the terrifying
observation in his Letter 190, written in 418, that God, by creating so
many men who, He foreknew, would not have any part in His grace,
thereby wished to show, by the very multitude of the lost, that their
great number was of no concern to Him.[4] Such teaching aroused
opposition among catholic Christians even in Augustine's own day.
John Cassian of Marseilles and his supporters declined to endorse
Augustine's denial of God's intention to save all men. 'If God does
not will that one of His little ones should perish,' wrote Cassian,
'how can we imagine, without the greatest sacrilege, that He does
not will all men, but only some in the place of all, to be saved? Those
who perish, therefore, whoever they may be, perish against God's
will.'[5] Cassian's protest against Augustine was uttered in the name of
Augustine's earlier and more optimistic theology, which had in large
measure disappeared from his later works, in which the sense of
God's irresistible power finally triumphed over Augustine's earlier
emphasis on God's love and human freedom. It is true that

Augustine, to the end, paradoxically defended human freedom in the interest of moral responsibility; but, from the individual's point of view, that freedom, in the face of the Divine Omnipotence which elects some to salvation and leaves the rest to reprobation, can at best be only a very limited and circumscribed endowment.

It has been argued that theologically speaking there are two Augustines: the earlier teacher, who proclaimed the freedom of the will; and the later Doctor of Grace and defender of Predestination. Like all generalisations, this is open to criticism on points of detail; but it is difficult not to feel that the intellectual conversion-experience which occurred while Augustine was replying to the question of Simplicianus of Milan in 396, and to which Augustine, at the end of his life, repeatedly appealed as evidence of his anti-Pelagian views long before Pelagius appeared on the scene (XI,63 note[43]), marks a stage in the development of his thought hardly less significant than his decision to seek Catholic baptism, in a garden at Milan in 386. His often-quoted remark in the *Retractationes* (II,1[27]): 'In the solution of this question I laboured for the free choice of the human will, but the grace of God conquered,' is not simply an effective epigram, but needs to be taken in all seriousness. Augustine's conviction of the absolute power of God would not admit that it could ever be defeated by the human will; even those who seem to reject God are in fact fulfilling His purposes.[6]

The difficulty of accepting that Augustine's final conclusions are the legitimate expression of his theology, and regarding his earlier and more optimistic writings as a line of thought which he initially pursued and then abandoned, is the place of love in his system. No theologian has been more conscious of the declaration that God is love than Augustine. His trinitarian theology turns upon it, and his notion of redemption and deification must of necessity take as its starting point the notion of Christ, the God-man, who out of love for fallen humanity takes upon Himself human flesh and dies upon the cross, and by so doing becomes the mediator between God and man, to bring redeemed humanity to His divinity in a union of love. Whatever Augustine may say in his later writings about the inscrutability of the divine judgements and the hidden justice of God, most Christian readers will revolt from an understanding of the divine mercy which abandons the greater part of humanity to eternal torment, and agree with John Stuart Mill in declining to call good a being conceived as doing things which would be condemned in a man.

In this respect it is possible to hold that when John Cassian and the Massilian theologians protested against Augustine's final teachings, with their denial of an absolute divine will to save all men, they were being true to Augustine's fundamental assumptions and were in fact defending Augustine against himself. In some measure Augustine recognised this, and refused to regard the Semi-Pelagians as heretics, as he regarded Pelagius and Julian of Eclanum. Inflexible in maintaining his position, he may in his heart have acknowledged that in refusing to place a limit on the love of God for His creatures the Massilian theologians were maintaining a principle on which his own theology was based. They too might have quoted the words of St Paul: *O the depth of the riches!* and applied them, in an Augustinian sense, to the love of God, as the later Augustine applied them to God's justice and foreknowledge.

It has been argued that the final views of any thinker are to be regarded as the true state of his mind, and that it is misleading, and indeed wrong, to ascribe to him sentiments which he subsequently discarded. Historically speaking, this is undeniable: it is dishonest, on a final evaluation of any thinker, to ascribe to him as characteristic opinions which by the end of his life he had disowned. In seeking however to make a general assessment of a man's thought, we are not required to regard him as being necessarily his own best critic. Once an idea has been given to the world it acquires a value independent of its author's subsequent evaluation and it is therefore not improper for later generations to select as typical conceptions which the originator himself eventually rejected, or to decline to endorse his final opinions, on the ground that they represent a diversion from the true tenor of his mind. This is what many theologians have done with regard to Augustinian predestination, from the Semi-Pelagians onwards, and this is certainly a prevailing attitude in the last years of the twentieth century. 'No Christian thinker in his senses', observed N. P. Williams, 'will maintain that Augustinianism [i.e. Augustinian predestinarianism] is a heresy. Yet a theological opinion may be profoundly erroneous without being either formally or materially heretical.'[7] Throughout the centuries, while rigorous Augustinianism has been continually maintained by theologians like Gottschalk, Bradwardine, Wycliffe, Calvin and Cornelius Jansen, it has never won the mind of Western Christendom as a whole, to say nothing of the Eastern Orthodox Church. It is probable that Semi-Pelagianism, as expressed by John Cassian, comes closer to the instinct of the generality of Christian believers, and to Augustine himself if his theology is taken as a whole, than does the teaching of his last years.

It is here that the significance of Augustine's spiritual teaching becomes significant; for this, while recognising the fact of the Fall and its influence upon the human soul, accepts that there is, even in fallen man, a desire for God, a desire which might be termed ontological, since man is a being created out of nothing and utterly dependent upon God. Man without God is, indeed, literally nothing. Yet God loves man, to the degree of becoming man and dying upon the cross, in order that man redeemed may participate in the divinity of his creator. It is this aspect of Augustine's thought which is most likely to appeal to the modern theologian, seeking inspiration from so great a mind, and the aspect most likely to be fruitfully developed in the thought of the present day. Nevertheless we cannot ignore the other side of Augustine's thought; for whether we accept it or not, it represents a system which for centuries influenced the course of Western theological thinking. It is these considerations which have inspired my own Augustinian studies over the past quarter of a century, and if I can persuade others to share my interests, my researches will have been worth-while.

One thing remains to be said. Augustine's output is so vast that no single author can hope to do justice to all his interests. Isidore of Seville declared that if anyone claimed to have read all the works of Augustine, he was a liar. The same holds even more true for the man who claims to have discussed the whole range of Augustine's thought. One can only do what one can, and hope that one's conclusions will not be invalidated by the researches of another Augustinian scholar in another field, though with the reassuring knowledge that, whether one agrees with him or not, time spent with the Bishop of Hippo is never wasted.

GERALD BONNER

Durham,
September 1986

[1] 'Augustine's conception of Deification,' *Journal of Theological Studies*, NS, Vol.37 (1986), 369–86.

[2] Victorino Capánaga, 'La deificacíon en la soteriología augustiniana,' *Augustinus Magister: Congrès International Augustinien* (Paris 1954), ii. pp. 745–54.

[3] Thomas Allin, *The Augustinian Revolution in Theology* (London 1911), 141, 125.

[4] Augustine, *Ep.* 190, iii, 12: 'Tam multos autem creando nasci voluit, quos ad suam gratiam non pertinere praescivit, ut multitudine incomparabili plures sint illis quos in sui regni gloriam filios promissionis praedestinare dignatus est; ut etiam ipsa reiectorum multitudine ostenderetur, quam nullius momenti sit apud Deum iustum quantalibet numerositas iustissime damnatorum.'

[5] Cassian, *Conl.* xiii, 7.

[6] Augustine, *Enchiridion* xxvi, 100: 'Haec sunt *magna opera domini, exquisita in omnes voluntates eius*, et tam sapienter exquisita, ut cum angelica et humana creatura peccasset, id est, non quod ille, sed quod voluit ipsa fecisset, etiam per eandem creaturae voluntatem, qua factum est quod creator noluit, impleret ipse quod voluit, bene utens et malis, tamquam summe bonus, ad eorum damnationem, quos iuste praedestinavit ad poenam, et ad eorum salutem, quos benigne praedestinavit ad gratiam. Quantum enim ad ipsos attinet, quod deus noluit fecerunt; quantum vero ad omnipotentiam dei, nullo modo id efficere valuerunt. Hoc quippe ipso quod contra voluntatem fecerunt eius, de ipsis facta est voluntas eius.'

[7] N. P. Williams, *The Ideas of the Fall and of Original Sin* (London, reissue of 1938), 382.

ACKNOWLEDGEMENTS

The permission of the following journals and institutions to reproduce the various articles which have appeared in them or in their publications is gratefully acknowledged: The Council of the Fellowship of St Alban & St Sergius and *Sobornost* (London) for Nos I, V and VI; the Pontifica Università S. Tommaso and *Angelicum* (Rome) for II; the Institutum Patristicum Augustinianum and *Augustinianum* (Rome) for No III; the Council of the Ecclesiastical History Society of Great Britain and *Studies in Church History* Vol. 13 for No IV; *Augustinian Studies* (Villanova, Pa.) for Nos VII and X; *Augustinus* (Madrid) for No VIII; the Akademie-Verlag, Berlin and *Studia Patristica* VI for No IX; The Augustinian Institute, Villanova University (Villanova, Pa.) for No XI; and Etudes Augustiniennes (Paris) for No XII.

I

The spirituality of St Augustine and its influence on Western mysticism*

No one is more aware than myself of the presumption implicit in the title of this paper. The spirituality of St Augustine is a theme for a book in itself and its influence on Western mysticism the theme for another; I am trying to comprehend these vast topics in a paper of less than an hour. Inevitably I can do no more than provide the skeleton of an outline, an epitome of an epitome. But there is more to the matter than that; for if there is one thing which is necessary at the outset, it is to agree about the meaning of our terminology.

Mysticism and spirituality

Few words are more vaguely employed than mysticism and spirituality; we use them as if everybody understood their meaning, when in fact it is all too easily possible to conduct a discussion involving them on a basis of complete mutual misunderstanding. Consider, for example, the wide range of signification of that much-abused adjective 'mystical'; everything from Aldous Huxley's experiments with mescalin[1] to the precision of St John of the Cross. Or again, with the word 'spirituality', let us take heed to the warning of a Jewish writer, Lionel Blue, that Christian piety seems 'too religious to be Jewish. There is more cake than daily bread in the diet, and a Jew gets worried by spiritual indigestion [...]. For Jews religious experience can lead away from the religious duty to which God called us, and for which he gave us so many laws and commandments'.[2] Blue, who has

*   A paper read at the Fellowship Conference 1981 and subsequently to the Durham University Lightfoot Society, 26 February 1982. Following this second reading the Revd Dr John Gaden pointed out to me that there was little, if anything, which I ascribed to Augustine in the paper which would not hold equally true for the Greek Fathers. I am only too happy to agree with this observation, which confirms my own view that theological differences between the Greek and Latin Fathers are commonly exaggerated and that there is a patristic tradition common to East and West alike. I would however defend the propriety of the term 'Augustinian spirituality' in the present context, since in the first place it is not clear that Augustine owed any *direct* debt to Eastern theology in developing his own; and, secondly, it is certain that Western spirituality in the early Middle Ages was dominated by Augustine, and by his populariser, Gregory the Great, and owed relatively little to the Greeks until the works of Dionysius the Areopagite was made available by John Scotus Eriugena in the ninth century.

1. *The Doors of Perception* (London 1954) and *Heaven and Hell* (London 1956). See the ironic description by R.C. Zaehner of his own experiences with mescalin in *Mysticism: Sacred and Profane* (Oxford 1957), pp.212-26.
2. *To Heaven with Scribes and Pharisees* (London 1975), p.21.

I

Christian friends and who has, I am told, considerable experience of Christian devotion, is at some pains to emphasise the difference between the religious practices of Judaism and Christianity. 'Holy argument', he observes, 'is the greatest path to God in Jewish experience, and dialectic is as effective for a Jew as a rosary for a Catholic, in approaching the Almighty'. In view of the tendency today to emphasise the Jewishness of Christian origins, it is useful to be reminded by a Jew what a difference has been made in the devotional life of the two great religions by the doctrine of the Incarnation. 'Occasionally', says Blue, 'we feel God's presence, but his centre is far away, and very different from any man's [...]. A Jew feels that he has to take reality "neat". He is not allowed to sentimentalise the transcendent'.[3]

In the face of this warning, I propose to suggest definitions of what we mean — or, at any rate, what I understand — by mysticism and spirituality. My definition of mysticism will be that of André Lalande in the *Vocabulaire technique et critique de la philosophie*, which has the approval of so discriminating a scholar as the late Professor Dodds: 'Belief in the possibility of an intimate and direct union which* constitutes at once a mode of existence and a mode of knowledge different from and superior to normal existence and knowledge'.[4] This definition, it will be observed, avoids any introduction of the word God, a word which some Oriental and some Western nature-mystics would reject, and stresses both existential and the cognitive aspects of the experience. The Christian mystic will, of course, understand by the term 'the fundamental principle of being' the God of Abraham, of Isaac and of Jacob, the Father of our Lord and Saviour Jesus Christ, and will probably, for his own purposes, employ an abbreviated paraphrase of Lalande's definition, defining mysticism as 'the experiential knowledge of God' and understanding by experiential 'based on experience'. Any understanding of mysticism which does not include this element of experiential knowledge of God will be, for the Christian theologian, inadequate.

Spirituality is, in some ways, more difficult to define than mysticism, partly because it can be used simply as an equivalent of ascetic and mystical theology, as in F.P. Harton's manual, *The Elements of the Spiritual Life* (London 1932). It has, however, a wider signification. Reginald Cant, in his article for *A Dictionary of Christian Theology*, cites Hans Urs von Balthasar: 'The way a man understands his own ethically and religiously committed existence, and the way he acts and reacts habitually to this understanding' and adds: 'Basically Christian spirituality means the real, effective apprehension of Christian truth in the human consciousness[5] — a description which I prefer to that of von Balthasar, though I still do not find it wholly satisfying. My own definition of spirituality would be: 'an orientation of the mind and will to God expressed in a man's life and teaching', which agrees with Von Balthasar and Cant, but seems to me to be more direct and simpler.

---

3. Ibid., pp.79, 62.　　　　* Read: ' ... union with the fundamental principle of being which ... '.
4. Lalande, *Vocabulaire* (Paris 1956), col. 664; E.R. Dodds, *Pagan and Christian in an Age of Anxiety* (Cambridge 1965), p.70.
5. *A Dictionary of Christian Theology*, ed. Alan Richardson (London 1969), p.328.

THE SPIRITUALITY OF ST AUGUSTINE

With these two definitions, of mysticism as 'belief in the possibility of an intimate and direct union of the human spirit with the fundamental principle of being, a union which constitutes at once a mode of existence and a mode of knowledge different from and superior to normal existence and knowledge' and of spirituality as 'an orientation of the mind and will to God expressed in a man's life and teaching' I can address myself to the theme of this paper: the spirituality of St Augustine and its influence on Western mysticism.

Augustine 'Prince of Mystics'?

It will be generally agreed that Augustine of Hippo is to be reckoned one of the great masters of the early Western Middle Ages in all departments of theology, and, certainly not least in that of mysticism and spirituality. Abbot Cuthbert Butler, in his classic work, *Western Mysticism,* called Augustine 'the Prince of Mystics',[6] and associated with him his successors, Gregory the Great and Bernard of Clairvaux. Again, in the twelfth century the Victorines, Hugh and Richard, famous masters of the famous house of St Victor at Paris, whose writings so profoundly influenced the later course of Western mystical theology, were both Austin Canons. Hugh has been called a second Augustine; Richard 'the spiritual master of the Middle Ages'.[7] Both stood in a spiritual tradition which looked back to the Bishop of Hippo, their common master and teacher. Indeed, it is easy enough with almost any Western medieval theologian to identify ideas which are a legacy from Augustine (one might give as an example the images of Leah and Rachel signifying action and contemplation, to be developed by Richard of St Victor in his treatise *De Praeparatione Animae ad Contemplationem,* popularly called *Benjamin Minor*)[8] but to do so would be beyond the capacity of the present paper. Rather, we shall concern ourselves with a broader set of themes, with general ideas and conceptions which later generations inherited from Augustine.

At the outset we must notice, since we cannot avoid it, the difficult question of Augustine's personal mysticism. Is he to be regarded as a mystic, in the sense that we say that St Teresa of Avila or St John of the Cross were mystics? On this issue scholars are sharply divided. On the one hand Abbot Butler, in a phrase already quoted, described Augustine as 'the Prince of Mystics'. At the other extreme we have the judgement of the Dutch Augustinian scholar Ephraem Hendrikx that Augustine was no mystic but a great enthusiast *(ein grosser Enthusiast)*[9] – a phrase

6. *Western Mysticism* (London 1967), p.20; cf. Paul Henry, *La vision d'Ostie* (Paris 1938), p.88: 'Augustin est un mystique né'.
7. *Mediaeval Mystical Tradition and St John of the Cross* by a Benedictine of Stanbrook Abbey (London 1954), pp.25, 43.
8. c. *Faust.* 22, 52-7. See F. Cayré, *La contemplation augustinienne,* (Bruges 1954), pp.37-42. Richard of St Victor's treatise is printed in Migne, *PL* 196.1-64.
9. *Augustins Verhältnis zur Mystik. Eine patristische Untersuchung* (Würzburg 1936), p.176. See further Hans Meyer, 'War Augustin Intellektualist oder Mystik?', *Augustinus Magister* (Paris 1954), iii. 429-37; also his remarks, op.cit., p.166, agreeing with André Mandouze's summary of his position (p.121): 98% intellectualism, 2% mysticism.

which has caused difficulty to other scholars, less at home in the subtleties of the German language than Hendrikx, but which seems to suggest that for him Augustine's quest for God was essentially one pursued in the mind and described with a felicity and fervour which has misled later readers into supposing that Augustine's descriptions of his mental processes were to be identified with the experiences of accepted mystics of a later date.

Faced with these apparently contradictory judgements by scholars of the calibre of Butler and Hendrikx, most of us will probably be persuaded to suspend judgement in default of convincing evidence. For myself, I am prepared to believe that the spiritual experiences at Milan and Ostia which Augustine records in the *Confessions* did involve moments of illumination, ascents of the mind to God or to the Absolute, such as we find described in both theistic and nature mysticism. Further than that I am not prepared to go. There is no convincing evidence that these experiences were repeated in later life, when Augustine's heavy commitments as a presbyter and a bishop, together with his enormous literary output, might well have prevented any development of his contemplative capacity. Not even an Augustine can do everything.

This being said, we are faced with an immediate problem: if Augustine were not a mystic, why has he apparently been accepted as one by people like St Teresa, whose qualifications in this respect are hardly open to question?[10] The answer is that while Augustine may not have been a mystic in the strict sense of the word (and, let me emphasise, there are scholars of distinction who hold that he was), the way in which he writes, and the character of much of his discussion, do have remarkable affinities with the language of later mystics. To give a concrete example: in the *Confessions* Augustine describes an attempted ascent of the mind to God made at Milan in 386 before his conversion. The passage is so revealing and so important for our discussion that it is worth quoting it at length.

> Thus by stages I passed from bodies to the soul which uses the body for its perceiving, and from this to the soul's inner power, to which the body's senses present external things, as indeed the beasts are able; and from there I passed on to the reasoning power, to which is referred for judgement what is received from the body's senses. This too realised that it was mutable in me, and rose to its own understanding. It withdrew my thought from its habitual way, abstracting it from the confused crowds of fantasms that it might find what light suffused it, when with utter certainty it cried aloud that the

10. See St Teresa's remarks in *Life* 9 (tr. J.M. Cohen [Harmondsworth 1957], p.69).

AURELII AUGUSTINI DOCTORIS
DE CIUITATE
INCIPIT CO[NTRA]
GLORIOSISSI[MAM]

A

SIVE INHOC TEO
g'nat' ex fide 1
quá nc expecta
in iudicui. den
ultima & pace
p'missione deb
deor suos p'fe
ni op' exardui
ribz op' sic ur j
q'sic ut omnia cū

tancta. non humano usurpaca factu sed diuina gra do

immutable was to be preferred to the mutable, and how it had come to know the immutable itself; for if it had not come to some knowledge of the immutable, it could not have known it as certainly preferable to the mutable. Thus in the thrust of a trembling glance my mind arrived at THAT WHICH IS [*et pervenit ad id quod est in ictu trepidantis aspectus*]. Then indeed I saw clearly [God's] *invisible things which are understood by the things that are made* (Rom. 1:20); but I lacked the strength to hold my gaze fixed, and my weakness was beaten back again so that I returned to my old habits, bearing nothing with me but a memory of delight and a desire for something of which I had caught the fragrance but which I had not yet the strength to eat.[11]

Now this passage, together with another recorded slightly earlier in the *Confessions*,[12] point to a spiritual experience or experiences of some sort; the problem is to determine their character. It has been remarked that the passage which I have just quoted as an ascent of the mind to God also provides a description of Augustine's theory of cognition – bodies; sensation; inner sense; judgement; pure thought; intuition[13] – which parallels his account of the ascent to reality given in his work *On the Greatness of Soul*, written in 388, nearly a decade before the *Confessions*.[14] Similar notions of a 'ladder of intellectual ascent to God' which also appears to be an analysis of the process of human cognition occur in other Augustinian writings,[15] leaving the reader in some doubt as to whether he is concerned with an account of contemplation or a theory of epistemology. The answer seems to be that for Augustine the two enquiries cannot be separated. In the words of Etienne Gilson: 'One never really knows whether Saint Augustine is talking as a theologian or a philosopher, whether he is proving the existence of God or developing a theory of cognition, whether the eternal verities about which he is speaking are those of understanding or morality, whether he is expounding a doctrine of sensation or the consequences of Original Sin; everything holds together so well that Augustine cannot seize one link of the chain without drawing the entire chain

11. *Conf.* 7, 17, 23 (tr. F.J. Sheed [London 1944], pp.127-8).
12. *Conf.* 7, 10, 16: 'When first I knew thee, thou didst lift me up so that I might see that there was something to see, but I was not yet the man to see it. And thou didst beat back the weakness of my gaze, blazing upon me too strongly, and I was shaken with love and with dread. And I knew that I was far from thee in the region of unlikeness [*regio dissimilitudinis*], as if I heard thy voice from on high: "I am the food of grown men: grow, and you shall eat me. And you shall not change me into yourself as bodily food, but into me you shall be changed" ' (tr. Sheed, p.113). Note the eucharistic and deificatory character of the last sentence, reminiscent of Gregory of Nyssa, *Oratio Catechetica*, 37: 'For in the manner that, as the Apostle says, *a little leaven* assimilates to itself *the whole lump*, so in like manner that body to which immortality has been given by God, when It is in ours, translates and transmutes the whole into itself. For as by the admixture of a poisonous liquid with a wholesome one the whole draught is deprived of its deadly effect, so too the immortal Body, by being within that which receives it, changes the whole to its own nature' (tr. in *NP-NF Library*).
13. Meyrick H. Carré, *Realists and Nominalists* (Oxford 1946), p.7.
14. *quant. an.*33, 70-7: life; perception; reasoning; moral judgement; confidence in virtue; understanding of reality; the vision of truth. See Carré, *Realists*, pp.7-8.
15. *Gn.c.Man.* 1, 24, 42; *doctr.chr.* 2, 7, 9-11; *trin.* 12, 15, 25.

THE SPIRITUALITY OF ST AUGUSTINE

to himself'.[16] Thus the experiences described in the seventh book of the *Confessions* cannot be simply treated as an account of a mystical experience as Christian theologians currently understand the term, and even the Vision of Ostia, that shared meditation with his mother which Augustine describes in the ninth book of the *Confessions*,[17] however beautiful and moving it may be (and it is very beautiful and very moving), lacks something of the passionate intensity and ardent love which we find in St Bernard's sermons on the Song of Songs. A clue may be found in the fact that at the very beginning of the Canticle we have the words: *Let him kiss me with the kisses of his mouth* (1:2 [1 Vg]), which inspire Bernard to expound his doctrine of the three kisses of the feet, the hand, and the lips of the Lord. In Augustine's writings there are very few references to kisses.[18] There is intensity of devotion and a burning thirst for God — much of both — but Augustine's encounter with God always retains an intellectual element; he needs to love the Lord with his mind as well as with his heart.[19]

Augustine and Neoplatonism

Some clue to this intellectualism — an intellectualism which is never divorced from love, which remains for Augustine the only way to God — may be found in Augustine's dramatic discovery of Neoplatonism at Milan in 386, at the time when he was beginning to take seriously the claims of catholic Christianity. I cannot myself accept the views of those scholars who hold that there was a period in Augustine's life when he was a Neoplatonist rather than a Christian, and that his true conversion came only after his return to Africa in 388. I do, however, agree that Neoplatonism played a major role in his decision to seek baptism by providing a key to some of the intellectual difficulties which had hitherto hindered his acceptance of catholic Christianity and that it remained a powerful influence upon his thinking as a catholic theologian.

Neoplatonism is a system of intellectual mysticism which involves an attempt by the human soul to leave the lower world of the senses and to return to the One, the Ground of Being, in an act of union in which it realises its true nature;[20] and while

16. Gilson, *Introduction à l'étude de saint Augustin*, (Paris 1969), pp.311-2.

17. *Conf.* 9, 10, 23-26. See Henry, *La vision d'Ostie* (Paris 1938).

18. See Peter Brown, *Augustine of Hippo* (London 1967), p.83: '[Ambrose's] sermons are studded with the language of the Song of Songs: "kissing" — so seldom mentioned by Augustine — recurs constantly in Ambrose'.

19. Augustine's suspicion of sexuality after he had become a catholic Christian, so vividly expressed in certain passages of his anti-Pelagian writings, may help to explain his reluctance to make use of the image of the kiss. There is a certain paradox (no doubt easily explicable psychologically) in the fact that Augustine, who had had a concubine and a son, avoids using the image of the kiss while Bernard, the monk, preaches sermons on the theme.

20. See J.M. Rist, *Plotinus. The Road to Reality* (Cambridge 1977), p.230: 'The soul, then, by its natural kinship with the One can return to the source and be "oned" with it'. Note Rist's comment (p.246) on pseudo-Dionysius: '[. . .] the Christian doctrine of the Incarnation frees Dionysius from a charge of imposing mere magic and theurgy [so popular in later Neoplatonism] upon the philosophical schema'.

Plotinus can use language about the vision of the One in terms of love and even of spiritual inebriation,[21] Neoplatonism never has that element of personal love and devotion that we find in the greatest Christian mystics, for the very good reason (as Augustine recognised) that it had no place for any doctrine of the Incarnation.[22] Such a doctrine Augustine of course had; we shall indeed see that his Christocentricity is one of his major legacies to later generations; but some element of Neoplatonist intellectualism remained throughout his life, to influence the form of his theologising and to colour his attitude to contemplation. I do not imply by this that Neoplatonism and the teaching of the Church were in any sense equal partners in Augustine's thought. On the contrary, Neoplatonism was always the junior partner, to be jettisoned if ever it came into conflict with the Word of God; but its method, and to some extent its outlook, continued to influence Augustine's thinking to the end of his life.

The influence of Neoplatonism on Augustine is manifest in the *Confessions,* written at the beginning of his episcopate in 396/7, which constitutes the principal — though by no means the only — source for any discussion of his mysticism. Much labour has been expended by scholars identifying Plotinian echoes in Augustine's account of his conversion given in the *Confessions,*[23] and there can be no doubt that the Neoplatonist element here is very strong. Yet there is in the *Confessions* a quality which makes it unique in patristic literature, which sets it apart from Neoplatonism: a sense of intimacy with God. This was noticed many years ago by E.R. Dodds in a perceptive comment: 'Plotinus never *gossiped* with the One, as Augustine gossips in the *Confessions*';[24] though to my mind the word 'gossips' was ill-chosen. Augustine's intimacy never degenerates into the sort of familiarity or triviality which gossip commonly implies. Augustine, it is clear, talked a lot; but I doubt whether he had much small-talk, at least in his later, Christian life.[25] It has been observed that his letters, which so often reveal the personality of the writer, lack the point and passion of Jerome or the movement and poetic touch of

---

21. *Enneads* 6.7.33-5: '*Nous* (Intellect) has one power for thinking, by which it looks at its own contents, and one by which it sees THAT WHICH IS above it by a kind of intuitive reception, by which it first simply saw and afterwards, as it saw, acquired intellect and is one. The first is the contemplation of *Nous* in its right mind, the second that of *Nous* in love. When it goes out of its mind, being drunk with the nectar, it falls in love and is simplified into a happy fullness; and drunkenness like this is better for it than sobriety' (tr. A.H. Armstrong, *Plotinus* [London 1952], p.156). See the remarks of Rist, *Plotinus,* p.228.

22. *Conf.* 7, 9, 14.

23. Pierre Courcelle, *Recherches sur les* Confessions *de saint Augustin* (Paris 1950), may be said to have marked an epoch in this particular field of study. See further Robert J. O'Connell, *St Augustine's Early Theory of Man* (Cambridge, Mass. 1968) and *St Augustine's* Confessions (Cambridge, Mass. 1968).

24. *Hibbert Journal* xxvi (1927-8), p.471.

25. See J.H. Baxter, *St Augustine: Select Letters* (Loeb ed.) (London/Cambridge, Mass. 1953), p.xl: 'Of a sober and introspective nature, he is too much in earnest about the truth to be anything but direct, weighty and unadorned'.

THE SPIRITUALITY OF ST AUGUSTINE

Ambrose.[26] So in Augustine's talk with God, however close he may be, there is always that sense of restraint which the Romans called *gravitas*, which prevented men from overstepping the boundaries which convention imposes. I doubt if Augustine would ever have written, like St Teresa, 'Often I beseech the Lord, if he must upset me so much, to let me be free from it at times like this. "My God", I say to him sometimes, "when shall my soul be wholly employed in thy praise, instead of being torn to pieces in this way, and quite helpless?" '[27] On the other hand, Augustine's Roman reserve and sense of propriety in no way inhibits him from speaking to God with complete confidence. Baron Von Hügel noted as one of the characteristics of the *Confessions* '*Reality, Distinctness, Prevenience of God, our Home*' and commented: '[. . .] how this fundamental fact pervades St A.! It is because of this mighty fact, ever taken in all its seriousness, that the soul is left rock-based, serene, unshaken; even though it wander far away from God, its Home. Yet that Home continues ready to receive it back'.[28]

This then is the first element in the spirituality of St Augustine which he transmitted to later ages: a sense of frankness and intimacy with God devoid of any element of sentimental and vulgar familiarity, and it is this element, I think, which accounts for the popularity of the *Confessions* down the ages with spiritual souls from St Bernard[29] and St Aelred of Rivaulx[30] to St Teresa, who found great consolation when she read a Spanish translation published in 1554:

> At this time I was given St Augustine's *Confessions,* seemingly by the ordainment of the Lord [. . .]. When I began to read the *Confessions* I seemed to see myself portrayed there, and I began to commend myself to that glorious saint. When I came to the tale of his conversion, and read how he heard the voice in the garden, it seemed exactly as if the Lord has spoken to me. So I felt in my heart.[31]

Interiority

Again, a characteristic of the spirituality of St Augustine is its interiority. 'Being admonished by all this to return to myself', he says to God, 'I entered into my own depths, with you as guide; and I was able to do it because *you were my helper*'.[32]

26. Ibid., p.xxxix.
27. Letter 17 (tr. E. Allison Peers, *The Complete Works of Saint Teresa of Jesus* [London/ New York 1946], ii.103).
28. Letter to his niece (1919) in Friedrich Von Hügel, *Selected Letters 1896-1924* (London 1933), p.280 and *Letters* [. . .] *to a Niece* (London 1929), p.49.
29. See P. Courcelle, *Les Confessions de saint Augustin dans la tradition littéraire* (Paris 1963), pp.280-5.
30. Courcelle, *Les* Confessions [. . .], pp.291-301; Aelred Squire, *Aelred of Rivaulx: A Study* (London 1969), pp.37-50. According to Aelred's biographer, Walter Daniel, the *Confessions* was among the books which Aelred had by him when he was dying, because it was to this work he owed his initiation into theology: *Vita Ailredi*, 42: 'Legebat autem libros, quorum litera lacrimas elicere solet et edificare mores, et maxime Confessiones Augustini manibus portabat assidue, eo quod illos libros quasi quasdam introductiones habebat cum a saeculo converteretur'.
31. Teresa, *Life* 9 (tr. S.M. Cohen, p.69).
32. *Conf.* 7, 10, 16.

I

The inspiration of this technique seems to be Neoplatonic; it followed almost immediately upon reading a work or works which have been identified as the Plotinian treatises *On the Beautiful; On Omnipresence;* and *On Intelligible Beauty*,[33] but the Christian element is safeguarded, in Augustine's account in the *Confessions,* by the reference to Ps 29 [30]:11, *The Lord has become my helper.*[34] For Augustine, the encounter with God is an interior process, a process of introversion, preceded by a period of purgation of the mind of all sensual images, in order that it may see itself and know itself. So he declares, in his sermon on Psalm 41:

> I return to myself, and look closely at myself, who I may be who seek such things [. . .]. Seeking my God in visible and corporeal things and not finding him, seeking his substance in myself, as though it were something such as I am and not finding this either, I perceive that God is something above the soul.[35]

It is easy to see how such a process of seeking God, even if it were in Augustine's case a mental exercise accompanied by prayer, and not mystical in the later, technical sense, would have been read by subsequent generations of mystics as being the description of an experience equivalent to their own.

Self-knowledge

With this principle of interiority Augustinian spirituality emphasises the need for self-knowledge. 'I desire to know God and the soul', says Augustine in the first book of the *Soliloquies,* written at the very beginning of his career as a catholic Christian in the winter of 386-7;[36] and again, in an often-quoted phrase: 'O God who art ever the same, let me know myself and let me know thee',[37] and this requirement of self-knowledge as a preparation for knowing God may be said to be implicit throughout the *Confessions.* At a later date Bernard of Clairvaux is to lay down a similar principle as a preparation for the mystic union of the soul with God:

> Fitting indeed it is that when the soul shall emerge from this school of humility wherein, under the tuition of the Son, she has learnt to enter into herself in accordance with the warning: *If thou knowest not thyself, go out and feed thy flock* [Cant. 1:7 Vg.] — fitting it is that now, under the

33. Plotinus, *En.* 1, 6; 6, 4-5; 5, 8. See Paul Henry, *Plotin et l'Occident* (Louvain 1934), pp.78-119, 128; Id., *La vision d'Ostie,* 17; P. Courcelle, *Recherches sur les* Confessions, 160-7; R.J. O'Connell, *St Augustine's Early Theory of Man,* pp.206-8. Courcelle, *Les lettres grecques en Occident* (Paris 1948), pp.163-8 would add Porphyry's *De Regressu Animae* to the list of Neoplatonist works read by Augustine before his conversion.

34. Augustine's account of his mystical experiences at Milan was, of course, only written ten years afterwards, when he was a Christian bishop. One cannot therefore exclude the possibility that he introduced into his narrative Christian elements which were not there at the time. I do not myself believe this; and in any case, we are here concerned with the influences of Augustine's writings rather than the historical accuracy of his descriptions.

35. *en.Ps.* 41.7, 8.

36. *sol.* 1, 2, 7: 'AVGVSTINVS: Deum et animam scire cupio. RATIO: Nihilne plus? AVGVSTINVS: Nihil omnino'.

37. Ibid., 2, 1, 1: 'Deus semper idem, noverim ne, noverim me. Oratum est'.

guidance of the Holy Spirit, she be introduced through affection into the store-rooms of charity, by which assuredly we must understand the hearts of our neighbours.[38]

In a similar fashion Walter Hilton declares:

> There is one work in which it is both very necessary and helpful to engage, and which — so far as human efforts are concerned — is a highway leading to contemplation. This is for a person to enter into himself and to understand his own soul with all its powers, virtues and sins.[39]

Dame Julian of Norwich echoes the principle:

> [. . .] our soul is so deep-grounded in God and so endlessly treasured, that we may not come to the knowing thereof until we have, first, knowing of God, who is the Maker; to whom it is oned. But notwithstanding I saw that we have, of our fullness, the desire wisely and truly to know our own soul; whereby we are learned to seek it where it is; and that is, in God.

And again:

> [. . .] notwithstanding all this, we may never come to the full knowledge of God until we know, first, clearly, our own soul.[40]

We have here clear evidence of the prevalence of the Augustinian idea of the need for self-knowledge as a preparation for contemplation.

Contemplation

With regard to this contemplation, it has already been suggested that it cannot indisputably be identified with the mystic way as described by contemplatives like St Teresa and St John of the Cross. For myself — and this is an issue on which the historian of doctrine is constrained to speak personally — I am inclined to agree with the late David Knowles that Augustinian contemplation involves an intense, though not technically speaking a mystical, experience and that it is possible that Augustine on occasion describes a supernatural, but not strictly mystical, enlightenment of the mind in proportion to its purity and degree of charity, or an occasional intellectual enlightenment regarding God himself and other theological truths, given to the mind in an experiential, but not a strictly mystical way.[41] This view should, I think, agree with what Knowles says elsewhere about Walter Hilton: that he 'does

38. *De Gradibus Humilitatis*, 7, 21: 'Digna certe, quae de schola humilitatis, in qua primum sub magistro Filio ad seipsam intrare didicit, iuxta comminationem ad se factam, *Si ignoras te, egredere et pasce haedos tuos* (Cant. 1:7 Vg.); digna ergo, quae de schola illa humilitatis, duce Spiritu sancto in cellaria charitatis (quae nimirum proximorum pectora intellegenda sunt) per affectionem introduceretur' (*PL* 182. 953 CD). I borrow the translation in E. Gilson, *The Mystical Theology of St Bernard*, tr. A.H.C. Downes (London 1940), pp.102-3.
39. Hilton, *Scale* i.42 (tr. L. Sherley-Price, *The Ladder of Perfection* [Harmondsworth 1957], p.48).
40. Julian, *The Revelations of Divine Love* (Longer Version), 56 (tr. James Walsh [London 1961], pp.154, 155).
41. D. Knowles, *The English Mystical Tradition* (London 1961), p.27.

not touch upon the highest point to which the soul made perfect may attain; there is nothing to set against the many chapters in *The Living Flame* and *The Spiritual Canticle* of St John of the Cross that describe the spiritual marriage and the life of the soul on ever higher levels'.[42] This would be easily understandable in a mind nourished upon Augustinian theology; as Oliver O'Donovan has recently remarked: 'The mature Augustinian was not interested in spiritual or moral progress as a matter for speculative theorising [...]. For him there was no ladder of progress by which the soul's movement from one level of moral achievement to a higher one could be charted. The struggle rather consisted in a series of recapitulations of Adam's choice between good and evil'.[43]

This does not mean, however, that the mature Augustine abandons any thought of contemplation as part of the Christian life. How could he, when on his own first principles the end and crown of the life of the elect will be the vision of God? What moreover the mature Augustine was concerned to do in his polemics against the Pelagians was to emphasise the sinfulness of all men, however holy an individual might be, and to maintain that perfection is possible only in the world to come; as long as they live in this world, the saints of God must continue to pray that their trespasses may be forgiven. Yet this does not imply that no progress is possible; on the contrary, the earthly life of the Christian is a reformation of the image of God, which is the human soul, to conformity with the divine exemplar.

The image restored

This theology of the image[44] seems to me to be one of the major contributions made by Augustine to Christian spirituality. Starting from the words of God in Genesis 1:26: *Let us make man in our image and likeness,* Augustine lays down a number of important exegetical principles: firstly, that the creation of man is the work of the whole Trinity – a notion which will contribute to Augustine's trinitarian speculations, in which he will explore the human mind as providing some analogy of the being of the Trinity which created it;[45] secondly, that it is not enough for an image to be merely 'like' its model: it must in a sense be 'born' of its model if it is truly to be called an image – a principle which inevitably leads to the conclusion that the only true image of God is God the Son, and the corollary that man can therefore only be the divine image by grace.[46] This corollary, in turn, leads to a third and vital principle: that the likeness of man to his creator is by participation: man becomes like God by participating in him.[47]

42. Ibid., p.115.
43. Oliver O'Donovan, *The Problem of Self-Love in St Augustine* (New Haven/London 1980), p.150.
44. Of which I have spoken before at a Fellowship Conference in days long past; see 'The Glorification of the Image', *Sobornost* 4: 7 (1962), pp.358-73.
45. *Gn.litt.imp.* 16, 55-6; *trin.*1, 7, 14; 1, 8, 18; 7, 6, 12; 12, 6. 7,
46. *Gn.litt.imp.* 16, 57.
47. Ibid. Cf. *trin.* 14, 12, 15. I have discussed this topic in a paper 'Augustine's doctrine of Man: Image of God and sinner' in a paper read to the Académie Internationale des

THE SPIRITUALITY OF ST AUGUSTINE

Participation is itself a Platonic concept, which Augustine may well have taken from Plotinus; but in using it, Augustine radically christianises it and so brings it into harmony with Christian doctrine. By the Fall, man has wounded and distorted the likeness of God in which he was originally created. Of himself he is utterly powerless to heal and restore that image. Healing and restoration can only come by the action of God in the Incarnation; if Christ had not willed to be deformed, mankind would not have recovered the form which it had lost.[48] Christ, being God, and remaining wholly in his nature, was nevertheless made a partaker of our nature, so that we, while remaining in our nature, might be partakers of his nature. By this participation, the divine in the human, and the human in the divine, man's soul, perverted and distorted by sin, is restored to wholeness.[49]

We find this doctrine, of course, in Walter Hilton. Indeed, one might say that the opening chapters of the second book of *The Scale* amount to an admirable summary of Augustinian teaching. Space does not permit extensive quotation to illustrate this point, but I cannot resist a citation from the conclusion of chapter 3:

> If, then, you wish to learn which souls are re-formed here in this life to the image of God by the merits of Christ's passion, it is only those who believe in him and love him. In these souls God's image, which was deformed by sin into that of an evil beast, is restored to its original form, and to the dignity and honour which it once enjoyed. And no soul can be saved or come to the joys of heaven unless it has been restored and reformed.[50]

Christocentricity

Augustine's doctrine of the restoration of the image of God in man by participation in God, made possible by the Incarnation of Jesus Christ the God-man, leads to another, and very important, element in his influence on later Western spirituality, namely his Christocentricity. In his *Confessions*, having described the unsatisfactory character of the Neoplatonist mystical experiences which he had enjoyed at Milan, Augustine goes on to say:

> So I set about finding a way to gain the strength that was necessary for enjoying you [O God]. And I could not find it until I embraced *the Mediator between God and man, the Man Christ Jesus, who is over all things, God blessed for ever,* who was calling unto me and saying: *I am the Way, the Truth and the Life.*[51]

Christ is the Way, the only Way to God. 'The God Christ is the home where we are going; the man Christ is the Way by which we are going;'[52] and again: 'He says: *I*

Sciences Religieuses in April 1980, which is to be published (I hope) at some future date by the Académie.

48. *serm.* 27, 6, 6.
49. *ep.* 140 (*ad Honoratum de Gratia Novi Testamenti*), 4, 10.
50. Hilton, *Scale*, Sherley-Price, p.119.
51. *Conf.* 7, 18, 24 (tr. Sheed, p.118); cf. *civ.* 9, 15.
52. *serm.* 123.3, 3: 'Ista est via; ambulate per humilitatem, et venias ad aeternitatem. Deus Christus est quo imus; homo Christus via est qua imus. Ad illum imus, per illum imus: quid timemus ne erremus?'

I

am the Way and the Truth and the Life, that is, "by me men come, to me they attain, in me they abide".[53] Devotion to the humanity of Christ, which became so characteristic in the West in the Middle Ages, could only be strengthened by the teaching of Augustine. Harnack was led to remark that the contemplation of Christ in theology was a new element which Augustine reintroduced after Paul and Ignatius; and while the Abbé Portalié found 'some exaggeration' in this assertion, he recognised its fundamental truth: 'from the time of his conversion, Jesus Christ was the guiding light of Augustine's soul'.[54]

To find echoes of this Christocentricity in the English medieval mystics of the fourteenth century — and indeed in the spirituality of an earlier epoch, if the famous *Iubilus rhythmicus de nomine Iesu* ('Jesus, the very thought of thee/With sweetness fill the breast') is indeed the work of an English Cistercian of the late twelfth century[55] — is so easy as to make citation almost superfluous. I will content myself with two examples. From *The Cloud of Unknowing:*

> How right you are to say 'for the love of Jesus' for it is in the love of Jesus that you have your help. The nature of love is such that it shares everything. Love Jesus, and everything he has is yours. Because he is God, he is maker and giver of time. Because he is man, he has given true heed to time. Because he is both God and man he is the best judge of the spending of time. Unite yourself to him by love and trust, and by that union you will be joined both to him and to all who like yourself are united by love to him.[56]

and Walter Hilton:

> Whoever imagines that he can attain to the full state and practice of contemplation in some other way — that is, without continual recollection of the precious Humanity and Passion of Jesus Christ, and the pursuit of all virtues — does not come in by the door, and will therefore be cast out like a thief. I do not deny that by the grace of God a man may sometimes have some foretaste and limited experience of contemplation, for some have been granted this early in their spiritual life,[57] but they cannot retain it permanently. For Christ is both the door and the porter, and no one may enter unless he shares his life and bears his sign. As he himself has said: *Nemo venit ad Patrem nisi per me* [John 14: 6] — *No one comes to the Father except through me* — meaning that no one can come to the contemplation of the Godhead unless he is first conformed by perfect humility and charity to the likeness of Jesus in his Humanity.[58]

53. *doctr.christ.* 1, 34, 38.
54. Harnack, *History of Dogma* (London 1898), v.127-8; Eugène Portalié, *A Guide to the Thought of Saint Augustine,* tr. R.J. Bastian (London 1960), p.152.
55. See André Wilmart, *Le 'Jubilus' dit de S. Bernard* (Rome 1944). Text in *The Oxford Book of Medieval Latin Verse* ed. F.J.E. Raby (Oxford 1959), pp.347-53 (and note, pp.493-4).
56. *The Cloud,* 4 (tr. Clifton Wolters [Harmondsworth 1961], p.56).
57. A remark which could well apply to Augustine's early experiences.
58. Hilton, *Scale* i.92 (tr. Sherley-Price, p.110).

THE SPIRITUALITY OF ST AUGUSTINE

Deification

There is, however, in Augustine's spirituality another element, perceived as a consequence of Christ's taking human nature upon himself; for it is in Christ and through Christ, and only in and through Christ, that man becomes a partaker of God's nature: 'He who was God was made made to make gods those who were men'.[59] These words, which parallel the more-often-quoted words of St Athanasius in his *De Incarnatione*,[60] show that Augustine did not shrink from using the language of deification, often said to be peculiar to the Greek Fathers.[61] The influence of this doctrine upon later Western mysticism, outstandingly in the theology of St Bernard and St John of the Cross, is well known. It may seem curious – and to some a contradiction in terms – that Augustine, the Doctor of Grace and the theologian of Original Sin *par excellence*, should have tolerated a concept like deification, which would seem to take a far more optimistic view of human nature and even, if misapplied, to lead to a view of the human soul which comes dangerously close to implying that it enjoys a kind of natural divinity, in the worst traditions of Platonic thought. This was, of course, very far from being Augustine's view. The former Manichee had every reason as a catholic theologian to reject any suggestion that the soul was by nature divine and immortal. Rather, Augustine's view of deification is conditioned by his understanding of what the Incarnation has done. By the union of the two natures of God and man in himself, Christ brought about an elevation of the humanity which he assumed, and by being made members of Christ, who was a partaker of our human nature, men may be made partakers of the divine nature:

> We too were made by his grace what we were not, that is, sons of God. Yet we were something else, and this much inferior, that is sons of men. Therefore he descended that we might ascend, and remaining in his nature was made a partaker [*particeps*] of our nature, that we remaining in our nature might be made partakers [*participes*] of his nature. But not simply this; for his participation [*participatio*] in our nature did not make him worse, while participating in his nature makes us better.[62]

Augustine's language here, with its reference to participation, is of the greatest importance for a right evaluation of his doctrine of deification – and also for the evaluation of his more familiar teaching about Free Will and the Fall, for in the *Enchiridion* he writes: 'For even though [Adam's] sin stood in free choice and nothing else, free choice itself did not suffice for the conservation of righteousness, unless by participation in the immutable goodness it were furnished by divine aid'.[63]

59. *serm.* 192.1, 1: 'Deos facturus qui homines erant, homo factus est qui Deus est'. Cf. *civ.* 9, 15: '[. . .] beatus et beatificus Deus factus particeps humanitatis nostrae compendium praebuit participandae divinitatis suae'.

60. Athanasius, *De Incarnatione*, 54.3.

61. See Victorino Capánaga, 'La deificación en la soteriología agostiniana', *Augustinus Magister* (Paris 1954), ii.745-54.

62. *ep.* 140.4, 10.

63. *ench.* 28.106 (tr. Ernest Evans, *Saint Augustine's* Enchiridion [London 1963], p.92).

Again, in *The City of God,* Augustine speaks of the hopes of the saints still on earth for heaven where, free from all distresses, they will have the society of the angels 'in participation of the highest God': *in participatione summi Dei.*[64] But the word *participatio* has a Platonic ring, and there is no question that in using it, Augustine would not have been aware of its Platonic associations. We find them, indeed, in his teaching concerning the divine Ideas, the uncreated archetypes of all individuals and species existing in the mind of God.[65] Created things simultaneously enjoy two modes of existence, one in their own natures, the other in the Ideas. Augustine certainly believed that he could find this doctrine in the Bible; but it is also the teaching of the Neoplatonists, which Augustine believed to come very close to Christianity, lacking only the saving doctrine of the Incarnation.[66]

It is the doctrine of the Incarnation, however, that makes the decisive difference. It is here that Augustine's teaching on deification parts company, as it is bound to part company, with the teaching of Plotinus and Porphyry.[67] Man is a being made by God, and wholly dependent upon God. He cannot rise to God except by divine grace, a grace which comes only through the voluntary flesh-taking of the Word — a conception which, for the Platonist, is either ridiculous or degrading.[68] Whether he consciously drew upon Augustine or not, the author of *The Cloud* was standing directly in the tradition of Augustinian thought when he wrote to his disciple:

> Certainly you are 'above yourself', because you have succeeded in reaching by grace what you could not achieve by nature. And that is, that you are united with God, in spirit, in love, and in harmony of will. You are beneath God, of course; for though in a manner of speaking you and God could be said at this time [that is, when your mind is engaged solely with God] not to be two spiritually, but one — so that you or whoever it is that perfectly contemplates may, because of this unity, truthfully be called *a god* as the Bible says (Ps. 81 [82]:6; John 10:34) — you are nonetheless beneath God. For he is God by nature, and without beginning; and you were once nothing at all. And when afterwards you, by his power and love, were made something, you by your deliberate act of will made yourself less than nothing. And it is only by his wholly undeserved mercy that you are made a god by grace, inseparably united to him in spirit, here and hereafter in the bliss of heaven, world without end! So though you may be wholly one with him in grace, you are still infinitely beneath him in nature.[69]

This is Augustinian doctrine in all but one small detail: Augustine would not be prepared to assert that a human being is made a god by grace in this life, but only in the life to come.[70] He would, however, have emphatically agreed with the propo-

64. *civ.* 11, 12.
65. *div.quaest.* q.46, 1-2.
66. *Conf.* 7, 9, 13-14; cf. *civ.* 10, 29.
67. See the appendix, below.
68. See Augustine's remarks in *civ.* 10, 24: 'But Porphyry was under the influence of evil powers [...]. Through pride Porphyry failed to understand that great mystery' (tr. J.W.C. Wand, *St Augustine's City of God* [Oxford 1963], p.175).
69. *The Cloud,* 67 (tr. Wolters, p.133).
70. See for example, *doctr.chr.* 1, 39, 43; *spir. et litt.* 22, 37; *trin.* 14, 17, 23.

THE SPIRITUALITY OF ST AUGUSTINE

sition that man remains man even when glorified, and would have approved the words of St Bernard:

> [. . .] with the saints, their human love will then ineffably be melted out of them and all poured over, so to speak, into the will of God. It must be so. How otherwise could God be *all in all* if anything of man remained in man. And yet our human substance will remain. We shall still be ourselves, but in another form, another glory and another power.[71]

Bernard's description of the process of deification, when the human will of the saints 'will then ineffably be melted out of them and all poured over, so to speak, into the will of God' is but another expression of what Augustine had written at the end of *The City of God:*

> There we shall be still and see; we shall see and we shall love; we shall love and we shall praise. Behold what will be, in the end, without end.[72]

Whether a practising mystic or not, there can be no question of the influence which Augustine's teaching exercised over later Western mystical theology.

The soul athirst for God

Considerations of space and time constrain me to bring this paper to a close. I have deliberately omitted many aspects of Augustine's spirituality which demand attention: his emphasis on illumination (*God is light and in him is no darkness at all*), which Abbot Butler noted;[73] the elements of apophatic theology which exist in his works, as Vladimir Lossky demonstrated;[74] his discussion of prayer in his letter to Proba, which shows him to have been aware of the ejaculatory prayers of the monks of Egypt, familiar to us from the writings of John Cassian;[75] and the evangelical basis of his *Rule,* such a potent influence upon the Middle Ages, where all piety was fundamentally monastic.[76] All of these aspects of Augustine's spirituality are important, and their omission testifies only to the amplitude of the subject.

Perhaps in concluding I might cite a passage of St Augustine quoted by the author of *The Cloud* at the end of his treatise:

> All the life of a good Christian is nothing else but holy desire.[77]

71. Bernard, *De Diligendo Deo,* 10, 28 (tr. A Religious of C.S.M.V. [London 1961], p.45).
72. *civ.* 22, 30: 'Ibi vacabimus, et videbimus; videbimus et amabimus; amabimus et laudabimus. Ecce quod erit in fine sine fine'. See the remarks of Henry, *La vision d'Ostie,* pp.126-7.
73. Butler, *Western Mysticism* (London 1967), pp.123-4.
74. V. Lossky, 'Les élements de "Théologie négative" dans la pensée de Saint Augustin', *Augustinus Magister* i.575-81.
75. *ep.*130 (*ad Probam de orando Deo*), 10, 20.
76. See T.J. Van Bavel, 'The Evangelical Inspiration of the Rule of St Augustine', *The Downside Review* xciii (1975), pp.83-99; George P. Lawless, 'Enduring Values of the Rule of St Augustine', *Angelicum* lix (1982), pp.59-78.
77. *The Cloud,* 75: 'Of this holy desire spekith Seint Austyne & seith that ' "al the liif of a good Cristen man is not elles bot holy desire" ' (ed. Hodgson, p.133).

I

This comes from Augustine's commentary on the first Epistle of St John: *Tota vita christiani boni, sanctum desiderium est* and Augustine continues: 'What you desire you do not as yet see; but desiring makes you able to be filled, when that which you are to see shall have come'.[78] That haunting Latin word *desiderium*[79] surely expresses the essence of the Christian spiritual life: *My soul is athirst for God, yea even for the living God* (Ps. 41:3 [42:2]), says the contemplative, as he awaits with patience the words of the Master: *Well done, good and faithful servant, enter thou into the joy of thy Lord* (Matt. 25:21).

78. *Io.ep.tr.* 4,6: 'Tota vita christiani boni, sanctum desiderium est. Quod autem desideras nondum vides; sed desiderando capax efficeris, ut cum venerit quod videas, implearis [...]. Desideremus ergo, fratres, quia implendi sumus'.
79. Never more poignantly expressed than in Abelard's description of heaven in his great hymn *O Quanta Qualia:*

> Vere Hierusalem est illa civitas,
> cuius pax iugis est, summa iucunditas,
> ubi non praevenit rem desiderium,
> nec desiderio minus est praemium

(Truly Jerusalem name we the shore/'Vision of Peace' that brings joy evermore;/Wish and fulfilment can severed be ne'er,/Nor the thing prayed for fall short of the prayer).

THE SPIRITUALITY OF ST AUGUSTINE

APPENDIX

When this paper was first read, I suggested that Augustine's doctrine of deification by participation also differs from Neoplatonism in respect of the Christian doctrine of creation from nothing. This would seem to be implied by James F. Anderson, *St Augustine and Being. A Metaphysical Essay* (The Hague 1963), 55: '[. . .] if things in the Augustinian universe exist by participating in the Ideas, this "participation" is radically different from that of Plotinus because it is creationist and not exemplarist'. I am now doubtful about this. It is, of course, true that the Christian doctrine of creation out of nothing makes a fundamental distinction between pagan and Christian thought from Theophilus of Antioch, *Ad Autolycum* ii.4: 'Plato and his followers acknowledge that God is uncreated, the Father and Maker of the universe; next they assume that matter is coeval with God' (tr. R.M. Grant [Oxford 1970], p.27) to Athanasius, *De Incarnatione*, 3: '[. . .] the world did not come into being of its own accord because it did not lack providence, and that neither was it made from pre-existent matter since God is not weak, but that through the Word, God brought the universe, which previously in no way subsisted at all, into being from non-existence [. . .]' (tr. R.W. Thomspon] Oxford 1971] p.141). As late as the mid-fourth century the pagan theologian Saturninus Salutius Secundus (usually and incorrectly called Sallustius) was still maintaining that matter was imperishable and uncreated: 'The universe itself must be imperishable and uncreated, imperishable because if it perishes God must necessarily make either a better or a worse, or the same or disorder [. . .]. That it is uncreated even what I have said suffices to show, because if it does not perish, neither did it come into being, since whatever comes into being perishes, coupled with the fact that since the universe exists because of God's goodness, it follows that God is ever good and the universe never exists' (*Sallustius: Concerning the gods and the universe*, 7, ed./tr. A.D. Nock [Cambridge 1926], pp.13, 15). This view, however, although characteristic of Plato himself (*Tim.* 41B) and of a certain type of popular Platonism (as Augustine recognised, *civ.* 10, 31) is not the doctrine of Plotinus. J.M. Rist, *Plotinus, The Road to Reality* (Cambridge 1967), p.26, draws attention to the fact that the Plotinian One is the creator of all finite beings. He refers to *En.* 6.8.19, where it is stated no less than four times that the One has 'made' (*epoiēse*) Being; and this assertion seems to be confirmed by Augustine himself, in describing the impression made on him on first reading Neoplatonist works: 'in them I found, though not in the very words, yet the thing itself and proved by all sorts of reasons, that *in the beginning was the Word and the Word was with God and the Word was God; the same was in the beginning with God; all things were made by him and without him was made nothing that was made; in him was life, and the life was the light of men, and the light shines in darkness and the darkness did not comprehend it.* And I found in those same writings that the soul of man, although *it gives testimony to the light, yet is not itself the light;* but the Word, God himself, is *the true light which*

I

enlightens every man that comes into this world; and that *he was in the world and the world was made by him, and the world knew him not.* But I did not read in those books that *he came unto his own and his own received him not, but to as many as received him he gave power to be made the sons of God* [cf. Rist, *Plotinus,* p.225: 'We have the power derived from the One of reascending. We must make use of the power available to us], *to them that believed in his name.* Again I found in them that the Word, God, was *born not of flesh nor of blood, nor of the will of man nor of the will of the flesh, but of God;* but I did not find that *the Word became flesh'* (*Conf.* 7,9, 13-14; tr. Sheed, p.111).

This passage suggests that, at least at the time of writing the *Confessions,* Augustine did not deny a doctrine of creation in Neoplatonism.

A NOTE ON THE ILLUSTRATION

Our illustration comes from a manuscript of St Augustine's *The City of God* in the Cathedral Library at Durham (B.II.22). It dates from the late eleventh century and apparently formed part of the collection presented to the Cathedral by the founder of the present church, Bishop William of St Carilef, who was consecrated in 1081 and died in 1098. R.A.B. Mynors, *Durham Cathedral Manuscripts* (Oxford 1939), pp.6 and 33, believes the manuscript to have been written at Durham and that two 14th-century copies of *The City of God,* Durham MSS. B.II.23 and B.II.24, were copied from it. The manuscript contains 231 folios and measures 12.6 by 9.3 inches (320 x 240mm), with 44 lines to the page. It is described in detail by Mynors, op.cit., no 33, pl.22 and by Franz Römer, *Die Handschriftliche Überlieferung der Werke des heiligen Augustinus* Bd II/2: *Grossbritannien und Irland: Verzeichnis nach Bibliotheken* (Vienna 1972), p.107.

The illustration shows an illuminated initial G with St Augustine at work on one of his books. Note the penknife in his left hand. He is vested, with a monastic tonsure, and his hair is (improbably) blue. All around him is a pack of grotesque monsters, who do not, apparently, cause him much concern. The colours of the initial are red, blue, purple and greenish-yellow.

The photograph is reproduced by courtesy of the Dean and Chapter of Durham.

Christ, God and Man, in the Thought of St Augustine*

In the eighteenth chapter of Book VII of the *Confessions* Augustine describes his intellectual condition at Milan in the critical period 385-386 when, after the discovery of the Neoplatonist philosophers, he had at last (to his own satisfaction at least) solved the problem of the existence of evil in a world made by a good Creator by discovering that it was nothing positive, only a privation, a mere absence of substance. Furthermore, he had enjoyed a spiritual experience which, for an instant, had provided a vision of eternal Truth. The transitory character of his vision, and the revelation of his own spiritual immaturity, caused Augustine to consider how he might come to a more enduring experience of God.

> So I set about finding a way to gain the strength that was necessary for enjoying You. And I could not find it until I embraced the *Mediator between God and man, the man Christ Jesus, who is over all things, God blessed for ever,* who was calling unto me and saying: *I am the Way, the Truth, and the Life;* and who brought into union with our nature that Food which I lacked the strength to take: for *the Word was made flesh* that Your Wisdom, by which You created all things, might give suck to our souls' infancy. For I was not yet lowly enough to hold the lowly Jesus as my God, nor did I know what lesson His embracing of our weakness was to teach. For Your Word, the eternal Truth, towering above the highest parts of Your creation, lifts up to Himself those who were cast down. He

* This text was read at the Pontifical University of Saint Thomas Aquinas on 14 April 1983 as part of the lecture series, *The Spirituality and Ministry of Saint Augustine,* sponsored by the Institute of Spirituality.

built for Himself here below a lowly house of our clay, that
by it He might bring down from themselves and bring up to
Himself those who were to be made subject, healing the swol-
lenness of their pride and fostering their love; so that their self-
confidence might grow no further but rather diminish, seeing
the deity at their feet, humbled by the assumption of our coat
of human nature; to the end that weary at last they might cast
themselves down upon His humanity and rise again in its
rising [1].

It might be said that Augustine's whole theology of Christ,
God and man, is comprehended in this short chapter. Jesus
Christ, the eternal Word, by taking flesh and becoming man,
raises fallen mankind and heals the pride which brought about
the Fall by His own divine humility. In the *Confessions* Augustine admits that he did not have this understanding as a result
of reading the Neoplatonists, but thought of Christ simply
as a man of marvellous wisdom and pre-eminent authority [2].
His recognition of Christ's divinity came from his subsequent
reading of St. Paul [3], and Augustine, when he came to write
the *Confessions*, considered that it might have been through
God's providence that he encountered the Neoplatonists before
studying the Scriptures, since their self-confidence might have
had the effect of undermining the authority of Scripture if
the order of reading had been reversed [4]. As it was, the
Neoplatonists had removed Augustine's fears that God might
be the creator of evil and had shown him the goal to which
he must strive. To this goal, Christ was the Way; but He could
only be the Way by being in one and the same Person both
God and man.

(1) *Conf.* VII, xviii, 24. Tr. by F.J. SHEED (1944), p. 118.
(2) *Ibid.*, VII, xix, 25 (SHEED, pp. 118-9).
(3) *C. Acad.* II, ii, 5; *Conf.* VII, xxi, 27. See the note by J.J. O'MEARA,
St. Augustine: Against the Academics (Ancient Christian Writers No 12)
(Westminster, Maryland/London 1950) p. 178 note 26.
(4) *Conf.* VII, xx, 26: « Nam si primo sanctis tuis litteris informatus
essem et in earum familiaritate obdulcuisses mihi et post in illa volu-
mina incidissem, fortasse aut abripsuissent me a solidamento pietatis,
aut si in affectu, quem salubrem inbiberam, perstitissem, putarem etiam
ex illis libris eum posse concipi, si eos solos quisque didicisset ».

Accordingly, the unity of Christ's person was a doctrine which was, one might say, forced upon Augustine by his own spiritual experiences; but it was also both to determine and to be influenced by his doctrine of grace. In the *Enchiridion*, written in 421 and of all Augustine's writings the one which can most easily be regarded as a systematic exposition of his beliefs, we find Augustine using the unity of Christ's Person as an argument for the grace of God. What, he asks, had the human nature in the man Christ deserved, that it should be joined in unity of Person with the only Son of God? There was, indeed, no human merit; « for the Truth itself, by nature and not by grace the only-begotten Son of God, did by grace assume manhood in such close unity of person, as Himself and of Himself to be also the Son of Man » (5). Augustine here is by anticipation anti-Nestorian, because he is already anti-Pelagian. Manhood is ennobled by union with the Godhead through a divine act of humility and without any merit, and it is because of this union of sinless manhood with divinity that it becomes possible for fallen man, by the sacrifice of Christ on the Cross, to become a partaker of divinity in the Body of Christ.

The theological problem which is solved for Augustine, as for the other Fathers, by the concept of the mediation of Christ, is the reconciliation of God's transcendence and His immanence. Put in another way, Augustine needs to affirm God's otherness, not simply as the highest being and the source of

---

(5) *Ench.* xi, 36: « Hic omnino granditer et evidenter Dei gratia commendatur. Quid enim natura humana in homine Christo meruit, ut in unitatem personae unici filii dei singulariter esset assumpta? Quae bona voluntas, cuius boni propositi studium, quae bona opera praecesserunt, quibus mereretur iste homo una fieri persona cum Deo? Numquid antea fuit homo, et hoc ei singulare beneficium praestitum est, cum singulariter promereretur deum? Nempe ex quo esse homo coepit, non aliud coepit esse, quam Dei Filius; et hoc unicus; et propter Deum Verbum, quod illo suscepto caro factum est, utique Deus, ut quemadmodum est una persona quilibet homo, anima scilicet rationalis et caro, ita sit Christus una persona, Verbum et homo.. Veritas quippe ipsa, unigenitus Dei Filius non gratia, sed natura, gratia suscepit hominem tanta unitate personae, et idem ipse esset etiam hominis filius ».

being, but as the Creator who has brought all things into existence from nothing, while at the same time recognising that, because man is made in the image and likeness of God (Gn 1:26), and has as his chief end to praise God([6]) and to enjoy him for ever([7]) he has a particular relationship with his Creator, since in all creation, nothing is nearer to God than man's soul([8]).   Man is, therefore, a special creature, designed to be a fellow-citizen with the angels in the eternal Jerusalem; but he is also a fallen creature, whose being has been damaged and distorted as a consequence of the sin of Adam, though it still retains something of its original capacity to enjoy God and to participate in His goodness. Augustine expresses the matter in an important passage in the *De Trinitate*:

> Now we have reached the point in our discussion at which we have undertaken to consider that highest element in the human mind whereby it knows or can know God, with a view to our finding therein the image of God. Although the human mind is not of that nature which belongs to God [i.e. it is something created and not self-existent like God], yet the image of that nature which transcends every other in excellence is to be sought and found in the element which in our own nature is the most excellent. But first we have to consider the mind in itself, before it has participation in God, and discover His image there. We have said that it still remains the image of God, although an image faded and defaced by the loss of that participation. It is in virtue of the fact that it has a capacity

---

(6) *Enar. Ps.* 44, 9: «... Ut et illud quod adiunctum est, *Dico ego opera mea regi*, significare voluerit summum hominis opus non esse, nisi Deum laudare. Illius est specie sua placere tibi, ad te pertinet eum in gratiarum actione laudare ».

(7) *De Doctr. Chr.* I, v, 5: « Res igitur quibus fruendum est, Pater et Filius et Spiritus sanctus, eodemque Trinitas, una quaedam summa res, communisque omnibus fruentibus ea »; cf. *Conf.* VII, xviii, 24: « Et quaerebam viam comparandi roboris, quod esset idoneum ad fruendum te... ».

(8) *De Civ. Dei* XI, 26: « Et nos quidem in nobis, tametsi non aequam, imo valde longeque distantem, neque coaeternam, et quo brevius totum dicitur, non eiusdem substantiae, cuius est Deus, tamen qua Deo nihil sit in rebus ab eo factis natura propinquius, imaginem Dei, hoc est summae illius Trinitatis, agnoscimus, adhuc reformatione perficiendam, ut sit etiam similitudine proxima ».

for God (*eius capax est*) and the ability to participate in God, that it is His image; only because it is His image can so high a destiny be conceived for it (⁹).

This passage admirably expresses Augustine's understanding of man's relation to God. Although itself a creature, man's soul reflects in a certain fashion its uncreated Creator and can therefore in some degree participate in Him. The notion of participation is originally a Platonic one, used to describe the relation between an individual, existing thing and its archetype or form, from which it derives its being; but the idea was taken over and developed by the Fathers (¹⁰): man exists by participating in God, who is Being and the source of Being. This rather obvious understanding of participation is adopted by Augustine in Question 46 of his work *On Eighty-Three Diverse Questions*, in which he identifies Plato's ideas with thoughts in the mind of God: « Not only do Ideas exist, but they are true because they are eternal and remain unchangeably what they are; and it is by participating in them that everything is made which exists, whatever may be its mode of being » (¹¹).

The Christian Fathers, however, were not prepared to consider participation only in a philosophical sense. For them, God not only existed as Being and the cause of Being, but also as Goodness and the cause of Goodness, and Blessedness and the cause of Blessedness. Man is unable to be good or happy by his own efforts and resources, but only by participation in God. So Augustine writes: « God is the supreme reality, with His Word and the Holy Spirit — three who are

---

(⁹) *De Trin.* XIV, viii, 11. Tr. by JOHN BURNABY, *Augustine: Later Works* (The Library of Christian Classics Vol. VIII) (London/Philadelphia 1955), pp. 108-09.

(¹⁰) See DAVID L. BALÁS, METOUSIA THEOU. *Man's participation in God's Perfections according to Saint Gregory of Nyssa* (Studia Anselmiana Fasc. LV) (Rome 1966).

(¹¹) *De Div. Quaest. LXXXIII*, q. 46, 2: « non solum sunt ideae, sed ipsae verae sunt, quia aeternae sunt, et eiusmodi atque incommutabiles manent, quarum participatione fit ut sit quidquid est, quomodo est ». See É. GILSON, *Introduction à l'étude de saint Augustin* ⁴ (Paris 1969), 109ff.

one. He is the God omnipotent, creator and maker of every soul and every body; participation in Him brings happiness to all who are happy in truth and not in illusion » (¹²). (It may be added, though it is not our present concern, that angels no less than men, participate in God who is their creator) (¹³). Thus the blessedness of Adam in Paradise before the Fall was due to his unhindered participation in God: « He lived in the enjoyment of God and derived his own goodness from God's goodness (*vivebat fruens Deo, ex quo bono erat bonus*) » (¹⁴). This relationship was broken by the Fall. By his own action man turned away from God and became alienated from the source of his goodness. In the purely philosophical sense he did not cease to participate in God, for if he had done so, he would have passed out of existence; but in the moral and spiritual sense man ceased to be a partaker of the divine nature, became a slave of sin, and fell into the power of the devil. From this state of sin and slavery he was powerless to raise himself; and because of the gulf which had been created between sinful man and sinless God, a Mediator was required, who should unite in Himself both alienated humanity (though without sharing in its sin) and the Godhead upon which humanity absolutely depended.

This is, of course, the message of the Gospel; this is what Christianity is about, and constitutes the essence of the Christian religion. Yet the Atonement, although a vital religious truth, is not the sole doctrine of Christianity. If man is to be saved, he must be saved for an end: to glorify God and to enjoy Him for ever in His kingdom; as Augustine put it, at the conclusion of *The City of God*: « There we shall be still and see; we shall see and we shall love; we shall love and we shall praise. Behold what will be, in the end, without end! For what is our end but to reach that kingdom which has no end? » (¹⁵).

(¹²) *De Civ. Dei* V, 11. Tr. by HENRY BETTENSON (Penguin Books, London 1972), p. 196.
(¹³) *Ibid.*, XI, 12.
(¹⁴) *Ibid.*, XIV, 26.
(¹⁵) *Ibid.*, XXII, 30 (Bettenson, p. 1091).

And yet more: the glorification and enjoyment of God is not to be understood as a servile activity, but as one in which man finds his true happiness. The nature of human happiness, like the origin of evil, had been one of the problems which had haunted Augustine all his life. At Milan, before his conversion, he had put forward the suggestion that an Epicurean notion of perpetual physical pleasure might represent the ideal of happiness ([16]), without taking account, as he afterwards realised, of the loveliness of virtue and of that beauty — « so old and so new » ([17]) — which compels love for its own sake, and without any thought of sensual gratification. After his conversion, at Cassiciacum, he proposed another definition of true happiness: « Whoever has God is happy... whoever comes to the Highest Measure, through the Truth, is happy. This means to have God within the soul, that is, to enjoy God » ([18]). Nearly forty years later, in the nineteenth book of *The City of God*, Augustine, the mature theologian, says roundly: « ... Indeed, the only purpose man has in philosophizing is the attainment of happiness; but that which makes him happy is the Supreme Good itself » ([19]) and goes on to define the Supreme Good as eternal life and eternal death as the Supreme Evil, « and that to achieve the one and escape the other, we must live rightly. That is what the Scripture says: *The just man lives on the basis of faith*. For we do not yet see our good, and hence we have to seek it by believing; and it is not in our power to live rightly, unless while we believe and pray we receive help from

---

([16]) *Conf.* VI, xvi, 26: « ... et quaerebam, si essemus inmortales et in perpetua corporis voluptate sine ullo amissionis terrore viveremus, cur non essemus beati aut quid aliud quaereremus, nesciens id ipsum ad magnam miseriam pertinere, quod ita demersus et caecus cogitare non possem lumen honestatis et gratis amplectandae pulchritudinis, quam non vidit oculus carnis, et videtur ex intimo ».

([17]) *Ibid.*, X, xxvii, 38.

([18]) *De Beata Vita* iv, 34: « Deum habet igitur quisquis beatus est. ... Quisquis igitur ad summum modum per veritatem venerit, beatus est. Hoc est animis deum habere, id est deo perfrui. Cetera etiam quamvis a deo habeantur, non habent deum ». Tr. by LUDWIG SCHOPP (1939), slightly modified.

([19]) *De Civ. Dei* XIX, 1 (BETTENSON, p. 846); cf. *De Trin.* XIII, v, 8; viii, 11.

Him who has given us the faith to believe that we must be
helped by Him » ([20]).

It would seem, then, that the Augustinian conception of
the work of Christ the Mediator implies not only the remission
of sins, but the fulfillment of the destiny for which human nature
was originally created. The Incarnation did not take place
simply to redeem man from his sins. That, indeed, is its
primary purpose; and Augustine specifically says that while the
angels who did not fall have no need for a mediator and the
fallen angels are not given one, man, who was cast down
by the mediation of the proud devil persuading him to pride,
may be raised up by Christ, the humble mediator, persuading
him to humility. As so often in the thought of Augustine, it is
the humility of Christ which is the most striking feature of the
Incarnation:

> And so the only Son of God was thus made the mediator
> of God and man, when being the Word of God with God, He
> both brought down His majesty to human affairs and raised
> human lowliness to the realms of the divine, that He might be
> a Mediator between God and men, being made a man by God
> above men ([21]).

Here, in the phrase « he raised human lowliness to the
realms of the divine » (*et humilitatem humanam usque ad divina*

([20]) *Ibid.*, XIX, 4 (BETTENSON, p. 852).

([21]) *Ep. ad Gal. exp.*, 24: « Mediator ergo inter Deum et Deum esse
non potest, quia unus est Deus: *mediator autem unius non est*, quia
inter aliquos medius est. Angeli porro, qui non lapsi sunt a conspectu
Dei, mediatore non opus habent, per quem reconcilientur. Item angeli
qui nullo suadente spontanea praevaricatione sic lapsi sunt, per media-
torem non reconciliantur. Restat ergo ut qui mediatore superbo diabolo
superbiam persuadente deiectus est, mediatore humili Christo humilitatem
persuadente erigatur. Nam si Filius Dei in naturali aequalitate Patris
manere vellet, nec se exinaniret, *formam servi accipiens*, non esset mediator Dei et hominum: quae ipsa Trinitas unus Deus est, eadem in tribus,
Patre et Filio et Spiritu sancto, deitatis aeternitae et aequalitate constante.
Sic itaque unicus Filius Dei, mediator Dei et hominum factus est, cum
Verbum Dei Deus apud Deum, et maiestatem suam usque ad humana
deposuit, et humilitatem humanam usque ad divina subvexit, ut mediator
esset inter Deum et homines homo per Deum ultra homines ». Cf. *De
Trin.* IV, x, 13.

subvexit) we find again the notion of participation in God by man, His creation, through the flesh-taking of the Son.

This notion is so admirably expressed in the passage in Augustine's work on the Trinity as to invite quotation at some length.

> Our illumination is indeed participation in the Word, in that *life*, that is, *which is the light of men*. But on account of the defilement of our sins we were utterly incapable and unworthy of that participation. We had therefore to be cleansed. Moreover the one cleansing of wicked and proud men was the blood of the Just One and the humility of God; and by this we became able to come to the contemplation of God, which we cannot do by nature, through being cleansed by Him, who was made what we are by nature [sinless] and are not by sin. Now we are not divine by nature; by nature we are men, and through sin we are not righteous men. And so God, being made a righteous man, interceded with God for man who is a sinner. The sinner has nothing in common with the Righteous One, but man has humanity in common with man. Therefore joining to us the likeness of His humanity, He took away the unlikeness of our iniquity, and being made a sharer (*particeps*) of our mortality, He made us sharers of His divinity(22).

This last phrase will readily recall the famous words of St Athanasius: « He was made man that we might be made gods » (23) which are almost exactly echoed by Augustine in his

---

(22) *De Trin.* IV, ii, 4: « Illuminatio quippe nostra participatio Verbi est, illius scilicet *vitae* quae *lux est hominum*. Huic autem participationi prorsus inhabiles et minus idonei eramus, propter immunditiam peccatorum. Mundandi ergo eramus. Porro iniquorum et superborum una mundatio est sanguis iusti, et humilitas Dei: ut ad contemplandum Deum quod natura non sumus, per eum mundaremur factum quod natura sumus, et quod peccato non sumus. Deus enim natura non sumus: homines natura sumus, iusti peccato non sumus. Deus itaque factus homo iustus, intercessit Deo pro homine peccatore. Non enim congruit peccator iusto, sed congruit homini homo. Adiungens ergo nobis similitudinem humanitatis suae, abstulit dissimilitudinem iniquitatis nostrae: et factus particeps mortalitatis nostrae, fecit nos participes divinitatis suae ».

(23) ATHANASIUS, *De Incarnatione*, 54; see also IRENAEUS, *Adv. Haer.* V *Praef.*: « ... Verbum Dei, Iesum Christum Dominum nostrum: qui

sermon 192 (²⁴): « To make those gods who were men, He was made man who is God ». This bold language emphasises the significance for the Fathers of what the Incarnation accomplished; and it is worth considering this against another view of the Incarnation in the early Church held by the Arians. It will be recalled that, for the Arians, the Logos, who is created by the Father, participates in His divinity and is divine, not by nature but by grace. At an early stage of the Arian Controversy St Athanasius decided that what was at stake was not simply the place of the Logos in the Holy Trinity, but man's salvation: if Christ were not fully God, but only God by participation, then he could not make men partakers of the divinity which is not his by nature but only by grace (²⁵). Now Arius apparently taught such a doctrine — « And if He is called God, He is not a true God, but by grace of participation, as are all others » (²⁶) — and Maurice Wiles has argued that it may well not have been as logically inconsistent, as Catholic controversialists like St Athanasius maintained: « The deification which is man's goal is not to become [God], *ho theos* but [gods by grace] *theoi kata charin*. The Son, on the Arian understanding, is the prototype of *theoi kata charin*. It is not clear, therefore, why he should not logically be able to bring men to be what he is » (²⁷).

Let us accept this argument. What does it imply? The answer, surely, is that the Arians were anxious above all else to preserve the Old Testament teaching of the Oneness of God

propter immensam suam dilectionem factus est quod sumus nos, uti nos perficeret esse quod est ipse ».

(²⁴) AUG., *Serm.* 192, i, 1: « Deos facturos qui homines erant, homo factus est qui Deus est ».

(²⁵) ATHANASIUS, *De Synodis*, 51.

(²⁶) ARIUS, *Thalia*, fragm. *apud* ATHANASIUS, *Or. adv. Ar.* I, 6: ...Εἰ δὲ καὶ λέγεται Θεός, ἀλλ'οὐκ ἀληθινός ἐστιν· ἀλλὰ μετοχῇ χάριτος ὥσπερ καὶ οἱ ἄλλοι πάντες, οὕτω καὶ αὐτὸς λέγεται ὀνόματι μόνον Θεός. Cf. Athanasius' reply, § 9: Διὸ Θεός ἐστιν ἀληθινός, ἀληθινοῦ Πατρὸς οὐσίας γέννημα. τὰ δ'ἄλλα, οὓς εἶπεν, « Ἐγὼ εἶπα Θεοί ἐστε », μόνον μετοχῇ τοῦ Λόγου διὰ τοῦ Πνεύματος ταύτην ἔχουσι τὴν χάριν παρὰ τοῦ Πατρός.

(²⁷) « In Defence of Arius », *The Journal of Theological Studies*, NS xiii (1962), 346.

while doing justice to the language of the New Testament, which implied that the Son and the Holy Spirit were real, subsistent entities, and not mere appearances of the One God, as the Sabellians taught. But there was another consideration. The God of Arius was a high and transcendent being, who had, so far as possible, to be kept apart from the created world. « God was alone », declared Arius in the *Thalia*, « and the Word and Wisdom did not yet exist. When afterwards He wished to create us, He then made a certain Being, whom He named Logos and Wisdom and Son, that He might create us through Him » (²⁸). Thus between God and the created world was imposed the Logos which, though created, had a special role as mediator between God and the lower creation. What Arianism, then, did was to adapt the theory of emanation, employed earlier by the Gnostics and, with suitable modifications, by the Neoplatonists. As Bible Christians the Arians had to take account of the statement in Genesis that God created the heavens and the earth; but they endeavoured to shield Him, as far as possible, from creation, by interposing the Son who, although Himself a created being, enjoyed a special relationship to the Creator — « a perfect creature of God, but not as one of the creatures » (²⁹) — and who, in turn, separated himself from the lower order of creation by Himself creating the Holy Ghost. This adaptation of emanationism to biblical creationism remained a feature of Western Arianism in Augustine's lifetime; thus, in the *Sermo Arianorum*, to which Augustine composed a reply (³⁰), probably in the winter of 418-9, we have the assertion that the Son is begotten of the Father and the Spirit made by the Son; while a decade later the Arian bishop, Maximinus,

---

(²⁸) ATHANASIUS, *Or. adv. Ar.*, 5.

(²⁹) ARIUS, *Ep. ad Alexandrum apud* ATHANASIUS, *De Synodis*, 16; EPIPHANIUS, *Haer.* 69.7: κτίσμα τοῦ Θεοῦ τέλειον, ἀλλ' οὐχ ὡς ἕν τῶν κτισμάτων.

(³⁰) *Serm. Ar.*, 10-12: « Ergo Filius a Patre est genitus: Spiritus sanctus per Filium est factus. Filius Patrem praedicat: Spiritus sanctus Filium annuntiat. Primum et praecipuum opus est Filii, genitoris gloriam revelare: primum et praecipuum est opus Spiritus sancti, in animas hominum Christi dignitatem manifestare ». *PL* xlii, 680.

was to distinguish between *honouring* the Spirit as teacher, *reverencing* the Son as creator, and *adoring* the Father as First Cause ([31]).

It is against this background of Arian theologizing that the sheer audacity of the doctrine formulated in the first four General Councils and in the treatises of the Catholic Fathers becomes apparent. Far from being the bold blasphemers of orthodox Christian tradition, Arius and his followers appear to the modern student as cautious thinkers, anxious to preserve the mystery of the Christian revelation by safeguarding, as far as possible, the transcendence of God. They could not bear to admit that the Godhead could have become involved with His creation: their God was *the high and lofty One who inhabits eternity* (Isai. 57.15), and He could have no dealings with man except through an intermediary. As against this, the Catholic response to Arianism was to proclaim the consubstantiality of the Son with the Father and, as a consequence, the unity of Godhead and manhood in the One Person of Christ. The Nicene Fathers were bold enough to affirm

> that a higher gift than grace
> Should flesh and blood refine;
> God's presence and His very self
> And essence all divine.

The confession of Jesus Christ, true God and true man, has become so familiar to us by habitual repetition that we often fail to appreciate the portentous content of what we affirm; and it is not altogether surprising that some modern theologians, like the Arians before them, have found the Catholic doctrine of the Incarnation intellectually unacceptable. If we think them wrong, we ought at least to bear in mind the nature of our claim: that we take literally the words of St Paul: *that*

([31]) AUG., *Coll. cum Maximino*: [Max. dixit]: « ... Nos enim Spiritum sanctum competenter honoramus et doctorem, ut ducatorem, ut illuminatorem, ut sanctificatorem: Christum colimus ut creatorem: Patrem cum sincera devotione adoramus ut auctorem, quem et unum auctorem ubique omnibus pronuntiamus ». *PL* xlii, 725; cf. *C. Max.*, II, 5; *ibid.*, cols 760-1.

in Christ the whole fulness of deity dwells bodily and accept
the necessary implication that God,

> giver of breath and bread,
> World's strand, sway of the sea,
> Lord of living and dead

— has lived and died in this world, His creation, in a human
body. This affirmation is easily made; but the implications
are terrifying.

Augustine did accept these implications; indeed, they colour
his whole theology. We may here note one particular phrase
from the *Enchiridion* ([32]): « This at least we say: that the Word
was made flesh through the assuming of flesh by divinity, not
by the conversion of divinity into flesh ». In this phrase, which
anticipates and probably inspires the language of the Athan-
asian Creed, Augustine provides the clue to his understanding
of the Incarnation: it was the Word of God descending to man,
so that man might in turn ascend to God. The gulf which
opened between God and man through Adam's sin has been
bridged — but from the divine side.

> The more credible and probable position is that all [fallen]
> men, as long as they are mortals, must needs be also wretched.
> If this is so, we must look for a mediator who is not only
> human but also divine, so that man may be brought from mortal
> misery to blessed immortality by the intervention of the blessed
> mortality of this mediator. It was necessary that He should not
> fail to become mortal, equally necessary that He should not
> remain mortal. He was in truth made mortal, not by the weak-
> ening of the godhead of the Word but by the assumption of
> the weakness of the flesh. But He did not remain mortal in
> that flesh which He raised from the dead. For the fruit of His
> mediation is just this: that those for whose liberation He was

([32]) *Ench.*, x, 34: « De quo mediatore longum est, ut quanta dignum
est, tanta dicantur, quamvis ab homine dici digna non possint. Quis
enim hoc solum congruentibus explicet verbis, quod *verbum caro factum
est, et habitavit in nobis*, ut crederemus in Dei patris omnipotentis
unicum Filium, natum de Spiritu sancto et Maria virgine? Ita quippe
verbum caro factum est, a divinitate carne suscepta, non in carnem
divinitate mutata ».

made a mediator should not themselves remain for ever in
death, even the death of the flesh [33].

Even more vivid is the language of Sermon 121, a paschal
homily of uncertain date, perhaps earlier than 410. The sermon
was addressed to the newly-baptised; hence the text is taken
from the Prologue to St John's Gospel, with its triumphant
declaration that *the Word was made flesh*, as a consequence
of which those who receive Him are given power to become
sons of God. Space forbids us to quote the whole of this
admirable, short homily, but the conclusion must be given:

> He came to us but did not depart much from Himself —
> rather He never removed from Himself what is divine, but
> added what was of our nature. He added what He was not,
> He did not lose what He was, He was made son of man but
> did not cease to be Son of God. For that reason He is the
> mediator *in the midst* (John 20:19,26). What is *in the midst*?
> Neither above nor below. How neither above nor below? Not
> *above* because flesh, not *below* because not a sinner, yet how-
> ever, inasmuch as He is God, always above; for He did not so
> come to us as to desert the Father. He has gone from us and
> has not deserted us; He will come to us again and not desert
> the Father [34].

Thus, it is essential in Augustine's view of the Mediator
that He should not only be *in the midst*, between God and man;
but that He must also *be* both God and man and not merely
participate in the two natures, divine and human. This is why
the Arian Christ, who is neither fully God nor fully man, was

---

[33] *De Civ. Dei* IX, 15 (BETTENSON, pp. 359-60).
[34] *Serm.* 121, 5: « Ad nos accessit sed a se non multum recessit.
Immo a se quod Deus est numquam recessit sed addidit quod erat
naturae nostrae. Accessit enim quod non erat, non amisit quod erat,
factus filius hominis, sed non cessavit esse Filius Dei. Per hoc mediator
in medio. Quid est *in medio*? Nec sursum nec deorsum. Quomodo nec
sursum nec deorsum? Nec sursum quia caro; nec deorsum quia non
peccator, sed tamen in quantum Deus, semper sursum. Non enim sic
venit ad nos, ut dimitteret Patrem. A nobis ivit, ivit et non nos dimisit;
ad nos veniet, et illum non dimittet (ed. Poque, AUGUSTIN: *Sermons pour
la Pàque*, p. 232).

unacceptable to Augustine, not simply because Arianism was repugnant to Catholic doctrine, but because as a theology it would have made meaningless Augustine's understanding of mediation. In his work *Against a Sermon of the Arians* Augustine understands the declaration there made that the Lord Jesus « deigned to take human flesh » as implying an Apollinar- ian conception of Christ's manhood: Christ assumed human flesh but without taking a human soul [35]. In his treatise against the Arian bishop Maximinus, Augustine makes the rather obvious claim that the Arians, by confessing the Son to be God and Lord, while at the same time denying His identity of sub- stance with the Father, teach a doctrine of two gods, in defiance of the Deuteronomic declaration: *Hear, O Israel, the Lord thy God is one God* (Deut. 6:4) [36]. This was a good debating point, given that one of the principal concerns of Arianism was to preserve the divine unity; but it was more than a debating point. Arianism wished to preserve the transcendent God from contact with human baseness [37] and so held that He had created

---

[35] *C. Serm. Ar.* v, 5: « Dicunt etiam: "Et quia de omnibus spiri- tualibus et rationalibus gradibus, propter qualitatem et fragilitatem corporis paulo minus ab Angelis inferior minoratus homo videbatur; ne se vilem speraret, et de salute sua desperaret, Dominus Iesus honorans facturam suam, dignatus est humanam carnem suscipere, et ostendere quia non est homo vilis, sed pretiosus, sicut scriptum est: *Magnus homo et pretiosus vir* (Prov. 20:6 LXX). Et ideo solum hominem Patri suo haeredem, sibi enim cohaeredem facere dignatus est: ut quod minus acceperat in natura, plus haberet in honore" [*Sermo Ar.*, 5, *PL* xlii, 679]. Haec dicentes, hoc volunt intelligi, quod humanam carnem sine humana anima Christum assumpserit. Quae propria haeresis Apollinaristarum est: sed etiam istos, id est Arianos, in eorum disputationibus, non solum Trinitatis diversas esse naturas, sed etiam hoc sentire deprehendimus, quod animam non habeat Christum humanam ». *PL* xlii, 686-7.

[36] *C. Max. Ar.* II, 15, 1: « In forma Dei Filium esse non negas, et Deo Patri aequalem negas, maiorem Patris formam putans esse quam Filii: tanquam non habuit Pater unde forman suam compleret in Filio, quem de se ipso genuit, non fecit ex nihilo, non ex alio. Aut si formam suam in unico Filio plenam gignere potuit, nec tamen genuit plenam, sed minorem; quid sequatur attendite, et in viam redite, ne cogamini Patrem invidum dicere. Dicitis Deum Filium, dicitis Dominum; sed ut duos deos dominosque faciatis, contra Scripturam clamantem: *Audi, Israel: Dominus Deus tuus, Dominus unus est* ». *PL* xlii, 777.

[37] *Coll. c. Max.*: « Max. respondit: "Nos enim unum auctorem

a Son who only participated in the Father's divinity and was
therefore not naturally divine. The Son took flesh for man's
salvation, but only flesh, and was therefore not fully man. He
was therefore an intermediate being, a kind of virtuous equivalent of the demons, whose activities are discussed and denounced in the ninth book of *The City of God*. The Arians saw
Him acting in the Incarnation by the will and precept of the
Father [38] — the whole economy of the redemption is effected
by God at one remove through a created agent. Augustine,
on the other hand, saw the act of redemption as the work of
the entire Trinity, acting through the Son, in a human being,
Jesus Christ, the second Adam, in whom the entire human race
can be comprehended [39].

It is for that reason that Augustine insists on the unity
of Christ's person:

> Consequently Christ Jesus, the Son of God, is both God and
> man: God before all ages, man in our age: God because He
> is God's Word, for *the Word was God*, man however because
> into unity of person with the Word has been joined a rational

Deum Patrem cognoscimus, a quo illuminatio omnis *per gradus* descendit.
... Sive ergo Christus docens nos illuminat, Pater illuminat qui eum des-
tinavit; sive Spiritus sanctus illuminat, illuminatio ad auctorem recurrit,
qui est fons bonitatis... A nobis unus colitur Deus, innatus, infectus,
invisibilis, qui ad humana contagia et ad humanam carnem non descendit"». *PL* xlii, 711-2, 718. Cf. *C. Max. Ar.* I, 2, 3. *PL* xlii, 744-6.

(38) *Serm. Ar.*, 6: « *Cum*, inquit, *venit plenitudo temporis, misit Deus
Filium suum natum ex muliere* (Gal. 4:4). Ipse qui voluntate Patris
carnem suscepit, ipse et voluntate et praecepto ipsius in corpore con-
versatus est, sicut ipse ait: *Descendi de caelo, non ut faciam voluntatem meam, sed voluntatem eius qui me misit* (Ioh. 6:38) ». *PL* xlii, 679.

(39) *Ench.* xii, 38: « Sed cum illam creaturam, quam virgo concepit et
peperit, quamvis ad solam personam Filii pertinentem, tota trinitas fe-
cerit, neque enim separabilia sunt opera trinitatis, cur in facienda solus
Spiritus nominatus est? An et quando unus trium in aliquo opere nominatur, universa operari trinitas intelligitur? Ita vero est, et exemplis
doceri potest »; *De Trin.* I, iv, 7: « ... Pater et Filius et Spiritus sanctus,
sicut inseparabiles sunt, ita inseparabiliter operentur. Haec et mea fides
est, quando haec est catholica fides »; *ibid*, I, vi, 12, 13: « Aequalis est
ergo Patri Filius, et inseparabilis operatio est Patris et Filii... Similiter
et de Spiritu sancto... Ergo Patri et Filio prorsus aequalis, et in Trinitatis unitate consubstantialis et coaeternus »; *Enar. Ps.* 20, II, 5: « ... omnis
homo in Christo unus homo est, et unitas Christianorum unus homo ».

soul and flesh. Therefore in that He is God, He *and the Father are one,* while in that He is man, *the Father is greater than* He. For being the only Son of God, by nature and not by Grace, that He might even be full of grace, He was made also Son of Man; and He, being one, is both things, One Christ constituted of both (⁴⁰).

And again:

I have come down from heaven not to do My own will but the will of Him who sent me (⁴¹). ... This is said on account of the unity of person, since Christ, God and man, is one person. On this account He also said: *No one has ascended into heaven but He who descended from heaven, the Son of Man* (John 3:13). If you take account of the distinction of substances, it was the Son of God who descended from heaven and the Son of Man who was crucified; if you take account of the unity of person, the Son of Man also descended from heaven and the Son of God also was crucified. For He Himself is the Lord of Glory, of whom the Apostle says: *If they had understood, they would not have crucified the Lord of Glory* (I Cor. 3:8). On account, therefore, of this unity of person, not only did He say that the Son of Man descended from heaven, but said that He was in heaven when he was speaking on earth (⁴²).

(⁴⁰) *Ench.* x, 35. Tr. by E. EVANS (1953), p. 33.

(⁴¹) JOHN 6: 38. This was, of course, a proof-text for the Arians, because they could apply it to the Word. So in the *Sermo Arianorum,* 6, quoted above, note 38. See Augustine's reply, *C. Serm.* Ar. vi, 6: « His testimoniis sanctarum Scripturarum quid persuadere conantur, nisi propterea Patris et Filii diversas esse naturas, quia obediens Patri ostenditur Filius? Quod tamen de hominibus non utique dicerent: neque enim si homo filius homini patri est obediens, ideo amborum diversa natura est ». *PL* xlii, 687.

(⁴²) *C. Max. Ar.* II, 20, 3: « ...Hoc enim propter unitatem personae dictum est, quoniam una persona est Christus Deus et homo. Propter quod etiam: *Nemo,* inquit, *ascendit in caelum, nisi qui de caelo descendit, Filium hominis, qui est in caelo* (Ioh. 3: 13). Si ergo attendas distinctionem substantiarum, Filius Dei de caelo descendit, Filius hominis crucifixus est; si unitatem personae, et Filius hominis descendit de caelo, et Filius Dei est crucifixus. Ipse est enim Dominus gloriae, de quo ait Apostolus: *Si enim cognovissent, numquam Dominum gloriae crucifixissent* (I Cor. 2: 8). Propter hanc ergo unitatem personae, non solum Filium hominis dixit descendisse de caelo, sed esse dixit in caelo, cum loqueretur in terra ». *PL* xlii, 789-90. Cf. *C. Serm. Ar.* vii. 6, viii. 6. *PL* xlii, 687-9.

Augustine, then, long before the Tome of Pope Leo and
the Chalcedonian definition of faith, confessed « one and the
same Christ, Son, Lord, Only-begotten; acknowledged in Two
Natures unconfusedly, unchangeably, indivisibly, inseparably;
the difference of the Natures being in no way removed because
of the union, but rather the property of each nature being
preserved, and both concurring into One Prosopon and One
Hypostasis ». Furthermore, for Augustine this confession was
not a mere exercise in academic theology but a vital religious
truth if Christ were truly to be the mediator between God and
man. For him, in the words of St. Paul: *God was in Christ
reconciling the world to Himself* (II Cor. 5:19).

What are the consequences of Augustine's view of Christ,
God and man, for his theology as a whole? A comprehensive
answer would require a book, or several books, for of Augustine
we might say what Nietzsche said about Thucydides: « You
must read and mark him line by line till you can read between
the lines as clearly as in them. There are few thinkers with
so many ideas brooding in the background » ([43]). The more one
reads Augustine, the more one notices his tendency, when writing
upon a particular theme to refer, almost as it were in passing,
to an idea which he has developed elsewhere. Furthermore,
in view of the centrality of the Incarnation in any system of
Christian theology, we shall not be surprised to find it at the
centre of Augustine's own thinking, informing and determining the course of his reflexions. Accordingly, in this present
lecture, I can only give a very general indication of the consequences for Augustine of his understanding of Christ, true God
and true man, the Mediator between God and man.

The purpose of the Incarnation, for Augustine as for others
of the Fathers, is the salvation of mankind. Augustine discusses
the question in the thirteenth book of the *De Trinitate*, in which
he maintains that no more appropriate way could be found
to save man who, by the sin of Adam, had fallen into the power

---

([43]) NIETZSCHE, « Gotzen-Dämmerung », *Works* viii, 168-9 quoted by
A. Zimmern, *The Greek Commonwealth* [5] (1931), 199.

of the devil, than for the Son of God to take human nature and, by suffering an unjust death at the hands of the devil, to release from the devil's power fallen men over whom the devil had been permitted to rule by God's justice ([44]). Nevertheless, the benefits of the Incarnation were not limited to the Atonement for, as Augustine notes,

> there are many other things in Christ's incarnation, which so displeases the proud ([45]), which may profitably be considered and reflected upon. One of these is that it demonstrated to mankind what place it had in God's creation; seeing that human nature was so capable of being joined to God that out of two substances might be made one Person and, as a consequence, that Person might be formed out of three: God; soul; and flesh, so that those proud and evil spirits, who take their station between God and man, as though ready to help though really to deceive, may not dare to prefer themselves to mankind because they do not have flesh; and above all, because the Son of God has deigned to die in the same flesh, they may not on that account persuade men to adore them as gods, because they seem to be immortal ([46]).

The Incarnation, then, reveals a special characteristic of human nature: namely, that it is capable of being united to God; man, fallen man, weighed down by the burden of the sin of Adam, is shown that the « immortal longings » which he sometimes experiences are not mere illusion; man is made in the image of God, and is therefore *capax Dei* — « capable of God » — even though the image has been worn and defiled by sin ([47]). It is because of the Incarnation that man has some vision of the Divine Trinity. In his disputes with the Arians, Augustine firmly maintains that the divine epiphanies recorded in the Old Testament were not visions of the Son, but angels sent at the behest of the whole Trinity ([48]), for it is only through

---

([44]) *De Trin.* XIII, x, 13-xvl, 21.
([45]) Augustine is here thinking of Neoplatonists like Porphyry; cf. *De Civ. Dei* X, 28, 29.
([46]) *De Trin.* XIII, xvii, 22.
([47]) *Ibid.*, XIV, v, 6; viii, 11.
([48]) *C. Max. Ar.* II, 26. 10-12. *PL* xlii, 311-3; cf. *De Trin.* III, xi, 27.

the humanity of Christ, prefigured in the cleft in the rock
through which Moses saw the back of God, that we may hope,
after this life, to see Him *face to face* [49] (I Cor. 13: 12).

> That Mediator in whom we can participate, and by partici-
> pation reach our felicity, is the uncreated Word of God, by
> whom all things were created. And yet He is not the Mediator,
> in that He is the Word, for the Word, being pre-eminently
> immortal and blessed, is far removed from wretched mortals.
> He is the Mediator in that He is man, by His very manhood
> making it plain that for the attainment of that good, which is
> not only blessed but beatific also, we have not to look for
> other mediators, through whom, as we may think, we can
> achieve the approach to happiness. God Himself, the blessed
> God, who is the giver of blessedness, became partaker of our
> human nature, and thus offered us a short cut [50] to parti-
> cipation in His own divine nature [51].

We come to God, then, only through the humanity of
Christ; and Christ, the Son of Man, offers us, as His body, in
sacrifice to God. But to be in His body, we must be members
of His Church:

> ... Without Him we are nothing; but in Him there is both
> Christ Himself and ourselves. How? Because the whole Christ
> means both Head and Body. He is the Head, the saviour of the
> Body, who has already ascended into heaven; but the Body is
> the Church, which labours yet on earth [52].

[49] *De Trin.* II, xvii, 28.

[50] *compendium praebuit.* Augustine probably has in mind the complicated magical practices of the later Platonists called theurgy, which
he discusses in *De Civ. Dei* X, 9.

[51] *De Civ. Dei* IX, 15 (BETTENSON, p. 361).

[52] *Enar. Ps.* 30, II, *serm.* 1,3: « Nam sine illo, nos nihil; in illo
autem, ipse Christus et nos. Quare? Quia totus Christus caput et corpus.
Caput ille salvator corporis, qui iam ascendit in caelum; corpus autem
Ecclesia, quae laborat in terra »; *Serm.* 91, 7: « Ambulandum ergo est,
nec pedes ungendi, nec iumenta quaerenda, nec navis providenda. Affectu curre, amore ambula, caritate ascende. Quid quaeris viam? Inhaere
Christo, qui descendendo et ascendendo se ipsum fecit viam. Vis ascendere? Ascendentem tene. Etenim per te ipsum levari non potes. Quia
*nemo ascendit in caelum, nisi qui de caelo descendit, Filius hominis, qui
est in caelo* (Ioh. 3: 13). Si nemo ascendit, nisi qui descendit, ipse autem

For Augustine Christology can never be separated from
ecclesiology; the risen Christ is with His body, which is the
Church (53), and the life of the Church, which is a continual
act of praise, is comprehended in the offering of the eucharist,
of which Christ is the true minister. This is the theme of
chapter twenty of the tenth book of *The City of God*, in which
Augustine contrasts the true sacrifice of Christ, offered on
Calvary and shown forth in the daily sacrament of the sacrifice
of the Church with the ineffective sacrifices of the pagans.
The passage is a familiar one, but so important that it must
be quoted, if justice is to be done to the boldness of Augustine's
thought:

> Hence it is that the true Mediator, in so far as He *took
> the form of a servant* and was thus made *the Mediator between
> God and mankind, the man Christ Jesus*, receives the sacrifice
> *in the form of God*, in union with the Father, with whom He
> is one God. And yet *in the form of a servant* He preferred to
> be Himself the sacrifice than to receive it, to prevent anyone
> from supposing that sacrifice, even in these circumstances,
> should be offered to any created being. Thus He is both the
> priest, Himself making the offering, and the oblation. This is
> the reality; and He intended the daily sacrifice of the Church
> to be the sacramental symbol of this; for the Church, being
> the body of which He is the head, learns to offer herself through
> Him. This is the true sacrifice; and the sacrifices of the saints
> in earlier times were many different symbols of it. This one

est Filius hominis, Dominus noster Iesus; vis et tu ascendere? Membrum
ipsius esto, qui solus ascendit. Etenim ille caput cum caeteris membris
unus homo est ».

(53) *De Trin.* III, x, 20: « ...Ergo virga [Moysi] in serpentem, Christus
in mortem; et serpens rursus in virgam, Christus in resurrectionem
totus cum corpore suo, quod est Ecclesia »; *Enar. Ps.* 26, II, 2: « Hoc
habet titulus Psalmi: *Psalmus David priusquam liniretur*, hoc est, priusquam ungeretur. Unctus est enim ille ut rex. Et solus tunc ungebatur
rex et sacerdos: duae istae illo tempore unctae personae. In duabus
personis praefigurabatur futurus unus rex et sacerdos, utroque munere
unus Christus, et ideo Christus a chrismate. Non solum autem caput
nostrum unctum est, sed et corpus eius nos ipsi. Rex autem est, quia
nos regit et ducit; sacerdos, quia pro nobis interpellat. Equidem solus
ille sacerdos talis extitit, ut ipse esset etiam sacrificium. Sacrificium
obtulit Deo non aliud quam seipsum ».

sacrifice was pre-figured by many rites, just as many words are
used to refer to one thing, to emphasise a point without
inducing boredom. This was the supreme sacrifice, and the true
sacrifice, and all the false sacrifices yielded place to it [54].

I do not know of any other passage in Augustine which
better expresses how the mediatorial role of Christ is expressed
in the offering of the eucharist. Yet Augustine goes further:
the consecrated bread and wine upon the altar are the sacrament
of *both* the Body and Blood of Christ *and* of the worshipping
Church. So Augustine can declare:

> What you see is bread and a cup — that is what your eyes
> tell you; what your faith asks for enlightenment is how the
> bread is the Body of Christ and the cup the Blood of Christ...
> These things, my brethren, are called sacraments, because in
> them one thing is seen and another is understood. What is
> seen has a physical appearance, what is understood has spiritual
> fruit. If therefore you wish to understand what is the Body of
> Christ, hear the Apostle saying to the faithful: *Now you are
> the body of Christ and individually members of it.*
>
> If therefore you are the Body of Christ and its members,
> your mystery is placed on the Lord's table: you receive your
> own mystery [55].

and again:

> This bread which you see on the altar, sanctified by the
> word of God, is the Body of Christ. This cup — or, rather, what
> this cup contains — being sanctified by the word of God, is
> the Blood of Christ. Through these our Lord Jesus Christ
> willed to entrust to us His Body and Blood, which He poured

---

[54] *De Civ. Dei* X, 20 (BETTENSON, pp. 400-01).

[55] *Serm.* 272: « Quod ergo videtis, panis et calix; quod vobis etiam
oculi vestri renuntiant: quod autem fides vestra postulat instruenda,
panis est corpus Christi, calix sanguis Christi... Ista, fratres, ideo dicuntur sacramenta, quia in eis aliud videtur, aliud intelligitur. Quod videtur,
speciem habet corporalem, quod intelligitur, fructum habet spiritualem.
Corpus ergo Christi si vis intelligere, Apostolus audi dicentem fidelibus:
Vos autem estis corpus Christi et membra (I Cor. 12:27). Si ergo vos
estis corpus Christi et membra, mysterium vestrum in mensa dominica
positum est: mysterium vestrum accipitis ».

out for us for the remission of sins. If you have received them in good faith (*bene*), you are what you have received. ... The Holy Spirit has come, fire after water [of baptism] and you become the bread which is the Body of Christ... Then after the sanctification of the sacrifice of God, because He willed that we ourselves should be His sacrifice, as was shown when He instituted that first sacrifice of God, which we also are — or, rather, which we represent — then after the sanctification, we say the Lord's Prayer[56].

It is of interest to compare Augustine's theology of the eucharist, which is both the Body of Christ which, being worthily received, gives life, and also the Church, which is herself offered in the sacrament, with Gregory of Nyssa's famous doctrine that, in receiving the immortal Body of God, the communicant is himself made immortal:

The reason, moreover, that God, when He revealed Himself, united Himself with our mortal nature, was to deify humanity by this close relation with Deity. In consequence, by means of His flesh, which is constituted by bread and wine, He implants Himself in all believers, following out the plan of grace. He unites Himself with their bodies, so that mankind too, by its union with what is immortal, may share in incorruptibility. And this He confers on us by the power of the blessing [of consecration], through which He changes the nature of the visible elements into that immortal body[57].

Augustine, to my knowledge, does not speak in exactly similar language, though the words which he records in the

---

[56] *Serm.* 227: « Panis ille quem videtis in altari sanctificatus per verbum Dei, corpus est Christi. Calix ille, immo quod habet calix, sanctificatus per verbum Dei, sanguis est Christi. Per ista voluit dominus Christus commendare corpus et sanguinem suum quem pro nobis fudit in remissionem peccatorum. Si bene accepitis, vos estis quod accepistis... Accedit ergo Spiritus sanctus, post aquam ignis et efficimini panis quod est corpus Christi... Deinde post sanctificationem sacrificii Dei, quia nos ipsos voluit esse sacrificium suum, quod demonstratum est ubi impositum est primum illud sacrificium Dei et nos — id est signum rei — quod sumus, ecce ubi est peracta sanctificatio dicimus orationem dominicam » (POQUE, pp. 234, 238, 240).

[57] Greg. Nyss., *Or. Catechetica*, 37. Tr. by E.R. HARDY (The Library of Christian Classics, Vol. III [1954], p. 321).

Confessions: « I am the food of full-grown men: grow and
you shall eat Me; and you shall not change Me into yourself
as bodily food, but into Me you shall be changed » ([58]) may
point to a doctrine like Gregory's. Augustine does, however,
teach a doctrine of deification not less than Gregory of Nyssa,
and this deification must be seen as a consequence of the ∨
Incarnation of the Son of God.

Western theologians are apt to be suspicious of the term
deification — it seems to imply too much, to raise man so far
from his creaturely status as to trespass on the divine transcendence. It is recognised that defication (*theosis; theopoi-
esis*) is a familiar concept in the Greek Fathers; but it is felt
that the Latin tradition, ever anxious to avoid giving fallen
man more than his due, avoids it, preferring to talk of redemption from sin and sanctification. Yet the notion of deification
is to be found in Augustine, not as something added to his
system as an afterthought, but as integral to the whole. In
itself, the notion of deification is no more than what is implied
by the New Testament term *uiothesia* — sonship by adoption
— by grace, that is to say, and not by nature ([59]). It is, indeed,
the consequence of human flesh being assumed by the divinity
in the Incarnation ([60]): that flesh has been taken into heaven

---

([58]) *Conf.* VII, x, 16: « Cibus sum grandium: cresce et manducabis
me, nec tu me in te mutabis sicut cibum carnis tuae, sed tu mutaberis
in me ». The inspiration of this passage would seem to be Hebrews 5:14:
Perfectorum autem est solidus cibus.

([59]) *Ep. ad Gal. exp.*, 30: « *Ut adoptionem* inquit, *filiorum recipiamus.*
Adoptionem propterea dicit, ut distincte intelligamus unicum Dei Filium.
Nos enim beneficio et dignatione misericordiae eius filii Dei sumus: ille
natura est Filius, qui hoc est quod Pater. Nec dixit, accipiamus, sed
recipiamus, ut significaret hoc nos amisisse in Adam, ex quo mortales
sumus... Hinc enim adoptionem recipimus, quod ille Unicus non dedig-
natus est participationem naturae nostrae, factus ex muliere, ut non
solum Unigenitus esset ubi fratres non habet, sed etiam Primogenitus
in multis fratribus fieret ».

([60]) *Ep.* 140, iv, 11: « proinde cum dixisset, *Ut eos, qui sub lege erant,
redimeret*, continuo subiunxit, *Ut adoptionem filiorum reciperemus*, ut
videlicet huius gratiam beneficii discerneret ab illa Filii natura, qui mis-
sus est Filius, non adoptione factus sed semper genitus Filius, ut parti-
cipata natura filiorum hominum ad participandam etiam suam naturam
adoptaret filios hominum ».

by the ascended Christ, and if men participate in Him through membership of the Church, the Body of Christ, they too may hope, after death, to enjoy the divinisation effected by His flesh-taking. So Augustine writes, in the last chapter of the last book of *The City of God*:

> We ourselves shall become that seventh day [i.e. the eternal Sabbath], when we have been replenished and restored by His blessing and sanctification. There we shall have leisure to be still, and we shall see that He is God, whereas we wished to be that ourselves when we fell away from Him, after listening to the seducer saying: *You will be like gods.* Then we abandoned the true God, by whose creative help we should have become gods, but by participating in Him, not by deserting Him. For what have we done without Him? We have *fallen away in His anger* (Ps. 89 [90]:9/LXX). But now restored by Him and perfected by His greater grace, we shall be still and at leisure for eternity, seeing that He is God, and being filled by Him when He will be *all in all* (I Cor. 15:28)([61]).

But the mediation of Christ is effective, not only for the world to come, but also for the present age, where Christians are even more divided than in Augustine's day. In our divisions, let Augustine remind us of the high-priestly prayer of Christ the mediator:

> Thus the Son of God Himself, the Word of God, and Himself the mediator of God and Men, Son of Man, equal to the Father through His divinity, and our brother through participation, through the taking of our humanity, interceding with the Father in that He was man, and not being silent because as God He was one with the Father, said among other things: *I do not pray for these only, but also for those who believe in Me through their word, that they may all be one; even as Thou, Father, art in Me and I in Thee, that they may also be in Us, so that the world may believe that Thou hast sent Me. The glory which Thou hast given Me I have given to them, that they may be one, even as we are one* (John 17:20-22)([62]).

([61]) *De Civ. Dei* XXII, 30 (BETTENSON, p. 1090).
([62]) *De Trin.* IV, viii, 12: « Sic ipse Filius Dei, Verbum Dei, et idem ipse mediator Dei et hominum, Filius hominis, aequalis Patri per divini-

It seems fitting to close upon these words; but one further point should perhaps be made. It may seem to some that the Augustine whose thought I have tried to expound in this paper, the Doctor of Participation and Deification, is a very different theologian from the Augustine more commonly presented in text-books, the Doctor of Predestination and Grace, the defender of religious coercion of schismatics and heretics, or even the busy and active episcopal administrator revealed in the new letters published by Johannes Divjak in 1981. It may be that some will find the Augustine whom I have tried to show a more appealing thinker than the conventional figure, and be tempted to think of two Augustines, with two different theologies which were never properly reconciled in the mind of their originator.

Attractive though such a tendency may be, I think that it should be resisted; for Augustine's teaching regarding Christ, God and man, is not out of harmony with the fundamental principles informing his other writings. Thus he sees the Incarnation as the highest example of divine grace without regard to human merit; he holds that man is incapable of himself of participating in God, and can hope to do so only as a member of Christ's Church. If the Augustine whom I have depicted seems a different thinker from the author of the later anti-Pelagian treatises, it is because these reveal, as it were, the other side of the medal. Augustine is concerned both with the heights to which man can be raised by God's grace, and the depths into which he has fallen through his own sin. There is, indeed, an underlying unity in Augustine's thinking which must impress the reader of his voluminous writings.

This is not to say that certain aspects of Augustine's thinking may not be more appropriate to the spiritual needs

---

tatis unitatem, et particeps noster per humanitatis susceptionem, Patrem interpellans pro nobis per id quod homo erat, nec tamen tacens quod Deus cum Patre unum erat, inter cetera ita loquitur: *Non pro his autem rogo*, inquit, *tantum, sed et pro eis qui credituri sunt per verbum eorum in me: ut omnes unum sint, sicut tu Pater in me, et ego in te, ut et ipsi in nobis unum sint; ut mundus credat, quia tu me misisti. Et ego claritatem quam dedisti mihi, dedi eis, ut sint unum, sicut et nos unum sumus* ».

of the present day than others, and that in the twentieth century we may perhaps gain more from Augustine, the spiritual and ascetical teacher, than from Augustine the unyielding opponent of Julian of Eclanum; but the student of Augustine, seeking to understand his thought as a whole, is inevitably constrained to marvel at its internal coherence no less than at its extraordinary comprehensiveness.

University of Durham - England

III

Augustine's Doctrine of Man: Image of God and Sinner

At the beginning of the first book of his *Soliloquies*, written shortly before his baptism at the end of 386 or the beginning of 387, Augustine declares that his desire is to know God and the soul. « Nothing more? Nothing whatever. »[1] In the second book, he narrows the field of enquiry still further. « O God, who art ever the same, let me know myself and Thee. That is my prayer. »[2] It might be said that Augustine's doctrine of man is comprehended by these two short petitions. The desire to know God is constant; but Augustine will never be able to consider the nature of man with a purely academic detachment. His experience of himself, at once a sinner and drawn to God by love — *pondus meum, amor meus*[3] — will provide practical evidence of the nature of man; and if the *De Trinitate* is the work which, outstandingly among Augustinian writings, discusses the doctrine of man as the image of God, the *Confessions* provide an individual case-history — admittedly a highly subjective one — to illustrate that theology. « Man desires to praise Thee, He is but a tiny part of all that Thou has created. He bears about him his mortality, the evidence of his sinfulness, and the evidence that Thou *dost resist the proud*; yet this tiny part of all that Thou hast created desires to praise Thee ». [4] It is this paradox of man's sinfulness which procures his aversion from God, and the desire for God felt

---

[1] *Solil.* I,2,7: « *A.* Deum et animam scire cupio. *E.* Nihilne plus? *A.* Nihil omnino. »
[2] *Ibid.* II,1,1: « *A.* Deus semper idem, noverim me, noverim te. Oratum est. »
[3] *Conf.* XIII,9,10.
[4] *Ibid.* I,1,1: « Et laudare te vult homo, aliqua portio creaturae tuae, et homo circumferens mortalitatem suam, circumferens testimonium peccati sui et testimonium, quia *superbis resistis.* » E.T. by F.J. Sheed, *The Confessions of Saint Augustine*, London 1944.

by some men — *Fecisti nos ad te* — which constitutes the problem with which Augustine struggles throughout the *Confessions*. Man is made for God, who is the source of his being and life; and yet man, by the abuse of the God-given gift of free-will, turns away from God to sin, which is nothingness. It is the mystery of sin, the appeal of the shadow over against the substance, which explains (for me at least) Augustine's concern, in the opening chapters of the *Confessions*, with what appear to be mere trivialities: infant rage and jealousy,[5] schoolboy indolence and deceit.[6] Augustine's recording of the notorious episode of the stolen pears, which has provoked so much surprise, amusement and learned explanation from his readers,[7] becomes intelligible as a paradigm, not of the worst sin which Augustine ever committed, but of the essentially negative character of sin. « What was it then that in my wretched folly I loved in you, O theft of mine, deed wrought in that dark night when I was sixteen? For you were not lovely: you were a theft. Or are you anything at all that I should talk with you? »[8] It might be said that in this banal and frequently misunderstood episode Augustine contrives to illustrate his conception of the anhypostatic nature of evil, while his conclusion enshrines his understanding of man as the image of God, which is the subject of this paper.

> The soul is guilty of fornication when she turns from You and seeks from any other source what she will nowhere find pure and without taint unless she returns to You. Thus even those who go from You and stand up against You are still perversely imitating You. But by the mere fact of their imitation, they declare that You are the creator of all that is, and that there is nowhere for them to go where You are not.[9]

---

[5] *Ibid*. I,6,8; 7,11.

[6] *Ibid*. I,9,14-10,16; 19,30.

[7] *Ibid*. II,4,9. See, for example, Leo C. Ferrari, *The Pear-Theft in Augustine's Confessions*, REAug 16 (1970) 233-42.

[8] *Ibid*. II,6,12: « Quid ego miser in te amavi, o furtum meum, o facinus illud meum nocturnum sexti decimi anni aetatis meae? Non enim pulchrum eras, cum furtum esses. Aut vero aliquid es, ut loquar ad te? » Tr. by Sheed.

[9] *Ibid*. II,6,14: « Ita fornicatur anima, cum avertitur abs te et quaerit extra te ea quae pura et liquida non invenit, nisi cum redit ad te. Perverse te imitantur omnes, qui longe se a te faciunt et extollunt se adversum te. Sed etiam sic te imitando indicant creatorem te esse omnis naturae et ideo non esse, quo a te omni modo recedatur. » Tr. by Sheed.

In my discussion of Augustine's doctrine of man, image of
God and sinner, we have to take account of a thinker whose
views on many subjects changed and developed over the years.
Because of the inevitably limited compass of this paper, while
I hope to demonstrate the development of Augustine's views
chronologically, it will on occasion be necessary to present his
doctrine systematically rather than historically, taking his mature opinions as being representative of his thought as a whole.
That Augustine's views on certain issues changed during the
course of his life is undeniable, though it is possible to exag-
gerate the extent of the changes.[10] At all events, it is reasonable to regard his opinions on most theological issues as having
been established by the time he became sole bishop of Hippo
in 396,[11] though controversy with the Pelagians constrained
him to clarify his understanding of the effect of sin on the
image of God in the human soul.

Long before the Pelagian Controversy, however, Augustine
was forced to consider the paradox of man, image of God and
sinner, once he had discarded what he conceived to be the
Manichaen doctrine of the Two Souls: a Good Soul, which is
a part of God; and an Evil Soul, the cause of sin in man,
which is not created by God but pertains to the Kingdom of
Darkness. (Whether the Manichees actually held such a doctrine is, for our purpose, irrelevant. Augustine may well have
misunderstood and misrepresented their teaching; but it is
with his own conceptions that we are here concerned.)[12]
In the treatise *De Duabus Animabus*, written while still a presbyter in 391 or 392, Augustine enunciates two principles which
are to be of vital importance for his subsequent theology of
the image: first, that God is the creator of everything that
exists; and, secondly, that God is not the cause of sin, which
is a negation. Souls become good or bad in the degree to

---

[10] As does, for example, Robert J. O'Connell, *St. Augustine's Early
Theory of Man, A.D. 386-391*, Cambridge Mass. 1968, and *St. Augustine's
Confessions. The Odyssey of Soul*, Cambridge Mass. 1969, who, in my
opinion, greatly exaggerates the influence of Neo-Platonism on Augustine's later thought. Cf. the comments of Gerald J. P. O'Daly, *Did
St. Augustine ever believe in the soul's pre-existence?*, Augustinian Studies
5 (1974) 227-35.

[11] His attitude to the coercion of the Donatists is, of course, a
notorious exception.

[12] See F. C. Baur, *Das Manichaeische Religionssystem*, Tübingen 1931,
repr. Göttingen 1928, 162-77.

which they adhere to, or depart from, God who is the source of all goodness. [13] Augustine further declares that mind (*mens* or *intelligentia*) is the highest point of the soul — the instrument by which intelligible truth is apprehended, and equates it with life. [14] The significance of the *De Duabus Animabus* is that in it Augustine, without specifically speaking of the image of God in man, sketches the theological framework in which he will develop the concept. The image of God in man must necessarily be God's creation and not a part of His substance; it is to be located in the highest part of the soul; and its resemblance to God will be determined by its obedience to its creator. In another anti-Manichaean work the *Contra Adimantum* (394), the notion of the image is specifically discussed in relation to two classic texts: *Gen* 1,26 and *1Cor* 11,7. The Manichees, says Augustine, deny the Genesis assertion that man was made in the image and likeness of God, *ad imaginem et similitudinem Dei*, because, they allege, it conflicts with Christ's words to the Jews in the Gospel of John (8,44): *You are of your father the devil.* [15] Augustine replies by quoting St. Paul: *A man indeed ought not to have his head veiled, since he is the image and glory of God* (a text which would later demand further exegesis to establish that woman is, like man, made in God's image), [16] and gives his own explanation:

---

[13] *De duabus animabus* 1,1: « ... nullam esse quamlibet vitam, quae non eo ipso, quo vita est et in quantum omnino vita est, ad summum vitae fontem principiumque pertineat: quod nihil aliud quam summum et solum et verum deum possumus confiteri »; 6,8-9; 8,10: « etenim anima quamvis sit inmortalis, tamen quia mors eius rite dicitur a dei cognitione aversio, cum se convertit ad deum, meritum est aeternae vitae consequendae, ut sit aeterna vita, sicut dictum est, ipsa cognitio, converti autem ad deum nemo, nisi ab hoc mundo se averterit, potest »; 13,20: « Quamquam etiam si eis concedatur inferiore alio genere animarum nos inlici ad turpia, non inde conficiunt aut illas natura malas esse aut istas summum bonum. fieri enim potest, ut propria illae voluntate adpetendo, quod non licebat, hoc est peccando, ex bonis factae sint malae rursusque fieri bonae possint. »

[14] *Ibid.* 2,2: « ... summam esse dementiam id praedicare pertinere ad deum, quod per corpus intuemur, quod vero non solum animo, sed ipsa sublimitate animi, mente scilicet atque intellegentia caperemus, id est vitam, qualiscumque illa diceretur, tamen vitam eodem deo auctore privandam et viduandam putare, num enim quid sit vivere quamque secretum ab omni corporis sensu quamque omnino incorporeum, si me ipsum invocato deo interrogarem, respondere non possim? »

[15] *C. Adim.* 5,1.

[16] *De Gen. ad lit.* II,22,34. See Kari Elisabeth Børresen, *Subordination et équivalence*, Oslo-Paris 1968, 25-42, 74-75, and Cornelia W. Wolfskeel,

The sons of God are men renewed according to His image and made like to Him, even to the love of an enemy, since the Lord has told us that we ought to love our enemies. ... Men are, however, called sons of the devil when they imitate his impious pride, and decline from the light and the height of wisdom, and do not believe the truth, even as the Lord accuses them. [17]

Augustine's point is that the image of God is present in man by a spiritual fashioning (*secundum spiritalem conformationem*), effected by *putting off the old man with his doings* and *putting on the new man, who is being renewed unto knowledge after the image of Him who created him* (Col 3, 9.10). [18] We have here the foreshadowing of a theme which was destined to be powerfully developed in later writings, notably in the *De Trinitate*, namely the re-creation and glorification of the image of God in fallen man by the grace of Christ, by which men are made sons of God.

At some point during the period between his return to Africa in 388 and his episcopate in 396 — we cannot, unfortunately, be more precise in our dating — Augustine provided, in the fifty-first question of the *De diversis quaestionibus LXXXIII*, one of the key texts for the understanding of his doctrine of the image by formulating a crucial distinction between the Son, who is the true image (*imago*) of God, and man, who is made *ad imaginem*, in the image. [19] This likeness Augustine sees in the inner man (*is qui intus est* of 2Cor 4,16), who can participate in wisdom (*sapientia*). [20] In his later

---

Augustine's conception of man as the image of God, VigChr 30 (1976) 63-71.

[17] *C. Adim.* 5,2: « filii ergo dei sunt homines renovati ad eius imaginem et ei similes facti usque ad dilectionem inimici, sicut dominus dicit diligere nos debere inimicos nostros, ut similes simus patri nostro, qui in caelis est. quod in potestate nostra ab ipso deo esse positum docet scriptura, cum dicit: *dedit eis potestatem filios dei fieri.* filii autem diaboli dicuntur homines, cum imitantur eius inpiam superbiam et a luce atque celsitudine sapientiae decidunt et non credunt veritati, quales dominus arguit, cum dicit: *vos ex patre diabolo estis* et cetera. »

[18] *Ibid.*: « et ut manifeste intellegatur non secundum vetustatem peccati, quae corrumpitur, sed secundum spiritalem conformationem factum esse hominem ad imaginem dei, item apostolus monet, ut exuti consuetudine peccatorum, id est vetere homine, induamus novam vitam Christi, quem novum hominem appellat. »

[19] *De div. quaest. LXXXIII*, q. 51,4: « Neque inscite distinguitur, quod aliud sit imago et similitudo Dei, qui etiam Filius dicitur; aliud ad imaginem et similitudinem Dei, sicut hominem factum accipimus. »

[20] *Ibid.* 2: « Quod enim participat sapientiae, et vivit et est: quod

writings, notably the *De Trinitate*[21] and the *Retractationes*,[22] Augustine was to concede that the words of the Apostle in *1Cor* 11,7 justified the convention by which man is called the image of God in his own right; but there nevertheless remains as the basis of his thought the conviction that the only true image of God is the Son. This is implied in the *Incomplete Commentary on Genesis*, begun about 393 though retouched and completed in 426 or 427.[23] Here Augustine, discussing the words of Genesis 1,26: *Let us make man in our image after our likeness*, enunciates three exegetical principles. First, that the creation of man is the work of the whole Trinity — a doctrine which will be developed in the *De Trinitate*, when the human mind will be seen as providing by its character some analogy with the creator whose image it is.[24] Secondly, that it is not enough for an image to be like its model; if it is not « born » of that model, it cannot be called an image.[25] Thirdly — and this is crucial for the whole conception of man being made in the image of God — Augustine understands likeness (*similitudo*) in terms of participation: man becomes like God by participating in Him;[26] and he is able to do so because he

autem vivit, necesse est ut sit, non necesse est ut sapiat. Quare cum homo possit particeps esse sapientiae secundum interiorem hominem, secundum ipsum ita est ad imaginem, ut nulla natura interposita formetur; et ideo nihil sit Deo coniunctius. Et sapit enim, et vivit, et est: qua creatura nihil est melius. »

[21] *De Trin.* VII,6,12: « Sunt enim qui ita distinguunt, ut imaginem velint esse Filium: hominem vero non imaginem, sed ad imaginem. Refellit autem eos Apostolus, dicens: *Vir quidem non debet velare caput, cum sit imago et gloria Dei.* Non dixit *ad imaginem*, sed *imago*. Quae tamen *imago*, cum alibi dicitur: *Ad imaginem*, non quasi ad Filium dicitur, quae *imago aequalis* est Patri; alioquin non diceret *ad imaginem nostram*. »

[22] *Retract.* I,26[25],2: « Item dixi: " Neque inscite distinguitur, quod aliud sit imago et similitudo Dei, aliud ad imaginem et similitudinem Dei, sicut hominem factum accipimus. " Quod non ita intelligendum est, quasi homo non dicatur imago Dei, cum dicit Apostolus: *Vir quidem non debet revelare caput, cum sit imago et glorai Dei*; sed dicitur etiam ad imaginem Dei, quod Unigenitus non dicitur, qui tantummodo imago est, non ad imaginem. »

[23] See Mary Inez Bogan, *Saint Augustine: The Retractations* [The Fathers of the Chuch, 40], Washington D.C. 1968, 78.

[24] *De Gen. ad lit. lib. imperf.* 16,55-56: *De Trin.* IX.

[25] *De Gen. ad lit. lib. imperf.* 16,57: « Omnis imago similis est ei cuius imago est; nec tamen omne quod simile est alicui, etiam imago est eius; sicut in speculo et pictura, quia imagines sunt, etiam similes sunt; tamen, si alter ex altero natus non est, nullus eorum imago alterius dici potest. Imago enim tunc est, cum de aliquo exprimitur. »

[26] *Ibid.*: « Castitas autem nullius participatione casta est, sed eius

is a reasonable being (*rationalis substantia*), made by God for Himself without any intermediate nature.[27] When Augustine came to revise and complete the *De Genesi liber imperfectus* at the end of his life, he added a short concluding section in which he deliberately emphasised what he held to be implied in the work as a whole: that the Son is the only true image of the Father; even if man had not sinned he would not, like the Son, have been equal and coeternal with the God whose image he is.[28] It is here that the Augustinian notion of participation becomes of vital importance; by sin, men fall away from God, become unlike Him and lose His image in which they were made. « Men », Augustine tells the congregation in one of his sermons,

> rendering back to God His image, lift up their minds, not to themselves but to their Creator and to the light from whence they come; to a certain spiritual heat from which they grow warm, and removed from which they grow cold, and departing from which they are darkened and by returning again they are enlightened.[29]

Or again:

> what does it mean *Begin to the Lord in confession* (*Ps* 146,7)? Begin to be joined to God. In what way? By letting that

participatione sunt casta quaecumque casta sunt. Quae utique in Deo est, ubi est etiam illa sapientia, quae non participando sapiens est, sed cuius participatione sapiens est anima quaecumque sapiens est. Quapropter etiam similitudo Dei, per quam facta sunt omnia, proprie dicitur similitudo; quia non participatione alicuius similitudinis similis est, sed ipsa est prima similitudo, cuius participatione similia sunt, quaecumque per illam fecit Deus. »

[27] *Ibid.* 60: « Rationalis itaque substantia et per ipsam facta est, et ad ipsam: non enim est ulla natura interposita. Quandoquidem mens humana (quod non sentit, nisi cum purissima et beatissima est) nulli cohaeret nisi ipsi veritati, quae similitudo et imago Patris et sapientia dicitur. Recte igitur secundum hoc quod interius et principale hominis est, id est secundum mentem, accipitur, *Faciamus hominem ad imaginem et similitudinem nostram*. Ex illo enim quod in homine principatum tenet, quod eum disiungit a belluis, totus est homo aestimandus. »

[28] *Ibid.* 61: « Sed haec imago ad imaginem Dei facta, non est aequalis et coaeterna illi cuius imago est; nec esset, etiam si nunquam omnino peccasset. »

[29] *Enar. in Ps. 103, serm.* 4,2: « Homines ergo reddentes Deo quae Dei sunt, si Caesari reddunt quod Caesaris est; id est, reddentes Caesari imaginem suam et reddentes Deo imaginem suam, erigunt ipsam mentem suam, non ad se, sed ad artificem suum, et ad lumen unde sunt, et ad calorem quemdam spiritualem unde fervescunt, et unde remoti frigescunt, et unde recedentes contenebrantur, et quo revertentes illuminantur. »

displease you which displeased Him. Your evil life displeases Him; if it pleasures you, you are separated from Him: if it displeases you, you are rejoined by confession. See to what extent you are unlike. You assuredly displease because of that unlikeness, since you have been made in the image of God; but by a perverse and evil life you are troubled in yourself and have destroyed in you the image of your founder. Being thus made unlike, look to yourself and be displeased with yourself; and from that very moment you will have begun to be made like, since that thing displeases you which also displeases God. [30]

Augustine sees fallen man as being alienated from God and dwelling in that region of unlikeness (*regio dissimilitudinis*) mentioned by Augustine in the *Confessions* — a phrase which, itself inspired by Platonic thought, was destined to exercise a profound influence on the language of Christian spirituality. [31]

However, fallen man's alienation from God, while it involves every man as an individual, is also the result of a collective act — the sin of Adam — in which all the human race is, mysteriously, involved, and from which it can be set free only by the action of the God-man, Jesus Christ. No one is likely to dispute the harshness of the Augustinian doctrine of Original Sin; but it must be recognised that it was from the notion of the coinherence of fallen humanity in Adam that Augustine derived his vision of the coinherence of redeemed humanity in the Body of Christ. Against the *massa peccati*, the lump of sin, Augustine sets the *corpus Christi*. « *Communis fuit perditio, sit communis inventio* », he says. « There was a common loss, let there be a common finding ». [32] And again:

All who are reborn are made His members, and Christ alone who is born of Mary is one Christ, and with His Body the

---

[30] *Enar. in Ps.* 75,3: « Quod est, *Incipite Domino in confessione?* Incipite adiungi Deo. Quomodo? Ut hoc vobis displiceat quod et illi displicet. Displicet illi vita tua mala: si placeat tibi, disiungeris ab illo; si displiceat tibi, per confessionem ill coniungeris. Vide ex quanta parte dissimilis es, quando utique propter [ipsam] dissimilitudinem displices. Factus enim es, o homo, ad imaginem Dei; per vitam vero perversam et malam perturbasti in te, et exterminasti in te imaginem Conditoris tui. Factus dissimilis, adtendis in te, et displices tibi: iam ex eo coepisti similis fieri, quia hoc displicet quod displicet et Deo. »

[31] *Conf.* VII,10,16: « ... et inveni longe me esse a te in regione dissimilitudinis. » See Pierre Courcelle, *Les Confessions de Saint Augustin dans la tradition littéraire*, Paris 1963, Appendix 5, pp. 623-40.

[32] *Serm.* 115,4,4.

one Christ is the Head. Therefore it was His will to say: *No man hath ascended into heaven but He that descended out of heaven.* No man has therefore ascended except Christ. If you wish to ascend, be in the Body of Christ. [33]

The incarnation and death of Christ are, therefore, of necessity at the centre of Augustine's system; and it is not an accident that one of the most comprehensive statements of his doctrine of the Atonement is to be found in the *De Trinitate.* [34] Christ's humanity is the means whereby the souls of men are healed.

> God, being made a righteous man, has interceded with God for man who is a sinner; for though there is no harmony between the sinner and the righteous, there is harmony between man and man. Therefore joining to us the likeness (*similitudinem*) of His humanity, He took away the unlikeness (*dissimilitudinem*) of our iniquity; and having been made a partaker of our mortality, made us partakers of his divinity; [35]

and again:

> Our illumination is participation in the Word, in that *life,* that is, *which* is *the life of men.* But on account of the defilement of our sins we were utterly incapable and unworthy of that participation. [36]

The essence of Adam's sin was pride: his refusal as a being created from nothing to recognise absolute dependence upon his Creator.

---

[33] *Serm.* 294,10,10: « Omnes qui renascuntur, membra ipsius fiunt; et solus Christus de Maria natus unus est Christus, et cum corpore suo caput unus est Christus. Hoc ergo dicere voluit: *Nemo ascendit, nisi qui descendit.* Nemo ergo ascendit, nisi Christus. Si vis ascendere, esto in corpore Christi. »

[34] *De Trin.* XII,10,13-15,19.

[35] *Ibid.* IV,2,4: « Deus itaque factus homo iustus, intercessit Deo pro homine peccatore. Non enim congruit peccator iusto, sed congruit homini homo. Adiungens ergo nobis similitudinem humanitatis suae, abstulit dissimilitudinem iniquitatis nostrae: et factus particeps mortalitatis nostrae, fecit [nos] participes divinitatis suae. » Cf. *Conf.* 10,42,67: « Mediator autem inter deum et homines opportebat ut haberet aliquid simile deo, aliquid simile hominibus, ne in utroque hominibus similis longe esset a deo aut in utroque deo similis longe esset ab hominibus atque ita mediator non esset. »

[36] *De Trin.* IV,2,4: « Illuminatio quippe nostra participatio Verbi est, illius scilicet vitae quae *lux* est *hominum.* Huic autem participationi prorsus inhabiles, et minus idonei eramus, propter immunditiam peccatorum. »

No nature can be depraved by vice except such as is made out of nothing. Its nature it derives from the fact that it was made by God; but its fall derives from the fact that it was made out of nothing. Man did not fall to the extent that he became nothing at all, but by stooping to follow his own inclination he became less than he was when he clung to God, who is Being in the highest degree. When man abandoned God and lived to himself to do his own pleasure he did not become nothing, but approached nothingness. [37]

So Augustine, in a passage of the *City of God* written about 420, described the metaphysics of the Fall, in words which could equally be applied to his mature view of the effect of the Fall upon the image of God in man. In his earlier writings Augustine speaks as if the image of God had been totally obliterated by sin. Even in Book VI of the *De Genesi ad Litteram*, written between 401 and 415, and thus to be reckoned among the productions of his theological maturity, he could still write: « By sin Adam lost this image imprinted in the spirit of the mind which we receive by the grace of righteousness » [38] — an expression which he later modified in the *Retractationes*, explaining that it should not be understood as implying that no image remained, but that the image was so deformed as to be in need of reformation. [39] Again, in his sermon on Psalm 72, apparently delivered before 411, judging from references to Donatism in the text, Augustine explains the verse: *O Lord, thou shalt bring their image to naught in thy city*: « Are they not worthy to suffer such things, that God should bring their image to nothing in His City, because they

---

[37] *De Civ. Dei* XIV,13: « Sed vitio depravari, nisi ex nihilo facta, natura non posset. Ac per hoc ut natura sit, ex eo habet quod a Deo facta est: ut autem ab eo quod est deficiat, ex hoc quod de nihilo facta est. Nec sic defecit homo, ut omnino nihil esset: sed ut inclinatus ad se ipsum, minus esset, quam erat, cum ei qui summe est inhaerebat. Relicto itaque Deo, esse in semetipso, hoc est sibi placere, non iam nihil esse est, sed nihilo propinquare. » Tr. by J. W. C. Wand.

[38] *De Gen. ad lit.* VI,27,38: « Hanc imaginem in spiritu mentis impressam perdidit Adam per peccatum; quam recipimus per gratiam iustitiae; non spirituale atque immortale corpus, in quo ille nondum fuit, et in quo erunt omnes sancti resurgentes a mortuis: hoc enim praemium est illius meriti, quod amisit. »

[39] *Retract.* II,25[51],2: « In sexto libro quod dixi Adam imaginem Dei, secundum quam factus est, perdidisse peccato, non sic accipiendum est, tamquam in eo nulla remanserit, sed quod tam deformis, ut reformatione opus haberet. »

themselves have likewise brought the image of God to nothing in the Earthly City? »[40]

Such a notion of the total obliteration of the image of God in fallen man may seem a strange aberration in a thinker like Augustine, since it apparently runs counter to the whole tenor of the argument which he had directed against the Manichees. There are, however, a number of considerations which help to explain the character of Augustine's reasoning. In the first place, we cannot ignore the influence of Neo-Platonism. According to Plotinus, an image can only obtain a true likeness to its model if it is turned to it in contemplation.[41] If Augustine had read this particular section of the Enneads (as seems not unlikely),[42] it would have been easy for him to conceive that the Fall, by turning the soul from the contemplation of God, had destroyed His image in itself. Again, Augustine regards the image of God in man as being found in the *mens*, the highest part of the soul, which is capable of supernatural life.[43] If that supernatural life were brought to an end by sin, God's image would perish, and man would live an animal life, like the beasts that perish, in the *Civitas terrena*, the Earthly City.[44] Finally, account should be taken of the parallel in Augustine's mind between man's creation in Adam and his recreation in Christ by reform and renewal. As G. B. Ladner has expressed it: « (For Augustine) Pauline *reformatio-renovatio* meant a new creation which implies an overcoming of sin and evil, a victory from which all further improvement can flow. But, in one sense, sin and evil are only an absence of good, and therefore but the remnants in the created world of the pre-creational nothing. Reformation-renovation, then, is a second turning to God from nothingness, starting with a new conversion, a renewal this

---

[40] *Enar. in Ps. 72,26*: « Domine, in civitate tua imaginem illorum ad nihilum rediges. Nonne digni sunt haec pati, ut Deus in civitate sua imaginem illorum ad nihilum redigat; quia et ipsi in civitate terrena imaginem Dei ad nihilum redegerunt? *In civitate tua imaginem eorum ad nihilum rediges*. »

[41] *Enn.* V,3,7 (ed. Bréhier, vol. 5, Paris 1931, 57-58).

[42] See A. Solignac, *Oeuvres de Saint Augustin*: *Les Confessions* [Bibliothèque Augustinienne 13], 1962, 110.

[43] See above, n. 14. Cf. J. E. Sullivan, *The Image of God*, Dubuque, Iowa 1963, 42.

[44] See above, n. 40.

time to the creational condition of formation ».[45] With such a conception in his mind, it would have been very easy for Augustine to have regarded the image of God in man as having been destroyed by the Fall to be re-created in Christ.

It might be thought that this theology of the divine image in the mind of man would keep uneasy company with Augustine's traducian doctrine of Original Sin with its decidedly materialistic character — Original Sin is transmitted in the physical process of generation — but there is no evidence that he felt any particular difficulty in reconciling the two. Indeed, the idea of physically inherited sin and guilt, first overtly expressed in 396/7 in the treatise *Ad Simplicianum*,[46] would help to explain how the divine image has perished in each new-born individual in a way that would be difficult with a creationist view of the human soul. However, the origin of the soul remained a problem for Augustine and he was never able to discard creationism entirely. We find him writing an anguished letter to Jerome on the subject as late as 415,[47] and at the end of his life he admitted that the origin of the soul remained an unsolved problem.[48] Augustine's inability wholly to discard creationism may explain why he came to hold that while the Fall has darkened and obscured God's image in man, it has not wholly extinguished it.

Controversy with the Pelagians, and the charge that under the cloak of the doctrine of Original Sin he had revived Manichaean opinions, undoubtedly encouraged Augustine to define more precisely his beliefs about the image of God in the soul. In the *De spiritu et littera*, written in 412 at the very beginning of the Pelagian Controversy, he declares that « the image of God in the human soul has not been so completely obliterated

---

[45] G. B. Ladner, *St. Augustine's Conception of the Reformation of Man to the Image of God*, in *Augustinus Magister*, Paris 1954, vol. 2, p. 872.

[46] *De Div. quaest. ad Simplic.* I, q. 2,16-22. See G. Bonner, *Augustine and Modern Research on Pelagianism* [The Saint Augustine Lecture 1970], Villanova Pa. 1972, 16-17.

[47] *Ep.* 166.

[48] *Retract.* II,56[83]: « Eodem tempore quidam Vincentius Victor in Mauritania Caesariensi invenit apud Hispanum quemdam presbyterum Petrum, nonnullum opusculum meum, ubi quodam loco de origine animae hominum singulorum, utrum ex illa una primi hominis ac deinde ex parentibus propagentur, an sicut illi uni sine ulla propagatione singulae singulis dentur, me nescire confessus sum, verumtamen scire animam non corpus esse sed spiritum. »

by the stain of earthly affections that no faint outlines of the
original remain ». [49] Given both the early date of this treatise
in the Pelagian debate and the fact that it was addressed, at
his own request, to Augustine's friend, Count Marcellinus, and
was therefore not polemically inspired, it seems reasonable to
assume that this change of opinion was due rather to Augustine's own thinking than to any controversial necessity. At any
rate, the change was to be permanent. In 426, in the last
book of *The City of God*, Augustine speaks of the « spark of
reason » in man, in virtue of which he was made in the image
of God, and which sin has not utterly extinguished. [50] Finally
in the *Retractationes*, published about 427/8, Augustine specifically referred to the statement which he had made earlier
in the *De Genesi ad litteram*, that Adam by sin lost the image
of God in which he was made, and insisted that it must be
understood to mean that the image persisted, though so deformed as to need reformation. [51] Nor did he hesitate to admit,
at the end of his life, in controversy with Julian of Eclanum
that in the damnation of unbaptised infants the image of God
is subjected by God's judgement and permissive will to the
power of the devil. [52]

This last affirmation, while indicating as it was intended
to do the absolute need of the grace of baptism for all ages
and classes of humanity, also reveals how completely Augustine
was determined to sever the idea of the mind of man as being
made in the image of God from any suggestion of natural
divinity. Nothing, he admits, has been created better in its
nature than that which is made in the image of its Creator;
but the image remains a creature; it is nature, and not grace. [53]

---

[49] *De spir. et lit.* 28,48: « Verumtamen quia non usque adeo in anima
humana imago Dei terrenorum affectuum labe detrita est, ut nulla in
ea velut lineamenta extrema remanserint ... »

[50] *De Civ. Dei* XXII,24: « Ex quo enim homo in honore positus, postea
quam deliquit, comparatus est pecoribus, similiter generat; non in eo
penitus exstincta est quaedam velut scintilla rationis, in qua factus est
ad imaginem Dei. »

[51] *Retract.* II,24[51],2, cited above, n. 39.

[52] *Op. imp. c. Iul.* VI,20: « Nec tibi videatur indignum, quod subiecta
est diabolo imago Dei; hoc enim non fieret, nisi iudicio Dei; nec remo-
vetur ista damnatio, nisi gratia Dei. Qui enim naturae excellentia, ut
imago esset, ad similitudinem Dei factus est, non est mirandum, quia
naturae depravatione, vanitati similis factus est, unde dies eius velut
umbra praetereunt. »

[53] *De gra. et lib. arbitrio* 13,25: « Nam et hoc Pelagiani ausi sunt

508

Augustine here, of course, has in mind the Pelagian tendency to see grace in creation, in man's natural endowments, and not as the divine power by which each and every good action is done; but he is also determined to maintain the absolute gulf between God's transcendence and man's contingent existence and to emphasise that it cannot be bridged from man's side, but only from God's, through Jesus Christ the God-man.

It is here that the paradoxical character of Augustine's theology becomes apparent. Few Christian writers have painted the state of fallen man in darker colours than he. « His theology is *really a pathology* », wrote one indignant critic, « he is *par excellence* a penologist; » and again: « Instead of a theology, he gives us an elaborate criminology ».[54] Extravagant though this language may be, it expresses an impression which has been shared by many students of Augustine, who were nevertheless disposed to number him among the greatest teachers of the Christian Church.[55] Yet side by side with Augustine's doctrine of Original Sin and the *massa damnata* from which only a very small part of mankind will be set free,[56] we find in his teaching of the glorification of the image of God in the souls of the elect a doctrine which is reminiscent of the deification taught by the Greek Fathers — indeed, Augustine does not shrink from using the word *deificatio*, as we shall see. Two scholars who have been particularly concerned with elucidating this aspect of Augustinian soteriology are Victorino Capánaga[57] and G. B. Ladner,[58] and they

---

dicere, gratiam esse naturam, in qua sic creati sumus, ut habeamus mentem rationalem, qua intelligere valeamus, facti ad imaginem Dei, ut dominemur piscibus maris, et volucribus caeli, et omnibus pecoribus quae repunt super terram.' Sed non haec est gratia, quam commendat Apostolus per fidem Iesu Christi. » Cf. *De Trin.* XIV,2,4.

[54] Thomas Allin, *The Augustinian Revolution in Theology*, London 1911, 129, 175.

[55] e.g. N. P. Williams, *The Ideas of the Fall and of Original Sin*, London, ed. of 1938, 389: « ... the fact that we must needs reject the ideas of " original righteousness " and " original guilt " as Augustine formulated them involves no disparagement of the spiritual greatness of this heroic saint and doctor. »

[56] *De Civ. Dei* XXI,12: « ... si omnes remanerent in poenis iustae damnationis, in nullo appareret misericors gratia [redimentis]; rursum, si omnes a tenebris transferrentur in lucem, in nullo appareret severitas ultionis. In qua propterea multo plures quam in illa sunt, ut sic ostendatur quid omnibus deberetur. »

[57] Capánaga, *La deificación en la soteriología agustiniana*, in *Augustinus Magister*, vol. 2, pp. 745-54.

have helped us to perceive an aspect of his thought which
has often, in the past, been neglected.

The foundation of Augustine's teaching of the glorification
of the image of God in man is Jesus Christ. Without His
incarnation, death and resurrection there could be no healing
of diseased humanity.[59] « Let the deformity of Christ form
you », he told his congregation,

> for if He had not willed to be deformed, you would not
> have recovered the form which you lost. He, therefore, hung
> upon the cross, deformed; but His deformity was our beauty.
> In this life, therefore, let us hold the deformed Christ. What
> is the deformed Christ? *Far be it from me to glory, save
> in the cross of our Lord Jesus Christ, through which the
> world hath been crucified unto me and I unto the world.*
> This is the deformity of Christ.[60]

The sermon from which these words are taken, has a
strongly anti-Pelagian tendency, and can hardly have been
preached before 418. We may note its emphasis upon Christ
crucified — an emphasis which will become a tradition in
Western devotion and Western iconography in the centuries
after Augustine's life. Ladner has pointed out that this emphasis was to have important consequences for belief about
the destiny of redeemed humanity in Augustine's thought, which
eventually meant that the idea of the reform of man had to
move away from the notion of an *apokatastasis eis to archaion*,
a return to Adam's primal state, to a higher condition. As
Ladner puts it: « If God really was crucified as man, man
could never again be quite the same ».[61] Rather, he must be

---

[58] G. B. Ladner, *St. Augustine's Conception of the Reformation of
Man to the Image of God*, in *Aug. Mag.* 2, pp. 867-78; *The Idea of Reform*,
Cambridge Mass. 1959.

[59] Ladner, *The Idea of Reform*, 193: « Even though the Neoplatonic
background of patristic thought, and in particular Augustine's own
indebtedness to Platonism, are clearly perceptible also in his ideas of
man's image-likeness to God, it is alone the sacrifice of Christ which
in his view can reform the image of God in us. »

[60] *Serm.* 27,6,6: « Deformitas Christi te format. Ille enim si deformis
esse noluisset, tu formam quam perdidisti non recepisses. Pendebat
ergo in cruce deformis; sed deformitas illius pulchritudo nostra erat.
In hac ergo vita deformem Christum teneamus. Quid est, deformem
Christus? *Absit mihi gloriari nisi in cruce domini nostri Iesu Christi,
per quem mihi mundus crucifixus est, et ego mundo.* Haec est deformitas Christi. »

[61] Ladner, *The Idea of Reform*, 154.

III

510

renewed *in melius*,[62] to a better condition. Augustine's great rhapsody upon this renewal in the *De Correptione et Gratia* (426) is well known: « The first liberty of the will was to be able not to sin; the last will be much greater, not to be able to sin; the first immortality was to be able not to die; the last will be much greater, not to be able to die; .... etc. »[63] and this reformation is dependent solely upon Christ. Thus Augustine writes to his correspondent, Honoratus, in 412:

> We too are made by His grace what we were not, that is, sons of God. Yet we were something else, and this much inferior, that is, sons of men. Therefore He descended that we might ascend, and remaining in His nature was made a partaker of our nature, that we remaining in our nature might be made partakers of His Nature; but not simply thus; for His participation in our nature did not make Him worse, while participating in His nature makes us better.[64]

We have here a reaffirmation of the doctrine of participation, which we encountered earlier in the *De diversis quaestionibus LXXXIII*.[65] It is through this participation, which is made possible by the reception of baptism, which makes us members of Christ, that man's deformity is healed.[66] This sacrament is received within the church, and it is within the Church, the Body of Christ, that the image of God is reformed in the

---

[62] *De Gen. ad lit.* VI,20,31: « Hic occurrit alia quaestio, quomodo renovemur, si non ad hoc per Christum revocamur, quod in Adam prius eramus. Quamquam enim multa non in pristinum, sed in melius renoventur, ab inferiore tamen statu, quam quo erant antea, renovantur. »

[63] *De corrept. et grat.* 12,33: « Prima ergo libertas voluntatis erat, posse non peccare; novissima erit multo maior, non posse peccare; prima immortalitas erat, posse non mori; novissima erit multo maior, non posse mori; prima erat perseverantiae potestas, bonum posse non deserere; novissima erit felicitas perseverantiae, bonum non posse deserere. Numquid, quia erunt bona novissima potiora atque meliora, ideo fuerunt illa prima vel nulla vel parva? »

[64] *Ep.* 140,4,10: « Nos quoque per eius gratiam facti sumus quod non eramus, id est, filii Dei; sed tamen aliquid eramus, et hoc ipsum aliquid multo inferius, hoc est, filii hominum. Descendit ergo Ille ut nos ascenderemus, et manens in sua natura factus est particeps naturae nostrae, ut nos manentes in natura nostra efficeremur participes naturae ipsius. Non tamen sic: nam illum naturae nostrae participatio non fecit deteriorem; nos autem facit naturae illius participatio meliores. »

[65] See above, n. 20.

[66] *In Ep. Iohan. Tr.* 5,6: « Ecce accepit sacramentum nativitatis homo baptizatus. Sacramentum habet et magnum sacramentum, divinum, sanctum, ineffabile. Considerate quale: ut novum faciat hominem dimissione omnium peccatorum. »

mind of man; [67] and while this renewal is not effected in a moment of time, as is the remission of sins in baptism, [68] it will, at the end of their lives, bring the faithful to the vision of God, in which the image of God in man will have been perfected. [69] Augustine is prepared to use the word deification to describe this condition, in language so reminiscent of that of St. Athanasius as to suggest the possibility of direct borrowing: « He who was God was made man to make gods those who were men ». [70] That Augustine did not in principle regard such language as inappropriate to the life of the ordinary Christian is apparent from the fact that he was prepared to use it in a sermon on the prosaic theme of not telling lies. « Do not lie, my brethren, » he says,

---

[67] See above, n. 33.

[68] *De Trin.* XIV,17,23: « Sane ista renovatio non momento uno fit ipsius conversionis, sicut momento uno fit illa in baptismo renovatio remissione omnium peccatorum, neque enim vel unum quantulumcumque remanet quod non remittatur. Sed quemadmodum aliud est carere febribus, aliud ab infirmitate, quae febribus facta est, revalescere; itemque aliud est infixum telum de corpore demere, aliud vulnus quod eo factum est secunda curatione sanare: ita prima curatio est causam removere languoris, quod per omnium fit indulgentiam peccatorum; secunda ipsum sanare languorem, quod fit paulatim proficiendo in renovatione huius imaginis. »

[69] *Ibid.*: « In agnitione igitur Dei, iustitiaque et sanctitate veritatis, qui de die in diem proficiendo renovatur, transfert amorem a temporalibus ad aeterna, a visibilibus ad intelligibilia, a carnalibus ad spiritalia; atque ab istis cupiditatem frenare atque minuere, illisque se charitate alligare diligenter insistit. Tantum autem facit, quantum divinitus adiuvatur. Dei quippe sententia est: *Sine me nihil potestis facere.* In quo profectu et accessu tenentem Mediatoris fidem cum dies vitae huius ultimus quemque conperit, perducendus ad Deum quem coluit, et ab eo proficiendus excipiendus ab angelis sanctis, incorruptibile corpus in fine saeculi non ad poenam, sed ad gloriam recepturus. In hac quippe imagine tunc perfecta erit Dei similitudo, quando Dei perfecta erit visio. De qua dicit apostolus Paulus: *Videmus nunc per speculum in aenigmate, tunc autem facie ad faciem.* Item dicit: *Nos autem revelata facie gloriam Domini speculantes, in eamdem imaginem transformamur de gloria in gloriam, tanquam a Domini spiritu*: hoc est quod fit de die in diem bene proficientibus. »

[70] *Serm.* 192,1,1: « Deos facturus qui homines erant, homo factus est qui Deus erat. » This, and similar examples collected by Capánaga and Ladner (see above, nn. 57, 58) disprove the assertion by Myrrha Lot-Borodine, *La déification de l'homme*, Paris ed. of 1970, p. 39, that Augustine's spirit is drawn to beatitude, but not to deification. An exclusive reliance on the statement of Mme Lot-Borodine seriously vitiates an essay on deification by Dr. Ben Drewery in *Christian Spirituality: Essays in Honor of Gordon Rupp*, ed. by Peter Brooks, London 1975, 35-62.

for you were formerly the old man, but you have come to God's grace and have been made *new men*. The lie pertains to Adam, the truth to Christ. *Putting away lying*, therefore, *speak truth*, so that this mortal flesh which you have up to now from Adam may, after the renewing of the spirit, itself deserve renewal and transformation in the time of its resurrection; and thus the whole man, being deified, may cleave to the perpetual and unchanging Truth.[71]

Augustine is however clear that in deification there is no change in the nature of man's being: he remains a creature, and is deified only by God's grace. Accordingly, in expounding the words of the psalmist: *I said, Ye are gods* (*Ps* 81,6/82,6) Augustine declares:

It is clear that He (i.e. God) calls men *gods* through their being deified by His grace and not born of His substance. For He justifies, who is just of Himself and not of another; and He deifies, who is God of Himself and not by participation in another. Now He who justifies, Himself deifies, because by justifying He makes sons of God. For *to them gave He power to become the sons of God*. If we are made *sons of God*, we are also made *gods*; but this is done by grace of adoption, and not by generation.[72]

---

[71] *Serm.* 166,4,4: « Nolite ergo mentiri, fratres. Iam enim veteres homines eratis: accessistis ad gratiam Dei, facti estis homines novi. Mendacium ad Adam pertinet, veritas ad Christum. *Deponentes* ergo *mendacium, loquimini veritatem* (*Eph* 4,25), ut et caro ista mortalis quam adhuc habetis de Adam, praecedente novitate spiritus, mereatur et ipsa innovationem et commutationem tempore resurrectionis suae; ac sic totus homo deificatus inhaereat perpetuae atque incommutabili veritati. »

[72] *Enarr. in Ps.* 49,2: « Manifestum est ergo, quia homines dixit deos, ex gratia sua deificatos, non de substantia sua natos. Ille enim iustificat, qui per semetipsum non ex alio iustus est; et ille deificat, qui per seipsum non alterius participatione Deus est. Qui autem iustificat, ipse deificat, quia iustificando, filios Dei facit. *Dedit enim eis potestatem filios Dei fieri* (*Jo* 1,12). Si filii Dei facti sumus, et dii facti sumus: sed hoc gratiae est adoptantis, non natura generantis »; *Serm.* 166,4,4: « Deus enim deum te vult facere: non natura, sicut est ille quem genuit, sed dono suo et adoptione. Sicut enim ille per humanitatem factus est particeps mortalitatis tuae, sic te per exaltationem facit participem immortalitatis suae »; *Enarr. in Ps.* 146,11: « Igitur si ipse idem ipse est, et mutari ex nulla parte potest, participando eius divinitatem erimus et nos immortales in vitam aeternam. Et hoc nobis pignus datum est de Filio Dei, quod iam dixi Sanctitati vestrae, ut antequam efficeremur participes immortalitatis ipsius, fieret ipse prius particeps mortalitatis nostrae. Sicut autem ille mortalis, non de sua substantia, sed de nostra; sic nos immortales, non de nostra substantia sed de ipsius. »

For Augustine, then, deification is not by nature, but by grace and adoption; and he emphasises that deification by grace is on earth only in hope, not in reality, *in spe* not *in re*, for *it is not yet made manifest what we shall be* (*1Jo* 3,2).[73]

Thus Augustine, no less than, though in a manner somewhat different from that of the Greek Fathers, speaks of the destiny of the elect in terms of deification, a doctrine which has left its traces upon Latin theology, particularly in the writings of Christian mystics like St. Bernard and St. John of the Cross,[74] but a doctrine destined in the West to be overshadowed by the doctrine of justification and sanctification, for which Augustine had himself to a large degree prepared the terminology.[75] Yet the Augustinian doctrine of the glorification of the image by deification, which at one and the same time emphasises the great dignity of the human soul in its creation, the depth of its fall, and its renewal to a greater

---

[73] *Enar. in Ps.* 49,2: « *Videte*, inquit apostolus, *qualem dilectionem nobis dedit Deus, ut filii Dei vocemur et simus.* Et in alio loco: *Dilectissimi, filii Dei sumus, et nondum apparuit quid erimus.* Ergo sumus in spe, nondum in re. *Scimus autem*, inquit, *quoniam cum apparuerit, similes ei erimus, quoniam videbimus eum sicuti est.* Unicus similis nascendo, nos similes videndo. Non enim ita similes ut ille, qui hoc est quod ille a quo genitus est; nos enim similes, non aequales; ille quia aequalis, ideo similis »; *De Trin.* XIV,17,23 (cited above, n. 69); *De pecc. mer. et rem.* II,8,10: « Adoptio ergo plena filiorum in redemptionem fiet etiam corporis nostri. Primitias itaque spiritus nunc habemus, unde iam filii Dei reipsa facti sumus; in caeteris vero spe sicut salvi, sicut innovati, ita et filii Dei; re autem ipsa quia nondum salvi, ideo nondum plene innovati, nondum etiam filii Dei, sed filii saeculi. Proficimus ergo in renovationem iustamque vitam. »

[74] Bernard, *De Diligendo Deo* 10,28: « O amor sanctus et castus! o dulcis et suavis affectio! o pura et defaecata intentio voluntatis! eo certe defaecatior et purior, quo in ea de proprio nil iam admistum relinquitur; eo suavior et dulcior, quo totum divinum est quod sentitur. Si affici, deificari est. Quomodo stilla aquae modica, multo infusa vino, deficere a se tota videtur, dum et saporem vini induit et colorem; et quomodo ferrum ignitum et candens, igni simillimum fit, pristina propriaque forma exutum; et quomodo solis luce perfusus aer in eamdem transformatur luminis claritatem, adeo ut non tam illuminatus, quam ipsum lumen esse videatur; sic omnem tunc in sanctis humanum affectionem quodam ineffabili modo necesse erit a semetipso liquescere, atque in Dei penitus transfundi voluntatem. Alioquin quomodo *omnia in omnibus* erit Deus, si in homine de homine quidquam supererit? Manebit quidem substantia, sed in alia forma, alia gloria, alia potentia. » See E. Gilson, *The Mystical Theology of St. Bernard*, Eng. Tr., London 1940. For St. John of the Cross, see the passages collected by E. Allison Peers, *Spirit of Flame*, London 1943, 141-44.

[75] See Ladner, *The Idea of Reform*, 195.

glory, while maintaining the absolute gulf between the Creator and the creature, deserves more consideration than it commonly receives as a means of understanding the eternal destiny of the redeemed in Christ. In saying this, however, it is necessary to keep in mind another consideration: the fact that for Augustine the number of the elect, great as it is, was but small in comparison with the number of those left in the mass of perdition.[76] The modern student of Augustine's writings, while making every allowance for the circumstances of the age and the presuppositions of the author, may well feel surprise and regret that the great Doctor of Love should have felt constrained to limit the operation of the divine charity to so small a part of humanity. It is true that Augustine's harshness springs paradoxically from the Christocentricity which is the basis of his thought; for him, salvation could only be by Christ, through the reception of the sacrament which He had instituted. Augustine was certainly not indifferent to the fate of the lost; but he preferred to echo the Apostle: *O homo, tu quis es qui respondeas Deo — But who art thou, O man, that repliest unto God* (*Rom* 9,20), rather than indulge in personal speculation. Nevertheless, it is possible to count oneself one of his admirers and still to wish that on this particular issue he had shown something of the speculative boldness which has given Origen, whatever his errors, a special place among Christian theologians.

Durham University,
England

---

[76] *De Civ. Dei* XXI,12 (quoted above, n. 56); *De corrept. et gratia* 10,28: « Quod ergo pauci in comparatione pereuntium, in suo vero numero multi liberantur. »

IV

VERA LUX ILLA EST QUAE ILLUMINAT: THE CHRISTIAN HUMANISM OF AUGUSTINE

IN 427, three years before his death, Augustine of Hippo compiled the *Retractations*, a kind of critical bibliography in which he passed in chronological review his writings as a catholic Christian, clarifying, defending and, where necessary, correcting passages which the course of events or his own theological development had called in question. In a very human way Augustine tended, in practice, to defend his previously-expressed views to a rather greater degree and to criticise them less than had been his original intention;[1] but this means that where he declares a change of opinion, this statement may fairly be regarded as his final and definitive view. Two such statements are relevant to our purposes here: in his review of his earliest Christian work, *Against the Academics*, which appeared in 386, Augustine expresses his displeasure at the praise he there bestowed on the Platonist and Academic philosophers;[2] while in his discussion of the two books *On Order*, which were written at the end of the same year, he regrets that he attributed too much to those liberal studies, of which many of the saints had been ignorant and many of their most enthusiastic disciples lacking in sanctity.[3] Such views would seem, on first reading, to be exactly what we should expect of Augustine in the last years of his life, the result of an increased rigorism brought about by many years of controversy, which had left little of the humanism which had marked his first years as a Christian.

There is, however, another piece of information, provided almost accidentally by Augustine's biographer Possidius, who records that in his last days, when the Vandal armies were over-running Africa,

---

[1] See John Burnaby, 'The *Retractationes* of Saint Augustine: Self-criticism or Apologia?' *Augustinus Magister: Congrès international augustinien* (Paris 1954) 1, pp 85–92.

[2] *Retract[ationum Liber]* I 1 12: Laus quoque ipsa, qua Platonem vel Platonicos seu Academicos philosophos tantum extuli, quantum inpios homines non oportuit, non immerito mihi displicuit. praesertim contra quorum errores magnos defendenda est Christiana doctrina.

[3] *Ibid* I 3 2: Verum et in his libris displicet mihi . . . quod multum tribui liberalibus disciplinis, quas multi sancti multum nesciunt, quidam etiam sciunt et sancti non sunt.

and the society which Augustine had known was falling into ruin, the saint consoled himself with the maxim of a certain wise man: 'He will not be great who thinks it a great matter that wood and stones fall and mortals die.'[4] The wise man, whose name Possidius omits—whether from ignorance, considerations of literary style, or a desire to avoid scandal we do not know—was Plotinus,[5] and thus we find Augustine, in the last months of his life, finding comfort in the words of the great pagan philosopher, whose writings had so powerfully affected his spiritual development more than forty years before.

Too much should not, of course, be made of Augustine's Plotinian citation. The thought expressed is no more than a literary commonplace and in no way characteristically Neo-Platonic; but even if this be granted, it remains significant that at the end, Augustine was prepared to cite a pagan author, when he might have turned so easily and, it might be thought, so predictably, to the scriptures. In the event, Augustine by his own words revealed how profoundly his mind had been formed by the cultural tradition which, as a Christian, he was disposed to reject on first principles. Augustine's dilemma in this matter has long been recognised by scholars. The aim of this paper is to try to discuss, inevitably in a rather superficial fashion, the degree and manner in which Augustine assimilated the classical tradition with his Christianity and transmitted the result to his fellow-Christians and to future generations, thereby bringing about in some measure reform and renewal in the church.

A warning must, however, be given at the outset against over-estimating the extent and immediacy of Augustine's influence. Because Augustinian theology has, at certain periods, played a decisive rôle in determining the development of Latin theology, it is all too easy to assume that it was already dominant in the whole Christian church within the saint's own lifetime. This is certainly an error; for in the first place, Augustine's influence throughout the middle ages was confined to the Latin west. His place in the Greek east has been examined by Berthold Altaner in a magisterial article and need not be

---

[4] Possidius, *Vita Augustini*, ed M. Pellegrino (Cuneo 1955) 28 11: 'Et se inter haec mala cuiusdam sapientis sententia consolabatur dicentis: 'Non erit magnus magnum putans quod cadunt ligna et lapides, et moriuntur mortales' (ed M. Pellegrino, p 154 lines 77–80).

[5] Plotinus, *Enneads* I 4 7. See note by Pellegrino in his ed, p 226 and Pierre Courcelle, 'Sur les dernières paroles de Saint Augustin', *Revue des études anciennes* 46 (Bordeaux 1944) pp 205–7.

The Christian humanism of Augustine

recapitulated here.[6] It is enough to say that although according to Possidius[7] Greek translations of Augustine's writings were made during his lifetime and one of them—the *De Gestis Pelagii*, not commonly reckoned among his greatest—was apparently available to the patriarch Photius in the ninth century,[8] it was only in the first half of the fourteenth century that Byzantine scholars like Maximus Planudes and Demetrius and Procheros Kydones began to produce translations of his major works. But despite their efforts, Augustine long remained for eastern orthodoxy symbolic of that element in Latin Christianity which it finds unacceptable, and this suspicion is only slowly disappearing. Vladimir Lossky, one of the most resolute exponents of an uncompromising Orthodoxy, considered that a theological analysis of Augustine's *De Trinitate* by an Orthodox—an exercise which he was himself admirably equipped to undertake—was a great desideratum; but this is still unprovided.[9] In short we may say that for our purposes Augustine's influence in the east was non-existent.

Secondly, if Augustine brought about reform and renewal in the western church—and few medieval historians are likely to contest the remark of Charles Homer Haskins that 'no writer had a more persistent influence on the higher ranges of mediaeval thought'[10]—this was due more to the long-term effect of his life and writings than to his immediate impact. At the time of his death Augustine was indeed regarded as the most distinguished Latin theologian of his age, as was shown by the imperial summons to attend the ecumenical council of Ephesus;[11] but the predestinarian doctrines which he was then maintaining against Julian of Eclanum had attracted strenuous opposition in southern Gaul from theologians who could not be dismissed as mere Pelagians.[12] Furthermore, the Vandal conquest of Africa destroyed the flourishing monasticism which Augustine had so powerfully influenced and hampered any immediate development of his teaching.

---

[6] [Berthold] Altaner, ['Augustinus in der griechischen Kirche bis auf Photius'], *HJch* 71 (1952) pp 37–76, repr in *Kleine patristische Schriften, TU* bd 83 (Berlin 1967) pp 57–98.

[7] Possidius, *Vita* 11 5 (Pellegrino p 74 lines 20–6). Altaner, pp 52–3, doubts whether many works were in fact translated.

[8] Photius, *Bibliotheca*, cod 54, ed R. Henry, *Photius: Bibliothèque*, 1 (Paris 1959) pp 42–5.

[9] V. Lossky, 'The Procession of the Holy Spirit in Orthodox Trinitarian Doctrine' in *The Image and Likeness of God* (ET London 1975) pp 95–6.

[10] C. H. Haskins, *The Renaissance of the Twelfth Century* (New York 1957) p 80.

[11] Liberatus Carthaginensis, *Breviarium*, 5, PL 68 (1866) col 977A. See G. Bonner, *St Augustine of Hippo* (London 1963) p 156.

[12] See Owen Chadwick, *John Cassian* (2 ed Cambridge 1968) pp 127–32.

Thus I would consider that Augustine's real influence began in the sixth century, through the work of theologians like Caesarius of Arles, Primasius of Hadrumetum, and Gregory the Great, and thereafter was steadily strengthened until it was modified, though certainly not superannuated, by the rise of scholasticism. Augustine did not, like Francis of Assisi or Luther, see any dramatic changes effected in the church by his influence in his own lifetime. Indeed, I am inclined to think that the influence of Augustine encouraged, rather than initiated, developments which were already latent in Latin theology. But to discuss this aspect of Augustinianism would take us outside our theme.

Augustine's attitude to secular studies, and especially to philosophy, has long been discussed in a number of works of outstanding quality. The essential problem is how we are to reconcile the influence which classical literature and Neo-Platonist philosophy undoubtedly exercised over him with his apparent rejection of both these influences in his later life as a Christian. One may mention in this connexion two well-known works: Prosper Alfaric's *L'évolution intellectuelle de saint Augustin* (Paris 1918) and H.-I. Marrou's *Saint Augustin et la fin de la culture antique* (4 ed Paris 1958). In the former Alfaric argued that Augustine's conversion at Milan in 386 was really a conversion to philosophy, and that his true Christian conversion came later; and this view, although extravagant, cannot merely be rejected out of hand, since it is apparent that Augustine's early Christianity was unquestionably deeply influenced by Neo-Platonism. Marrou, in his great study, showed how much Augustine the theologian continued to be *un lettré de la décadence*, a characteristic product of the schools of the later Roman Empire.[13] How, then, are we to reconcile the apparent contradiction between Augustine's own assertions and the testimony of his writings? We may assent to John Burnaby's trenchant observation that 'Augustine is not a compound of Plotinus and Luther, but a Father of the Catholic Church';[14] but the problem of reconciling apparently irreconcilable elements in his thought remains. The issue is not so much the question of Augustine's honesty as of the accuracy of his own understanding of his intellectual development. How did he move from his earlier philosophic humanism to the characteristic theological position of his later years?

[13] [H-I] Marrou, [*Saint Augustin et la fin de la culture antique*] (4 ed Paris 1958) cap 5: 'La bible et les lettrés de la décadence.'
[14] John Burnaby, *Amor Dei. A Study of the Religion of St Augustine* (London 1938) p 21.

4

The Christian humanism of Augustine

I would suggest that some of the difficulties surrounding the problem of Augustine's intellectual development can be resolved if we recognise that his conversion to Christianity was a process which was spread over many years, rather than a momentary experience dividing his life into two parts.[15] The traditional tendency to regard Augustine as having been 'converted' at Milan in 386, with the result that he becomes what William James called a 'twice-born' man, is historically misleading, in that it underestimates that other conversion, specifically recorded by Augustine as having occurred while he was composing his reply to the questions of Simplicianus of Milan in 396/7, and also makes difficult any attempt to harmonise the various influences on Augustine's thinking, on the principle that his pre-conversion experience cannot, by definition, have any real relevance to his 'converted' Christian life. But this is a theological, not an historical judgement, and a narrow one at that (Gerard Manley Hopkins, with a surer theological judgement, spoke of the 'lingering-out swéet skíll' of Augustine's conversion). I would not deny the importance of Augustine's decision to seek baptism in 386—it was undoubtedly the great decision of his life; but I would nevertheless maintain that it must be understood in the context of Augustine's religious development over many years. I therefore propose to consider briefly the intellectual and spiritual career of Augustine, in the hope of finding a key to his eventual understanding of the place of humanism in the Christian life.

Augustine, in the circumstances of his birth and education, was a characteristic product of the later Roman empire, except in one particular, that he was born into a family with a devoutly Christian mother and a father who was sympathetic to Christianity. In this respect, and in this respect only, he differed from his contemporaries, in that he took Christianity without question as the religious norm. Augustine is, indeed, an example of a type of Christian leader which becomes increasingly common in the fourth century: the product of a Christian home, who takes Christianity for granted and, in that sense, never has to make any conscious act of renunciation of paganism, which always had for him something of an academic and bookish quality. On the other hand, again like other Christian leaders of the fourth century coming from Christian homes, Augustine's education was the standard education of his day, as we find it embodied in one

---

[15] See Max Wundt, 'Ein Wendepunkt in Augustins Entwicklung,' *Zeitschrift für die Neutestamentliche Wissenschaft* 21 (Giessen 1922) pp 53–64.

of its most successful products, Decimus Magnus Ausonius, professor and poet, imperial tutor, pretorian prefect and consul—a paradigm of the sort of career which Augustine himself might have hoped to enjoy in other circumstances. The qualities valued by this educational system were wholly at variance with those enjoined by Christianity; yet the young Augustine was able to accept them as easily as did the majority of educated Christians; and it is worth noting that they were called into question not, so far as we can tell, by any religious considerations, but by reading Cicero's *Hortensius* in the normal course of study.[16] Augustine's assertion that it was the *Hortensius* which first turned his aspirations towards God seems, so far as we can judge from the available evidence, to be true;[17] and we may compare this initial conversion at the age of nineteen with Newman's Calvinist conversion at fifteen 'of which', he was later to write as a Catholic, 'I still am more certain than that I have hands and feet.'

The conversion experience effected by reading the *Hortensius* had certain features which apply to Augustine's later conversions and to their effect upon his attitude to humanism. First, the *Hortensius* persuaded him that the love of wisdom, which he unhesitatingly identified with Christianity, was the only true object of study. Secondly, that what was said was more important than the manner of saying it—a doctrine to which he could assent in principle, but not yet accept in practice, as was speedily shown by his revulsion from the style of the Latin bible. Thirdly, the reading of the *Hortensius* taught Augustine that philosophy was not a merely intellectual exercise but a way of life, a discipline of conduct as well as a process of thought. Accordingly, he turned to prayer and to the study of the scriptures without, it must be admitted, much result, for the style of the old Latin bible repelled him, and he continued to keep the mistress whom he had recently acquired.

The sequel to reading the *Hortensius* is notorious: Augustine became a Manichee. His motives were complex, but certain must be noted here as being relevant to his later religious development. First, he did not, in his own eyes, cease to be a Christian by becoming a Manichee—

---

[16] *Conf*[*essionum Liber*] III iv 7: . . . et usitato iam discendi ordine perveneram in librum cuiusdam Ciceronis . . .

[17] See the testimony in *De Beata Vita* i 4: Ego ab usque undevicesimo anno aetatis meae, postquam in schola rhetoris librum illum Ciceronis, qui Hortensius vocatur, accepi, tanto amore philosophiae successus sum, ut statim ad eam me ferre meditarer. Compare *Solil*[*oquia*] I x 17. On the influence of Cicero on Augustine see [Maurice] Testard, [*Saint Augustin et Cicéron*], 2 vols (Paris 1958).

The Christian humanism of Augustine

even if his mother, a woman born to believe, thought otherwise. Secondly, Augustine's adoption of Manichaeism did not impose any obligation to renounce his rhetorical studies, such as he subsequently felt as a catholic Christian. The Manichaean double standard imposed no such demands upon its catechumens. On the other hand, as a result of his conversion to philosophy, Augustine continued as a Manichee to read works of a philosophical character; and the fact that such studies had no financial motivation no doubt helped to consolidate that esteem for philosophy which he felt throughout his life. But there is another factor, which I cannot prove but of which I am fully persuaded. Manichaeism offered Augustine the inspiration of an ideal of continence in the lives of the elect, while at the same time permitting him to keep his mistress as long as he was an auditor. This situation, I suggest, satisfied a psychological need in Augustine, who experienced only too powerfully that combination of sexual attraction and revulsion which was later to cause him to pray: 'Give me chastity and continence, but not yet.'[18] In the continence of the Manichaean elect he would find a degree of devotion for which there would have been no parallel in the African church, where monasticism was unknown. Indeed by Augustine's own account it was only on the eve of his decision to seek baptism at Milan in 386 that he first heard of Saint Antony and of the great tradition of the Egyptian desert, which showed that the Manichees had no monopoly of dedicated chastity, and this discovery aroused in him the greatest enthusiasm.[19]

I would lay some stress upon the hypothesis I have just put forward, not because it is in itself either new or very original, but because it helps to explain the development of Augustine's attitude to humane studies; for his final outlook needs to be understood, in my opinion, in terms of the monastic ideal to which he became, at a later date, so enthusiastic a convert. Augustine's austerity with regard to secular culture is only part of the totality of self-denial which the monastic

[18] *Conf* VIII vii 17. See the discussion of marriage in the *Soliloquies*, in which Augustine declares: Prorsus nihil huiusmodi quaero, nihil desidero; etiam cum horrore atque aspernatione talia recordor (I x 17) and contrast with the later admission: Quam tibi sordidus, quam foedus, quam exsecrabilis, quam horribilis complexus femineus videbatur, quando inter nos de uxoris cupiditate quaesitum est! Certe ista nocte vigilantes, cum rursus eadem nobiscum ageremus, sensisti quam te aliter quam praesumpseras, imaginatae illae blanditiae et amara suavitas titillaverit; longe quidem longe minus quam solet, sed item longe aliter quam putaveras (I xiv 25).

[19] *Conf* VIII vi 14: Cui ego cum indicassem illis me scripturis curam maximam inpendere, ortus est sermo ipso narrante de Antonio Aegyptio monacho, cuius nomen excellenter clarebat apud servos tuos, nos autem usque in illam horam latebat.

state involves, a self-denial which extends not only to property and sexuality, but to the very principle of self-hood. This is why humility came to play such a part in Augustine's moral theology. He had still very far to go before he understood the need for humility; but the conversion effected by the *Hortensius* began the process within him.

The story of Augustine's eventual disillusionment with Manichaeism, though important, does not concern us here. The next episode which is essential in our discussion is the character of the conversion at Milan in 386, with the long-standing problem: to what extent was this a conversion to Christianity, as opposed to Neo-Platonism? In the past, the two professions were commonly deemed to have been mutually incompatible: if Augustine had been truly converted to catholic Christianity, then Neo-Platonist influence on him could, by definition, only have been superficial. If, on the other hand, Neo-Platonism represented a real influence, then Augustine's baptism was no more than a formality which he later, as a mature Christian, invested with a significance which it did not have at the time. Today, however, scholars are less inclined to adopt such a rigorous attitude of either-or. We can believe that a Christianised-Neo-Platonism was popular in the intellectual circles of Milan which Augustine frequented; and we can recognise the effect made upon him by the Neo-Platonic works which he read at that time, and even agree that certain Neo-Platonic doctrines, such as the characteristic view of man which sees him as a soul fallen into a body, continued to affect his thinking long after he had become a catholic.[20] At the same time, it is still possible to believe that Augustine's conversion at Milan was essentially Christian and not Neo-Platonic.

Here, I would suggest, the fact that Augustine sought and received baptism at Easter 387 is crucial, and its significance is deliberately thrown into relief in the *Confessions* by the story of Marius Victorinus, the Platonist philosopher who, before his conversion, was accustomed to declare that he was already a Christian, and when challenged to prove his claim by coming to church would ask: 'Do walls then make Christians?' Victorinus here expresses the view, held by certain pagan intellectuals, that the outward forms of religion, though necessary for the multitude of men, were of little account to the philosopher. But it was precisely this attitude which was unaccept-

[20] See Robert J. O'Connell, *St Augustine's Early Theory of Man A.D. 386–391* and *St Augustine's Confessions: the Odyssey of Soul* (Cambridge, Mass., 1968, 1969) and my review in *JTS* ns 22 (1971) pp 248–51.

The Christian humanism of Augustine

able to catholic Christianity, which insisted that the one road to God was through an exclusive belief in Christ and the reception of the sacraments, which alone gave the power necessary for right living. It was precisely this power which Augustine found lacking in Manichaeism, and subsequently in Neo-Platonism: both failed to make him personally chaste, and neither was able to influence the great majority of men in the way that catholic Christianity seemed able. Augustine makes this clear in certain of the writings which followed his conversion. In what I take to be a crucial passage in the treatise *On True Religion*, written in 389 or 390, he points to the fact that Christianity, in persuading so many thousands of its followers, men and women alike, to live in chastity, had accomplished what Plato could only commend without success.[21] A year or two before the composition of *On True Religion*, in the work *On the morals of the Manichees and of the Catholic Church*, written at Rome, Augustine had, in a rather ungenerous fashion, sought to disparage the celibacy of his former co-religionists the Manichees and to contrast it with the disciplined and self-supporting lives of Christian ascetics.[22] The burden of Augustine's argument is clear: whatever may be the ideals and the claims of others, it is only within the catholic Church that these ideals are realised.

Given this view, what was Augustine's attitude towards literary and philosophical studies at the time when he determined to seek catholic baptism? He resigned his official post as the teacher of rhetoric at Milan, though without any ostentation, urging as a reason weak health, as well as the desire to devote himself to God's service;[23] but he was prepared to continue to read Virgil with private pupils.[24] Furthermore, precisely as a consequence of his conversion, he was moved to envisage the composition of a series of works on the liberal arts—of which the only certain survivor is the *De Musica*—designed 'to reach things incorporeal through things corporeal and to lead others to them!'[25]—an undertaking which indicates the influence which both traditional culture and Neo-Platonism alike exercised over his

---

[21] *De Vera Religione* iii 5.

[22] *De Moribus Catholicae Ecclesiae* xxx 64–xxxi 68.

[23] *De Beata Vita* i 4: . . . Itaque tantus me arripuit pectoris dolor, ut illius professionis onus sustinere non valens, qua mihi velificabam fortasse ad Sirenas, abicerem omnia et optatae tranquillitati vel quassatam navem fessamque perducerem. See also *De Ord[ine]* I ii 5; *Solil* I ix 16; *Conf* IX ii 2–4.

[24] *De Ord* I viii 26: . . . nihilque a me aliud actum est illo die, ut valetudini parcerem, nisi quod ante cenam cum ipsis dimidium volumen Vergili audire cotidie solitus eram.

[25] *Retract* I 5 [6]: . . . per corporalia cupiens ad incorporalia quibusdam quasi passibus certis vel pervenire vel ducere.

9

mind. Nor is this surprising, considering the part which philosophy had played in bringing Augustine to the acceptance of catholic Christianity. Through his reading of the Platonists he had come to believe—mistakenly, as it happened, but to his own satisfaction—that catholic doctrine was in accord with the most advanced, the most brilliant, and the most profoundly religious philosophy of the Greco-Roman world; and if, as seems possible, he had enjoyed some kind of mystical experience a little time before his conversion,[26] he would easily have been persuaded that the Platonist philosophers had contrived, in some degree, to see the truth from afar, even though they failed to attain to it, lacking the power which was given only by Christ in the catholic church.

The respect which Augustine, at the time of his baptism, entertained for Platonic thought, has recently been emphasised by Pierre Courcelle,[27] who draws attention to the fact that the statement by Porphyry in the *De Regressu Animae*[28] that there is no one way for the deliverance of the soul, not even in the *verissima philosophia*, is echoed by Augustine in the *Soliloquies*[29] (386–7); while in the *Contra Academicos* (386) the *verissima philosophia* is defined as a philosophy 'not of this world—such a philosophy our sacred mysteries most justly detest—but of the other, intelligible world.'[30] Thus it appears that in Augustine's view, Platonism is a philosophy not only recognised by, but positively acceptable to, Christianity.[31] Furthermore, in the *De Ordine*[32] (386)

---

[26] *Conf* VII iii 5; xx 26. See Pierre Courcelle, *Les Confessions de Saint Augustin dans la tradition littéraire* (Paris 1963) pp 43–58.

[27] Pierre Courcelle, '*Verissima philosophia*' in *Epekstasis: mélanges patristiques offerts au Cardinal Jean Daniélou* (Paris 1972) pp 653–9.

[28] *De Regressu Animae, Fragm* 12 (preserved by Augustine, *De Civ[itate] Dei* X 32).

[29] *Solil* I xiii 23.

[30] *Contra Academicos* III xix 42: Non enim est ista huius mundi philosophia, quam sacra nostra meritissime detestantur, sed alterius intellegibilis, cui animas multiformibus erroris tenebris caecatas et altissimis a corpore sordibus oblitas numquam ista ratio subtilissima revocaret, nisi summus deus populari quadam clementia divini intellectus auctoritatem usque ad ipsum corpus humanum declinaret atque summitteret, cuius non solum praeceptis sed etiam factis excitatae animae redire in semet ipsas et resipiscere patriam etiam sine disputationum concertatione potuissent.

[31] *Ibid* III xx 43: Quod autem subtilissima ratione persequendum est—ita enim iam sum affectus, ut quid sit verum non credendo solum sed etiam intellegendo apprehendere impatienter desiderem—apud Platonicos me interim, quod sacris nostris non repugnet, reperturum esse confido.

[32] *De Ord* I xi 32: Unde etiam divinae scripturae, quas vehementer amplecteris, non omnino philosophos, sed philosophos huius mundi evitandos atque inridendos esse praecipiunt. Esse autem alium mundum ab istis oculis remotissimum, quem paucorum sanorum intellectus intuetur, satis ipse Christus significat, qui non dicit: 'regnum meum non est de mundo', sed: *regnum meum non est de hoc mundo.*

The Christian humanism of Augustine

Augustine assures his mother that scripture itself teaches that not all philosophers are to be shunned, but only the philosophers of this world, 'for that there is another world, far removed from these human eyes, which the understanding of a few, healthy souls apprehends, Christ Himself aptly indicates, who did not say: "My kingdom is not of any world" but *My kingdom is not of this world*.' Philosophy is, indeed, simply the love of wisdom, which is pursued alike by Platonists and students of the scriptures. But what is significant in Augustine's statement in the *Soliloquies* that there is no one way of deliverance for the soul, is that it is superficially in agreement with the view of pagans like Symmachus, and Augustine's African correspondent Maximus of Madaura: *Nam deus omnibus commune nomen est. Ita fit, ut, dum eius quasi quaedam membra carptim variis supplicationibus prosequimur, totum colere profecto videamur.*[33] Maximus expressed his view in a letter of 390, by which time Augustine was prepared to administer a sharp rebuff; and it is clear that even when writing in 386, he did not intend to include the pagan cults among the ways of deliverance for the soul; but, as he afterwards noted in the *Retractations*, when he echoed Porphyry in the *Soliloquies*, he had overlooked the Dominical saying: *I am the way*.[34]

Augustine's return to Africa in 388 and the three years which followed it, culminating in his ordination as presbyter of Hippo in 391, represents another stage in his conversion, for the decision to return to Africa determined Augustine's life to a degree which he could never have anticipated. In the first place, Augustine moved from the cosmopolitan intellectual atmosphere of Milan to the narrower and more puritanical atmosphere of African Christianity. Secondly, and apart from that external influence, the triennium 388–91 saw a development in Augustine himself. The academic community which he established at Thagaste appears superficially to owe more to Neo-Platonic and Stoic doctrine than to Christian monasticism; but the appeal of the cloister may be discerned under the appearance of cultured leisure.[35] Moreover, in the works composed during this period, like the *De Magistro* and the *De Vera Religione*, we can see the developing operation of Augustine's Christianity upon his thought.

---

[33] *Inter* Aug, *Ep* 16.
[34] *Retract* I 4 3: item quod dixi: *ad sapientiae coniunctionem non una via perveniri* non bene sonat; quasi alia via sit praeter Christum, qui dixit: *ego sum via*.
[35] See Adolar Zumkeller, *Das Mönchtum des heiligen Augustinus*, 2 ed, *Cassiciacum* bd XI (Würzburg 1968) pp 56–68.

Christ is the only true teacher. Divine authority precedes and prepares the way for the exercise of reason—a view already proposed in the *De Ordine* which will be developed in the *De Utilitate Credendi*, written soon after Augustine's ordination in 391.

This ordination, administered against Augustine's will, when he was on the point of transforming the community of Thagaste into something more formally monastic, brought about a revolution in Augustine's relationships. Up to this point he had moved largely in a world of Christian intellectuals, men for whom a knowledge of classical culture was taken for granted. From 391 onwards he was to be concerned with a different type of Christian, the *rudes ac simplices* for whom he was to compose his *Abecedarian Psalm against the Donatists* and his work on *The Christian Combat*, men for whom Christianity was, in a very real sense, an alternative way of life to that offered by the classical tradition. With a sure instinct for the requirements of the task which lay ahead, Augustine prepared himself for his priestly duties by a study of the Christian scriptures, which he recognised as providing the foundation and guide for the Christian life. For the rest of his life the bible was to be his rule and norm. Significantly, the canon of scripture was defined for Africans at the council of Hippo in 393, at which Augustine delivered his sermon on the creed, the *De Fide et Symbolo*, and again at the council of Carthage of 397—a process of definition which must have emphasised the authority of the sacred text for Augustine. From 391 onwards, then, Augustine's mind was professionally orientated towards biblical study. His concern for philosophy, except as an aid to exegesis, is abruptly cut short. As a new Christian convert, he was prepared to read Virgil with his pupils; but inquiries made to him as a bishop about Cicero received a dusty answer. A bishop has better things to do than expound Ciceronian treatises.[36]

Furthermore, although Augustine's ordination prevented him from pursuing the sort of monastic life which he had proposed for himself in 391, he still contrived to live a community-life according to rule, so that Hippo became a kind of monastic episcopal seminary. Even

[36] *Ep* 118 (*ad Dioscorum*, written in 410; see A. Goldbacher, *CSEL* 58 (1904) p 34): ... sed in hac re nihil esse dedecoris, non mihi videtur. Non enim dedecora facies rerum attingit sensum meum, cum cogito episcopum ecclesiasticis curis circumstrepentibus districtum atque distentum, repente quasi obsurdescentem cohibere se ab his omnibus et dialogorum Tullianorum quaestiunculas uni scholastico exponere? Nevertheless, the whole letter bears witness to the influence exercised by Cicero on Augustine's mind. See Testard 2, pp 94–106.

The Christian humanism of Augustine

after becoming sole bishop of Hippo in 396 Augustine continued, so far as he could, to live like a monk, requiring his clergy to bestow their property upon the church of Hippo, and himself displaying the greatest circumspection in his relations with women, even when dealing with them as a bishop.

This background of monastic living and a growing preoccupation with biblical study as a guide to the Christian life underlies Augustine's conversion experience of 396 or 397, when he was at work on his reply to the exegetical problems raised by bishop Simplicianus of Milan, an experience which he subsequently recognised as having been one of the decisive events in his life. In a sudden flash of apprehension Augustine came to understand the wholly gratuitous character of grace, as expressed in the words of St Paul: *What have you that you did not receive? If then you received it, why do you boast as if it were not a gift?* 'In the solution of this question', Augustine was later to write, 'I indeed laboured in defence of the free choice of the human will; but the grace of God conquered.'[37]

It was about the time of his conversion-experience while replying to Simplicianus, or shortly afterwards, that Augustine composed the *Confessions*, which equally and more famously emphasise the absolute gratuity of grace, and which are regarded by a leading authority (H. Hagendahl) as exhibiting 'a deep-seated hostility to the old cultural tradition.'[38] Too much emphasis should not, perhaps, be laid upon Augustine's language in the *Confessions*, if only because that work, while avowedly hostile to rhetoric, is itself very much a product of the rhetorical tradition. Of more significance for a balanced understanding of Augustine's attitude is the evidence provided by the work on Christian culture, *De Doctrina Christiana*, begun about the same time as the *Confessions* and completed to a little way after the middle of the third book, the remainder of that book and book IV being added thirty years later, about 426 or 427; for here Augustine provides what is, in effect, a Christian alternative to the classical education of his day, with the bible replacing the pagan literary texts, and ancillary studies like history and philosophy being employed as aids to exegesis,

---

[37] *Retract* II 1 [27]. See G. Bonner, *Augustine and Modern Research on Pelagianism* (The Saint Augustine Lecture for 1970) (Villanova, Pa., 1972) pp 15–18.

[38] H. Hagendahl, *Augustine and the Latin Classics*, Studia Graeca et Latina Gothoburgensia no 20 (Gothenburg 1967) 2, p 715. See also pp 726–7: 'The *Confessions* represent the climax of an attitude of unconcern, aversion, even hostility that subsisted, though occasionally less austerely, to the end of his life.'

with the specific warning that they should not be studied to excess. The deliberate restriction of the course of studies envisaged by the *De Doctrina Christiana* is striking. It may be true, as H.-I. Marrou asserts, that Augustine was providing a course of study for intending preachers and did not mean to imply that Christians should contract out of secular life or forbid young Christian men to pursue the necessary studies to become magistrates, physicians or civil servants;[39] but the intellectual narrowness of the *De Doctrina* is striking. Augustine does not go so far as Tertullian in rejecting pagan learning; but he certainly accepts in practice his view that 'when we believe, we desire no further belief.' The only value of secular studies, according to Augustine, is that they may help us to understand the sacred text.

Yet Augustine's narrow biblicism differs from the biblicism of later protestantism. For Augustine, even the bible itself is but a means to an end: the love of God, who is to be enjoyed, and of our neighbour, who is able to enjoy God with us and the study of Scripture is but the third stage of seven, which lead to wisdom—the vision of God (*De Doctrina Christiana II*, vii 11–viii 12), to be used to the enjoyment of some other thing. Having established in his first book that God alone is the thing to be enjoyed, and all other things used to obtain that enjoyment, Augustine then proceeds in the second to discuss the nature of signs, by which truth is communicated from man to man and from one generation to another, in order to provide an epistemological basis for biblical exegesis. Now the nature of signs had already attracted Augustine's attention in 389 in the *De Magistro*, where he had come to the conclusion that the true teacher is Christ, 'Whom to love and to know is the happy life, which all men claim that they seek, though few there are who rejoice in having truly found it';[40] and it may seem surprising that he returns to the topic afresh in the context in which he was writing. The reason, I would suggest, is that Augustine wished to take into account an intellectual austerity even greater than his own, which not only rejected any study of pagan literature whatever, but even held that the bible itself was not essential for the mature Christian—a view with which Augustine

---

[39] Marrou p 380.

[40] *De Magistro* xiv 46: ut iam non crederemus tantum, sed etiam intelligere inciperemus quam vere scriptum sit auctoritate divina, ne nobis quemquam magistrum dicamus in terris, quod unus omnium magister in coelis sit. Quid sit autem in coelis, docebit ipse a quo etiam per homines signis admonemur et foris, ut ad eum intro conversi erudiamur; quem diligere ac nosse beata vita est, quam se omnes clamant quaerere, pauci autem sunt qui eam vere se invenisse laetentur.

The Christian humanism of Augustine

agrees: '. . . The man who is supported by faith, hope and charity and maintains the same unshaken has no need of the scriptures, except to instruct others. And so by these three, many live even in solitude, without books.'[41] Augustine accepts the monastic ideal, even in the anti-intellectual form sometimes found in the Egyptian desert, where books could be regarded as the plunder of widows and orphans; yet he is prepared to offer an argued defence of the propriety both of scriptural study and of secular reading to advance that study. And from that he produces a genuine, if grudging, outline of a Christian culture; but a Christian culture designed solely to further the growth in grace of the baptised believer.

In the event, Augustine's ideal failed to transform the educational system of his age, which continued to cling to the study of the classical authors as the foundation and the norm of culture. It was the ideals of Symmachus and Ausonius, and not those of Augustine, which determined the shape of education in western Europe down to the renaissance and long afterwards. Once and once only in medieval history, to the best of my knowledge, was Augustine's ideal realised, three centuries after his lifetime, in the culture of Christian Northumbria represented by Benedict Biscop's foundation of Wearmouth-Jarrow and expressed in the writings of its brightest ornament, the venerable Bede; for Bede's work was accomplished within the framework which Augustine had envisaged, inasmuch as Bede passed from elementary grammar directly to Christian authors without any intervening study of classical models, and thereafter devoted himself to a career of teaching which found its end and fulfilment in the exposition of the scriptures to the increase of faith, hope and charity. But Bede's career remains the brilliant anomaly, made possible only because Northumbrian Christianity was a monastic culture imposed upon a Germanic society ignorant of the classical tradition. Elsewhere, outside the monasteries and sometimes within them, educational tradition proved too strong, even for the victorious Christian church, and throughout the middle ages the specious charms of the pagan classics continued to disturb the consciences of zealous churchmen.

It is however important to recognise that the *De Doctrina Christiana*, despite its deliberate limitations of outlook, does not represent a complete rejection of non-Christian culture. Secular studies which

---

[41] *De Doct[rina] Christ[iana]* I xxxix 43.

may be useful for biblical exegesis are permitted, and it is noteworthy that the writings of the philosophers, and especially the Platonists, are specifically commended, where they declare truths in agreement with the Christian faith, on the traditional Christian principle that the Children of Israel when they came out of Egypt despoiled the Egyptians.[42] This concession is, of course, hardly surprising, when we remember that in the *Confessions*, written at about the same time, Augustine had paid tribute to the part which they had played in bringing him to the Catholic church.[43]

With the *De Doctrina Christiana* and the *Confessions* we have reached the point at which Augustine's views on the value of secular studies for the Christian have become reasonably fixed and it will be convenient to recapitulate their development. The reading of Cicero's *Hortensius* at the age of nineteen, turned Augustine's thoughts to Christianity, which in turn led him to Manichaeism, partly, according to his own testimony, because his literary tastes were offended by the style of the Latin bible. Acquaintance with Neo-Platonism at Milan in 386 helped to make possible his acceptance of catholic baptism, and left him with an enthusiasm for a kind of Christian humanism, expressed in the *De Musica*. However, besides the Neo-Platonists, Augustine at Milan also discovered Christian monasticism, which seems from his own account to have played a decisive part in bringing about his conversion, and to have left him with an ideal which continued steadily to attract his allegiance over the years, and was intensified by the three years spent at Thagaste, after his return to Africa in 388. His involuntary ordination in 391 both brought him into contact with the uneducated Christian who formed the majority in the African church, and also directed him to intensive biblical study. Finally the conversion experience which occurred while he was at work on the answers to the biblical questions of Simplicianus of Milan, leaving him convinced of the absolutely gratuitous character of grace, completed the transformation of Augustine the Christian humanist to Augustine the Doctor of Grace, and explains the hostility to humanism revealed in the *Confessions* and the *De Doctrina Christiana*, while still leaving him convinced of the truth and the utility of much of the teaching of the Platonists.

This evaluation of Augustine's eventual attitude to secular studies is confirmed by the evidence provided by his treatise *On Catechizing*

---

[42] *Ibid* II xl 60.
[43] *Conf* VII ix 13–xxi 27.

The Christian humanism of Augustine

the Uninstructed (De Catechizandis Rudibus), composed in 399, in which he provides a practical guide to the instruction of candidates for baptism. Here, in order to provide the most effective instruction, Augustine recognises three classes of catechumens: the ordinary uneducated; well-educated persons who have received a thorough training in liberal studies (liberalibus doctrinis excultus);[44] and, finally, those who have received the general literary education of the schools (de scholis usitatissimis grammaticorum oratorumque venientes)[45] 'who seem to surpass other men in the art of speaking.' Of these three classes, special consideration should be given to the highly-educated, who are accustomed to make diligent inquiry into matters which interest them, and who may already have discovered a good deal about Christian doctrine on their own account, in order to spare them a tedious recital of what they already know. On the other hand, Augustine shows markedly less sympathy with the third category, composed of those who have received a general literary and rhetorical education. Such persons must be warned against presuming on their literary skills and despising simpler believers who can more easily avoid faults of conduct than of grammar. They must not let themselves be deterred by the uncouth style of the scriptures or fall into the error of taking literally what is to be understood metaphorically, nor must they ridicule any bishop or minister of the church who lacks their literary training. These recommendations seem to have an autobiographical flavour. Augustine has in mind his own experience when, after reading Cicero's Hortensius, he turned to the scriptures, only to find their style inferior to that of Cicero; and the distaste for grammarians and rhetoricians revealed in the Confessions reappears in the De Catechizandis Rudibus. On the other hand, it is equally clear that Augustine's concern for those who come to be made Christians after prolonged inquiry conducted on a high intellectual level is based on personal experience, and constitutes a recognition of the value of secular learning as a preparation for the gospel message.

It would therefore appear that about the year 400 Augustine had come to reject the classical culture in which he had been educated, while retaining a measure of regard for non-literary studies, and especially philosophy, which he had acquired on his own account. Yet we have to take account of the regret, expressed in the Retractations,

---

[44] De Catechizandis Rudibus viii 12.
[45] Ibid ix 13.

that in his early writings he had over-valued the Platonists, which implies that his respect for the pagan philosophers had by this time still further diminished. Is it possible to establish to what extent there was a real change in his opinions, and if so, how this change came about?

In the *Confessions* Augustine likens the Neo-Platonists to men who see the country of peace from afar, but fail to find the way, because they do not keep to the road that leads there.[46] This recognition of the ability of the human mind, even when fallen, to see the truth, and to come to some knowledge of God from the evidences of His creation, reappears in the second tractate on St John's Gospel (perhaps to be dated 406–7): '[The philosophers] saw where they had to come; but they were ungrateful to Him who furnished what they saw, and wished to attribute what they saw to themselves, and becoming proud lost what they saw and were turned away from it to idols and images and to the cult of demons, adoring the creature and scorning the Creator.'[47] This, for Augustine, constituted the great error of the Platonists: they failed to recognise the Incarnation, and their failure was due to pride.[48] 'Oh had you but recognised the grace of God in Jesus Christ our Lord, and that very Incarnation of His, wherein He assumed a human soul and body, you might have seen it to be the brightest example of grace!'[49] It was the humility of God revealed in the Incarnation which particularly moved Augustine, and it was in this divine virtue of humility that the Platonists were deficient.

This dissatisfaction only increased in the years following the sack of Rome of 410, when Augustine was at work on the anti-pagan polemic of *The City of God*; for he now had to deal with the Platonists, no longer as the philosophers whose teaching afforded the strongest endorsement of Christian doctrine, but as the embittered defenders of later Roman paganism, who patronised the sacrificial cultus, that aspect of paganism most repulsive to Augustine. Here the tenth book of the *De Civitate Dei*, written in about 417, is particularly revealing. The Platonists are still 'the noblest of all the philosophers' (*Platonicos*

---

[46] *Conf* VII xxi 27; compare *De Civ Dei* X 29.

[47] *In Evang[elium] Ioh[annis] Tr[actatus]* 2, 4.

[48] *De Civ Dei* X 24: Eum quippe in ipsa carne contempsit, quam propter sacrificium nostrae purgationis adsumpsit, magnum scilicet sacramentum ea superbia non intellegens, quam sua ille humilitate deiecit verus benignusque Mediator.

[49] *Ibid* X 29: O si cognovisses Dei gratiam per Iesum Christum dominum nostrum ipsamque eius incarnationem, qua hominis animam corpusque suscepit, summum esse exemplum gratiae videre potuisses!

The Christian humanism of Augustine

omnium philosophorum merito nobilissimos),[50] Plotinus is 'that great Platonist' (*ille magnus Platonicus*),[51] while Porphyry is a man 'of no mean intellect' (*homo non mediocri ingenio praeditus*);[52] yet despite their wisdom, all fell alike into the popular error of polytheism, and some even maintained that divine honours might be accorded to demons. 'Porphyry was under the influence of evil powers, of which he was ashamed and yet dared not freely contradict them. He would not acknowledge Christ the Lord, by whose Incarnation we are cleansed, to be the First Principle. He even despised Him in the very flesh which he assumed for the sacrifice of our purification, failing to understand the great mystery by the very pride which the true and loving Mediator destroyed by His humility'.[53] It is not surprising that in the last twenty years of his life Augustine came to see the Platonists, not simply as more doubtful guides to Christianity than he had assumed in the enthusiasm of 386, but as the enemies of Christianity and advocates of idolatry and sorcery.

Thus his earlier enthusiasm for Neo-Platonism came (in the words of Portalié) 'to die a slow death in the heart of Augustine',[54] and this process seems to have been accomplished during the period of the composition of *The City of God*, 413–26; yet even in the last book of that work, Augustine could still quote the Platonists in defence of the Christian doctrine of the resurrection of the body, and observe that 'Plato and Porphyry each made certain statements which might have brought them both to become Christians if they had exchanged them with one another.'[55] Furthermore, we have a revealing insight into Augustine's attitude to the great pagan writers and thinkers in a letter to his friend Evodius, written in 414–5, discussing the question of Christ's descent into Hell, in which Augustine asks who would not rejoice if all the souls in Hades were set free, and especially those who have made themselves familiar by their writings—not only poets and orators who exposed the follies of polytheism, but also the philosophers.[56] This attitude is more significant, because it was about this time that Augustine was writing the fifth book of *The City of God*, in

---

[50] *Ibid* X 1.
[51] *Ibid* X 2.
[52] *Ibid* X 32.
[53] *Ibid* X 24.
[54] Eugène Portalié, *A Guide to the Thought of Saint Augustine*, trans R. J. Bastian (London 1960) p 95.
[55] *De Civ Dei* XXII 27.
[56] *Ep* 164 ii 4. For date, see Goldbacher, *CSEL* 58, p 42.

which he was concerned to refute the suggestion that virtuous pagans might deserve a place in Heaven for their good deeds, arguing that their virtues were made of no effect because they were practised for the sake of fame, and quoting with supreme irony the Dominical words: *They have received their reward.*[57] Writing in private, to a fellow-Christian and personal friend, Augustine did not hesitate to express his regard for the pagans whom he was obliged to disparage for the sake of controversy. Dante, when he placed the virtuous pagans in the noble castle of Limbo, was writing in the spirit of Augustine.

There would therefore seem to be some difference between what Augustine formally said about pagan literature as a Christian controversialist, and what he privately felt as an individual; and this dichotomy helps to explain his continued regard for pagan philosophy, and the fact that he continued to quote Plotinus in the last months of his life, the very time when he was engaged upon his last and most uncompromising anti-Pelagian work, the *Opus Imperfectum contra Iulianum*. The tension between Augustine the Christian humanist and Augustine the predestinarian theologian was never entirely resolved. It is expressed vividly in the twenty-fourth chapter of the last book of *The City of God* (written in 426) when Augustine, after pronouncing an enthusiastic encomium on man's achievements and the beauty of the created world, concludes that these are only the consolations of humanity under judgement, and asks rhetorically what God will give to those whom He has predestinated to life, if He has given all this to those whom he has condemned to death. The grimness of Augustine's conclusion does not altogether obscure his enthusiasm for man's abilities and achievements even in a fallen world. The divine spark of reason implanted by God in man is not wholly extinguished by Adam's sin.

If the argument which has been followed in this paper is valid, we may say that although Augustine formally rejected the literary and rhetorical training of his youth, he never wholly divested himself of its influence; and he continued to have a real regard and admiration for philosophy to his life's end, regarding the Platonic philosophy as being in large measure in agreement with the inspired teaching of Christianity. The fatal weakness of Platonism in his eyes, the deficiency which made it fundamentally insufficient to bring man to the truth, was the absence of any recognition of Christ, the true light, 'for the man

[57] *De Civ Dei* V 15.

The Christian humanism of Augustine

who is enlightened is also called a light; *sed vera lux illa est quae illuminat*—but the true light is that which enlightens.'[58] For Augustine —and this is as true of him when he first read the *Hortensius* as of the mature theologian—the way to God is through Christ, 'by whom man comes, to whom man attains, in whom man abides.'[59] Philosophising is a religious activity, a form of contemplation.

It is this consideration which provides the key to Augustine's influence on Latin Christian culture in the later middle ages. He helped, more perhaps than anyone else, to bring into western monasticism that intellectual and academic element which contrasts so strongly with the traditional asceticism of the Christian east. This he did, not so much by his specific recommendations of a programme of studies, which was realised, as we have seen, only in a particular locality and for a limited time, but rather by the general influence of his life and writings. Gregory the Great's famous dictum on Saint Benedict, *scienter nescius et sapienter indoctus*, could never have been applied to Augustine who was, and always remained, a learned intellectual. Yet Augustine was also a monk, the author of a rule which was to exercise an influence in the west second only to the Benedictine. Augustine thus combined in himself the scholar's love of learning and the contemplative's desire for God, and could commend these in that moving style of which the *Confessions*—already a favourite in his own lifetime[60]—was the supreme expression. Furthermore, Augustine not only commended the Platonists as the philosophers who came closest to Christianity, but provided in his own writings a very considerable part of the knowledge of Platonism available in western Europe in the early middle ages. Augustine can therefore be seen as the ideal monastic philosophical theologian, and it is no accident that Saint Anselm, perhaps the supreme Latin Christian intellect of the pre-scholastic era, should have been soaked in the writings of Augustine, so that his works, however original they are in their matter, could well be mistaken for Augustine's own as regards style.

Yet style was precisely that element in a piece of writing which Augustine had learned, from the first reading of the *Hortensius*, to be of no account in respect to what was said; and there is a certain irony

---

[58] *In Evang Ioh Tr* 2, 6: *Erat lux vera.* Quare additum est: *vera*? quia et homo illuminatus dicitur lux; sed vera lux illa est quae illuminat.

[59] *De Doct Christ* I xxxiv 38: Sic enim ait: *Ego sum via et veritas et vita*, hoc est 'per me venitur, ad me pervenitur, in me permanetur.'

[60] *Retract* II 6 [32] 1: Quid de illis alii sentiant, ipsi viderint; multis tamen fratribus eos multum placuisse et placere scio.

in the fact that the one Christian father to have written a work which posterity has decided was a literary classic should have reacted so violently against the educational system of his day, which sought above all else to develop a moving and persuasive style. Yet the irony is more apparent than real; for although Augustine long continued—like other Christian fathers—to employ the rhetorical techniques acquired in his school education, he informed them with a personal enthusiasm and devotion, to produce a style which was both characteristic and wholly appealing. If Augustine was, in effect, the universal doctor of the early middle ages in the west, it was because his personality coloured the vast store of information which he provided. It was for this reason that Augustine became, in the words of Harnack, 'not only a paedagogue and teacher, but a Father of the Church.' Something of the charm which his biographer Possidius recognised, when he said that he thought that those gained most from Augustine who heard him preaching in church or witnessed his dealings with men, continues to haunt his pages. Sir Ernest Barker has observed that to read *The City of God* is an education, and a very liberal education. The judgement may be extended to Augustine's writings as a whole.

University of Durham

V

ST. AUGUSTINE'S DOCTRINE OF THE HOLY SPIRIT

*A Paper read at the Fellowship Conference, Broadstairs,
September, 1959*

I begin with a quotation from the prayer with which
Augustine closes his great treatise on the Trinity :
'Directing my attention to the rule of faith, as far as I was
able and Thou hast made me able, I have sought Thee, and I
have desired to see by my understanding what I have believed.
I have disputed and laboured greatly. O Lord my God, my one
hope, do Thou hear me, lest, being wearied, I should not wish
to seek Thee. Let me rather always seek Thy face with burning
zeal. Give the power to seek, who hast made me find Thee and
given the hope of finding Thee more and more. Before Thee is
my strength and my weakness; preserve the one, and heal the
other. Before Thee is my knowledge and my ignorance; where
Thou hast opened to me, receive me going in; where Thou hast
barred the door, open to him who knocks. Let me be mindful
of Thee, let me understand Thee, let me love Thee. Increase in
me these things, until Thou reform me to wholeness.'[1]
A paper on the Holy Spirit must inevitably also deal with
the doctrine of the Trinity as a whole; for the Trinity, to use
Augustine's phrase, is 'ineffably inseparable',[2] and we should be
on our guard against any tendency to dwell upon one Person,
to the exclusion of the others. Furthermore, it will be necessary,
as a preliminary, to consider, very briefly, the general background to Augustine's Trinitarian writings. I have emphasised
in the past that he is an occasional writer in the strictest sense
of the term; his crowded life left him little leisure; and his
widely ranging and deeply original mind had to express itself,
not in formal treatises, but in pamphlets, produced to refute the
doctrines of religious opponents, like the Donatists or the
Pelagians; to edify and instruct the faithful; or to answer the
questions of a correspondent. Similar considerations, of course,
inspire systematic theologians, for few men are inclined to
speculate in a void, or care to divorce their work from questions
of immediate interest; but it is clear that there will be a difference between the carefully planned writings of the scholar in
his study, and the *ad hoc* writings of the man of action. Now
Augustine wrote, not from the professorial chair, but from the

[1]*De Trinitate,* XV, xxviii, 51. (*M.P.L.* xlii, 1098).

[2]Aug., *Ep.* 120, iii, 13: 'ipsa ineffabiliter inseparabilis trinitas'. (*C.S.E.L.*
xxxiv, 715). Cf. *De Trin.,* XV, xxiii, 43, (*M.P.L.* xlii, 1090).

episcopal throne, devoting his energy to inspiring that increase of faith, hope, and charity which he regarded as the goal of all scriptural and secular study. For that reason, it is essential to begin with a brief examination of the conditions in the Latin west in general and in Roman Africa in particular, at the time when he produced his Trinitarian writings.

It is clear to the point of being platitudinous that the Christian doctrine of One God in three Persons makes possible the formulation of two opposite types of error. On the one hand, men may so emphasise the Unity, as to reduce the Persons to mere appearances of God in His activity in the world. Such a proceeding leads to the heresy commonly called Sabellianism. At the opposite extreme are the views generally comprehended under the name of Arianism. Here, the intention is to safeguard the reality of the three Persons while avoiding any lapse into polytheism and this is done by calling the Son a created being, immeasurably exalted above all other creatures, created beyond and before time, to whom divine honours may be accorded, but who remains, in the last resort, a being created by the Father out of nothing. Such was the heresy which convulsed the Christian Church for sixty years during the Fourth Century, and whose refutation drew from the pens of St. Athanasius and the Cappadocian Fathers some of their noblest writings. Now, while in the east, the Fifth Century saw Arianism virtually a dead issue, and Nestorius, newly arrived in Constantinople in 428, displaying his zeal for the faith by suppressing the remnants of the Arians there, in the west the Latins were having the unwelcome experience of dealing with an agressive Arianism on their own ground. By one of the tragedies of history Ulfilas, the missionary of the Goths, whose labours among them must always command our admiration, was present at the council of Constantinople of 360 and accepted the Arian doctrine which triumphed there, so that his converts learned and nourished a hatred of the Nicene formula of *homoousios*. To be a Goth became, in effect, to be an Arian; it was almost the distinguishing badge of the German. Already, in the Fourth Century, the presence of German soldiers in the Roman army meant that Arianism had secured a place in the Roman body politic—Alaric, it will be recalled, was nominally a general in the imperial service—but, from 406 onwards, when the Vandals, Suevians and Alans crossed the Rhine, and poured into Gaul, whence they were to spread to Spain, and Africa itself, the Latin Catholics were to find themselves living side by side with the barbarian invader, victorious, confident, and in many cases, bitterly hostile to the doctrine of Nicaea.

The fact of the Challenge of Arianism must be remembered when we discuss Augustine's trinitarian writings. It is never far from his thoughts, though he has to deal with more than one form, from the extreme Anomoeanism of Eunomius, inspired by a study of the Categories of Aristotle, to the more popular subordinationism of the Goths, as expressed for example by the

Arian bishop, Maximinus. Furthermore, there seems to have existed a subordinating tendency in African thought, apart from Arianism; Donatus the Great, the effective founder, and the great doctor of the schismatic church, had written a work on the Holy Spirit which, in Jerome's opinion, was Arian in tone.[3] Augustine is more explicit; according to Donatus, he says, the Son is of the same substance as the Father, but lesser than He; and the Spirit less than the Son. Augustine admits that the majority of the Donatists of his day, knew nothing of these views, but claimed to hold the same Trinitarian doctrine as the Catholics.[4] Nevertheless, the knowledge of the existence of views like those of Donatus besides the direct threat of Arianism, ensured that Augustine would continually be sensible of the need to emphasise the consubstantiality, coeternity and co-equality of the Son, and this, in turn, would be likely to affect his doctrine of the relationship of the Holy Spirit to the Son.

Augustine's debt to the Greek Fathers in the formulation of his trinitarian doctrine is difficult to estimate, since it involves the much debated issue of his general familiarity with the Greek language and literature. Controversy has raged, and is still not finally ended, on the question of Augustine's linguistic ability; but the consensus of opinion can now be said to be that, by the end of his life, Augustine had a working knowledge of New Testament Greek and could, on occasion, refer, to and translate, a portion of Patristic Greek. For his knowledge of classical Greek literature, including Plato and the Neoplatonists, he relied upon translations. Altogether, while there is no evidence to justify those scholars who have denied him any knowledge of Greek it is apparent that such knowledge as he possessed was essentially that of the study, and relied much upon the dictionary.

Nevertheless, while Augustine can hardly have had much knowledge of the Greek Fathers in the original, this does not mean that he was unacquainted with Greek Trinitarian theology. Translations from the Greek undoubtedly existed; those by Rufinus of nine homilies of St. Gregory Nazianzen have survived to the present. In his writings against the Pelagian Julian of Eclanum, Augustine speaks of translations of St. John Chrysostom which the Pelagians used to their own advantage and, in order to refute them, reproduces the original Greek text, and offers his own version.

Irénée Chevalier, in his book, S. *Augustin et la pensée grecque*, has established that Augustine was familiar with works of Athanasius, Basil, Gregory Nazianzen, Epiphanius, and Didymus the Blind, and has demonstrated his debt to them in the formulation of his doctrine of the relations of the persons of the Trinity to one another. Augustine therefore, was not divorced from the teaching of the Greek Fathers, and we have

[3]*De Viris Illustribus*, 93: 'de Spiritu sancto liber, Ariano dogmati congruens'. *(M.P.L.* xxiii, 695).

[4]Aug., *Ep.* 185, 1; *(C.S.E.L.* lvii, 1). *De Hæres. ad Quidvultdeum,* 69 *(M.P.L.,* xlii, 43).

his own statement that from what he had read, he did not doubt that if sufficient Greek books on the Trinity were to be translated into Latin, they would supply the answer to all questions which might be asked with any profit.[5]

At all events, Augustine was sufficiently familiar with Greek theology to recognise that there was a difference in terminology between Greek and Latin theologians. The Greek say μίαν οὐσίαν, τρεῖς ὑποστάσεις which Augustine translates as "one essence, three substances";[6] but the Latins dare not use such language, since in their tongue, 'substance' and 'essence' have the same meaning,[7] though of the two, the word 'substance' has the wider currency. Augustine is, nevertheless, aware that, when the Greeks talk of three *hypostases*, they understand by that what the Latins mean by three *personae*.[8] The difference is simply one of usage, due to the poverty of human language; we have not found any better way of expressing in words what we understand without words. We know, indeed, that the Father is not the Son, and the Son is not the Father, and the Holy Spirit is neither the Father nor the Son so that They are indeed three; and therefore the Scripture uses the plural: *I and the Father are one*, (John 10[30]). If however, the question is put: What three? the resources of human language fail us, and we say 'three Persons' to avoid falling into Sabellianism.[9] We must not, however, talk about 'three essences', since that would lead us into the errors of the Arians; for whatever is said of God regarded in Himself, (*ad se ipsum*), or concerning one Person of the Trinity considered as one Person, (*singulariter*), or concerning the Trinity itself, is not said in the plural, but in the singular number.[10] Yet all these expressions have their origin in the necessity of disputing with heretics, in the attempts to convey by speech what one holds as a belief in the inmost part of the mind from God either by pious faith, or by a certain understanding.[11]

The fact that Augustine recognises the inadequacy of language to express the ineffable, governs his approach to theology. 'When you consider these matters', he wrote to his correspondent Consentius, 'whatever corporeal similitudes come to your mind, refuse them, reject them, repel them, abandon them, flee them! For it is no small beginning of thinking about God, if, before we begin to know what He is, we first begin to know what He is not.'[12] Similarly, at the beginning of the Eighth

---

(5) *De Trin.*, III, *Proem.* (*M.P.L.* xlii, 868-9).

(6) ibid., V, viii, 10. (*M.P.L.* xlii, 917).

(7) ibid., V, ix, 10. (*M.P.L.* xlii, 918).

(8) ibid., VII, iv, 8: 'Quod enim de personis secundum nostram, hoc de substantiis secundum Graecorum consuetudinem, ea quae diximus, opportet intelligi.' (*M.P.L.* xlii, 941).

(9) ibid., V, ix, 10. (*M.P.L.* xlii, 918).

(10) ibid., V, viii, 9. (*M.P.L.*, xlii, 917).

(11) ibid., VII, iv, 9. (*M.P.L.* xlii, 941).

(12) Aug., *Ep.* 120, iii, 13. (*C.S.E.L.* xxxiv, 716).

Book of the *De Trinitate*, when he passes from the exposition of the faith in the Trinity to an attempt to explain it, he again urges the rejection of all corporeal images.[13]

Readers of Vladimir Lossky's book, *The Mystical Theology of the Eastern Church*, will observe that Augustine's doctrine is as fully apophatic as that of the Greek Fathers. The way to God is, initially, a way of negation, by the rejection of carnal images. But this discipline of rejection does not mean that we are to despise, or reject, the intellect; on the contrary, in the same letter to Consentius in which he exhorts him to purge his mind as a first step to thinking of God, Augustine urges him to love the intellect. We must both hold the doctrine of God by faith and endeavour to apprehend it by reason; for God does not endow us with reason without intending it to be used.[14] The exercise of faith presupposes a rational intelligence; the Scriptures themselves, which urge Faith before understanding, cannot be of use, unless they are rightly understood.[15] Belief indeed precedes understanding;[16] but from belief, with the aid of the reason by which we understand, we may come to understanding.[17] Though we cannot comprehend God, who is, by His nature, incomprehensible,[18] yet we seek to see Him, who has been declared to us; who has inspired faith in us through the humanity of Christ, and the ministry of His preacher; and who has made us able to find Him, and given the hope of finding Him more and more.[19] Moreover, although God is wholly other than His creation, He is Himself nearer to us than the things which He has created,[20] and has left, in that creation, images of Himself, of which Man, made in the image of God, is an outstanding example.[21] For this reason, although nothing can worthily be said of God, in another sense, all things can be said of Him. 'You seek a fitting name, and you find none; you seek in what way soever to speak of Him, and thou findest Him all things.'[22] We have, in fact, the familiar paradox, upon which all that we can say about God, (other than what we have by revelation in Holy Scripture), is based : that no human attribute may be predicated about God, but that human language may be used to describe Him by analogy, since Man has been created in the image of God. Because of this, in Augustine's opinion, the Neoplatonist philosophers had come very near to discovering the

(13) *De Trin.*, VIII, ii, 3. (*M.P.L.* xlii, 948-9).

(14) Aug., *Ep.* 120, i, 3. (*C.S.E.L.* xxxiv, 706).

(15) ibid., iii, 13: 'Intellectum vero valde ama, quia et ipsae scripturae sanctae, quae magnarum rerum ante intelligentiam suadent fidem, nisi eas recte intellegas, utiles tibi esse non possunt'. (*C.S.E.L.* xxxiv, 716).

(16) Aug., *Serm.* 118, 1. (*M.P.L.* xxxviii, 672).

(17) *Serm.* 43, ii, 3. (*M.P.L.* xxxviii, 255).

(18) *Serm.* 117, iii, 5. (*M.P.L.* xxxviii, 663).

(19) *De Trin.*, XV, xxviii, 51. (*M.P.L.* xlii, 1098).

(20) *De Gen. ad Litt.*, V, xvi, 34. (*M.P.L.* xxxiv, 333).

(21) *De Trin.*, VII, vi, 12. (*M.P.L.* xlii, 946).

(22) *In Iohan. Evan.*, *Tr.* xiii, 5. (*M.P.L.* xxxv, 1495).

Christian doctrine of God, though at the vital point they failed, seeing the promised country from afar, but lacking the power to enter therein, and failing to render to God the worship which is due. Hence it is that Augustine, while firmly maintaining that the first approach to a doctrine of God must be a negative one, is nevertheless prepared, on the basis of the revelation of Holy Scripture and the teaching of the Church, as expressed in the creeds, and the writings of her Doctors, to explain and defend the doctrine of the Trinity, and so lay the foundation of the trinitarian doctrine with which his name will always be associated.

We are taught by ecclesiastical writers that the Father, the Son, and the Holy Spirit, being of one and the same substance, imply, in their inseparable equality the divine unity; and therefore there are not three gods, but one God, although the Father begot the Son, and therefore He is not the Son who is the Father; and the Son is begotten of the Father and therefore is not the Father; and the Holy Spirit is neither the Father nor the Son, but the Spirit of the Father and the Son, being Himself co-equal with the Father and the Son, and pertaining to the Unity of the Trinity.[23] So Augustine summarises the teaching of his predecessors at the beginning of the *De Trinitate*. The intention of the book, and indeed of all Augustine's trinitarian writings, is to show 'that the Trinity is the one and only and true God, and that Father, Son and Holy Spirit may be rightly said, believed, and understood to be of one and the same substance or essence.'[24] Augustine, then, begins from a concept of one God in three Persons. These three Persons are distinct, and can act directly, and yet the whole Trinity works inseparably in every operation of God.[25] The reason why we assign particular actions to particular Persons is 'propter insinuationem Trinitatis'—on account of the insinuation of the Trinity.[26] Nor does differentiation imply any inequality. The Son says to the Father : *Glorify me*, but He also declares that the Holy Spirit will glorify the Son, and that the Son has glorified the Father upon earth. Such mutual glorification implies equality.[27] And, against the Arians, special stress is laid by Augustine on the use, in connexion with the Holy Spirit, of the Greek verb λατρεύειν which is used of the service of God[28] and in the case of the Incarnate Son, of the distinction between *forma dei* and *forma servi*, in passages where He is spoken of as less than the Father.[29]

But how can we arrive at any knowledge of the Trinity? If God has left images of Himself in His creation, we may seek it

(23) *De Trin.*, I iv, 7. (*M.P.L.* xlii, 824).
(24) ibid., I, ii, 4. (*M.P.L.* xlii, 822).
(25) ibid., I, v, 8. (*M.P.L.* xlii, 824).
(26) ibid., ix, 19. (*M.P.L.* xlii, 834).
(27) ibid., II, iv, 6. (*M.P.L.* xlii, 848).
(28) *De Trin.*, I, vi, 13. (*M.P.L.*, xlii, 827).
(29) ibid., vii, 14. (*M.P.L.* xlii, 828-9).

in that quality which is so highly prized in His Word, namely Love.

'What is the Love or Charity which Holy Scripture so greatly praises and preaches, except love of the good? But love supposes a lover and a beloved. So there are three things : the lover, the beloved, and love. And what is love, except a certain life, joining or seeking to join two beings, the lover and the beloved? This is the case even in external and carnal loves; but that we may draw from a purer and clearer fount, let us leave the flesh, and ascend to the soul. What does the soul love in the friend, except the soul? And so there also are three : the lover, the beloved, and love.'[30]

Augustine takes care to emphasise that we have not solved our problem, but only discovered where we are to look :

'It remains for us to ascend, and to seek these things—as far as it is given to man to do so—in a higher realm. But let our attention rest here for a little, not as thinking that it has already found what it seeks, but just as if a place has been found, as commonly happens, where the thing looked for is to be sought. The thing itself is not yet found; but we have found where it is to be sought.'[31]

The passage just quoted comes from the eighth book of the *De Trinitate*, and introduces the famous psychological discussion of the Trinity in which Augustine find traces of the highest Trinity in Man, who is created in the image of God. So we see a trinity in the human mind, and the knowledge by which it knows itself, and the love by which it loves itself; or again, in the triad of memory, understanding, and will. The psychological doctrine of Augustine does not, at this moment, concern us, and it is necessary to pass on to his application of it, in his doctrine of the Holy Spirit.

Augustine has already established that the Holy Spirit is co-equal and co-substantial with the Father and the Son :

'On this account, the Holy Spirit exists in the same unity of substance and equality. For whether He is the unity of both, or the sanctity, or the charity; or the unity because He is the charity, and therefore the charity because His is the sanctity, it is manifest that neither of those two is He by whom each is conjoined, by which the Begotten is loved by the Begetter and returns that love, *preserving the unity of the Spirit in the bond of peace*, not by participation, but by His own essence; not by the gift of any superior, but by His own.'[32]

To this, Augustine applies his formula : the lover; the beloved; and love. 'He who is the Holy Spirit, according to the Holy Scriptures, is neither of the Father alone, nor of the Son alone, but of both; and therefore intimates to us the mutual love, by which the Father and the Son love one another.'[33] The

(30) ibid., VIII, x, 14. (*M.P.L.* xlii, 960).
(31) ibid.
(32) ibid., VI, v, 7. (*M.P.L.* xlii, 927-8).
(33) ibid., XV, xvii, 27. (*M.P.L.* xlii, 1080).

Scriptures tell us that God is love, and they tell us also that the Holy Spirit is the gift of God. 'So, then, if among the gifts of God none is greater than Charity, and there is no greater gift of God than the Holy Spirit, what follows more necessarily than that He is Himself Charity, who is both called "God", and "of God"? And if the Charity with which the Father loves the Son and the Son loves the Father ineffably indicates the communion of both; what is more natural than that He should rightly be called Charity, who is the Spirit common to both?'[34]

It is this concept of the Holy Spirit demonstrating the mutual love of Father and Son which conditions Augustine's doctrine of the procession of the Spirit.

'Not without reason in this Trinity is the Son alone called the Word of God, and the Holy Spirit called the Gift of God, and God the Father He from whom the Word is born, and from whom the Holy Spirit principally proceeds (principaliter). I have added 'principally" for this reason, that the Holy Spirit is found to proceed from the Son as well.'[35]

This, of course, is the crucial point in Augustine's doctrine, in view of later controversies between eastern and western theologians. It might be well, at this stage, to notice certain facts relevant to the matter under discussion.

It may be remarked in the first place that the Holy Spirit had not been the subject of much debate, at least at the beginning of the Arian controversy. It was only after the middle of the fourth century, with the rise of the Macedonian heresy. which held that, while the Son was God and of the same essence as the Father, the Holy Spirit was a creature, that the Greek theologians began to address themselves seriously to the task of formulating the belief of the Church. Among them, St. Epiphanius, bishop of Salamis in Cyprus, comes nearest to the Latin view. In his *Ancoratus*, written in 374, with which Augustine may possibly have been familiar, he does not hesitate to declare that the Spirit is from both the Father and from the Son,[36] though he never in fact speaks of procession from the Son but only of the Spirit 'proceeding from ($\pi\alpha\rho\acute{\alpha}$ or $\dot{\alpha}\pi\acute{o}$) the Father and receiving of the Son,' ($\tau o\hat{\upsilon}$ $\Upsilon \acute{\iota}o\hat{\upsilon}$ $\lambda\alpha\mu\beta\acute{\alpha}\nu o\nu$).[37]

St. Epiphanius is, however, an anomaly among the easterns; more characteristic of the orientals is the view expressed by St. Gregory of Nyssa at the close of his treatise, *Quod non sunt tres dii*, (*M.P.G.* xlv, 133) that what accounts for the distinctions in the Trinity is that one of the Persons stands in the relation of Cause, to the other two. God is one, but within the divine being is both Cause, ($\alpha\check{\iota}\tau\iota o\nu$), which is called the Father, and that which is caused, ($\alpha\dot{\iota}\tau\iota\alpha\tau\acute{o}\nu$) which includes the immediately

(34) ibid., xix, 37. (*M.P.L.* xlii, 1086).
(35) ibid., xvii, 29. (*M.P.L.* xlii, 1081).
(36) *Ancor.*, 67: $\pi\alpha\rho'$ $\dot{\alpha}\mu\phi o\tau\acute{\epsilon}\rho\omega\nu$. (*M.P.G.* xliii, 137b) Cf. *Ancor.*, 6, 8, 9 (cols. 25c, 29b-c, 32c). and *Panar. haeres.*, 76. (*M.P.G.* xlii, 525b).
(37) *Ancor.*, 6, 7. (*M.P.G.* xliii, 25c, 28b).

caused, to which the name of Son is given, and the mediately caused, to which the name of Holy Spirit corresponds. The Holy Spirit may therefore rightly be said to be 'from the Father' and is also 'through the Son.' Further than this, St. Gregory does not go. As far as we know, St. Augustine was not familiar with the works of Gregory of Nyssa, though his statement that the Holy Spirit proceeds *principaliter* from the Father may look back to the Greek doctrine.

Secondly, we may consider the state of Latin theology with regard to the doctrine of the procession of the Holy Spirit before Augustine's labours. Briefly, it may be said to be undecided, but tending towards some statement of a double procession. Tertullian held the eastern view: 'I think the Spirit is from no other source than from the Father through the Son,'[38] and offered various images from nature: Root-shrub-fruit; spring-stream-river; sun-ray-point of the ray.[39] For Him, the Spirit is 'third' from the Father and the Son;[40] an assertion which implies subordinationism, but in no sense other than with regard to origin, for Tertullian is a firm exponent of the consubstantiality of the Son and the Spirit. Such is the Latin view of the Spirit in the third century; in the fourth, a deeper implication was being extracted from the formula: 'from the Father, through the Son.' St. Hilary of Poitiers, the most original among the Latin writers during the Arian controversy, uses the formula: 'of the Father, through the Son,' (*ex Patre per Filium*)[41] The Spirit is through Him through whom are all things, (the Son), and of Him of whom are all things, (the Father).[42] The Spirit receives from the Son, and so from the Father also, so that he may be said to receive of each; but St. Hilary does not decide whether receiving connotes proceeding, nor does he speak of any procession of the Spirit from both the Father and the Son[43]. A similar tendency may be seen in Gregory of Elvira in the treatise *De Fide Orthodoxa* which long went under the name of Phoebadius of Agen, and which has even been ascribed to Gregory Nazianzen, but which is now to be assigned to the Spanish author.[44]

St. Ambrose of Milan, the spiritual father of Augustine, marks a further stage in the development of a doctrine of double procession. Sometimes, he appears to endorse the Greek doc-

(38) *Adv. Prax.*, 4: 'Spiritum non aliunde puto quam a Patre per Filium'. (*M.P.L.* ii, 159).

(39) ibid., 8. (*M.P.L.* ii, 164).

(40) *ibid., 'Tertius enim est spiritus a Deo et Filio'* (*M.P.L.*, ii, 163-4). Cf. Epiphanius, *Ancor.*, 8: Πνεῦμα . . . ἐκ τοῦ Πατρὸς καὶ τοῦ Υἱοῦ τρίτον, τῇ ὀνομασίᾳ, (*M.P.G.*, xliii, 29c).

(41) Hilary, *De Trinitate* XII, 56. (*M.P.L.*, x., 470).

(42) ibid., II, 29. (*M.P.L.*, x, 70).

(43) ibid., II, 29; VIII, 20; 26. (*M.P.L.* x, 69; 250-1; 255).

(44) *De Fid. Orthod.*, 8. (*M.P.L.* xx, 49).

trine;[45] but he takes a different view in an explanation of the words of Psalm 35[10] [46]: *With Thee is the fountain of life*. Of these words he writes : 'Many interpret this to mean that the Son is the fountain of life, making the psalmist to say : "With Thee, Almighty God, Thy Son is the fountain of life," that is, the fountain of the Holy Spirit, for the Spirit is life.'[47] St. Ambrose, however, admits that others hold that here the Father alone is signified by the words 'the fountain of life'. We may say, then, that while St. Ambrose implies procession from the Son as well as the Father, he does not specifically teach an eternal procession from the Son. He nevertheless bears witness to a tendency in Latin theology, even before Augustine brought his genius to bear upon the theme.[48]

Thirdly, we must recognise that Augustine's doctrine of the Double Procession is a subtle one, which demands careful consideration. In the first place he does not simply and invariably affirm it. Indeed, in one of his earliest utterances on the subject, the address *De Fide et Symbolo*, delivered to the bishops of the African churches at the Council of Hippo in 393, when Augustine was still only a presbyter—an unusual honour, and one which affords evidence of the esteem in which he was held even at this early stage of his Christian career—his language is such as could come from any traditional Greek theologian. The great and learned commentators of Holy Scripture, he says, have not discussed the doctrine of the Holy Spirit so fully and carefully as that of the Son.

'However, they declare Him to be the Gift of God, so that we may believe that God does not give a gift inferior to Himself. They take care, however, to declare that the Holy Spirit is not begotten, as the Son is of the Father; for Christ is the only begotten; nor is the Spirit of the Son, as it were a grandson of the Father; nor yet does he owe His being to any, save the Father, of whom are all things, lest we should establish two principles without a beginning, which is most false and absurd, and the characteristic, not of the Catholic faith, but of the error of heretical sects.'[49]

This passage is of great interest, since it is in full agreement with Photius in rejecting two conceptions which he claimed to be the logical consequences of the *Filioque* : that the simplicity of the Godhead is destroyed if it have two principles; and that, according to the *Filioque* theory, it is impossible to see why the Holy Spirit may not be called the Grandson of the Father[50]. We

(45) Ambrose, *De Spiritu Sancto*, II, xi, 118; xii, 134. (*M.P.L.*, xvi, 768, 771).

(46) Ps. 36[9] in the A.V.

(47) *De Spiritu Sancto*, I, xv [xix], 152-4. (*M.P.L.* xvi, 739).

(48) See F. Holmes Dudden, *The Life and Times of St. Ambrose*, Oxford, 1935, ii, 574-5.

(49) *De Fide et Symbolo*, ix, 19. (*M.P.L.* xl, 191).

(50) Photius, *De Sancti Spiritus Mystagogia*, 11, 12, 61. (*M.P.G.* cii, 292, 340).

are not here concerned with the correctness or otherwise of Photius' view of the *Filioque*; the significant fact is that Augustine vehemently rejects two interpretations which Photius thought it implied.

It might be argued that the *De Fide et Symbolo* is an early work, and that Augustine may subsequently have changed his opinion as his trinitarian doctrine developed. Such a view, while plausible, is untenable. In the *Retractationes*, written at the end of his life, in 426 or 427, when the Saint passed in review his literary output to that date, and modified statements on which his opinions had altered, he saw nothing in the Trinitarian doctrine of the *De Fide et Symbolo* needing correction. Moreover in the *Enchiridion ad Laurentium*, written in 421, in the last decade of his life, when his theology was well established, and in which he lays down in the most rigorous terms his characteristic doctrine of Original Sin and Predestination, Augustine can declare :

'It suffices the Christian to believe that there is no cause of created things, whether of heaven or of earth, visible or invisible, except the goodness of the creator, who is the one true God; and that there is no nature, which is not either God Himself, or created by Him; and that He is a Trinity, namely the Father, and the Son, begotten of the Father, and the Holy Spirit, proceeding from the Father, but one and the same Spirit of the Father and of the Son.'[51]

It is clear, then, that Augustine did not regard his doctrine of a procession from the Son as conflicting with the Constantinopolitan credal formula of procession from the Father, and worship and glorification with the Father and the Son. On the contrary, he affirms them both simultaneously :

'Now just as to be born is, for the Son, to be of the Father, so to be sent is, for the Son, to be recognised that He is of Him; and just as, for the Holy Spirit, to be the gift of God is to proceed from the Father, so to be sent is to be recognised that He proceeds from Him. Nor are we able to say that the Holy Spirit does not also proceed from the Son; for it is not without a reason that the same Spirit is said to be the Spirit of the Father and the Son. Nor do I see what else he wished to signify when breathing on the faces of the disciples he said : *Receive the Holy Spirit*. Not that That corporeal breath, proceeding out of the body with the sensation of physical contact, was the substance of the Holy Spirit; but it was a demonstration, with an appropriate symbol, that the Holy Spirit proceeds not only from the Father but from the Son.'[52]

These are the views of the fourth book of the *De Trinitate*, composed about A.D. 400. In the ninty-ninth tractate on the Gospel of St. John, delivered at some date earlier than 418, when Book XV of the *De Trinitate*, in which Augustine quotes

(51) *Enchir.*, ix, 3. *(M.P.L.* xl, 235-6).
(52) *De Trin.*, IV, xx, 29. *(M.P.L.* xlii, 908).

61

from it, appeared, he repeats the argument. The Son is of the Father alone, and the Father is the Father of the Son alone; but the Spirit is of both. Augustine quotes Matthew 10^{20} : *For it is not you who speak, but the Spirit of your Father which speaketh in you*, and Galatians 4^6 : *God has sent the Spirit of His Son into your hearts*. Are there then two Spirits? he asks. On the contrary; 'since therefore there is one Father, and one Lord, that is, the Son, so there is also one Spirit, certainly of both.'[53] He once again urges the fact of the insufflation and the words, *Receive the Holy Spirit* as evidence for a double procession.[54] He discusses the significance of the words of John 15^{26} : *which proceeds from the Father*, by maintaining that as the Son has His being of the Father, since He is God of God, even so it is of the Father that the Holy Spirit proceeds from the Son; 'and through this it is that the Holy Spirit has from the Father Himself, that He may also proceed from the Son, as He proceeds from the Father.'[55]

It is to be observed that Augustine here asserts a procession *principaliter* from the Father, as he does in the *De Trinitate*. 'Whatever the Son has, He has of the Father; certainly He has of the Father that the Holy Spirit may proceed from Him.'[56] So, in his work against the Arian bishop, Maximinus, he says : 'The Father, therefore, is the beginning without any beginning; the Son is the beginning from the beginning (the Father); but both at the same time, not two, but one beginning; just as the Father is God, and the Son is God; but both together not two gods, but one God. Nor will I deny the Holy Spirit proceeding from both to be a beginning; but these three together, just as I say they are one God, so I say them to be one beginning.'[57]

It is clear from the foregoing that some attention must be given to the use of the verb *procedere* in Augustine, if we are to understand his teaching. We have already observed that Augustine makes a distinction between the procession of the Spirit from the Father, ('procedit principaliter'), and procession from the Son. To the question : how does the procession of the Spirit differ from the generation of the Son? he has no explanation. He affirms the distinction—indeed, any theologian who accepts a double procession is obliged to do so—but he attempts no explanation. The context in which he discusses it is, however, of interest, since it arises in his debate with the Arian bishop, Maximinus. The Arian had put the question : if both the Son and the Spirit are of the substance of the Father, why is the one the Son, and the other not? It was a reasonable debating point, from the Arian side, since their own answer was a simple one : neither the Son nor the Spirit is co-substantial with the Father,

(53) *In Iohan. Evang., Tr.* xcix, 6. *(M.P.L.* xxxv, 1889).
(54) ibid., 7.
(55) ibid., 8. *(M.P.L.* xxxv, 1889-90).
(56) *De Trin.,* XV, xxvi, 47. *(M.P.L.* xlii, 1094).
(57) *C. Max. Ar.,* II, xvii, 4. *(M.P.L.* xlii, 784-5).

V

and so one can easily make a distinction between them, in the
hierarchy of created beings. From a Catholic standpoint, the
explanation is less easy; St. John Damascene, with all the heritage of Greek patristic theology behind him, was content to
declare : 'We have learned that there is a distinction between
generation and procession; but of the manner of that distinction, we are utterly ignorant.'[58] Augustine was no more ready to
attempt an explanation; but he was able to make a distinction,
by reason of his doctrine of a double procession :

'If the Spirit should be born, he would consequently be
born, not only of the Father, but of both, and without doubt
would be called the Son of both. And for this reason, because
He is in no way the Son of both, it was not meet for Him to be
born of both. Therefore the Spirit is of both, by proceeding
from both. But what the difference may be between "to be born"
and "to proceed" who is able to explain, when speaking of that
most excellent Nature? Not everything that proceeds is born,
although everything that is born proceeds, just as not every
biped is a man, although every man is a biped. This much I
know : I do not know, I am unable, I lack the power to distinguish between the generation of the One, and the procession
of the Other.'[59]

In this passage, however, Augustine makes a distinction
between procession from the Father and from the Son; the
Father is the source of the procession, and it is by His gift that
the Spirit proceeds from the Son as well as from the Father.
In fact, 'procedere' is used in two different senses : 'procedere
principaliter' with regard to the Father, and 'procedere de Filio
per donum Patris', (quoniam Pater processionis eius est auctor,
qui talem Filium genuit, et gignendo ei dedit ut etiam de ipso
procederet Spiritus sanctus).[60]

We cannot, however, accept the opinion that the passage
in the De Trinitate, (XV, xvii, 29), in which Augustine speaks
of procession 'principaliter' from the Father, teaches modern
Eastern Orthodox doctrine, by making a distinction between the
Eternal Procession from the Father, and the Mission in time by
the Son. On the contrary, Augustine speaks of the procession
of the Holy Spirit from the Father and from the Son as being
timeless: 'Let him who is able to understand the timeless
generation of the Son from the Father, understand the timeless
procession of the Spirit from both . . . . let him understand
that as the Father has it in Himself that from Him the Holy
Spirit should proceed, so He has given to the Son, that from
Him also the same Holy Spirit should proceed—and in both
cases timelessly; and that the Holy Spirit so proceeds from the
Father, that it may be understood, that His procession from the

(58) De Fid. Orthod., I, viii: καὶ ὅτι μὲν ἔστι διαφορὰ γεννήσεως καὶ
ἐκπορεύσεως μεμαθήκαμεν·τίς δὲ ὁ τρόπος τῆς διαφορᾶς, οὐδαμῶς. (M.P.G. xciv,
824A).

(59) C. Max. Ar., II, xiv, i. (M.P.L. xlii, 770).

(60) ibid.

63

Son comes likewise from the Father to the Son, (ut intelligatur, quod etiam procedit de Filio, de Patre esse Filio).'[61]

Such a statement of procession from the Son seems, to me at least, to come very close to the classical Latin formula 'of the Father through the Son', which we have observed in Tertullian and St. Hilary, and to differ only in the employment of one word 'procedere' to describe two operations which are both similar, and yet disparate. In the light of subsequent history, we may regret that Augustine did not show more precision in his use of words though we can hardly blame him for not anticipating the disputes which were to arise from the application of his doctrine, first in Spain, and later in the kingdom of the Franks. But that he used the word in an imprecise fashion does not admit of any discussion. A good example occurs in one of his sermons, where he explains the mystery of how the Divine Word could both take flesh of the Virgin Mary, and walk this world as perfect man, without leaving the side of the Father in heaven :

'Regarding the Word of God, perhaps I myself and the human word can provide some analogy which, although quite inadequate, different in kind, and not to be compared in point of detail, may suggest what I mean, by a certain resemblance. Very well : I had in my mind the word I speak to you; it proceeded (processit) to you, and it has not receded (recessit) from me; it begins to be in you, which was not in you before; it remained with me, when it went out (exiret) to you. Now just as my word has been delivered to your sense, and did not recede from my mind; so was that Divine Word delivered to our senses, and did not recede from His Father. My word was with me, and proceeded (processit) into speech; the Word of God was with the Father, and proceeded (processit) into flesh.'[62]

Here we find 'procedere' being used to describe both the action of the Word in taking flesh, and the ordinary physical phenomenon of the spoken word affecting our hearing. There is nothing wrong, in itself, in such language—one has only to think of the use (and abuse) of the English word 'proceed' to understand that it is susceptible of a wide field of employment—but it is further evidence that, as Augustine used it, it had a number of different significations. We have noted four : (i) to describe the procession of the Holy Spirit from the Father *principaliter* in the Trinity; (ii) to describe the procession of the Spirit from the Son, the procession coming to the Son from the Father; (iii) to describe the action of the Son in taking flesh for our salvation. Here, its sense is that of 'prodeo' as used by St. Thomas Aquinas in his hymn for Lauds at Corpus Christi :

Verbum supernum prodiens,
nec patris linquens dexteram,
ad opus suum exiens
venit ad vitae vesperam;

(61) *De Trin.*, XV, xxvi, 47. (*M.P.L.* xlii, 1094).
(62) *Aug.*, *Serm.* 119, vii, 7. (*M.P.L.*, xxxviii, 675).

and (iv) in the purely physical sense of movement, the example being given in terms of sound waves.

Let us now try to estimate what has been discovered. Augustine undoubtedly teaches a doctrine of double procession, and a doctrine, moreover, of double procession beyond time. He specifically excludes the suggestion that procession from the Son may refer to the temporal mission of the Holy Spirit. Nevertheless, he distinguishes as firmly as Gregory of Nyssa between the Father, who is the Cause, and the other two persons who are Caused. Moreover, he rejects any interpretation of the procession which would imply a Neo-platonist system of emanations, and make the Holy Spirit, as it were, the grandson of the Father. We must not be misled on this point by the text-book assertion that it is a cardinal premiss of Augustine's theology that whatever can be predicated of one of the Persons can be predicated of the others. This is undoubtedly a truth; but it refers to their qualities 'according to substance', not 'according to relationship'. We must remember Augustine's warning that, while nothing which is said of God may be said accidentally, (*secundum accidens*), since God can have no accidental attributes; yet not everything that is said is said substantially (*secundum substantiam*), for the relationships of the Persons within the Trinity are 'secundum relativum', relative to one another. Such relationships are not accidental, for they are eternal.[63] Now, it is in this relative sense, that Augustine holds that the Father is the Source of the whole Godhead, and warns his readers that, when we say that the Holy Spirit is not begotten, we must avoid saying that he is unbegotten, lest we should introduce two Fathers into the Trinity, or two Persons who are not from Another: hence, it seems to me that Augustine's doctrine of the procession of the Holy Spirit is a great deal less revolutionary, and a great deal closer to the thought of the Greeks, than he has usually been given credit for, whether for praise or blame. As I read it, his teaching of procession 'from the Father and the Son' is equivalent to 'from the Father through the Son', and certainly does not imply that the mode of the procession is the same in both cases. The difficulty arises, from the eastern theological view, in his use of 'procedere' to describe both the procession from the Father, and for the relation of the Son to the Father in the unity of the Holy Spirit. In this, as we have seen, he is an innovator; we have not found any example of such a usage in Augustine's predecessors. What we have seen is a theological ethos in which Augustine took a step which might seem to be inevitable, but which was to have deplorable consequences in future ages. Seldom has a choice of word so effectively influenced the course of history; one can only regret that the combatants on both sides did not bear in mind the charitable good sense of Theophylact of Bulgaria when he commented that much of the difficulty about the double pro-

(63) *De Trin.*, V, v, 6. (*M.P.L.* xlii, 913-4).

cession arose from the poverty of the Latin language; the Latins had to use the one word 'procedere' when the Greeks had no less than four words, each with a different shade of meaning.[64]

It is not, however, on this note that I wish to end; for the Holy Spirit should be the object of our love and adoration, and not of our controversies. Indeed, we may recall that it was precisely his sense of the Holy Spirit, the gift of God, as Charity, which encouraged Augustine in his enquiry into the nature of His procession:

'To sum up, Holy Scripture proclaims that God is charity. Charity is of God, and its effect in us is that we dwell in God and He in us. This we know, because He has given us of His Spirit. It follows that the Spirit Himself is the God who is charity. If among God's gifts there is none greater than charity, and there is no greater gift than the Holy Spirit, we naturally conclude that He who is said to be both God and of God is Himself charity. And if the charity whereby the Father loves the Son and the Son loves the Father displays, beyond the power of words, the communion of both, it is most fitting that the Spirit who is common to both should have the special name of charity. The sounder way of faith or of understanding is to hold that while charity in the divine Trinity is not the Holy Spirit alone, yet the reasons given justify applying to Him this special name.'[65]

This is Augustine's doctrine of the Holy Spirit. 'Through Him we receive remission of sins; through Him we believe the resurrection of the flesh; through Him we hope for life eternal'.[66] Let us pray to the Lord that He will send His Holy Spirit to pour into our hearts that most excellent gift of charity, the very bond of peace and of all virtues, so that we may be united in this Fellowship in the present world, and hereafter may behold the unspeakable glories of the blessed Trinity, in the eternal fellowship of the Kingdom of God!

[64] Theophylact of Bulgaria, *De iis in quibus Latini accusantur, (M.P.G.* cxxvi, 228-9).

[65] *De Trin.*, XV, xix, 37, trans. by Professor John Burnaby, *Augustine: Later Works,* (The Library of Christian Classics), London, 1955, 165-6. (*M.P.L.* xlii, 1086).

[66] Aug., *Serm.* 215, 8. (*M.P.L.* xxxviii, 1076).

ADDITIONAL NOTES

To page 53 lines 41–44: 'Irénée Chevalier, in his book *S. Augustin et la pensée grecque*, has established that Augustine was familiar with works of Athanasius, Basil, Gregory Nazianzen, Epiphanius and Didymus the Blind.' This assertion is too absolute. Chevalier's book (published at Fribourg-en-Suisse in 1940) was criticised by Berthold Altaner in a review in the *Historisches Jahrbuch der Görresgesellschaft* 62–69 (1949), 654–5, and in the same author's

'Augustinus und die griechische Patristik: Eine Einführung und Nachlese zu den quellenkritischen Untersuchungen,' *Revue bénédictine* lxii (1952), 201–15 (reprinted in *Kleine patristische Schriften* [Berlin: Akademie-Verlag 1967], 316–31), as being too subjective. Parallels in thought between authors do not necessarily prove a direct dependence of one upon another, and while Augustine was clearly aware of the ideas of many of the Greek Fathers, there is no direct evidence that his knowledge came from study of the original Greek text. Augustine had a working knowledge of biblical Greek and a limited knowledge of patristic Greek, but he knew the world of Greek thought, both sacred and secular, essentially through Latin translations.

To page 62 lines 25–37: 'To the question: how does the procession of the Spirit differ from the generation of the Son? [Augustine] has no explanation.' And to page 63 lines 7–8: 'Augustine was no more ready to attempt an explanation; but he was able to make a distinction.' This, as Fr Charles Boyer, S.J. pointed out, in a very kind review of this article in *Doctor Communis. Acta Academiae Romanae S. Thomae Aquinatis* xiii (1960), 246–7, is an inexactitude; for Augustine does elsewhere attempt an explanation. It is, in fact, in one of his sermons (*Io.Ev.Tr.*99, 8–9, quoted in *De Trinitate* XV, xvii, 47) in which he argues the case for saying that the Holy Spirit proceeds, instead of being born:

'For if He also were called Son, he must be son of both the other Persons — which would be altogether irrational. A son can be son of two only if they be father and mother; and between God the Father and God the Son no relation of the kind is even to be thought of. Indeed, no human son proceeds at one and the same time from father and mother: he does not proceed from the mother when he proceeds from father into mother, and he does not proceed from the father at the time of his proceeding from the mother into visible existence. Whereas the Holy Spirit does not proceed from the Father into the Son and then from the Son to sanctify the creature: He proceeds at once from both, although His proceeding from the Son as from the Father is the Father's gift to the Son.' (Translation by John Burnaby.)

Boyer suggested, very reasonably, that in debating with Maximinus, Augustine observed the so-called 'discipline of the secret' (*disciplina arcani*) and declined to speculate about the deepest mysteries of the faith with a heretic. He was, however, prepared to do so in a sermon, before a congregation which could be assumed to be in sympathy with his fundamental doctrines.

For the relation of the respective dates of the *Collatio cum Maximino*, which inspired the *Contra Maximum*, Sermon 99 of the *Tractatus in Evangelium Iohannis*, and *De Trinitate* XV, see *Possidio, Vita di S. Agostino*, ed. M. Pellegrino (Alba: Cuneo 1955), 213 note[9]; Anne-Marie La Bonnardière, *Recherches de chronologie augustinienne* (Paris 1965), 69–72; and Edmund Hill, *The Mystery of the Trinity* (London 1985), 75–6.

For further discussion of the teaching of Augustine regarding the Double Procession of the Holy Spirit, see Hill, *op.cit.*, pp. 108–21.

VI

THE CHURCH AND THE EUCHARIST IN THE THEOLOGY OF ST AUGUSTINE*

Church and Eucharist: the setting

Although it is not the fashion in scientific manuals of theology, I have no doubt that discussion of the Church and the Eucharist in the thought of St Augustine should start from the concrete fact of the eucharistic worship which he conducted, Sunday by Sunday, in the Great Church of Hippo, whose remains have been revealed by excavation, and enable us to form some picture of how it must have appeared in Augustine's lifetime.[1] Do not let us be deceived by the title the Great Church *(basilica maior);* the building measured some 126 feet in length (147 including the apse) by 60 feet wide, and was thus somewhat larger, but not all that much larger, than the average English parish church.[2] At the east end was the semicircular apse with the bishop's throne raised on a few steps, with benches *(subsellia)* for his presbyters on either side. In the nave, in front of him, was the small, square wooden altar, surrounded by low rails *(cancelli),* which did nothing to impede the congregation's view—we are very far from the medieval rood-screen or the iconostasis. There would be little sign of impressive ornamentation in the church, apart from the floor mosaic—the one piece of luxury which no African congregation seems to have been able to resist. At the celebration of the Eucharist the altar will be covered with a cloth,[3] and the sacred vessels—normally indistinguishable at this time from secular plate—may be of silver, like those recently discovered at Water Newton in Huntingdonshire,[4] or even of gold—provided always that the bishop has not melted them down for the relief of the poor or the redemption of captives.[5] Augustine himself is simply attired, without either cross or ring, and is clad in a dark-coloured robe called a *birrhus,* of the sort commonly worn by laymen; and he discouraged attempts by his admirers to clothe him in what they deemed to be a fashion more suited to the episcopal dignity[6]—unlike some other bishops of his age, he did not want the episcopate to provide him with a higher standard of living than he would have enjoyed in his father's house. His head would have been shaven, as were those of his clergy; Augustine was a monk, and required his household to follow his own monastic way of life.[7] Yet there must have been something impressive in the man, especially when he preached from his episcopal throne—for in those days the bishop sat to preach and the congregation stood to listen. Those sermons of Augustine, delivered extempore—*Deo donante*—and taken down by

*A paper given at the Fellowship conference of August 1977.

professional shorthand-writers *(notarii, oxygraphoi, tachygraphoi)*, with a knowledge of what the Christian public wanted, thereby becoming Augustine's first publishers and editors—it was those sermons which held his people.[8] 'No one can read what he wrote on theology without profit', declared Augustine's biographer Possidius. 'But I think that those were able to profit still more who could hear him speak in church and see him with their own eyes and, above all, had some knowledge of him as he lived among his fellow-men'.[9]

But let us look away from the bishop to his people, standing in the body of the church, with the sexes decently separated—the Africans have a good deal of puritanism in their make-up, though it tends to be theoretical rather than practical—with the professed virgins and widows in their reserved places, the penitents and the catechumens in theirs. The worshippers are a strange collection; most of them are Berbers, dark-skinned and dark-eyed, only partly Romanised. Despite the popularity of the public baths they probably smell—if you commonly wear wool in a hot climate it is difficult not to.[10] The men, if they are shaved—and many of them probably will be, for the beard has become very much the badge of the pagan philosopher—will not be very well-shaved; being scraped with an iron razor without any previous soaping is a risky and unrewarding experience.[11] Altogether, with the exception of a few rich people, elegantly attired and accompanied by their crowd of clients, they will be an exotic, unsavoury, and perhaps rather sinister collection—the sort of people the northern visitor expects to find in a second-class North African port.

However, Christianity does not judge by externals. What is the spiritual state of these townsmen of Hippo, *called to be saints,* as the Apostle puts it? Augustine would probably admit that they were a difficult crowd to handle. Devoted to their bishop personally, they were by no means disposed to take his word for law, and their behaviour on occasion causes him great distress. Augustine, notoriously, is an advocate of extreme sexual asceticism; but in dealing with his parishioners he is more concerned to stop them committing adultery than to exhort them to embrace the state of marital continence which he admires.[12] They are, like other Africans, much given to swearing—a fault to which their bishop admits himself to have been prone in the past.[13] They are very fond of money, and on one disgraceful occasion came near to rioting in an attempt to secure the ordination of a rich nobleman, in the hope that he would bestow his wealth on their church.[14] (Augustine, rather obviously embarrassed, has tried to explain that what they wanted was not the money but the desirable visitor himself; but other people have their doubts.)[15] They are fond of wine—too fond, indeed;[16] and they are apt to attend church in the morning and go to the theatre in the afternoon—a practice Augustine deplores, because of the lewdness and paganism of the drama. In short, they are very much like a modern congregation, only rather more so.[17] Perhaps they are more intelligent. At any rate, then can hear Augustine explaining the non-material nature of the divine omnipresence without protest.[18] According to certain modern theologians they ought to conceive of God as an old man up in the sky, over their heads. Perhaps some of them do; but their bishop gives them no encouragement.

449

VI

The challenge of Donatism

Thus the Church of Christ, as represented in the eucharistic congregation of Hippo, is very much a congregation still pressing on to perfection and not yet made perfect. But outside the Catholic community of Hippo, throughout the province of Africa, is another Church, called the Donatist after its great prophet Donatus, divided from the Catholic, not by creed or rite, but on a question of purity. The Catholics, say the Donatists, are the descendants of men who betrayed Christ in the persecutions by giving up the Holy Scriptures to the pagans; for that reason their sacraments are invalid. Worse, they are defiling; and this defilement has been communicated to the whole world, which shares in these polluted sacraments. Only in Africa, and only in the Church of Donatus, has purity been preserved. What does scripture say? *As the judge of the people is himself, so are his ministers, and as the ruler of the city, so are they that dwell in it* (Ecclus 10:2); and again: *Let the priests that draw nigh to the Lord be sanctified, lest perchance the Lord abandon them; when the ministers approach the altar let them not bring a sin in themselves, lest they die* (Ex. 19:22; 30:20, 21). Augustine, the unremitting opponent of Donatism, is nevertheless only too well aware of his own personal sinfulness and that of his congregation. How can such men as he and they participate in the holy and spotless feast of God?

Popular devotion and the Eucharistic sacrifice

Such a thought must often have been present in his mind during the Sunday liturgy, after the sermon and the dismissal of the catechumens, when he had offered the eucharistic prayer of consecration, broken the holy bread and pronounced the Lord's Prayer, and the people came forward to communicate, receiving the consecrated bread in their right hands and sipping from the great chalice. The ceremony is simple, but dignified; eucharistic adoration at that time consists in the reverent reception of the sacrament and not in any act of worship divorced from it.[19] The adoration which the later Western Church will offer to the Sacrament is now expressed in another form of devotion, universal among the Christians and the object of a great deal of scorn and derision on the part of hostile pagans: the cult of the martyrs.[20] Devout souls, like Augustine's dead mother, Monica, are accustomed to visit the martyrs' shrines—and also the tombs of their own dead kindred who have died in the faith—and eat and drink in their honour, sometimes even pouring a little of the wine down a hole in the grave slab, to refresh the dead man below[21]—a frankly pagan and superstitious practice,[22] which bishops like Ambrose of Milan, Aurelius of Carthage and Augustine himself are anxious to suppress, by incorporating the cult of the martyrs in the action of the Eucharist.[23]

Here we have another feature of the Eucharist in Augustine's time: it is 'the sacrifice', offered to God at the burial of a Christian and on the anniversary of his death.[24] The name is no innovation of Augustine's; before his day St Cyprian has used the term, and also the terms altar *(ara, altare)* and priest *(sacerdos)* in a Christian sense.[25] On her death-bed Augustine's mother had asked to be

450

remembered at God's altar, and Augustine describes how the sacrifice of our redemption *(sacrificium pretii nostri)* was offered for her at the graveside before the body was placed in the tomb.[26] In the *Enchiridion* or *Handbook of Christian Doctrine,* written about 421, he declares that there is no place for any disbelief that the souls of the dead obtain relief through the pious services of the living, when the Mediator's sacrifice *(sacrificium mediatoris)* is offered for them or almsgiving made in the Church.[27] Thus the Eucharist is no mere memorial meal; it is a sacrifice which benefits alike the living and the dead. Yet although Augustine speaks of it with reverence, being mindful of its saving power, there is in his teaching (so far as I can see) none of that sense of mystery and awe which is beginning to appear in Syrian circles about this time. He has, undoubtedly, that sense of dignity and restraint which Edmund Bishop declared, in a famous article, to be characteristic of the old Roman rite. 'The true Roman cannot forget his dignity. The thing had to be done, and it was done in a plain and simple but the most practical manner'.[28] Now in this respect Augustine was a Roman as well as an African, and this fact may explain the disappointment experienced by some at the absence of emotion in his references to the sacrament of the Eucharist. He refers to it indeed as Christ's Body and Blood,[29] but he never approaches the devotional intensity of, let us say, the *Adoro devote.* Nor can Augustine's restraint be ascribed to any lack of emotion in himself—a very little reading of the *Confessions* will show that. To understand him we have to look at the times in which he lived when, as I have said, adoration of the Body and Blood of Christ consisted simply in the reverent reception and consumption. In consequence, religious emotion had to be directed elsewhere, to the cult of the martyrs. This, in turn, would lead—and was indeed already leading—to the cult of relics, and only in the thirteenth century, and in the West alone, would popular devotion be 'more surely directed to the Eucharist, and that in itself required monstrances, feast days and processions to make it attractive—as a relic!'[30]

These historical considerations will explain an aspect of Augustine's eucharistic theology which has often puzzled historians of dogma: his ability to speak of the Eucharist both in terms of the Body and Blood of Christ and also of a figure or a sign. The employment of these apparently contradictory views seems strange today, when it is assumed that one cannot logically hold both, but only one or the other; I doubt if Augustine ever realised the existence of such a dilemma, for both strains of thought were present in the ecclesiastical tradition which he had inherited. Thus from Tertullian he would have learned of the bread 'by which He makes manifest *(repraesentat)* His own body'[31] and which is 'a figure of His body'.[32] From Cyprian he would learn that the Eucharist is a true sacrifice which the priest 'offers to God the Father in the Church' when he celebrates the Eucharist on Christ's behalf *(vice Christi fungitur).*[33] Yet Cyprian can nevertheless talk of the blood of Christ being 'shewn forth' *(ostenditur)* in the cup.[34] Again, in Optatus of Mileve, his predecessor in the controversy with the Donatists, Augustine would have read that the altar is 'the seat of the body and blood of Christ [. . .] where His body and blood used to dwell for certain moments of time'.[35] For Optatus the chalice is a 'container of the blood of

Christ'.[36] Again, in Ambrose of Milan, whom he so greatly admired, Augustine would have found a realism to parallel that of Optatus, but also the statement that the oblation is the 'figure of the body and blood of our Lord Jesus Christ'.[37] In fact, Western eucharistic tradition which Augustine inherited combined both realistic and figurative elements, and Augustine accepted them both, since both derived from the teaching of orthodox theologians. We should not, however, suppose that he accepted them unthinkingly as two mutually contradictory doctrines which must be held by the faithful because both are part of the tradition of the Church; this would be wholly foreign to his temperament and outlook. Rather, I do not think that he would have seen the sort of opposition between talking about the 'body and blood of Christ' and 'the figure of the body and blood of Christ' in the way that we should see it today. I think that Frederick Van der Meer has expressed the matter very well: '[Augustine] wrote at an epoch when the worship of the body and blood of Christ consisted simply in reverent reception, handling and consumption; at such a time men had not yet adverted to the idea of looking for the factual presence, which can be continually worshipped, behind the signs which they grasped and the means of grace of which they availed themselves. And in consequence the words *figura* and *signum corporis Christi* sound otherwise in their ears than they do now'.[38]

Confirmation of Van der Meer's view is provided by an incident which also sheds a lurid light on the popular piety of Augustine's day. It is narrated by Augustine himself in the *Unfinished Work against Julian,* his last composition, written at the end of his life when his theology had reached its most predestinarian stage, and concerns a certain Acatius, known to Augustine, who had been born with his eyelids closed together, so that he could not see. For this reason his doctor wanted to open them with a scalpel; but his pious mother would not allow any such thing, preferring to place upon his eyes a poultice made from the Eucharist, which effectively opened them.[39] This extraordinary tale reveals an attitude to the Eucharist as a wonder-working charm which equals anything that later medieval superstition could produce; but it is difficult to imagine any orthodox Christian in the later Middle Ages subjecting the consecrated elements to such indignity. Clearly, from Augustine's point of view, the Eucharist was a thing of miraculous power; but his attitude was equally clearly rather different from that of a devout man of the thirteenth, or for that matter, the twentieth century.[40]

Thus, in discussing Augustine's theology of the Church and the Eucharist, we have to take into account a number of very different factors: ecclesiastical and liturgical tradition; popular religion, in which Augustine came increasingly to share as he grew older; religious controversy, both with the Donatists, who differed from the Catholics on the doctrine of the Church, and pagans, who differed from the Christians on the nature of worship; and Augustine's own thought, with its strongly Platonic element combined with a steadily-increasing biblicism, and a steadily-increasing sense of man's utter dependence on the grace of God. Of these elements, it is the first and the last—ecclesiastical tradition, and the Bible and the doctrine of grace—which were, in the long run, the most powerful, but not exclusively so; it is clear that, to the end of his life, however much he might find it necessary to attack them, Augustine retained an admiration for the thought of the Neoplatonists, who had helped him to come to a decision to seek baptism at Milan in 386; and however much he might deplore the separation of the Donatists, there is in Augustine something of their unyielding temper, and he never concealed his debt to their greatest theologian, Tyconius.

Augustine's answer to Donatism

In formulating his theology of the Church and the Eucharist Augustine had, as I have said, to take account of the Donatist ideal of the pure Church, without spot or wrinkle, and its reconciliation with the all too obvious fact that neither his own congregation at Hippo nor he himself had arrived at that state of purity which was to be reached, he held, only after death. He had also to take account of the African view of the Eucharist as a sacrifice, and maintain this against the pagans, and especially the Neoplatonists, to whom he owed so much, and to whom he was inevitably so strongly opposed as a Christian. And here the crucial factor—the factor which embraced and reconciled all oppositions—was Jesus Christ, 'by whom man comes, to whom man attains, in whom man abides'.[41] It is Christ crucified, through whom grace comes, who is at the centre of Augustine's thought,[42] and it is Christ, the Head of His Body the Church, who makes the Church holy, and not the holiness of her members.

This thought of Christ the Head lies at the heart of Augustine's reply to the Donatists: the Church in this world is not a congregation of saints—she cannot be, for she is still *in via*, on the road to perfection; but she is sanctified by her ruler, who alone is without sin, the High Priest who has entered the Holy of Holies. This is the answer to the text: *As the judge of the people is himself, so are his ministers: and as the ruler of the city, so are they that dwell in it.*

> Let them understand that the one prince of the city is our Lord Jesus Christ, whose ministers are good. He is the ruler of His city Jerusalem, whose citizens accord with the dignity of the ruler, not to equality but according to His measure who said to them: *Ye shall be holy since I am holy,* that is, according to a certain likeness, into which we are changed *from glory unto glory as by the Spirit of God,* the gift of Him who makes us to *be conformed to the image of His Son.*[43]

Of course Augustine is aware that in the congregation of the Church of Christ there are those who, although they share the sacraments on earth, will not enjoy the everlasting joy of the saints in heaven; he contrasts those who adore the body and blood of Christ by a worthy reception and are filled with those who merely adore by receiving;[44] but he makes no attempt, as the Donatists did, to anticipate the final judgement of God, and the great teacher of predestination never in pastoral practice despaired of any man, for God's judgements are unsearchable and His ways past finding out.

The Eucharistic sacrifice: Augustine's doctrine

By a curious paradox the work in which Augustine presents his clearest exposition of his doctrine of the Church and the Eucharist—or so it seems to me—is not formally addressed to Christians at all, but is supposed to be an apologetic work against the pagans, *The City of God*. I say 'supposed' deliberately, because I suspect that *The City of God,* like most apologies, was written more for the encouragement of Augustine's own party, the Christians, than for the conversion of his opponents, the pagans. Thus, when in *The City of God* Augustine deals with the Church and the Eucharist, we may guess that he is, so to say, looking over his shoulder at his own side, in the hope that they will benefit from what he is allegedly offering for the refutation of the pagans.

The context of Augustine's exposition is his dispute with the Neoplatonist philosophers, and especially Porphyry, about the nature of sacrifice. The argument arose because the Neoplatonists, in Augustine's view, were of all philosophers those closest to Christianity, and their endorsement of the pagan sacrificial cultus constituted a problem in a way that the practice of the ordinary pagan did not. Furthermore, as we have seen, the Christians called their eucharistic worship sacrifice, and in Africa much emphasis was laid upon the efficacy of that sacrifice for the dead as well as for the living. Logically the Neoplatonists might have been expected to reject the whole apparatus of pagan sacrifice, since the essence of their philosophy was the union of the individual soul with the One, the ground of all being, by a kind of intellectual mystical experience; but in practice, not only did they tolerate it, but became increasingly concerned with it, so that from being philosophers, many of them degenerated into mere occultists. For Augustine, as for other Christians of his day, pagan sacrifices offered no problem: they are, by an appalling perversion, offered to the demons, who had stolen from the true God what was his due.[43] The Jewish sacrifices of the Old Covenant were true worship offered to the true God, but they had been superseded by the one true sacrifice offered by Christ on Cavalry and commemorated and shewn forth in the eucharistic worship of the Christian Church.[46] Thus Augustine had to find some understanding of what constitutes a sacrifice, to show alike that the pagan sacrifices were wrong, and that the Jewish sacrifices, though of divine institution and right in the past, had now to give place to the sacrifice of our redemption, offered alike for the living and for the dead.

Augustine addresses himself to this issue in the tenth book of *The City of God,* written about 417, and concerned to maintain that there is only one God, who alone is to be worshipped and from whom all blessings come. This, says Augustine, the Platonists knew well: happiness is to cleave to the unchangeable God with a chaste and pure love; and yet they gave way to popular error, and thought that worship might be offered to many gods—or even to the evil beings that they themselves called demons.[47] This causes Augustine to ask what honours—if any—may be offered to lesser beings than God, like the angels? And his reply is that there is a species of worship which may properly be offered to God alone, called in the Greek *latreia*.[48] Augustine's choice of a Greek word (as he explains elsewhere)[49] is determined by the fact that there is no Latin word which has the sense of worship directed to God alone. *Servitus, cultus, pietas*—all these words can be applied to human relationships, *latreia* never. For men (and for angels) there is a Greek word *douleia;* and although *douleia* may be offered to God as Lord—Augustine finds the word so used in the Septuagint[50]—He can only be worshipped as God by *latreia*. Now this service or *latreia* we offer to God either in various sacraments or in ourselves, for we are both the congregation of His temple and individually His temples, since our bodies are temples of the Holy Ghost. Thus the whole Christian life is —or should be—an expression of *latreia*.

> When we lift up our hearts to Him, our heart is His altar. We propitiate Him by our priest, His only-begotten Son. We sacrifice blood-stained victims to Him when we fight for truth *as far as shedding our blood* [cf. Heb. 12:4]. We burn the sweetest incense for Him, when we are in His sight, on fire with devout and holy love. We vow to Him and offer Him the gifts He has given us, and the gift of ourselves; and we have annual festivals and fixed days appointed and consecrated for the remembrance of His benefits, lest ingratitude and forgetfulness should creep in as the years roll by. We offer to Him, on the altar of the heart, the sacrifice of humility and praise, and the flame on the altar is the burning fire of charity.[51]

Augustine has, in this passage, not only asserted the spiritual character of the Christian sacrifice, as against that of the pagans, but has as it were in passing incorporated the whole sacrificial cult of the Old Testament into the Christian life. On the other hand—and it was an essential point to make in controversy with the pagans, whose principle of worship was all too often *do ut des*—I give, in order that you may give—Augustine is emphatic that God has no need of sacrifices.

> Could anyone be such a fool [he asks] as to suppose that the sacrificial offerings are necessary to God—that they are of any use to Him? There are many passages in Holy Scripture to witness this point; but it will be enough to cut a long story short by quoting a short extract from one of the Psalms: *I said to the Lord, You are my God, for you have no need of my possessions* [Ps. 15(16):2].[52]

A sacrifice, then, does not consist in an external act; rather the sacrificial act is the visible sacrament of an invisible sacrifice, a sacred sign *(sacrificum ergo visibile invisibilis sacrificii sacramentum, id est sacrum signum est)*.[53] It is not a slaughtered animal that God desires from men but the sacrifice of a broken and contrite heart.

This leads Augustine to offer a definition of sacrifice as 'every act by which it comes about that we cleave to God in holy fellowship—directed, that is, to that Final Good by which we are truly made happy'.[54] More specifically, when applied to the worship of the Christian Church, it is the Eucharist.

This is the sacrifice of Christians, who are *many, making up one body in Christ*. This is the sacrifice which the Church continually celebrates in the sacrament of the altar, a sacrament well-known to the faithful, where it is shown to the Church that she herself is offered in the offering which she presents to God.[55]

In the passages which I have quoted Augustine has done three things. He has argued that the Christian God, unlike the so-called gods of the heathen, has no need of sacrifices, requiring only the sacrifice of a contrite heart; he has provided, from this, a definition of sacrifice as any act by which we cleave to God in holy fellowship; and has applied this definition in turn to the Church's principal act of worship, the Eucharist, which, he declares, is a sacrament in that it teaches the Church that in that which is offered, she is herself the offering.

There is, however, a further consideration: *We, being many, are one body in Christ*. If the Church is both the offerer and the Thing offered, then the same must be true of Christ; and this is indeed essential, for only in Christ and through Christ the God-man can we come to God. This notion of the coinherence of all the faithful in Christ is fundamental to Augustine's theology, and helps to explain his apparent harshness with regard to the fate of the unbaptised: apart from Christ, he cannot imagine any possibility of salvation.

It is in [Christ] that [men] find purification full of compassion, the purification of mind, spirit, and body. For He took upon Himself entire humanity, though without sin, for this precise purpose, that He might cure all the constituents of human nature of the plague of sins [...]. The grace of God could not be commended in a way more likely to evoke a grateful response than the way by which the only Son of God, while remaining unchangeably in His own proper being, clothed Himself in humanity and gave to men the spirit of His love by the mediation of a man, so that by this love men might come to Him who formerly was so far away from them, far from mortals in His immortality, from the changeable in His changelessness, from the wicked in His righteousness, from the wretched in His blessedness.[56]

It is from this theology of the Incarnation and of our incorporation in Christ that we can understand Augustine's view of Christ as the High Priest of the Eucharist.

The whole community, that is to say, the congregation and fellowship of the saints, is offered to God as a universal sacrifice, through the great Priest who offered Himself in His suffering for us—so that we might be the body of so great a head—under *the form of a servant*. For it was this form He offered, and in this form He was offered, because it is under this form that He is the Mediator, in this form He is the Priest, in this form He is the Sacrifice.[57]

Augustine's theory is never better expressed than in the twentieth chapter of Book X of *The City of God,* when he draws together the argument which he has been pursuing through the earlier chapters.

> Hence it is that the true Mediator (in so far as He *took the form of a servant* and was thus made *the mediator between God and mankind, the man Christ in Jesus*) receives the sacrifice *in the form of God*, in union with the Father, with whom He is one God. And yet *in the form of a servant* He preferred to be Himself the sacrifice than to receive it, to prevent anyone from supposing that sacrifice, even in this circumstance, should be offered to any created being. Thus He is both the priest, Himself making the offering, and the oblation. This is the reality, and He intended the daily sacrifice of the Church to be the sacramental symbol of this; for the Church, being the body of which He is the head, learns to offer herself through Him. This is the true sacrifice; and the sacrifices of the saints in earlier times were many different symbols of it. This one sacrifice was prefigured by many rites, just as many words are used to refer to one thing, to emphasize a point without inducing boredom. This was the supreme sacrifice, and the true sacrifice, and all the false sacrifices yielded place to it.[58]

This then is Augustine's doctrine of the eucharistic sacrifice: Christ is both priest and oblation; the Church also offers herself as the oblation through Christ, because He is the head and she the body. The one true Sacrifice *(hoc unum),* which has put an end to all preceding sacrifices, is shown forth daily in the sacrament of the Church (a piece of evidence, incidentally, that by Augustine's time some churches—and presumably his own—were having a daily Eucharist, though we know from other evidence which he gives that the practice was by no means universal). The whole of Augustine's thought, in this passage as elsewhere, is Christocentric: 'Christ is the truth, Christ the way. Do you walk therein';[59] 'whither do we go, except to Him? and what way go we, save by Him? He to Himself goeth through Himself, and we to Him through Him';[60] 'He Himself is the physician and the remedy [. . .]. He Himself the priest and the sacrifice'.[61] It is this theological Christocentricity, combined with his profound respect for the text of the Bible, which helps to explain why Augustine's language about the Sacrament often has a literal ring.

> That bread which you see on the altar, being sanctified by the word of God, is the body of Christ. That cup—nay, rather, what that cup holds—is sanctified by the word of God and is the blood of Christ.[62]
>
> He has committed to us in this sacrament His body and blood.[63]
>
> What you see is bread and a cup, what indeed your own eyes report to you; what however your faith, ready for instruction, requires is other: the bread is the body of Christ, the cup is the blood of Christ.[64]

Yet from this language we can also understand how it is that Augustine can speak of the Last Supper as 'the banquet in which He entrusted and delivered to the disciples the figure of His body and blood'.[65]

Augustine's doctrine: its significance

It is in the light of this theology that we can understand the importance in Augustine's theology of the view of the Eucharist as a sacrifice offered alike for the living and for the dead. The idea is not, of course, his own formulation; it was already a well-developed practice in his own day, so that his mother could ask, as she lay dying, to be remembered at God's altar.[66] Nevertheless, the idea of the Eucharist offered for the dead in Christ is wholly in keeping with Augustine's theology, for it is the 'whole of the redeemed city'—*tota ipsa redempta civitas*—which is offered by Christ the High Priest to God, both living and departed, for it is only sin, and not physical death, which can separate us from God.[67]

'The whole of the redeemed city ....' Students of Augustine have long discussed the relationship in his thought between the City of God, the home of the good angels and the elect, and the Church, that very mixed body, made up of the elect and the reprobate.[68] Can these two—the City and the Church—ever come together in this life? Surely, the answer is here: 'The whole of the redeemed city, the congregation and fellowship of the saints, is offered to God as a universal sacrifice, through the great Priest, who offered Himself in His suffering for us—so that we might be the body of so great a head—*under the form of a servant*'. Wherever the faithful of Christ are gathered together to celebrate the Eucharist, there the City of God is realized for a moment of time. The physical surroundings do not matter; cathedral or slum-church or hunted and fugitive congregation in a hostile society, it makes no difference. 'This is the sacrifice of Christians, who are *many, making up one body in Christ*. This is the sacrifice which the Church continually celebrates in the sacrament of the altar, a sacrament well-known to the faithful, where it is shown to the Church that she herself is offered in the offering which she presents to God'.

Afterword

I have said enough. Not that there is not much more that I could say—we have only begun to treat of a rich and much-debated topic to which one might easily devote a book. Let me end on a personal note. I have been a member of the Fellowship for twenty-seven years, which is not long by some standards, but a fair span of time nevertheless. During that period I have, whenever I have had the opportunity (which is less often that I would have wished), also been a student of Augustine of Hippo and have on occasion defended him and the Latin tradition in Fellowship circles, sometimes with more heat than I would now wish to display. Let me now, following Augustine's example, retract whatever I have said on those occasions which may have given pain or offence to any of my fellow-members; but let me also urge upon you the fact that in his doctrine of the Eucharist and the

Church, Augustine stands within the whole Patristic tradition, Eastern and Western.[69] I do not see than anything which I have quoted from his teaching could not, with equal propriety, have been uttered by one of the Greek Fathers. I would therefore appeal to my Orthodox brethren not to look on Augustine as an alien, but to embrace him with the same love and affection that I do the great saints of the East: Ignatius; Athanasius; Basil; the two Gregories; and Maximus the Confessor. May we find our common heritage in these, and may their teaching lead us to unity in our common membership of the Body of Christ.

NOTES

1. For the description of the church and worship of Hippo I have drawn on F. Van der Meer, *Augustine the Bishop*, E. T. (London 1961), though the French translation, *Saint Augustin: pasteur d'âmes*, 2 vols (Paris 1959) is to be preferred. See also E. Marec, 'Les dernières fouilles d'Hippo Regius' in *Augustinus Magister* (Paris 1954), i. 1-18 and *Monuments chrétiens d'Hippone* (Paris 1958).
2. Van der Meer, p. 22 (metric measurements: 42 metres [with apse 49] x 20).
3. *Optatus, vi, 1: 'quis fidelium nescit in peragendis mysteriis ipsa ligna linteamine cooperiri?'*
4. See K. S. Painter, *The Water Newton Early Christian Silver* (London 1977).
5. Possidius, *Vita Augustini*, 24. 15: 'Nam et de vasis dominicis propter captivos et quam plurimos indigentes frangi et conflari iubebat et indigentibus dispensari'.
6. *Serm.* 356, 13. See G. Bonner, *St Augustine of Hippo* (London 1963), p. 129.
7. Van der Meer, pp. 25, 390.
8. See the remarks of C. Lambot, *Sancti Aurelii Augustini Sermones de Vetere Testamento I-L* (*Corpus Christianorum* xli) (Turnhout 1961), pp. viii-ix.
9. Possidius, *Vita Augustini*, 31. 9, tr. F. R. Hoare, *The Western Fathers* (London 1954), pp. 243-4.
10. For a general description of the congregation, see Van Der Meer, pp. 389-90 and Maurice Pontet, *'L'exégèse de S. Augustin prédicateur'* (Paris n.d.), pp. 55-62.
11. On shaving, see Jérôme Carcopino, *Daily Life in Ancient Rome* (London 1964), 175-83; on the beard as a badge of paganism, Frank D. Gilliard, 'Notes on the coinage of Julian the Apostate', *The Journal of Roman Studies* liv (1964), pp. 135-6.
12. See, e.g. *Serm.* 132 and 161. Van der Meer (pp. 184-90) argues that Augustine's view of marriage was more sympathetic than is often maintained.
13. *Serm.* 180, 10.
14. Van der Meer, pp. 143-8.
15. See Augustine's embarrassed explanation to Albina, *Ep.* 126, 7.
16. Van der Meer, p. 131.
17. 'Parish life in one age is remarkably like parish life in another. The differences are mostly differences of local colour' (Van der Meer, p. 130).
18. *Serm.* 277, xiii, 13: '[....] quia ubique totus Deus: non alibi dimidius et alibi alio dimidio constitutus, sed ubique totus. Implet caelum et terram; sed totus est in caelo, totus in terra'.
19. Van der Meer, p. 312.
20. So Julian the Apostate scornfully declares: 'You have filled the whole world with tombs and sepulchres, and yet in your Scriptures it is nowhere said that you must grovel among tombs and pay them honour' (*Against the Galilaeans* 335C, ed. Wright, Loeb edn., iii. 415). Augustine is at pains in *De Civitate Dei* to emphasise that the honours paid to the martyrs involve no suggestion of deification (VIII, xxvii; XXII, x; cf. *Contra Faustum* XX, 21).
21. H.-I. Marrou, 'Survivances païennes dans les rites funéraires des Donatistes', in *Mélanges à Joseph Bidez et à Franz Cumont* Brussels 1949), pp. 193-203.

22. See the comments of E. R. Dodds, *The Greeks and the Irrational* (Berkeley and Los Angeles 1951), p. 136.
23. See Ernst Dassmann, 'Ambrose und die Märtyrer', *Jahrbuch für Antike und Christentum*, Jahrgang 18 (1975), pp. 49-68, esp. 54, 55.
24. See J. Lécuyer, 'Le sacrifice selon saint Augustin' in *Augustinus Magister* (Paris 1954), ii. 905-14; but even better is the pamphlet by an anonymous author, perhaps the nonjuror George Smith (1693-1756), entitled *An Epistolary Dissertation Addressed to the Clergy of Middlesex wherein the Doctrine of St Austin concerning the Christian Sacrifice is set in a true Light. By Way of Reply to Dr Waterland's late Charge to them.* By a Divine of the University of Cambridge. Reprinted as an appendix to W. Cunningham, *S. Austin and his place in the History of Christian Thought* (London 1886), pp. 201-76.
25. *De Cath. Eccles. Unitate*, 17. See H. B. Swete, 'Eucharistic Belief in the second and third centuries', *JTS* iii (1902), pp. 161-77, who points out (p. 166 n 6) that Tertullian had anticipated Cyprian in the use of *sacrificium, sacerdos* and *ara* in a Christian sense.
26. *Conf.* IX, xii, 32.
37. *Enchir.*, xxix, 110.
28. Edmund Bishop, 'The Roman Rite' in *Liturgica Historica* (Oxford 1918), p. 10.
29. See below, nn 62, 63, 64.
30. Denis Bethell, 'The making of a twelfth-century relic collection' in *Popular Belief and Practice* (*Studies in Church History* vol. 8), ed. G. J. Cuming and Derek Baker (Cambridge 1972), p. 62.
31. *Adv. Marc.*, i, 14. See Swete, art. cit. n 25 above, p. 175 n 3.
32. *Adv. Marc.*, iii, 19.
33. *Ep.* 63, 14.
34. Ibid.. 63. 2.
35. Optatus, vi, 1: 'quid est enim altare nisi sedes. et corporis et sanguinis Christi? [...] cuius illic per certa momenta corpus et sanguis habitabat'.
36. Ibid., vi, 2: [...] calices, Christi sanguinis portatores [...]'.
37. *De Sacramentis* iv, 5.21: '[...] quod figura est corporis et sanguinis domini nostri Iesu Christi' (cf. the Liturgy of St Basil: '[...] offering the types *(antitupa)* of the holy body and blood of Thy Christ').
38. Van der Meer, p. 312.
39. *Ôp. Imp. c Iul.*, iii, 162.
40. Augustine mentions the Acatius episode to refute Julian of Eclanum's argument that the work of the Creator needs no modification or improvement. He neither commends nor condemns the action of Acatius' mother who, presumably, made the poultice from the portion of the host which she had taken from church for self-administered communion at home. (By the late fourth century the ancient practice of lay self-communion was coming under criticism—laymen, it was felt, ought not to be allowed to handle the holy mysteries, and St Basil of Caesarea found it necessary to defend its legality [*Ep.* 93]).
41. *De Doctrina Christ.*, I, xxxiv, 38: 'Sic enim ait: *Ego sum via et veritas et vita*, hoc est 'per me venitur, ad me venitur, in me permanetur'.
42. See J. Plagnieux, 'Influence de la lutte antipélagienne sur le "de Trinitate" ou: Christocentrisme de saint Augustin' in *Augustinus Magister* ii. 817-26.
43. *C. Epist. Parm.*, II, iv, 9.
44. *Ep.* 140, xxvii, 66; *Enarr. in Ps.* 21, i, 30.
45. *De Civ. Dei*, XIX, 21.
46. *dCD*, XIX, 23: 'Cessaturas enim victimas, quas in umbra futuri offerebant Iudaei, et unum sacrficium gentes a solis ortu usque ad occasum, sicut iam fieri cernimus oblaturas'. Cf. *Enarr. in Ps.* 33, i, 6.
47. *dCD*, X, 1.
48. Ibid.
49. *C. Faust.*, XX, 21.
50. *Quaest. in Heptateuchum*, II, 94: '[...] *douleia* debetur Deo tamquam Domino, *latreia* vera nonnisi Deo tamquam Deo'.

51. *dCD*, X, 3. Translation by H. Bettenson, *Augustine: City of God* (Penguin Books: Harmondsworth 1972), p. 375.
52. *dCD*, X, 5. (Bettenson, p. 377).
53. Ibid.
54. *dCD*, X, 6: 'Verum sacrifium est omne opus quo agitur, ut sancta societate inhaereamus Deo, relatum scilicet ad illum finem boni, quo veraciter beati esse possimus'.
55. Ibid. (Bettenson, p. 380); cf. XIX, 23: 'Huius autem praeclarissimum atque optimum sacrificium nos ipsi sumus, hoc est civitas eius, cuius rei mysterium celebramus oblationibus nostris, quae fidelibus notae sunt'.
56. *dCD*, X, 27, 29 (Bettenson, pp. 411, 414-15).
57. Ibid., X, 6 (Bettenson, p. 380).
58. Ibid., X, 20 (Bettenson, pp. 400-1).
59. *Enarr. in Ps.* 66, 5.
60. *In Evang. Ioh. Tr.* 69, 2.
61. *Serm.* 374, 3.
62. *Serm.* 227: 'Panis ille, quem videtis in altari, sanctificatus per verbum Dei, corpus est Christi. Calix ille, imo quod habet calix, sanctificatum per verbum Dei, sanguis est Christi'.
63. *Serm.* 229: 'Commendavit nobis in isto sacramento corpus et sanguinem suum'.
64. *Serm.* 272: 'Quod ergo videtis, panis est et calix; quod vobis etiam oculi vestri renuntiant: quod autem fides vestra postulat instruenda, panis est corpus Christi, calix sanguis Christi'. Further examples in Karl Adam, *Die Eucharistielehre des hl. Augustin* (Paderborn 1908), pp. 62, 63; Van der Meer, pp. 371-76.
65. *Enarr. in Ps.* 3, 1: '[...] convivium in quo corporis et sanguinis sui figuram discipulis commendavit et tradidit'.
66. *Conf.* IX, xi, 27: '"Ponite" inquit "hoc corpus ubicumque: nihil vos eius cura conturbet; tantum illud vos rogo, ut ad domini altare meminertis mei, ubiubi fueritis".'
67. *dCD*, X, xxii: 'non enim nisi peccatis homines separantur a Deo, quorum in hac vita non fit nostra virtute, sed divina miseratione purgatio; per indulgentiam illius, non per nostram potentiam [...]. Hac Dei gratia, qua in nos ostendit magnam misericordiam suam, et in hac vita per fidum regimur, et post hanc vitam per ipsam speciem incommutabilis veritatis ad perfectionem plenissimam perducemur'.
68. *Serm.* 223, 2: 'Ecclesia [...] habens permixtos bonis malos; habitura post iudicium sine ullis malis omnes bonos'; *Enarr. in Ps.* 128, 8: 'Mali mixti sunt bonis, non solum in saeculo, sed et in ipsa intus ecclesia mali mixti sunt bonis'.
69. That this was recognised by Vladimir Lossky is apparent from his paper 'Les éléments de "Théologie négative" dans la pensée de saint Augustin' (*Augustinus Magister* i. 575-81). It is much to be regretted that Lossky's recognition of the need for a theological examination of Augustine's *De Trinitate* by an Orthodox (V. Lossky, *In the Image and Likeness of God* [London 1974], pp. 95, 96) has as yet evoked no response.

VII

QUID IMPERATORI CUM ECCLESIA? ST. AUGUSTINE ON HISTORY AND SOCIETY[1]

ROBERT MARKUS is unquestionably one of the most learned and perceptive English scholars currently engaged in Augustinian studies, a field for which he is particularly well equipped, since he is equally competent as an historian and a philosopher and is, in addition, a theologian as capable of discussing the thought of Barth or Cullmann as that of the Fathers or the Schoolmen. To these qualifications may be added a love of literature (displayed in the present work by apposite citations from T. S. Eliot, Gerard Manley Hopkins and Richard Crashaw) which produces a thinker who not only writes in the tradition of Christian humanism but who appreciates that the truth of Christ is expressed, not in theological propositions alone but in the apprehension of the poet and the creative artist. Dante, as our author recognises,[2] was a great theologian.

These qualities—all of them demonstrated in the study *Saeculum*—are somewhat daunting to a reviewer whose professional competence is limited to the field of history. It is true that the author disarmingly declares in his Preface that the book is "in the first place, a historical study";[3] but the reader is expected, from the first, to consider the processes of Augustine's thought on biblical theology, political authority, and the nature of the Church. This observation is in no way intended as a criticism. On the contrary, the book is to be welcomed as an outstanding contribution to our understanding of the mind of Augustine and as an indication of the relevance of a particular aspect of his thought to the problems of the present age. To read it and, still more, to reflect upon it, will provide admirable exercise for the minds of students of human thought in general and of Augustine in particular.

In view of the complex nature of the matter of the book a non-special-

---

[1] R.A. Markus, *Saeculum: History and society in the theology of St Augustine*, Cambridge: University Press, 1970, pp. xii + 252.

[2] p. 176.

[3] p. vii.

ist reader might paradoxically be well advised to begin at the last chapter
—significantly entitled "*Civitas peregrina:* signposts"—for it is here that
the author explains that his aim is not simply to investigate Augustine's
thought as an historical exercise but to show that it has a significance for
the present climate of Christian theology.

> At this point [he writes] the historian and the theologian have
> reached a parting of the ways. The historian, even if he confines his
> interest to the history of ideas, will wish to understand as fully as
> he can all the ideas which went into the making of Augustine's
> mind, and to seize the full complexity of their tangled interplay in
> its development. The theologian can recognise that, abstracted
> from the context of Augustine's attitude to the ecclesiastical estab-
> lishment of his place and time, in all its complicated detail, there
> are two quite distinct sets of questions to be distinguished here.
> One concerns the internal, pastoral activity of the Church; the
> other concerns wider questions about history, society, human
> destiny, and the Church's relation to them. In this final chapter I
> keep entirely to this second set of themes. I shall attempt to sketch
> the directions of the signposts provided by Augustine's reflection
> on history, on society and on the Church.[4]

The reviewer is therefore faced with two tasks. He must first discuss
the historical investigation which occupies the greater part of the book;
but he must also accept the fact that, by the seventh chapter, "the historian and the theologian have reached a parting of the ways," and follow
the author into the realms of constructive theological exposition. *Magnum
opus et arduum;* but there is some reassurance in the observation that:

> the theologian is of all men the most apt to look over his shoulder,
> if not for "authorities," at least for a tradition to locate his own
> thought. . . . In theology, true continuity is not so much a matter
> of drawing out implications from, still less of repeating the sub-
> stance of assertions made by, the Fathers; it is rather to be found in
> loyalty to their ultimate doctrinal aims.[5]

The themes of *Saeculum,* as the sub-title indicates, is Augustine's theological understanding of history and society. This association may seem
forced, especially in contemporary society which increasingly tends to regard them as independent; but, as Markus proceeds to show, Augustine's
attitude to human society is determined by his conception of history. In

---

[4] p. 155.
[5] p. 156.

VII

Quid Imperatori Cum Ecclesia? St. Augustine on History and Society   233

traditional history of the sort written by Tacitus and Amianus Marcellinus he had little interest. He recognized its utility for biblical exegesis and was capable, if need arose, of employing it for apologetic purposes; but he saw in it no profound religious significance. There was, however, one particular branch of history, a "privileged strand," in which Augustine, as a Christian, could not fail to be interested: "the biblical narrative of God's saving work among His chosen people." [6] This constitutes "sacred history," the story of God's plan of salvation for men. All the rest, all the "troubled careers of men, societies and their institutions," is secular history; and this applies to the history of the Church no less than to that of the state.

What, then, differentiates sacred from secular history? Essentially, the difference lies in the prophetic character of the writing. Markus has already dealt with this theme in an article published in 1967,[7] now reprinted as Appendix A. Here he shows that in Augustine's thought, history was originally regarded as being concerned with the past and prophecy with the future. However, by the time he came to write the *De Civitate Dei* the two terms, so far as they apply to Holy Scripture, are almost synonymous. Events in the past, as they are understood and interpreted by the prophetic quality of the biblical writers, provide the key to the future.

> Inspiration, the gift of prophecy . . . is the constitutive difference between "sacred" and "secular" history. . . . The [biblical] writer's inspired insight presents the past events he tells of in a pattern of significance, a significance which may not be disclosed by the immediate context but only in its full unfolding in a possibly remote future.[8]

Sacred history, then, is simply the writings comprehended by the Canon of Scripture, and this view conditions Augustine's understanding of the course of human history since the Incarnation. "On the map of sacred history the time between Incarnation and Parousia is a blank; a blank of unknown duration, capable of being filled with an infinite variety of happenings, of happenings all equally at home in the pattern of sacred history." [9] No event, however, has any significance for man's salvation, which has already been effected by Christ's death and resurrection.

---

[6] p. 9.

[7] 'Saint Augustine on History, Prophecy and Inspiration,' *Augustinus* (Madrid 1967) 271-80.

[8] pp. 14, 15.

[9] p. 23.

The same attitude determines Augustine's treatment of the concept of the Six Ages of the world. Since the Incarnation mankind lives in the Sixth Age, which will endure to the Second Coming. No new, decisive period will intervene. In his early years as a Christian Augustine had been prepared to entertain views of a millenarian character;[10] but when he came to write the *De Civitate Dei* he had abandoned all traces of millenarian literalism in his understanding of Scripture. "Since the coming of Christ until the end of the world, all history is homogeneous. . . . It cannot be mapped out in terms of a pattern drawn from sacred history. . . . It can no longer contain decisive turning-points endowed with a significance in sacred history." [11]

Augustine's attitude to history and his limitation of sacred history to the canonical Scriptures explains why, in contrast to so many of his contemporaries, including his friend and disciple Orosius, he never came to accept the Eusebian view of the Roman Empire as being, in some special sense, the instrument for the extension of God's Kingdom upon earth. It is true that for a short time the collapse of paganism in the 390's produced in Augustine a tendency to applaud the Theodosian settlement and to speak triumphantly of *tempora christiana;* but around 400 this view underwent a profound change and devaluation. The Christianization of the Empire became no more than a period in Roman history, specific and limited; and after 410 the very expression *tempora christiana*—a term of abuse on the lips of the pagans—hardly seemed a matter for boasting.

Augustine's understanding of *tempora christiana* provides the theme of Markus' second chapter. In the third he deals with Augustine's attitude to the Roman state and discusses the perennial problem of its relation to the *Civitas terrena.* Here he shows (and his demonstration is likely to be accepted by anyone who has tried to deal with this complicated matter in any detail) that "Augustine's indentification of the Roman state with the earthly city is as clear in his writings as is his refusal to abide by this identification. His logic is the logic of late antique rhetoric rather than modern formal logic." [12] In fact, when disentangled from his oratory, Augustine's doctrine of the state (*res publica*) and of the *saeculum* (the age in which the state has its operation) is that they are things neutral in themselves which provide the field of action for the citizens of the two supernatural societies, the City of God and the Earthly City. Markus quotes the famous Augustinian assertion that the two cities are made by the

---

[10] *De Civitate Dei* 20.7.

[11] pp. 20,21.

[12] p. 59.

VII

Quid Imperatori Cum Ecclesia? St. Augustine on History and Society   235

wills of their citizens—love of self to the contempt of God and love of God to the contempt of self—and observes that while membership of either city is exclusive of membership of the other, it is nevertheless compatible with membership of both the state and the Church.[13] It is this consideration which lies behind Augustine's definition of a people as "a multitude of reasonable beings united in agreement over the things they love." [14] The citizens of both cities agree about the need for earthly peace as the common means to their radically different ends, the one enjoying it as an end in itself, the other using it as a means of coming to the enduring peace of the eternal Sabbath.

So far Markus has first shown how Augustine came to confine sacred history to the events recorded in Scripture, so relegating all other history, including that of the Church herself, to the sphere of the secular; and has then established the essential theological neutrality of the state in relation to the two supernatural societies to which all men belong. In Chapter 4 he discusses Augustine's view of the foundations of authority in the state which, by definition, cannot claim any moral sanction other than the permissive will of God, showing how Augustine steadily moved away from the Platonism of his early days as a Christian, with its conception of the *polis* as the means by which men can achieve the good life, to an attitude which comes close to that of Hobbes: the state exists, not for the sake of the good life but as a curb on human wickedness consequent upon the Fall. Because of man's fallen nature society is always tending to revert to chaos and requires the coercive power of civil authority to secure a minimal cohesion for the sake of the common good. Certainly there are hints in Augustine that society will to some extent provide a culture common to all its members, both the elect and the reprobate; but by the time he came to write the *De Civitate Dei* Augustine had come to deny absolutely that society was in any way the agency of man's pursuit of his final good (one thinks of the famous encomium on human achievement in Book 22, with its brutal conclusion that all this is no more than the consolation of damned wretches).[15] Augustine had moreover by now come to abandon the Greek philosophical notion of man as being by nature a political animal. Man is indeed a social creature and would have been so even without the Fall; but the need for political organization is consequent upon the supervening fact of sin. Because of sin, and only because of sin, the state

---

[13] p. 60 (*De Civ. Dei* 14.28).

[14] *De Civ. Dei* 19.24: 'Populus est coetus multitudinis rationalis rerum quae diligit concordi communione sociatus' (ed. Hoffmann, CSEL 40 (2) 419. 6-7).

[15] Ibid. 22.24: 'Et haec omnia miserorum sunt damnatorumque solacia, non praemia beatorum' (649. 3-4 Hoffmann).

is necessary for this life, and all men, including citizens of the City of God, must play their part in it.

Up to this point the argument developed has been predominantly philosophical, though illustrated with a good deal of historical detail in passing. In his next two chapters Markus deals with the effect on Augustine's thought of the outlook of the African society in which he lived and worked, and of his own experience as a bishop and ecclesiastic. These two chapters are particularly impressive and reveal the author's mastery of the details of African church history quite apart from Augustine's personal career. He deals at length with the African ecclesiological tradition expressed in the writings of Tertullian and Cyprian: the notion of a pure Church, a Church of the elect, of which the Donatists were the great exponents; and the conviction—which was not peculiar to the Donatists and which persisted among African Christians down to the eve of the Arab invasion—that Africa was in some sense the guardian of the true faith, and which expressed itself in displays of rugged independence against pope and emperor alike. Justinian, it will be remembered, experienced little gratitude from the African divines whom he had freed from Vandal rule when he tried to compromise the sacred Chalcedonian settlement.

The bitterness of the dispute between Catholic and Donatist in Augustine's day has tended to obscure the degree to which they were fundamentally in agreement, and it is a great virtue of Markus' study that he stresses the extent to which the thought of Augustine was conditioned by the presuppositions of the Donatists and particularly by the theology of that remarkable thinker Tyconius. In common with many scholars Markus sees the Donatists as representing the true strain of African theology, the authentic legacy of Tertullian and Cyprian, and actually describes Catholicism as being "from an African point of view an import to Africa." "Nothing," he writes, "can disguise the fact which the Donatists . . . never tired of stressing, the fact which even Augustine was compelled to recognise, that theologically the Donatists were the true heirs of Cyprianic Christianity." [16] The reviewer has considerable reservations about this view. Granted that on a specific theological issue—namely, the invalidity of sacraments administered outside the unity of the Church—the Donatists inherited the views of Cyprian; the fact remains that they entirely lacked Cyprian's sense of the universality of the Catholic Church, which made him welcome allies like Firmilian of Neocaesarea and caused him to avoid a decisive break with Stephen of Rome even at the crisis of the baptismal controversy. Indeed, as T. G. Jalland long ago pointed out, one of the most

[16] p. 110.

VII

Quid Imperatori Cum Ecclesia? St. Augustine on History and Society   237

revealing features of Cyprian's correspondence is an omission: he does not tell his allies that Stephen had refused to receive his delegates at Rome. "Cyprian was unwilling that his strained relations with Stephen should be widely known, since he realized that communion with the apostolic see of the West was an essential element in his theory of an episcopate enjoying together a common Petrine inheritance." [17] Nor are signs lacking that the Donatists, in their early days at least, were aware of the importance of communion with the Roman see as evidence for the orthodoxy of their views. Hence their efforts to establish a Donatist episcopal succession at Rome in the days of Damasus and the rather half-hearted attempt at the Conference of Carthage to put forward a Donatist Roman bishop, even though by this time communion with the rest of the Christian world had ceased to be a serious element in their theology.[18]

These considerations lead to another question: what was the real essence of Donatism? It has been discussed as a theology; as a manifestation of incipient nationalism; as an expression of class-warfare and economic discontent (Markus himself speaks of Donatism as "the religion of the economically underprivileged, the African 'masses' of the countryside").[19] Yet is the essence of Donatism to be found in any of these? Is it not, rather, like Montanism, one of those strange enthusiastic movements which throughout history have continually broken out in the Christian Church and which are commonly characterised by an ascetic hostility to the social order (which sometimes carries with it a good deal of sensuality)[20] and an urgent expectation of the end of the world. Such movements, like Donatism, often involve an attempt to return to the early days of Christianity in a mood of reactionary millenarianism. In this context, on Markus' own arguments, Augustine's rejection of Donatism was the logical consequence of his theology of history and society. The Donatists were wrong because they wished to make a separation of the just and unjust as if the Day of Judgement were immediately at hand, whereas in fact we do not know how much longer the Sixth Age is destined to last. They com-

---

[17] Jalland, *The Church and the Papacy* (London: SPCK, 1944) 177.

[18] See Frend, *The Donatist Church* (Oxford 1952) 164,181 ("The curious incident of the dispatch of a Numidian bishop to Rome suggests that Donatus, too, considered that the unity of the Church entailed contact in some form with the see of Peter") 206, 207, 283.

[19] pp. 110-111.

[20] e.g. the polygamy of the Anabaptists at Münster 1534-35 and the promiscuity ascribed —probably justly—to the Ranters in seventeenth-century England (for details see Norman Cohn, *The pursuit of the Millenium* [rev.ed. London 1970]). On the drunkenness of the Circumcellions, Frend, *The Donatist Church*, 174-75 and references. On enthusiastic movements in general, see the comments on Montanism by E.R. Dodds, *Pagan and Christian in an Age of Anxiety* (Cambridge 1965) 63-68.

mitted the classic error, perpetrated by the Montanists in the past and destined to be repeated by other chiliastic movements in the future, of supposing that the canon of sacred history is still open and that an "Age of the Spirit" had succeeded to the "Age of the Son" recorded in the New Testament.[21] The scandal of separation apart, Augustine was obliged to oppose Donatism on the very principles which Markus has so effectively demonstrated.

Paradoxically, the Donatist error had something in common with the Eusebian deification of the Empire: both systems refuse to accept the desacralisation of history and neither has any real understanding of the nature of eschatology. Tyconius, the most original mind which Donatism produced, had seen the weakness of the Donatist position and it was Tyconius who "taught Augustine to transpose concepts which earlier African theology had understood in empirical, sociological or historical terms, into an eschatological key."[22] Markus does justice to that very able thinker whom his own church disowned but who could never bring himself to join the Catholics. Through the mediation of Augustine Tyconius must on any showing be reckoned one of the most influential Latin theologians of the fourth century.

With great perception Markus points[23] to the contrast which Augustine must have experienced on his return to Africa between the cosmopolitan Church which he had seen at Milan, deeply involved in the life of the state though always, in the person of Ambrose, maintaining its independence of action; and the parochialism of the African Church, with its tradition of hostility to secular authority. He emphasises the effect which African tradition exercised on the mind of Augustine during his ministry. Augustine was always psychologically an African, even though his culture was Roman. Yet one should not underestimate the importance of the fact that his conversion took place in Italy, far from the parochial dissensions of Donatist and Catholic. As a result of his earlier experience he could with confidence appeal to the judgement of the *securus orbis terrarum* against the particularism which was at once the blessing and the bane of African Christianity. And in this may be seen a further link with Cyprian; for it is precisely his sense of the wholeness of the Catholic Church which distinguishes Cyprian's personal theology from the "Cyprianic" the-

---

[21] This is, notoriously, the doctrine of Joachim of Flora in the twelfth century; but the notion is clearly present in the thought of the redactor of the *Passio Perpetuae,* 1 in the third century: '. . . Sed viderint qui unam virtutem Spiritus unius Sancti pro aetatibus iudicent temporum: cum maiora reputanda sunt novitiora quaeque ut novissimiora, secundum exsuperationem gratiae in ultima saeculi spatia decretam' (ed. W.H. Shewring, *The Passion of SS. Perpetua and Felicity* [London 1931] 3.10-14).

[22] p. 120.

[23] pp. 105,106.

ology of the Donatists. In this respect Augustine can fairly claim to stand more closely within the true Cyprianic tradition than did the African separatists.

Yet there remains a difficulty facing any attempt to place Augustine within the African tradition of ecclesiastical independence: his support of coercion by the state to bring the Donatists into unity; and this would, moreover, appear to constitute a positive and irrefutable objection to any attempt to show that for Augustine the state is something religiously neutral. Does not his approbation of the intervention of the secular authority in a religious controversy constitute an endorsement of the Christian state as positive as that of the Byzantine theologians? This is the question discussed in the sixth chapter of Markus' book.

Of the facts there can be no question. By Augustine's own admission he moved from his original position of opposing coercion in the belief that it would produce feigned and hypocritical conversions to acceptance on the pragmatic ground that in practice it worked. Furthermore, even before he came to endorse the coercion of schismatic Christians, Augustine had approved of the suppression of paganism by state action and never wavered in this approval. In the light of these facts the whole theory that Augustine's theology assigns a neutral rôle to the state appears untenable and his outlook would seem to be little different from that of his contemporaries who saw the Christian Empire as the divinely-appointed instrument of God's purposes.

Markus recognises this difficulty. He argues nevertheless that it is precisely the pragmatic nature of Augustine's acceptance of state intervention which preserves his doctrine from assimilation to the Eusebian view. It is to be observed that Augustine continued to approve of coercion even after he had abandoned the favourable view of the Theodosian settlement which he had held about the beginning of the fifth century. Markus emphasises that Augustine's theory of coercion was "from beginning to end, part of a pastoral strategy" [24]—a judgement with which the present reviewer would entirely agree. Much energy has been expended in the past by well-intentioned scholars deploring Augustine's loss of a liberalism which he never in fact possessed. One has only to read that extraordinary letter[25] written in 416 to the would-be suicide the Donatist presbyter Donatus to realise both the strange quality of Augustine's thought on this particular issue and the even stranger quality of the minds of the schismatics with whom he had to deal. It is a measure of the sickness of our

---

[24] p. 140.
[25] *Ep.* 173 (ed. Goldbacher, CSEL 44,640-48).

age that neither Augustine's arguments nor the conduct of Donatus seem wholly unfamiliar, as they might well have done to men of an earlier generation.

Augustine's eventual approval of coercion by the state is therefore to be understood as determined by pastoral necessity: the Church accepts such coercion because it is in the interest of the victim. But is it really correct in this context to speak of the Church "accepting" coercion? Is not coercion, properly speaking, the action of the Church through her children who are also secular officials? Markus notes[26] that Augustine, after he had abandoned any notion of a Christian Roman Empire on the Eusebian pattern, still continued to speak of Christian rulers and officials as owing service to God in their public capacity. If then they act in the interest of the Church they do so as Christians who have secular authority rather than as officials of a Christian state.

Such reasoning appears forced at the present day and only doubtfully honest. It seems to imply that it is proper for the Church to use the state to further her own interests and for Christians to employ their secular powers, which should be reserved for the neutral area in which the citizens of the City of God and the Earthly City live together, to favour Christians at the expense of the rest of the population. It is difficult to avoid the conclusion that within certain limits such a view is quite correct. One must, of course, make some allowance for the ethos of Augustine's age, when the *patronus*, the great man who was supposed to intervene in the interests of his clients was taken for granted; but when every excuse is made, Augustine's defence of coercion remains an anomaly in the theological system which Markus is trying to demonstrate.

Expediency can make men illogical as well as untrue to their highest ideals. One can understand that pastoral expediency not only caused Augustine to abandon his earlier opposition to the use of force but also made him act in a manner which was inconsistent with his true principles. In this connexion that affair of Crispinus of Calama—rather surprisingly omitted by Markus from his discussion[27]—is revealing, occurring as it did when Augustine was still in principle opposed to coercion. In the spring of 404, in order to compel Crispinus, the Donatist bishop of Calama, to restrain the activities of the local Circumcellions who had violently assaulted Augustine's friend Possidius, the Catholic bishop of the see, Augustine and Possidius brought an action against him apparently under the law of Theodosius I of 392, which decreed a fine of ten pounds of gold

---

[26] p. 147.

[27] Also by Peter Brown in 'Saint Augustine's attitude to religious coercion,' *The Journal of Roman Studies* 54 (1964) 107-16.

for anyone who, being in heresy, should ordain or be ordained.[28] Crispinus at first met the charge successfully by denying that he was a heretic and it required an appeal by the Catholics to secure his conviction, a verdict which was subsequently upheld on appeal to the imperial court at Ravenna, although the Catholics were careful to see that the fine was not actually exacted, to avoid any appearance of making Crispinus a martyr.[29]

Augustine maintained, and continued to maintain, that this action was essentially defensive. At the end of his life, when Julian of Eclanum described the imperial treatment of the Pelagians as persecution, he replied (in words which go far to support Markus' contention that he thinks of state coercion only in terms of action by individual Christian officials):

> Absit a christianis potestatibus terrenae reipublicae, ut de antiqua catholica fide dubitent, et ob hoc oppugnatoribus eius locum et tempus examinis praebeant. Quod enim propter Donatistas factum est, eorum violentissimae turbae fieri coegerunt, ignorantes quid ante sit gestum, quod eis fuerat ostendendum; quales vos turbas Deus avertat ut habeatis; Deo tamen propitio non habetis.[30]

Nevertheless, even when the need for curbing violence is conceded, some doubt must remain about the method actually adopted by Augustine and Possidius in the case of Crispinus. Ignoring the obvious issue, that of violent assault, they chose to bring an action on a specifically theological issue. It would, perhaps, be unfair to accuse Augustine of deliberately equating schism with heresy for the purposes of litigation, in view both of the fact that the two had already been coupled in the legislation of Constantine[31] and of the lack of any clear-cut distinction between the two on the part of the Fathers. Thus Augustine's formula: *Haeresis schisma inveteratum*[32] is in harmony, not only with the traditional Cyprianic view[33] but

---

[28] *Cod.Theod.* 16.5.21 (ed. Mommsen & Krüger pp. 862,863).

[29] The details of the affair of Crispinus are given by Augustine, *Contra Cresconium* 3.46.50-48.52; *Epp.* 88.7; 105.4; Possidius, *Vita Augustini* 12.

[30] *Op.Imp.c.Iul.* 1.10 (PL 45.1054).

[31] *Cod.Theod.*16.5.1 (law of 326): 'Privilegia, quae contemplatione religionis indulta sunt, catholicae tantum legis observatoribus prodesse oportet. Haereticos autem atque schismaticos non solum ab his privilegiis alienos esse volumus sed etiam diversis muneribus constringi et subici' (ed. Mommsen & Krüger p. 855). Significantly the words *autem atque schismaticos* are omitted by *Cod.Iustin.*1.5.1 (ed. Krüger p. 50).

[32] *C. Cresc.*2.7.9: 'Proinde quamvis inter schisma et haeresim magis eam distinctionem adprobem, qua dicitur schisma esse recens congregationis ex aliqua sententiarum diversitate dissensio—neque enim et schisma fieri potest, nisi diversum aliquid sequantur qui faciunt—haeresis autem schisma inveteratum . . . sed quoniam nec nullum est nec aliquid parvum quod diversum sequimini, cum ab unitatis vinculo separati etiam de repetitione baptismi dissentitis a nobis, fit, ut secundum istam ipsam definitionem tuam, qua dixisti: *haeresis est autem diversa sequentium secta*, et haeretici sitis et victi appareatis' (ed. Petschenig, CSEL 52.367. 12-16,25-27—368.3).

[33] Cyprian, *Epp.* 69.7; 71.1 (ed. Hartel, CSEL 3 (2) 756, 771).

also with that of Jerome, writing in 386-387: *Nullum schisma non sibi aliquam confingit haeresim.*[34] The fact remains that by equating Donatist schism with heresy, a breach had been made in the Donatist defences and the way opened to the full employment of the resources of the state. Augustine's biographer Possidius appreciated the significance of the case, to which he devoted a section of the *Vita Augustini* (" . . . silendum non est quod ad laudem Dei per illius tam egregii in ecclesia viri studium domusque Dei zelum adversus praedictos rebaptizatores Donatistas gestum et perfectum est").[35] For Possidius, the prosecution was a matter for triumph. A modern reader may be moved to reflect on the change in Augustine's outlook from the mood of the *Psalmus abecedarius* written ten years earlier:

> Nolite nobis, iam, fratres, tempus Macharii imputare. Si crudeles erant illi, et nobis displicent valde; si autem falsa de illis dicunt, deus potest iudicare. Nos amemus pacem Christi, gaudeamus in unitate.[36]

At the time when he brought the action against Crispinus Augustine still opposed the use of force to reconcile the Donatists to the Church. "Some time between 405 and 408 his consent followed, and thereafter he never wavered."[37] The action against Crispinus prepared the way for this change of mind and it is in this context significant that the request of the Council of Carthage of 404 for protection against the Donatists included the suggestion that the existing laws against heretical ordination should be applied.[38] There is, however, an even more significant piece of evidence. The action against Crispinus only put into effect a threat which Augustine had already uttered as early as 401,[39] that is to say, within the

---

[34] Hieron., *In Titum* 3.11: 'Inter haeresim et schisma hoc esse arbitrantur, quod haeresis perversum dogma habeat: schisma propter episcopalem dissentionem ab Ecclesia separetur: quod quidem in principio aliqua ex parte intelligi potest. Caeterum nullum schisma non sibi aliquam confingit haeresim, ut recte ab Ecclesia recessisse videatur' (PL 26. 598 A).

[35] Possidius, *Vita Augustini* 12.3 (ed. M. Pellegrino, *Possidio, Vita di S. Agostino* [Edizioni Paoline 1955] 76.15-78.18).

[36] *Psalmus abecedarius contra partem Donati* ll. 164-167 (ed. R. Anastasi [Padua 1957] p. 58).

[37] p. 138.

[38] PL 11.1203 B: '. . . simul etiam petendum, ut illam legem, quae a religiosae memoriae eorum patre Theodosio de auri libris decem in ordinatores, vel ordinatos haereticos, seu etiam in possessores, ubi eorum congregatio deprehenditur, promulgata est, ita deinceps confirmari praecipiant: ut in eos valeat, contra quos propter eorum insidias Catholici provocati contestationem deposuerint, ut hoc saltem terrore a schismatica vel haeretica pravitate desciscant.' Note the phrase *a schismatica vel haeretica pravitate.*

[39] *Ep.*66: '. . . nam possemus agere, ut decem libras auri secundum imperatoris iussa persolveres. an forte propterea non habes, unde reddas, quod dare iussi sunt rebaptizatores, dum multum erogas, ut emas, quos rebaptizes? sed nos, ut dixi, de homine te non terremus; Christus te potius terreat' (ed. Goldbacher, CSEL 34 (2) 235.8-15).

period when "he had no reservations about endorsing the Theodosian set-tlement, with its forcible methods of repressing paganism and heresy and its recourse to legislation to enforce Christian orthodoxy." [40] Viewed in this light Augustine's conversion to and continued endorsement of coer-cion may be seen as a survival from a theological outlook he had come to reject. "Although the chief theoretical foundation of religious coercion built into his theology had . . . disappeared, Augustine never repudiated the policies which had been based upon it."[41] Pastoral practice had failed to keep pace with theological development.

❋ ❋ ❋

So far we have considered the specifically historical part of *Saeculum*, in which Markus seeks to make clear the development of Augustine's thought in respect of the historical process and human society. The reviewer finds the argument, and the conclusions drawn from it, convincing. Augus-tine, during the last decades of his life, came to regard the events of human history in the Sixth Age of the world as being, from the Christian point of view, without significance, and the state as being an institution, consequent upon the Fall and necessary for fallen man, enjoying a right in the things which pertain to this life but with no special God-given prerogatives or functions. Now, however, it remains to consider the last chapter of the book, in which the author sets out to consider "some of the ways in which Augustine's thought can nourish, deepen and set the di-rection for relevant thought on these subjects [the theology of history, of society and of the Church] in our own day."[42]

In our discussion it is necessary to heed the author's warning. "Hav-ing observed Augustine's doctrinal aims taking shape with growing clarity of focus in his writings, I now trace the direction, without following the signposts very far, in which the insights Augustine can furnish to twentieth-century theology point. Naturally such a task cannot be confined to the horizons of Augustine's world."[43] The difficulty for the reader is to decide where Markus is developing Augustine's thought and where he is striking out on his own. In this connexion it is relevant that Markus is an English Roman Catholic, that is to say, a member of a religious mi-nority in a country still nominally Christian and provided with an es-tablished church, a minority with a long memory of persecution and hos-tile discrimination and a tradition of loyal obedience to the largest and

---

[40] p. 136.
[41] p. 139.
[42] p. 156.
[43] Ibid.

most exclusive Christian communion. Such a man is, of course, particularly well qualified to understand Augustine and African Christianity and to sympathise both with the Donatist conception of the persecuted, minority Church and, also, with Augustine's vision of the *Catholica*. But there is another factor in Markus' insight: he is an ecumenically-minded English Catholic standing in an intellectual tradition going back to Von Hügel, a tradition which is inclusive rather than exclusive and which understands and appreciates the spiritual richness of all Christian traditions. (His liking for Eliot's *Four Quartets*, the work of a High Anglican royalist which draws on an international cultural heritage, is a good indication of this). For such a man, both recent developments in his own church[44] and in the thought of non-Catholic theologians are likely to have a strong appeal; and this appeal is evident throughout the last chapter of *Saeculum*.

* * *

It would probably be a fair summary of Markus' assessment of Augustine's contribution to the theology of history and society to say that he sees the Bishop of Hippo as the theologian who, above all else, restored eschatology to the Christian thought of the fourth century. While other theologians—Latins like Orosius as well as the Greeks—accepted the Eusebian identification of the Church's destiny with that of the Empire, Augustine liberated the Church from dependence on any such secular framework.[45] This liberation leads to the secularisation of both history and politics. The Christian believer has no privileged insight enabling him to judge historical developments where the Bible is silent and, equally, the Christian's "homelessness" in the world is to be understood not in sociological but in eschatological terms. "There was no need for Christians to be set apart, sociologically, as a community separated from the 'world', hated and persecuted, uncontaminated by it and visibly 'over against the world.' On the contrary, the Christian community was, quite simply, the world as redeemed and reconciled."[46] This consideration in turn leads to the conclusion that the Christian has no right, on the terms of his own beliefs, to contract out of the world and seek to find an earthly home within the Christian community. On the contrary, it is his duty to discharge his obli-

---

[44] See his paper 'Vatican II: The end of an epoch,' *Sobornost*, Series 5: No 3 (1966) 160-70.

[45] One must beware of any facile contrast between the 'Eusebian Platonic East' and the 'Augustinian Eschatological West,' if only because this judgement depends too much on a certain type of literary source. Thus although the Eastern Church long entertained reserves about the Apocalypse and still does not employ it for liturgical purposes, the notion of the Last Judgement became a familiar iconographic theme (see Walter Lowrie, *Art in the Early Church*, 2nd ed. (New York: Harper Torchbooks 1965) 83-85.

[46] p. 167 (cf. *In Ev.Ioh.Tr.*87.2,3 [ed. R. Willems, CC36.544, 545]).

gations to society to the best of his ability, provided always that they do not conflict with his supreme duty to God. Thus Augustine can exhort Count Marcellinus to perform his judicial duties "as a tender father," [47] and dissuade Count Boniface from his desire to resign his military command and retire into the cloister.[48]

Now these views, as Markus points out, are in harmony with those of modern secular theologians, for:

> [Augustine's] "secularisation" of the realm of politics implies a pluralistic, religiously neutral civil community. Historically, of course, such a society lay entirely beyond the horizons of Augustine's world. After centuries of development it has begun to grow from the soil of what has been Western Christendom; but it is still far from securely established in the modern world. It is assailed from many sides. Even Christians have not generally learned to welcome the disintegration of a "Christian society" as a profound liberation for the Gospel. Augustinian theology should at least undermine Christian opposition to an open, pluralist, secular society.[49]

Two points seem to arise here. The first is historical. How far can Augustine be considered to be the originator of this "secular" view of the world and the Church in the world? The question arises in the face of a quotation from Karl Barth, cited by Markus as a "most powerful re-statement of [the Augustinian] tradition of political theology:

> [The civil community] serves to protect man from the invasion of chaos and therefore to give him time: time for the preaching of the Gospel; time for repentance; time for faith.[50]

Let us set beside these the words of another, earlier, theologian:

> There is another need, a greater one, for our praying for the Emperors, and for the whole estate of the empire and the interests of Rome. We know that the great force which threatens the whole world, the end of the age itself with its menace of hideous suffering, is delayed by the respite which the Roman empire means for

---

[47] *Ep.* 133.2: 'Imple, Christiane iudex, pii patris officium . . .' (ed. Goldbacher, CSEL 44.82.1).

[48] *Ep.* 189.4: 'Noli existimare neminem deo placere posse, qui in armis bellicis militat' (Goldbacher, CSEL 57.133.12-13).

[49] p. 173.

[50] p. 177 (Barth, 'The Christian community and the civil community,' in *Against the stream* [ET London 1954] 21).

us. We do not wish to experience all that; and when we pray for its postponement are helping forward the continuance of Rome.[51]

The speaker is Tertullian; and if we substitute the term "civil community" for the "Roman empire" of his language we have a doctrine of secularisation hardly different from Augustine's or Karl Barth's. In a similar manner Tertullian sees the present state of secular history, embodied in the fortunes of the Roman state, extending to the end of the world: *quousque saeculum stabit, tamdiu enim stabit.*[52] And this is the view of a theologian who is normally regarded as being, on first principles, bitterly hostile to the secular order. On this evidence I would suggest that before Augustine, and even before Tyconius, the potentiality for secular theology existed in African thought. One remembers the words of Optatus of Milevis: *Non enim respublica est in ecclesia, sed ecclesia in respublica, id est in imperio Romano.*[53] Optatus was concerned to defend the propriety of imperial intervention in the affairs of the Church; but the important consideration for our purposes is that he was determined to hold Church and Empire apart and maintain the authority of the state in its own sphere.

This, however, is an historical detail. More important is the question: does Augustinian theology indeed undermine Christian opposition to an open, pluralist, secular society? Are modern secular theologians indeed in the stream of Augustinian tradition? The reviewer has his doubts. Augustine, after all, never forgets the warped element in the nature of fallen man which continually threatens to transform the theologically neutral *terrena respublica* into a visible manifestation of the *Civitas terrena*, and

---

[51] Tert., *Apologeticum* 32.1: 'Est et alia maior necessitas nobis orandi pro imperatoribus, et ita universo orbe et statu imperii rebusque Romanis, qui vim maximam universo orbi imminentem ipsamque clausulam saeculi acerbitates horrendas comminantem Romani imperii commeatu scimus retardari. Itaque nolumus experiri et, dum precamur differi, Romanae diuturnitati favemus '(ed. E. Dekkers, *CC* 1.142.16-143.7). Tr. Glover (Loeb ed.).

[52] Tert., *Ad Scapulam* 2.6: 'Christianus nullius est hostis, nedum imperatoris, quem sciens a Deo suo constitui, necesse est ut et ipsum diligat et revereatur et honoret et salvum velit, cum toto Romano imperio, quousque saeculum stabit: tamdiu enim stabit' (ed. Dekkers, *CC* 2.1128.24-28).

[53] Optatus, 3.3: 'Non enim respublica est in ecclesia, sed ecclesia in republica, id est in imperio Romano, quod Libanum appellat Christus in canticis canticorum, cum dicit: *veni, sponsa mea inventa, veni de Libano,* id est de imperio Romano, ubi et sacerdotia sancta sunt et pudicitia et virginitas, quae in barbaris gentibus non sunt et, si essent, tuta esse non possent. merito Paulus docet orandum esse pro regibus et potestatibus, etiamsi talis imperator esset, qui gentiliter viveret: quanto magis quod christianus' (ed. C. Ziwsa, CSEL 26.74.3-11). J.-P. Brisson, *Autonomisme et Christianisme dans l'Afrique Romaine* (Paris 1958) 235, critices Optatus for his views: '. . . la position d'Optat était plus grave en profondeur pour l'avenir du christianisme que celle des donatistes: elle liait en effet explicitement les vertus chrétiennes, ou considérées comme telles, à la domination romaine et en déclarait l'exercice impossible en dehors de cette protection.' I have no desire to defend Optatus, but would merely point to the crucial phrase *et, si essent, tuta esse non possent* as indicating the rôle of the state in providing that stability in which the Gospel can be preached.

VII

Quid Imperatori Cum Ecclesia? St. Augustine on History and Society   247

is tendency to identify the two while refusing to abide by that identification though not, as Markus observes,[54] in accordance with formal logic, is psychologically wholly justified for, as Markus says: "The sphere of politics belongs irrevocably to the realm infected with sin."[55] Everything in Augustine's career would suggest that he considered a state governed by Christians to be a "better" political entity than a pagan state; and the general tendencies in open, pluralist, secular societies hardly suggest that the abandonment of religious norms has been a particular blessing for human society. It is a very debatable question whether a society can abandon Christian, or some other religious, principles and not experience moral deterioration; but modern experiments are not encouraging. There are hints that the secular house, swept and garnished, may invite the entrance of seven devils; and certainly, insofar as that elusive quality, happiness, is capable of quantification, he would be a rash man who asserted that the average citizen of Britain or America today is happier than was his predecessor in 1900. The secular city of Harvey Cox has lost its charm, not least in the eyes of the young.

*   *   *

Markus concludes his examination of the relevance of Augustine's doctrine to the present age with a consideration of the nature of the Church. This is far more tentative than his discussion of history and society, and it is here that he would appear to depart farthest from Augustinian teaching. He recognises that it is an essential part of Augustine's ecclesiology to hold that the Church in this world is a *corpus permixtum,* where good and bad live together side by side to be separated only on the Day of Judgement. Indeed, in chapter 5 he remarks: "For Augustine the Church is always caught up in the tension and duality between *qualis nunc est* and *qualis tunc erit.*"[56] With this assertion, so far as it concerns the Church Militant, no one will disagree; but what is one to make of the following?

> The Church proclaims the inauguration of God's Kingdom by Jesus, it is not identical with it. The Church is not this Kingdom, even in its germ or chrysalis. For there is no continuous development, no growth or maturation of the Church into the Kingdom.

---

[54] p. 59.
[55] p. 173.
[56] p. 120.

The Kingdom is established by God's act alone. Man can only wait in hope, with faith and repentance.[57]

This assertion, which is supported by a quotation from Hans Küng,[58] undoubtedly expresses a view which would be held today by many Christians of all denominations; but is it that of Augustine? What is to be made of his famous assertion: *Ergo et nunc ecclesia regnum Christi et regnum caelorum?*[59] It is true that scholars are not agreed about its interpretation; but this very fact constitutes a warning against sweeping generalisations. The present writer can here only give his view that Augustine meant what he said. The Kingdom of God, like the Church, belongs both to the present and to the future. As Professor Lamirande has admirably expressed it: "Au contraire d'Eglise' qui, sans exclusivité cependant, désigne plus volontiers la société des fidèles sur la terre, le terme 'Royaume' se réfère de façon habituelle à la communauté eschatologique."[60] This is, indeed, the whole point of Augustine's case against the Millenarianists. They were looking for a rule of Christ with His saints at some historical date in the future. Augustine maintained that the battle had been won and that the reign of Christ upon earth had already begun.[61] Such a view is in complete agreement with Augustine's theology of history as analysed by Markus. In the Resurrection of Christ the course of human history had been determined; no future historical event can have any ultimate significance. *The kingdom of the world has become the Kingdom of our Lord and of His Christ and He shall reign for ever and ever.*

The key to the tension between *qualis nunc est* and *qualis tunc erit* is to be found in the concept of realized eschatology.[62] In a mysterious way

---

[57] p. 181.

[58] pp. 181,182 ('While ekklesia is something essentially of the present, something finite, basileia is something which, although it has irrupted into the present, belongs fundamentally to the future . . .').

[59] *De Civ. Dei* 20.9 (ed. Hoffmann, CSEL 40 (2) 450.6-7). See E. Lamirande, *L'Église céleste selon Saint Augustin* (Paris 1963) 105-07.

[60] Lamirande, op. cit., p. 106.

[61] *De Civ.Dei* 20.9: 'Regnant itaque cum illo etiam nunc sancti eius, aliter quidem, quam tunc regnabunt; nec tamen cum illo regnant zizania, quamvis in ecclesia cum tritico crescant. Regnant enim cum illo, qui faciunt quod ait apostolus: *Si resurrexistis cum Christo, quae sursum sunt sapite, ubi Christus est in dextera Dei sedens; quae sursum sunt quaerite, non quae super terram;* de qualibus item dicit, quod eorum conversatio sit in caelis. Postremo regnant cum illo, qui eo modo sunt in regno eius, ut sint ipsi regnum eius' (450. 10-16 Hoffmann).

[62] See the remarks of Christopher Dawson, 'St Augustine and his Age,' in *A Monument to St Augustine* (London 1930) 72,75: 'Certainly the Church is not the eternal City of God, but it is its organ and representative in the world. It is the point at which the transcendant spiritual order inserts itself into the sensible world, the one bridge by which the creature can pass from Time to Eternity. . . . Thus the Church is actually the new humanity in process of formation.'

the future, although it has not yet arrived, is already present with the faithful within the Body of Christ, and especially in the sacrament of the Eucharist, in which the whole body of Christians are united with Christ who is their Head.

> It follows that the whole of the redeemed City, that is the congregation and fellowship of the saints, is offered as a universal sacrifice to God by the great High Priest, who also offered Himself in suffering for us in the likeness of a slave, in order that we might become the body of which He is so great a head. . . . This is the sacrifice of Christians: we being many are one body in Christ. This the Church celebrates in the sacrament of the altar, so well known to the faithful. And thus the Church is made to realise that in what is there offered she is offered herself.[63]

It would be unjust to Markus to say that he entirely ignores this aspect of the Church's life. He does indeed refer to the "sacramental worship [of the Church] wherein the Christian community becomes an anticipatory sign of the fully human community of love whose coming we are required to await in hope;"[64] yet one is aware that this definition lacks something—Augustine's sense of the union of all Christians, living and departed, in the Christian sacrifice, poignantly expressed in Monica's request that she should be remembered at the Lord's altar, and affirmed by her son in his exegesis of the text *They reigned with Christ a thousand years:*

> . . . that is to say, the souls of the martyrs which have not yet rejoined their bodies. The souls of the pious dead are not separated from the Church, which is even now the Kingdom of Christ. Otherwise no memorial of them would be made at the altar of God in the communion of the Body of Christ.[65]

In the face of such language one wonders how it is that so learned and sensitive a scholar can offer such an attenuated interpretation of Au-

---

[63] *De Civ.Dei* 10.6: '. . . profecto efficitur, ut tota ipsa redempta civitas, hoc est congregatio societasque sanctorum, universale sacrificium offeratur Deo per sacerdotem magnum, qui etiam se ipsum obtulit in passione pro nobis, ut tanti capitis corpus essemus, secundum formam servi. . . . Hoc est sacrificum Christianorum: *multi unum corpus in Christo.* Quod etiam sacramento altaris fidelibus noto frequentat ecclesia, ubi ei demonstratur, quod in ea re, quam offert, ipsa offeratur' (456.6-10, 26-30 Hoffmann). Tr. Wand.

[64] p. 185.

[65] Ibid. 20.9: 'Neque enim piorum animae mortuorum separantur ab ecclesia, quae nunc etiam est regnum Christi. Alioquin nec ad altare Dei fieret eorum memoria in communicatione corporis Christi' (451.13-16 Hoffmann). Tr. Wand.

gustine's doctrine of the Church.[66] It is always presumptuous to attempt to guess what has influenced an author's mind; but I cannot help suspecting that Markus has been affected, consciously or unconsciously, by that recoil from triumphalism which is so characteristic of ecumenically-minded Roman Catholics today. With the spirit behind this recoil one can have nothing but sympathy; it is right and proper that the Church Militant should regard herself as the servant of the servants of God and of all men, made as they are in God's image. There is, however, a danger that the recognition of the duty of service can lead to forgetfulness of the supernatural glory which the Church enjoys by participation in Christ, a glory which is independent of worldly circumstances. Much of the malaise which afflicts Western Christendom today can be ascribed to the loss of any sense of the supernatural; to study the Fathers is to be made to take seriously the claims of the unseen world.

The Church lives in two worlds: in the present age (*in hoc temporum cursu*) and in the age to come (*in illa stabilitate sedis aeternae, quam nunc expectat per patientiam*).[67] No ecclesiology which neglects either of these worlds can be called satisfactory, and it is precisely his consciousness of the tension between them which makes Augustine's ecclesiology so fruitful.

> Our meditation in this present life should be in the praise of God; for the eternal exultation of our life hereafter will be the praise of God; and none can become fit for the future life, who has not practiced himself for it now.[68]

* * *

The criticisms of the concluding chapter of *Saeculum* here expressed are not to be regarded as applying to the work as a whole. On the contrary it is an admirable piece of scholarship, displaying all the erudition and perceptive sensibility which we have come to expect from the author and reminding us afresh of the almost inexhaustible opportunities for in-

---

[66] It is to be noted that the author specifically declares (p. 156) that 'neither has Augustine's immensely rich ecclesiological thought been examined in this book nor have I sought to tap its resources in this epilogue in order to point to anything one might properly call an "ecclesiology."' But he goes on to say that he keeps 'fairly narrowly to the eschatological perspective on ecclesiology,' which hardly lends itself to the devalued estimate of the Church which he presents on his final pages.

[67] *De Civ.Dei* 1.1 (3.1-3 Hoffmann).

[68] *Enarr.in Ps.*148.1: 'Meditatio praesentis vitae nostrae in laude Dei esse debet: quia exsultatio sempiterna futurae nostrae vitae, laus Dei erit; et nemo potest idoneus fieri futurae vitae, qui non se ad illam modo exercuerit' (edd. Dekkers & Fraipont, *CC* 40.2165.1-4).

vestigation and reappraisal of the thought of the great theologian with which it deals. Moreover, in an age when "relevance" is constantly demanded of works in the divine as well as liberal studies, Markus' book reveals the astonishingly contemporary character of one aspect of Augustine's doctrine. It is to be hoped that it will be read, not only by theologians and historians, but by students of political theory and by all who are interested in the metaphysical foundations of human society.

Durham University
England

VIII

Les origines africaines de la doctrine augustinienne sur la chute et le péché originel

Personne ne songera à nier l'importance de saint Augustin dans la formulation de la doctrine catholique sur la grâce, la prédestination et le péché originel. Pour quelques-uns, c'est là sa contribution principale à la théologie: on pense à un admirateur comme Baius, qui se vante d'avoir lu les oeuvres augustiniennes entières neuf fois, mais les écrits sur la grâce soixante-dix fois, ou à Luther, qui déclara: *Augustinus ex contentione cum Pelagianis magnus est factus et fidelis gratiae assertor.* Pour Baius et Luther, il y a là de quoi se féliciter.

Il y a d'autres qui la considèrent une raison pour la dénonciation. C'était l'avis du savant anglais Thomas Allin, dans un livre posthume qui jouait une certaine renommée dans le temps, mais qu'on ne lit que rarement aujourd'hui, même en Angleterre. Dans son livre, Allin parle d'Augustin comme "le premier dans l'Église de Dieu qui nia que le Christ fût mort pour tous les hommes, qui nia le libre arbitre, qui encouragea le persécuteur par tous les moyens de la sophisterie, qui forgea une théologie si cruelle, si choquante, qu'à la fin l' auteur même reste, en effet, ébahi mais impassible, regardant l'édifice achevé"[1].

Plus récemment, le docteur Jacques-François Thomas, bien que dans un langage beaucoup plus moderé, a soutenu une thèse assez proche de celle d' Allin[2].

Néanmoins, tout en reconnaissant l'importance du rôle de saint Augustin dans l'histoire de la doctrine du péché originel et les nombreuses conséquences —dont quelques-unes peu heureuses— qui en ont découlé, il faut se rappeler que la question de la pensée augustinienne est plus compliquée qu'on ne le croit souvent. Augustin n'est pas seulement le Docteur de la Grâce; son

---

[1] ALLIN: *The Augustinian Revolution in Theology*, Londres 1911, p. 128: "...Augustine who first in the Church of God denied Christ's death for all men, who denied free will, who urged on the persecutor by every art of sophistry, who forged a theology so cruel, so shocking, that he himself at length virtually stands aghast, but unmoved, as he surveys the completed fabric".

[2] THOMAS, J.-F.: *Saint Augustin s'est-il trompé? Essai sur la prédestination*, Paris 1959.

98

génie a exploré toute l'entendue de la théologie chrétienne et comprend certaines tendances que pourrait considérer le regard superficiel étrangères à la tendance générale de sa pensée. Le Dr. Thomas s'adresse à la thèse bien connue de Jules Gross sur la doctrine de la déification chez les pères grecs[3], qu'il qualifie de:

> "Contribution historique à la doctrine de la grâce… où l'auteur dès l'Introduction peut écrire que si la conception paulinienne de la conversion et de la guérison du pécheur a été développée surtout par saint Augustin et les latins, la conception Johannique de l'adoption et de l'élévation de l'homme par son Créateur a été exploitée avec une enthousiaste prédilection par les Pères grecs, [et] nous montre que ceux-ci supposaient bien un Dieu plus généreux, plus attaché à la créature humaine malgré sa désobéissance, et même plus délicat à son égard en lui laissant mieux le libre-arbitre avec la grâce que le Dieu peut-être un peu dur, d'une apparence pas toujours équitable, à mon gout, que risque de nous donner un raisonnement logique, trop anthropomorphique pour un mystère, très conséquent aux textes de saint Paul pris à la lettre et plus digne de la sévérité du droit romain que de la pitié et de la charité de notre Rédempteur"[4].

Faut-il donc confronter la doctrine orientale de la déification et la doctrine augustinienne de la rédemption? Dans un article magistral le P. Capánaga a examiné cette supposition courante et a conclu que "en la soteriología agustiniana la deificación tiene una importancia considerable", et qu'il n'y a aucune opposition substantielle entre la doctrine d'Augustin et celle des Pères grecs[5]. Bien que la doctrine augustinienne de la prédestination garde toute sa rigueur, il reste que les contrastes simples avec, par exemple, la théologie grecque, sont faux et trompeurs. Il faut considérer la pensée augustinienne dans sa totalité, si on veut arriver à des conclusions satisfaisantes.

D'ailleurs, quand on parle de l'originalité de la pensée de saint Augustin, il importe de se faire une idée précise du sens de ce mot. Augustin fut un grand génie: cela ne vaut guère qu'on le dise. Mais si on veut suggérer qu'il fut un penseur qui introduisît à lui seul une doctrine nouvelle dans l'Église occidentale et l'imposât par la force de sa personnalité, c'est beaucoup dire, et l'affirmation doit être très soigneusement examinée. De temps en temps dans l'histoire, on voit surgir un penseur qui introduit quelque chose de nouveau

---

[3] Gross, J.: *La divinisation du chrétien d'après les Pères grecs*, Paris 1938.
[4] Thomas, J.-F.: *o. c.*, pp. 79, 80.
[5] Capánaga, Victorino: *La deificación en la soteriología agustiniana*, en *Augustinus Magister*, Paris 1954, II p. 754.

dans la pensée humaine; mais il s'agit pour la plupart de philosophes ou de scientifiques plutôt que de théologiens.

En vérité, même dans la science, prétendre à une originalité absolue est chose asséez rare et quelque peu difficile à soutenir — on pourrait citer le cas de Charles Darwin et la théorie du transformisme. Mais, dans les cas d'un scientifique, ses principes même lui octroient la possibilité de formuler une théorie absolument nouvelle. Un théologien, de l'autre côté, est lié par la tradition, par la *regula fidei*, à laquelle il doit soumettre toutes ses théories. Or, il est clair que pour Augustin, comme pour la plupart des chrétiens de son époque, la notion de la primauté de la tradition, de la *paradosis*, est souveraine — il ne voulait tenir une autre doctrina que celle des Pères.

Cette consideration était au fond de toute la dispute avec Julien d'Eclane. Julien accusa Augustin d'être resté manichéen en doctrine, même comme évêque catholique. Augustin, indigné, rejette l'accusation. "Vous m'appelez manichéen; je vous montrerai *quos et quales viros et quantos fidei catholicae defensores tam exsecrabili criminatione appetere audeas*"[6]. On peut prétendre qu'Augustin, même en voulant défendre la foi catholique, a formulé une doctrine nouvelle, sans le savoir. Cela est possible; les événements de la controverse pélagienne montrent qu'il y avaient des gens, qui n'avaient aucune sympathie avec Pélage, mais qui trouvaient pourtant certaine doctrines défendues par Augustin nouvelles et inouïes. Il est possibles d'en tirer la preuve que la doctrine qu'on appelle aujourd'hui l'Augustinisme n'était pas la foi de l'Église du vivant d'Augustin; mais cela n'est pas, en soi, une preuve qu'Augustin l'ait inventée. Nous reviendrons bientôt à cette question.

Encore une considération qu'il ne faut pas négliger: le rôle de l'épiscopat africain dans la controverse pélagienne et, en effet, dans tous les débats doc-trinaux du cinquième siècle. S'il y a un trait particulier qui caractérisait les évêques de l'Afrique du Nord pendant toute l'histoire orageuse de l'Église africaine, c'est sa confiance dans sa propre rectitude. Les Donatistes ne repré-sentaient qu'un développement de cette opinion: "Nous avons raison et tout le reste du monde a tort". Les Catholiques étaient plus modérés. Leur situation même les contraignit à avouer le principe: *Securus iudicat orbis terrarum,* mais ils avaient le sentiment très fort de leurs droits et de leur exactitude théologi-que; c'est ce qu'allaient découvrir le pape Zosime et quelquesuns parmi ses successeurs.

Dans ces circonstances, on peut bien concevoir qu'on n'aurait pas permis à Augustin lui-même, malgré tout son éclat intellectuel, de se faire établis comme dictateur doctrinal par ses collègues plus bornés. Naturellement, ils l'estimaient comme le grand porte-parole de la théologie africaine, mais rien ne nous permet

---

[6] *C. Iul.* I 3, 5. PL 44, 643.

de supposer qu'ils auraient cru nécessaire de toujours céder à ses opinions. Au contraire, nous savons, d'Augustin lui-même, que dans une question politique importante, c'est à dire la coercition des Donatistes, un grand nombre de ses collègues episcopaux n'hésitèrent pas à rejeter ses vues et que plus tard il arriva, lui-même, à admettre qu'ils en avaient eu raison[7]. On peut bien croire que des hommes qui tenaient si fermement à leurs opinions sur la question de la répression du Donatisme, n'auraient pas été moins fermes sur les doctrines de la foi.

De plus, si on examine le cours de la controverse pélagienne, il est clair que saint Augustin n'est pas l'initiateur. La première attaque sur le Pélagianisme en Afrique fut déclenché par le diacre milanais Paulin, le biographe de saint Ambroise[8], à une date incertaine, vers la fin de 411[9]. Or, Augustin nous apprend qu'il n'avait pas assisté au concile de Carthage qui condamna Céleste[10], et nous n'avons aucune preuve certaine qu'il en avait lu les Actes avant d'écrire le De peccatorum meritis[11]. Ces Actes, conservés en partie par Augustin dans le De peccato originali, ont pour cette raison une grande importance comme témoignage de la doctrine ecclésiastique africaine sur la chute et le péché originel.

Marius Mercator et Augustin nous apprennent qu'un libellus fut présenté contre Céleste lequel renfermait les six thèses suivantes qui cherchait à résumer sa doctrine (selon l'ordre de Marius Mercator):

1) *Adam mortalem factum, qui sive peccaret, sive non peccaret, moriturus fuisset;*

2) *peccatum Adae ipsum solum laesit et non genus humanum;*

3) *parvuli, qui nascuntur, in eo statu sunt in quo fuit Adam ante praevaricationem;*

4) *neque per mortem, vel praevaricationem Adae, omne genus hominum moritur, neque per resurrectionem Christi omne hominum genus resurgit;*

5) *Lex sic mittit ad regnum caelorum, quomodo et Evangelium;*

6) *et ante adventum Domini fuerunt homines impeccabiles, id est, sine peccato.*

---

[7] AUG.: *Ep.* 93, 5, 17 CSEL 34 (2), 461-62.

[8] Sur Paulin, cf. PAREDI, Angelo: *Paulinus of Milan*, en *Sacris Erudiri* 14, 1963, pp. 206-30.

[9] Cf. KOOPMANS, J. H.: *Augustine's first contact with Pelagius and the dating of the condemnation of Caelestius at Carthage*, en *Vigiliae Christianae* 8, 1954, pp. 149-63, compte rendu par F. Refoulé, *Datation du premier concile de Carthage contre les Pélagiens et du "Libellus fidei" de Rufin*, en *Revue des études augustiniennes* 9, 1963, pp. 41-49.

[10] *Retract.* II 33, 60: "Caelestius vero discipulus eius iam propter tales assertiones apud Carthaginem in episcopali iudicio, ubi ego non interfui, excommunicationem meruerat", CSEL 36, 171.

[11] Cf. REFOULÉ: art. cit., p. 43.

On peut dire que toutes les questions qui fuerent débattées plus tard dans la controverse pélagienne, sont contenues dans ces six thèses, ou explicitement ou par implication, mais il semble (au moins dans cette partie du procès-verbale conservée par Augustin) qu'on y accentuât la question de l'effet du péché d' Adam sur ses descendants. Céleste voulait la traiter comme une matière d' opinion, comme un *theologoumenon*. Il avait entendu, dit-il, des vues diverses exprimées par les prêtres de l'Église catholique. Le diacre Paulin, qui avait quelque-chose de l'avocat dans son tempérament, lui démanda immédiatement leurs noms. Céleste nomma un certain Rufin, *qui habitait à Rome chez le saint Pammaque.*

Ce Rufin est peut-être le véritable fondateur du Pélagianisme, comme nous le verrons bientôt. Palin démanda encore des noms, mais Céleste réfusa de répondre, et l'évêque de Carthage, Aurélius, commanda de passer outre, en demandant à Céleste s'il avait jamais enseigné, comme l'accusait Paulin, que les enfants nouveaux-nés fussent dans l'état d'Adam avant la Chute, *ante transgressionem*. Céleste répondit en demandant à savoir le sens des mots *ante transgressionem*, et le dialogue suivant eut lieu:

> "Aurelius episcopus dixit: rogo, quid collegerim ego ex huius obiectione, dico, Adam constitutus in paradiso quod ante dicatur inexterminabilis factus, postea per transgressionem praecepti factus sit corruptibilis. hoc dicis, frater Pauline?
>
> Paulinus diaconus dixit: hoc, domine.
>
> Aurelius episcopus dixit: status certe infantum hodie baptizandorum utrum talis sit, qualis fuit ante transgressionem Adae, an certe de eadem origine peccati, de qua nascitur, transgressionis culpam trahat, hoc vult diaconus Paulinus audire.
>
> Paulinus diaconus dixit: utrum docuit hoc an non neget?
>
> Caelestius dixit: iam de traduce peccati dixi, quia intra Catholicos constitutos plures audivi destruere necnon et alios astruere, licet quaestionis res sit ista, non haeresis. Infantes semper dixi egere baptismo ac debere baptizari. Quid quaerit alius?"[12].

Il est clair que la doctrine énoncée par Aurélius de Carthage au commencement même de la controverse pélagienne est, en effet, la doctrine dite augustinienne du péché originel, et que la même doctrine est maintenue par Paulin de Milan. On ne doit pas pour autant affirmer que nous avons là une démonstration irréfutable que les enseignements de Carthage et Milan sur ce sujet étaient à cette époque absolument identiques —il est possible que Paulin

---

[12] *De pecc. orig.* IV 3 *CSEL* 42, 169.

fût influencé par son séjour en Afrique— mais il reste significatif que le premier adversaire du Pélagianisme en Afrique était un milanais, comme plus tard les dénonciateurs de Pélage même en Palestine étaient un prêtre espagnol, Orose, et deux anciens évêques provençaux, Héros d'Arles et Lazare d'Aix. Orose, il est vrai, était un disciple d'Augustin; mais Héros et Lazare étaient responsables d'eux-mêmes.

Si les six thèses du concile de Carthage de 411 constituent un bon résumé du Pélagianisme naissant, les premiers neuf[13] canons de celui de 418 représentent la réponse finale des Africains au système développé. Les premier et second canons de 418 ne sont, en effet, que les trois premières thèses de 411 refondues[14]. Le contenu de la quatrième thèse peut avoir été réfléchi dans le second canon, tandis que les cinquième et sixième thèses sont remplacées par les canons 3-9. Ces derniers sept canons reflètent, sans doute, les questions soulevées dans la lutte avec Pélage. Ainsi le canon 3, s'il est authentique, s'occupe du troisième lieu entre le ciel et l'enfer pour les enfants morts sans baptême —question débattue de très bonne heure dans les oeuvres anti-pélagiennes d'Augustin[15], tandis que les canons 4-9 semblent être dirigés contre les sentiments attri-

---

[13] Nous supposons la validité du troisième canon du concile de Carthage de 418 (CCEA N.º 109).

Les thèses de 411	Les canons de 418
1 Adam mortalem factum qui, sive peccaret, sive non peccaret, moriturus fuisset.	1 Ut quicumque dixerit, Adam primum hominem mortalem factum, ita ut, sive peccaret, sive non peccaret, moreretur in corpore, hoc est, de corpore exiret, non peccati merito, sed necessitate naturae, A. S.
	2 Item placuit, ut quicumque parvulos recentes ab uteris matrum baptizandos negat, aut dicit in remissionem peccatorum eos baptizari, sed nihil ex Adam trahere originalis peccati, quod lavacrum regenerationis expietur, unde sit consequens ut in eis forma Baptismatis in remissionem peccatorum non vera, sed falsa intelligatur, A. S. Quoniam non aliter intelligendum est, quod ait Apostolus, *per unum hominem peccatum intravit in mundum, et per peccatum mors, et ita in omnes homines pertransiit, in quo omnes peccaverunt*, nisi quemadmodum Ecclesia catholica ubique diffusa semper intellexit. Propter hanc etiam regulam fidei etiam parvuli, qui nihil peccatorum in semetipsis adhuc committere potuerunt, ideo in remissionem peccatorum veraciter baptizantur, ut in eis regeneratione mundetur, quod generatione traxerunt.
2 Quoniam peccatum Adae ipsum solum laesit et non genus humanum.	
4 Quoniam neque per mortem vel praevaricationem Adae omne genus hominum moritur, neque per resurrectionem Christi omne hominum genus resurgit.	
3 Quoniam parvuli qui nascuntur in eo statu sunt in quo fuit Adam ante praevaricationem.	

[14] Les thèses de 411

[15] Cf. De pec. mer. et rem. I 20, 26 CSEL 60, 25; Sermo 294, 2, 2 3, 3 PL 38, 1336-1337.

bués à Pélage au concile de Diospolis ou exprimés dans la littérature soulevée par cette affaire[16]. Il est possible que la formulation de ces sept derniers canons était l'oeuvre d'Augustin, et il était certainement la grande autorité théologique qui devait les critiquer et retoucher (le canon 5, comme l'a noté Georges de Plinval, est une réfutation de la conception pélagienne de la Grâce ou, peut-être, de ce qu'Augustin regardait comme la conception pélagienne de la Grâce)[17]. Il est pourtant clair que les premiers deux canons de 418 sont un sommaire satisfaisant des quatre premières thèses de 411[18].

La doctrine africaine sur la Chute et le péché originel, déjà énoncée avant qu'Augustin ne prît part à la controverse, restait inaltérée jusqu'aux décisions de 418.

C'est dans ce contexte qu'il faut considérer le rôle de saint Augustin dans les premiers étages de la controverse pélagienne. On peut le regarder trop facilement comme le grand adversaire de Pélage dès le moment où l'hérésiarque publia son premier livre; mais c'est une image trompeuse. Augustin ne s'engagea dans l'affaire pélagienne que lentement et avec répugnance, quoique, une fois engagé, il se battit jusqu'au bout. Il ne faut pas attribuer son âpreté théologique croissante seulement à l'influence de sa théologie de la Grâce et de la prédestination, quoique ces considérations aient eu un rôle à jouer.

Dans toutes ses grandes controverses, avec les Manichéens et les Donatistes, aussi bien qu'avec les Pélagiens, Augustin montre ce durcissement progressif. Il commence par les invitations à des pourparlers amicaux; il finit avec amertume, très bien symbolisée sans cette remarque trop fameuse faite à Gaudence, évêque donatiste de Thamugadi, qu'il vaudrait mieux que périssent quelques fanatiques suicidomanes plutôt qu'avec eux brûllent à jamais en enfer les grandes multitudes qu'ils décevoient[19].

La controverse pélagienne suivit le même cours; mais il reste néanmoins vrai qu'au commencement Augustin n'avait aucune envie de s'embrouiller dans l'affaire. Pour longtemps il essayait d'éviter une confrontation directe avec Pélage. Quand celui-ci arriva en Afrique aux environs de mai 411, Augustin était absent d'Hippone et n'eut pas l'occasion de lui parler. Un peu plus tard, à la conférence de Carthage il le vit une fois ou deux, mais Augustin était vivement préoccupé des discussions avec les Donatistes, et les deux hommes ne

---

[16] Cf. la discussion par PLINVAL, G. de: *Pélage: ses écrits, sa vie et sa réforme*, Lausanne 1943, pp. 324-326.

[17] *Ibid.* p. 325 *n* 3.

[18] Les 5e et 6e thèses de 411 n'étaient pas répétés en 418. Il est possible qu'on considérait la 5me, qui niait que la Loi aussi bien que l'Évangile n'admet au royaume des cieux contenue dans le canon 4, et que les sens de la 6e thèse était mieux exprimé par les canons 6-9.

[19] *C. Gaud.* I 22, 25: "Tolerabilius enim longe pauciores pertinacissimi vestri suis praecipitiis vel submersionibus vel ignibus pereunt, quam innumerabiles populi illis eorum salutem impedientibus incendio cum illis aeterni ignis ardebunt", *CSEL* 53, 224.

se parlerent pas entre'eux. Ce fut dommage, car l'évèque d'Hippone avait déjà entendu un bruit selon lequel Pélage avait conçu des idées nouvelles sur la Grâce quoique, pendant son séjour à Hippone, il n'avait pas laissé entendre aucun bruit d'hétérodoxie, et Augustin voulait savoir la vérité sur ces faits[20].

Cependant, il paraît qu'à cette epoque environ, ou un peu plus tard[21], Augustin, en visitant Carthage, entendit dire à quelques-uns que ce que les enfants reçoivent au baptême n'était pas la rémission des péchés mais la sanctification dans Jésus-Christ. La nouveauté de cette doctrine le surprit, mais Augustin n'avait pas le temps de la réfuter et ne s'en sentait aucun goût non plus, et, d'ailleurs, les gens qui parlaient ainsi n'avaient pas une autorité qui vaille être contesté. Pour cette raison, dit Augustin, il oublia bientôt l'épisode[22].

Cela paraît assex curieux, vu la réputation quelque peu douteuse qui avait précédé Pélage lors de son arrivée en Afrique; et, en tout cas, la dissémination assez rapide du Pélagianisme en Afrique aux environs de Carthage ne permit pas à Augustin de rester longtemps dans cet état d'oubli, et il commença bientôt à dénoncer les doctrines pélagiennes caractéristiques, sans en nommer les auteurs[23]. Déjà à cette période, Augustin voulait fonder sa cause sur la tradition de l'Église. "Que personne ne nous présente des doctrines différentes", s'écria-t-il dans son sermon 176 —parmi les premiers, semble-t-il, de la controverse pélagienne. "L'Église a toujours cru cela, elle l'a toujours enseigné; elle l'a reçu de la foi des anciens et elle le gardera jusqu'à la fin"[24].

Mais, à ce moment-là, Augustin n'écrivit rien, et il lui fallut la demande du Comte Marcellin pour le faire écrire les premiers deux livres du *De peccatorum meritis et remissione*[25]. Ce n'est qu'après avoir écrit ces deux livres qu'Augustin lit le commentaire de Pélage sur *l'Epître aux Romains*, qui le décida à y ajouter un troisième livre, pour réfuter les doctrines pernicieuses qu'il y avait découvertes. Mais Augustin avait garde de nommer Pélage sauf avec

---

[20] *De gest. Pel.* 22, 45 CSEL 42, 100.

[21] REFOULÉ, F.: "*Datation du premier concile de Carthage*", p. 43, se soutenant sur les mots *ante parvum tempus* de *De pec. mer. et rem.* III 6, 12 suggère que l'occasion était le séjour d'Augustin à Carthage, où il prêcha sur le Psaume 72 (AUG. *Ep.* 140, 5, 13); mais cette théorie donne du poids à la phrase *ante parvum tempus*, et il semble plus prudent de ne pas préciser la date, qui tombe dans la période mai-septembre 411.

[22] *De pec. mer. et rem.* III 6, 12: "Nam ante parvum tempus a quibusdam transitorie conloquentibus cursim mihi aures perstrictae sunt, cum illic apud Carthaginem essemus, "non ideo parvulos baptizari, ut remissionem accipiant peccatorum, sed ut sanctificentur in Christ". Qua novitate permotus et quia opportunum non fuit, ut contra aliquid dicerem, et non tales homines erant, de quorum essem auctoritate sollicitus, facile hoc in transactis atque abolitis habui", CSEL 60, 139.

[23] *Retract.* II 33 59: "Venit etiam necessitas, quae me cogeret adversus novam pelagianam heresem scribere, contra quam, cum opus erat, non scriptis, sed sermonibus et conlocutionibus agebamus, ut quisque nostrum poterat aut debebat", CSEL 36, 170.

[24] *Sermo* 176, 2, 2 PL 38, 950.

[25] *De gest. Pel.* 11, 25 CSEL 42, 78, 79.

des éloges, et dans l'ouvre complète, il pensait qu'il fallait taire les noms des individus, espérant qu'il serait plus facile de les corriger[26].

En effet, dans sa première oeuvre antipélagienne, la tactique d'Augustin fut essentiellement défensive. Cela peut facilement s'expliquer. Au commencement de la lutte pélagienne, Augustin s'occupait du Donatisme. Rien ne nous permet de supposer qu'il eût, à cette époque, un grand désir de se mêler à une controverse nouvelle, pendant que l'amertume soulevée par le Donatisme restait à guérir. Aussi —c'est lui-ême qui le dit— tout ce qu'il savait de Pélage à cette période était à l'avantage de ce dernier. "Il y a quelques jours", dit-il dans le troisième livre du *De peccatorum meritis*, "j'ai lu quéques écrits de Pélage. homme saint, dit-on, et bien avancé dans le christianisme"[27]. Donc, peut-être Pélage enregistra-t-il ces doctrines nouvelles, non comme les siennes, mais en espérant qu'on les réfuterait?[28]. Que ces doctrines fussent nouvelles, à l'avis d'Augustin, était indisputable. Pélage avait exprimé un argument contre la preuve de la doctrine de la transmission du péché originel par l'*Epître aux Romains* v. 12, et Augustin dit franchement qu'il n'avait pas prévu cette argumentation dans ses premiers écrits, parce qu'il n'aurait jamais cru que les chrétiens eussent des pensées pareilles[29].

Les recherches récentes semblent confirmer la déclaration d'Augustin. Deux articles importants ont été consacrés à ce thème par le professeur Altaner et le P. Refoulé. Ces auteurs arrivent à des conclusions très différentes, mais le Père Refoulé, tout en disputant la conclusion du professeur Altaner, bâtit sa théorie sur l'argumentation de son prédécesseur pour en tirer une autre très persuasive sur les origines du Pélagianisme.

L'étude du professeur Altaner[30] essaye de démontrer que le livre *De fide*, publié par Sirmond en 1650 et qui tient lieu parmi les oeuvres apocryphes de Rufin d'Aquilée, a été en vérité écrit par un certain Rufin, un prêtre de Palestine, qui peut être identifié avec le Rufin *natione Syrus* lequel, selon Marius Mercator, était le premier semeur du Pélagianisme à Rome, et qui corrompit Pélage et en fit le vulgarisateur de ses vues.

---

[26] *Retract.* II 33, 59: "In his autem libris tacenda [*al.* tangenda] adhuc arbitratus sum nomina eorum sic eos facilius posse corrigi sperans, immo etiam in tertio libro, quae est epistula, sed in libris habita propter duos, quibus eam connectandam putavi, Pelagii ipsius nomen non sine aliqua laude posui, quia vita eius a multis praedicabatur, et eius illa redargui, quae in suis scriptis non ex persona sua posuit, sed quid ab aliis diceretur exposuit, quae tamen postea iam haereticus pertinacissima animositate defendit", *CSEL* 36, 171.

[27] *De pec. mer. et rem.* III 1, 1: "Verum post paucissimos dies legi Pelagii quaedam scripta, sancti viri, ut audio, et non parvo provectu Christiani, quae in Pauli apostoli epistolas expositiones brevissimas continerent", *CSEL* 60, 129.

[28] *Ibid.* III 3, 5 *CSEL* 60, 131, 132.

[29] *Ibid.* III 1, 1.

[30] ALTANER, Berthold: *Der "Liber de fide" ein Werk des Pelagianers Rufinus des Syrers*, en *Theologische Quartelschrift* 130, 1950, pp. 432-49.

Cette identification est encore plus vraisemblable, parce que tout le ton du livre est pélagien, comme le remarquent deux notes marginales dans un des manuscrits où se trouve l'oeuvre de Rufin. "Hic liber qui attitulatur Rufini, non te seducat, pie lector, quia Pelagianus est et blasphemiis Pelagianorum plenus…". "Hic liber non Rufini sed Pelagii haeretici, in quo contra fidem catholicam multae continentur blasphemiae"[31].

Quelle est la date de cette oeuvre du fondateur du Pélagianisme? Sirmond pense que Rufin l'écrivit en 399 environ. Jean Garnier crut que le *De fide* fut écrit en Italie avant 410. Le professeur Altaner réjette ces dates en soutenant que, si la datation de cette oeuvre fût vraiment si ancienne, il serait impossible qu'Augustin ne l'eût pas lue et dénoncée. Pour Altaner, la preuve de sa thèse se trouve dans le c. 41 du *De fide,* où la doctrine de la damnation des enfants non-baptisés est attaquée. Altaner considère que personne avant Augustin n'avait tenu cette doctrine dont Augustin (à son avis) est l'auteur. Mais deux références à cette doctrine se trouvent dans le *De peccatorum meritis* (I, 16, 21; I 28, 55) et une dans le sermon 294, 3, prêché le 27 juin 413. Donc, le c. 41 du *De Fide* doit réprésenter une réponse au *theologoumenon* augustinien de la damnation des enfants non-baptisés, et l'oeuvre doit être datée entre 413 et 428[32].

Voici la théorie du professeur Altaner. Elle tourne sur les suppositions que le *De fide* est une réponse au *De peccatorum meritis,* et que la doctrine de la damnation des enfants non-baptisés est un *theologoumenon* inventé par Augustin. Par contre le Père Refoulé, après un confrontation soigneuse des trente-quatre premiers chapitres du premier livre du *De peccatorum meritis* avec le *De fide* de Rufin, a fourni des preuves convaincantes pour considérer la première oeuvre anti-pélagienne d'Augustin comme une réponse à Rufin, et non le contraire[33].

"Le fait que le *libellus* de Rufin, écrit-il, loin d'être une réponse à Augustin, est antérieur au *De peccatorum meritis* et constitue même une des sources de cet ouvrage, nous oblige à penser que la conception dite augustinienne du péché originel et du sort des petits enfants morts sans baptême constituait un *theologoumenon,* non seulement en Afrique, mais aussi en Italie (puisque Rufin dut écrire son traité à Rome, où il résida de 399 jusqu'à au moins 410) avant même les débuts de la crise pélagienne en 411. En ce cas, ne devons-nous

---

[31] *Ibid.* p. 434.
[32] *Ibid.* pp. 447-49.
[33] REFOULÉ: art. cit., pp. 44-49. Refoulé note (p. 47) que le P. de Blic releva en 1927 qu'Augustin avait cité le *De fide* dans le *De pec. mer. et rem.* I 18, 23, mais il n' avait pas cherché systématiquement à retrouver les traces de cet écrit dans les autres chapitres.

pas conclure qu'Augustin fut plus traditionel et moins innovateur que le professeur Altaner le présumait?"[34].

Les arguments de Refoulé s'accordent assez bien avec la description que donne Augustin de son intervention dans la controverse. Il fut étonné, dit-il, la première fois qu'il entendit exprimer la théorie de la sanctification des enfants par le baptême, plutôt que leur purification, parce qu'elle était nouvelle, mais il ne l'avait pas jugée d'une importance suffisante pour le contredire sur-le-champ. Il lui fallut la demande du comte Marcellin pour se mettre à écrire. A ce temps là il n'avait pas lu le commentaire de Pélage sur l'*Epitre aux Romains*, lecture qu'il n'entreprit qu'après avoir fini les deux premiers livres du *De peccatorum meritis*.

Mais il restait circonspect, se gardant d'attribuer à Pélage lui-même les vues qui se trouvaient dans le commentaire, et il parle toujours du théologien britannique avec respect. Augustin, encore préoccupé du schisme donatiste, voulait éviter, si possible, une controverse littéraire nouvelle.

Qu'est ce qui changea, chez Augustin, cette position de restreinte à celle de lutte à outrance? L'explication la plus probable serait la conduite de Pélage au concile de Diospolis. Augustin avait lu dans l'intervalle le *De natura* de Pélage, et dans sa réponse à Timase et Jacques, il continua à parler de l'auteur avec respect, sans en mentionner le nom[35]; mais la lecture lui avait montré le danger croissant du Pélagianisme, et il dut été déconcerté à trouver ses propres mots du *De libero arbitrio* utilisés par Pélage à soutenir sa propre doctrine[36]. Alors arriva le livre intitulé les *Definitiones*, ouvrage supposé de Céleste[37], qui montra une grande habilité dialectique. Il était clair que le Pélagianisme grandissait et avait des propagandistes copables.

D'ailleurs, Augustin, effrayé, dut avoir observé que les Pélagiens avaient pu citer ses peuvres comme témoignage de la vérité de leur doctrine. Alors, au point où en étaient les choses, Augustin reçut les nouvelles de la disculpation de Pélage à Diospolis, et de l'usage peu scrupuleux qu'il avait fait pour impressioner les juges de la lettre qu'Augustin lui avait autrefois envoyée[38]. Augustin lit, aussi, une lettre dirigée à une certaine veuve, dont le nom, d'après Marius Mercator, était Livania. A Diospolis on avait accusé Pélage d'en être l'auteur —une accusation qu'il nia. Augustin entendit dire à quelques frères de bonne

---

[34] *Ibid.* p. 49.
[35] *De nat. et grat.* 1, 1: "...et vidi hominem zelo ardentissimo accensum adversus eos, qui cum in suis peccatis humanam voluntatem debeant accusare, naturam potius accusantes hominem per illam se excusare conantur"; *ibid.* 7, 7 CSEL 60, 233, 236-37. Cf. *De gest. Pel.* 23, 47 CSEL 42, 101.
[36] *Ibid.* 67, 80 CSEL 60, 293-94.
[37] *De perf. iust. hom.* 1, 1 CSEL 42, 3.
[38] *De gest. Pel.* 26, 51-28, 52 CSEL 42, 104-106.

foi que Pélage était en vérité l'auteur de cette lettre, dont ils produisirent une copie[39].

Sur la foi de cette copie, Augustin crut que Pélage avait dû mentir au concile, à moins qu'on ne lui attribuât la paternité de la lettre par erreur, chose qui était autrefois advenu à Augustin lui-même. Il décida d'accorda à Pélage le bénéfice du doute au sujet de cette lettre; mais, comme l'a bien dit Georges de Plinval, "ce n'était que par condescendance qu'il a consenti à la laisser hors du débat"[40]. Mais, en effet, après le concile de Diospolis, Augustin décida de ne pas se mettre sa confiance en Pélage à l'avenir[41]. Dès ce moment il lutta contre le contre le Pélagianisme de toutes ses forces. Toujours courtois, il ne se laissa jamais défléchir de la voie étroite de l'orthodoxie, dans le sens qu'il donnait au mot. Il n'avait pas voulu ce combat mais, une fois engagé, il était implacable.

Bientôt les Pélagiens accusèrent Augustin d'innovation —les Catholiques, selon eux, étaient les nouveaux Manichéens. L'évêque d'Hippone ne cessa de rejeter cette imputation. Il prétendit marcher sur les traces des Pères. Sa défense n'a pas convaincu tout le monde, ni dans son vivant ni de nos jours. Le professeur Altaner parle de sa tentative, certainement vaine (*allerdings missglückten Versuch*), pour soutenir son *theologoumenon* par la témoignage de la tradition[42].

Cependant, on ne peut pas douter qu'Augustin ne se considérât comme le protagoniste de la doctrine patristique, et tout ce que nous avons pu esquisser à l'égard de son rôle dans la controverse s'accord avec cette idée. "Vous dites que j'ai changé mes vues", écrit-il à Julien d'Eclane, "et qu'au commencement de ma conversion, je pensais comme vous. Mais vous trompez, ou l'on vous trompe, soit en calomnant les choses que je disais à ce temps, soit en nanquant de compréhension à leur égard, pour mieux dire, de les lire. Car depuis le commencement de ma conversion je tiens toujours que *par un seul homme le péché est entré dans le monde, et par le péché la mort, et qu'ainsi la mort s'est étendue sur tous les hommes, en celui qui pécha.* J'ai écrit quelques livres étant encore laïque, et quoique je ne susse pas alors les Saintes Écritures aussi bien que plus tard, et que je n'imaginasse rien à l'égard de l'affaire présente, et bien que je n'eusse suivi que là où les exigences de ma discussion m'avaient mené, néanmoins je ne disais que ce que l'antiquité a appris et que toute les églises enseignent"[43].

[39] *Ibid.* 6, 16-7, 19 CSEL 42, 68-72.
[40] PLINVAL: *Pélage: ses écrits, sa vie, et sa réforme*, p. 22. Sur les lettres à Livania, voir aussi MORRIS, John: *Pelagian Literature*, en *Journal of Theological Studies*, N. S., 16, 1965, p. 33: "Augustine ...records an open verdict on Pelagius' authorship, content to say that the Council was quite right to accept his denial in default of evidence".
[41] *Voir ses remarques dans De grat. Christ.* II, 2-III, 3 CSEL 42, 125-27.
[42] ALTANER: *a. c.*, p. 448.
[43] *C. Iul.* VI 12, 39 PL 44, 843.

Cette déclaration devait être quelque peu difficile à vérifiér car, dans ses premiers ouvrages, Augustin ne discuta jamais ce verset —*Ep. aux Romains* 5, 12— mais la déclaration indique bien la certitude avec laquelle Augustin maintient qu'il n'avait appris aucune doctrine sur le péché originel depuis sa conversion, à part celle qu'il défend contre Pélage et ses partisans.

Cette certitude n'est nulle part plus manifeste que dans la façon dont Augustin traite ce verset de l'*Ep. aux Romains* et particulièrement à l'expression *in quo omnes peccaverunt*, laquelle il applique à Adam, ignorant, en apparence, que le texte grec rend son interpretation impossible. Dans un passage assez long du *Contra Iulianum*, il réprimande son adversaire très sévèrement parce que Julien, tout justement, veut comprendre les mots *in quo* dans le sens de *propter quod*. Selon Augustin, c'est Julien qui, par cette traduction, est un novateur d'une impudence merveilleuse, qui n'est rien autre que la démence[44].

La chose est d'autant plus curieuse, qu'Augustin était bien habitué à vérifier ses références bibliques sur le grec originel. Ainsi, dans une lettre écrit en 414 ou au commencement de 415, il dit que certaines manuscrits ont, pour l' expression "ceux qui n'avaient pas péché par une transgression semblable à celle d'Adam", de l'*Ép. aux Romains* 5, 14, une variante: "ceux qui *ont* péché...", mais il ajoute que le plupart des manuscrits grecs portent la lecture normale[45]. Voici une preuve qu'il a dû voir le grec original, ce qui rend encore plus curieux son refus d'entendre l'expression *in quo* dans le sens *propter quod*. Il est possible qu'une mauvaise lecture des manuscrits grecs qui circulaient à ce temps en Afrique du Nord l'ait trompé —ce ne serait que l'affaire d'une seule lettre. Nous ne le saurons jamais, semble-t-il; mais l'obstination d'Augustin indique bien sa confiance absolue dans la justesse de son interprétation.

Cependant, la question de la lecture manuscrite mise à part, l'exégèse d' Augustin reste solidement sur les principes théolologiques. Il est significatif que le texte de l'*Ép. aux Romains*: *in quo omnes peccaverunt*, est souvent lié, dans sa pensée, avec celui de *I Corinthiens* 15, 22: *De même, en effet, que tous*

---

[44] C. *Iul.* VI 24, 75: "De illis quoque apostolicis verbis, in quibus impudentia mirabili, imo dementia, resistitis fundatissimae fidei, ubi ait: *Per unum hominem peccatum intravit in mundum, et per peccatum mors, et ita in omnes homines pertransiit, in quo omnes peccaverunt:* frustra sensum alium novum atque distortum et a vero abhorrentem moleris exculpere, affirmans ea locutione dictum esse *in quo omnes peccaverunt* ac si diceretur "propter quod omnes peccaverunt", sicut dictum est, *in quo corripit iunior viam suam;* ut scilicet, non in uno homine omnes homines peccasse intellegantur originaliter, et tamquam in massae unione communiter; sed propterea quia primus hominum ille peccavit, id est, com imitantur illum, non cum generantur ex illo. Non ergo huic sensui convenit illa locutio, ita dictum est *in quo,* velut dictum esset *propter quod*", PL 44, 868.

[45] *Ep.* 157, 3, 19: "nonnulli sane codices non habent *in eos qui non peccaverunt* sed *in eos qui peccaverunt in similitudinem praevaricationis Adae,* quibus quidem verbis nullo modo iste sensus aufertur. secundum hoc quippe intelleguntur peccasse *in similitudinem praevaricationis Adae,* secundum quod dictum est: *in quo omnes peccaverunt.* sed tamen Graeci codices, unde in Latinum scriptura translata est, illud plures habent, quod diximus", CSEL 44, 468.

meurent en Adam, tous aussi revivront dans le Christ[46]. La juxtaposition de ces deux textes par Augustin constitue pour lui une explication admirable. fondée sur les Écritures, de son exégèse de l'*Ép. aux Romains*.

Augustin, comme l'a très bien allégué E. R. Fairweather[47], n'est pas un *tortor infantium;* mais il avait ce sens fort de la *solidarité humaine*, qui agit pour le mal, dans le cas du péché originel, et pour le bien dans la régéneration baptismale. "Tous meurent en Adam —*in quo omnes peccaverunt*— tous aussi revivront dans le Christ". On comprend facilement pourquoi Augustin, avec une intelligence qui lui semblait si admirable de l'*Ép. aux Romains* 5, 12 dans la lumière de *I Cor.* 15, 22, et soutenu par l'usage commun de l'Église africaine à l'égard du baptême des enfants, aurait refusé de considérer aucune exégèse autre que la sienne, qu'il juge être le sens catholique.

L'attitude d'Augustin dans ces choses reste valable malgré le fait que, dans son *Exposition de quelques propositions tirées de l'Épître aux Romains* de 394, il exprime des vues théologiques qu'il modifia plus tard[48], et aussi que cette oeuvre, avec le *De libero arbitrio*, l'*Epistulae ad Romanos inchoata expositio*, et le *De diversis quaestionibus ad Simplicianum*, influencèrent Pélage[49], qui réclama leur doctrine comme étant la sienne.

Dans ces écrits, Augustin s'intéresse à la question du libre arbitre, et il ne veut pas discuter la question de la transmission du péché originel ou de l'état des enfants nouveaux-nés. Dans de telles circonstances, il lui serait parfaitement possible, dans les premières années de sa vie chrétienne, de tenir la doctrine de la culpabilité des enfants nonbaptisés, tout en maintenant une attitude semi-pélagienne quant au libre arbitre et à la grâce.

Cette interprétation est raffermie par quelques remarques dans le *Contra Faustum*, écrit en 397-398, c.-à-d. immédiatement après la composition des *Confessions*. Le fait que Fauste était manichéen est une raison pour supposer qu'Augustin n'aurait pas souligné les doctrines catholiques qui pourrait être confondues avec le point de vue manichéen. Dans son ouvrage, Augustin affirme que la mort est la punition du péché, parce que l'homme est devenu mortel par le péché[50], déclare que la péché est entré dans le monde par Adam,

---

[46] *C. Faust.* XXII 78; *De pec. mer. et rem.* I 8, 8; III 11, 19; *En. in ps.* 50, 10; *En. in Ps.* 70, 1, 2; *Ep.* 190, 1, 3; *Sermo* 293, 12; *Op. imp. c. Iul.* VI 31.
[47] Fairweather, E. R.: *St Augustine's interpretation of infant baptism*, en *Augustinus Magister* II, p. 899.
[48] *Retract.* I 22, 23. Cf. l'observation de G. Bardy, dans son édition (Bibliothèque augustinienne: *Oeuvres de saint Augustin*, I série, vol. 12), Paris 1950, p. 574 n. 33: "Les corrections que saint Augustin signale ici peuvent ne porter que sur les détails; elles n'en témoignent pas moins du sens très net dans lequel s'est fait le changement de sa pensée, afin d'accroître la place donnée à la grâce".
[49] Voir Bohlin, Torgny: *Die Theologie des Pelagius und ihre Genesis*, Uppsala-Wiesbaden 1957, pp. 46 *et seq.*
[50] *C. Faust.* XIV 3: "Mors hominis ex poena peccati est: unde et ipsa peccatum dicitur, non quia peccat homo dum moritur, sed quia ex peccato factum est, ut moriatur", *CSEL* 25, 404, 405.

en lequel tous meurent[51], et applique à Adam le fameux verset de l'*Ép. aux Romains* dans toute sa rigueur[52].

A ces passages du *Contra Faustum* nous pouvons en ajouter deux tirés du *De Genesi ad litteram*. La valeur de cette oeuvre comme témoignage de la pensée d'Augustin avant la controverse pélagienne est diminuée par le fait que, quoique l'oeuvre fût commencé en 401, elle ne fut achevée qu'en 414/15, c.-à-d. après la naissance du Pélagianisme, et il est donc impossible d'être sûr qu'Augustin ne l'aurait pas modifiée, vu les exigences de la situation. Dans le sixième livre, Augustin cite le psaume 50, 7: *In iniquitatibus conceptus sum et in peccatis mater mea me in utero aluit,* et le rapporte à *I Cor.* 15, 22 et *Rom.* 5, 12[53]. Semblablement, dans un second passage, Augustin dit franchement que les petits enfants ne peuvent pas être séparés des pécheurs adultes, parce que l'Apôtre dit d'Adam: *in quo omnes peccaverunt*[54]. Si ce passage était écrit avant la naissance du Pélagianisme elle serait décisive; mais toute la tendance du dixième live du *De Genesi ad litteram* suggère une révision en vue des questions soulevées par les Pélagiens.

Une tendance pareille se trouve dans le *De Trinitate,* mais dans ce cas-ci, la difficulté que nous venons de remarquer dans le *De Genesi ad litteram* reparaît avec une force redoublée, parce que le *De Trinitate,* quoique commencé avant le *De Genesi ad litteram,* ne fut achevé que beaucoup plus tard. La datation est de 399/400 à après 416, probablement 419. On sait qu'Augustin a longuement hésité à publier son ouvrage, et nous ne pouvons pas éliminer la possibilité de quelque interpolation tardive.

Mais, dans le premier de nos passages, qui se trouve sans le quatrième livre du *De Trinitate,* la citation de *Rom.* 5, 12 s'accorde si bien avec le thème général du passage, avec sa référence aux deux chemins menant à vie et à la mort, qu'on peut très vraisemblablement supposer qu'elle représente le texte original, dans lequel sont contrastés les deux Adam, le premier, dont le péché

---

[51] *Ibid.* XXII 78: "Proditum est enim nobis peccatum Adae fideli eloquio Dei; et quia in illo *omnes moriuntur,* et quia *per illum peccatum intravit in* hunc *mundum et per peccatum mors,* veraciter scriptum est", *CSEL* 25, 679.

[52] *Ibid.* XXIV 2: "Veterem autem hominem nihil aliud apostolus quam vitam veterem dicit, quae in peccato est, in quo secundum Adam vivitur: de quo dicit: *Per unum hominem peccatum intravit in mundum et per peccatum mors; et ita in omnes homines pertransivit, in quo omnes peccaverunt*", *CSEL* 25, 723.

[53] *De Gen. ad lit.* VI 9, 15: "Nec tamen frustra scriptum est nec infamtem mundum esse a peccato, cuius est unius diei vita super terram, et illud in psalmo: *ego in iniquitatibus conceptus sum et in peccatis mater mea me in utero aluit* et quod *in Adam omnes moriuntur, in quo omnes peccaverunt.* nunc autem liquido teneamus, quaelibet parentum merita traiciantur in prolem, quaecumque gratia dei, antequam nascatur quemque sanctificet, nec iniquitatem esse apud deum nec boni malive agere quemquam, quod ad propriam personam pertineat, antequam natus est", *CSEL* 28, 181.

[54] *Ibid.* X 16, 29: "Eosdem multos peccatores non quibusdam exceptis, sed omnes intelligi volens superius ait [Apostolus] de Adam: *in quo omnes peccaverunt,* unde utique infantum animas non posse secerni...?". *CSEL* 28, 317.

nous a apporté la mort, parce que nous avons peché en lui, et le second, dont la mort nous a apporté la vie[55]. Cette pensée est développée dans le treizième livre. Augustin y parle du premier Adam, dont le péché et la mort obligent sa posterité comme des maux héréditaires[56].

S'il est impossible de prouver sans aucun doute que ses passages sont antérieurs à la controverse pélagienne, la chose reste néanmoins probable, et s'accorde bien avec la figure générale de la situation. En effet, la tâche de prouver que ces passages sont ajoutés par Augustin en vue de son conflit avec les Pélagiens incombe à ceux qui, comme les Pélagiens, veulent le réprésenter comme innovateur.

Restent à considérer les circontances dans lesquelles pouvaient se développer les doctrines dont nous avons suggéré qu'Augustin était le défenseur et non l' auteur.

Dès le début il faut dire que la doctrine dite augustinienne du péché originel, si on regarde Augustin comme en étant l'inventeur ou non, a certaines caractéristiques qui lui sont propres. Il ne s'agit pas du péché originel, *peccatum originale*, tout court. Cette doctrine était tenue par un penseur comme Origène, dont la pensée diffère totalement de celle d'Augustin. Il s'agit aussi de la culpabilité originelle, *originalis reatus*[57], à laquelle se mêle une maladie héréditaire, qu'Augustin compare à la goutte, qu'un père intempérant transmet à ses fils[58]. Mais c'est une maladie coupable, laquelle comporte très justement les châtiments éternels pour tous ceux ne renaissent pas dans l'eau baptismale.

---

[55] *De Trin.* IV 12, 15: "Proinde, sicut Magi fecerunt divinitus moniti, quos ad humilitatem Domini adorandum stella perduxit, ita et nos, non qua venimus, sed per aliam viam redire debemus, quam rex humilis docuit, et quam rex superbus humili regi adversarius obsidere non possit. Et nobis enim, ut adoremus humilem Christum, caeli enarraverunt gloriam Dei, cum in omnem terram exiit sonus eorum, et in fines orbis terrae verba eorum. Via nobis fuit ad mortem per peccatum in Adam. *Per unum quippe hominem peccatum intravit in mundum, et per peccatum mors; et ita in omnes homines pertransiit, in quo omnes peccaverunt.* Huius viae mediator diabolus fuit, persuasor peccati, et praecipitator in mortem. Nam et ipse ad operandum duplam mortem nostram, simplam attulit suam. Per impietatem namque mortuus est in spiritu, carne utique mortuus non est; nobis autem et impietatem persuasit, et per hanc ut in mortem carnis venire mereremur afficit", (éd. Arias, *Biblioteca de autores cristianos: Obras de San Agustín*, Tomo V, Madrid 1948, p. 352).

[56] *Ibid.* XIII 16, 21: "Deinde subiungit Apostolus: *Propter hoc sicut per unum hominem peccatum intravit in hunc mundum et per peccatum mors, et ita in omnes homines mors pertransiit, in quo omnes peccaverunt;* et cetera, in quibus prolixius de duobus hominibus disputat; uno eodemque primo Adam, per cuius peccatum et mortem tamquam haereditariis malis posteri eius obligati sumus; altero autem secundo Adam, qui non homo tantum, sed etiam Deus est, quo pro nobis colvento quod non debebat, a debitis et paternis et propriis liberati sumus" (éd. Arias, pp. 748, 750).

[57] *De div. quaest. ad Simplic.* 1, 2, 20: "...sed concupiscentia carnalis de peccati poena iam regnans, universum genus humanum tanquam totam et unam conspersionem originali reatu in omnia permanente confuderat", PL 40, 126.

[58] *Op. imp. c. Iul.* II 177: "Aug.: Si quis intemperantia sibi podagram faciat, eamque transmittat in filios, quod saepe contigit; nonne recte dicitur, in eos illud vitium de parente transiisse?... Quod ergo aliquoties invenitur in corporis morbis, hoc in illo unius primi genitores antiquo magnoque peccato, quo natura humana vitiata est, factum esse

Or, les origines de la théologie africaine sont peu connues avant le commencement du troisième siècle, quand tout à coup elle manifeste une floraison extraordinaire dans les oeuvres de Tertullien. Tertullien, on le sait bien, parle du *vitium originis*, le vice d'origine de la nature[59], mais il semble penser plûtot aux influences démoniaques dues aux pratiques païnnes qu'au péché originel héréditaire[60].

Son attitude à l'égard du baptême des enfants est compliquée. Il insiste qu'il n'y a aucune raison pourquoi l'innocence de la jeunesse se dépêchât à la rémission des péchés[61], mais il semble faire exception pour une crise qui pouvait hasarder la vie de l'enfant (*si non tam necesse est*). Ainsi, Tertullien ne nie pas l'importance du baptême. Son argumentation se fonde précisèment sur la valeur qu'il assigne à ce sacrement; mais sa pensée manque du sens d'urgence qu'on remarquera plus tard. L'importance de ses vues se trouve dans le fait qu'elles constituent la preuve que certains chrétiens africains de ses jours affirmaient déjà la nécessité du baptême pour tous les ages de la vie, y compris l'enfance.

Si de Tertullien on se tourne à saint Cyprien, on y trouve une attitude tout à fait différente. Sa fameuse épître 64 — oeuvre à laquelle Augustin revient souvent comme autorité pour sa doctrine[62] et qu'il cita dans la fameuse sermon prêché à Carthage le 27 juin 413[63] — réprésente un point de vue tout différent de celui de Tertullien. Il faut admettre au baptême les petits enfants, dont toute la faute est de naître d'une race coupable[64]. On ne doit pas tarder, même les huit jours qu'exige la Loi de l'Ancien Testament pour la circoncision.

Peut-on trouver aucune explication pour ce changement d'avis de Tertullien à saint Cyprien? Ce n'était pas seulement une matière du développement d'habitudes; Cyprien ne répond pas à son interlocuteur Fidus: C'est la coutume. Il raisonne que le Fils de l'homme est venu pour sauver tous, les petits enfants non exceptès[65]. Pour Cyprien, d'une façon qu'on ne trouve pas chez Tertullien, il ne faut pas permettre un délai. Est-il possible de trouver quelque

---

noverat, qui lucidissima locutione, quam vos conamini tenebrare, dicebat: *per unum homincm peccatum intravit in mundum et per peccatum mors, et ita in omnes homines pertransiit, in quo omnes peccaverunt"*, PL 45, 1218.

[59] TERT.: *De anima* 41, 1 (éd. Waszink, p. 57). Cf. ses remarques, pp. 448, 454.

[60] *Ibid.* 39, 1-4 (éd. Waszink, p. 57).

[61] TERT.: *De baptismo*, 18 (éd. Evans, p. 38).

[62] *De pec. mer. et rem.* III 5, 10; *De nupt. et concup.* II 30, 52; *C. duas ep. Pel.* IV 8, 23; *C. Iul.* I 3, 6; *Op. imp. c. Iul.* I 106, 152.

[63] *Sermo* 294, 20, 19, PL 38, 1347-48.

[64] CYP.: 64, 5: "Si etiam gravissimis delictoribus... remissa peccatorum datur et a baptismo adque gratia nemo prohibetur, quanto magis prohiberi non debet infans qui recens natus nihil peccavit, nisi quod secundum Adam carnaliter natus contagium mortis antiquae prima nativitate contraxit, qui ad remissam peccatorum accipiendam hoc ipso facilius accedit quod illi remittuntur non propria sed aliena peccata", CSEL 3 (2), 720, 721.

[65] *Ibid.* 2 CSEL 3 (2), 718.

114

raison pour cette modification de perspective dans les documents de la première moitié du troisième siècle qui nous restent?

Une telle indication existe peut-être dans la *Passion de sainte Perpétue et de sainte Félicité*. Cette fameuse passion était encore très populaire dans l' Afrique de saint Augustin, et lui causa un certain embarras, parce qu'on en cite le cas du frère de Perpétue, Dinocrate, comme preuve que les âmes des enfants nonbaptisés pouvaient être sauvées par les prières des saints[66]. A cette argumentation, Augustin répond, premièrement, que la *Passion de sainte Perpétue* n'était pas une Écriture canonique et, en second lieu, qu'il n'y avait aucune preuve que Dinocrate ne fût pas baptisé. Il avait sept ans au moment de sa mort et fut, ainsi, capable de pécher. Augustin propose la vue qu'un père impie fît, peut-être, apostasier l'enfant, qui entra après la mort dans un état de punition, duquel il fut liberé par les prières de sa soeur, qui allait mourir pour le Christ[67].

C'est une théorie ingénieuse, mais historiquement peu convaincente. Sainte Perpétue elle-même n'était pas baptisée au moment de son arrestation[68], et ne reçut le baptême qu'immédiatement avant son entrée en prison, pendant qu' elle était déjà gardée par ses garants[69]. Son intercession pour son frère ne doit pas être considérée comme une anticipation de la doctrine du Purgatoire, mais comme une expression du grand mérite du martyr, qui osa demander une vi-sion de Dieu[70]. Mais on peut croire que cette vision, tout en contribuant à la gloire des martyrs, et à la croyance à l'efficacité de leur prières (Augustin re-fère à la croyance répandue de ses jours, que les méchants et les infidèles seraient épargnés au Dernier Jour par les intercessions des saints)[71] aurait aussi constitué une argumentation puissante pour la nécessité du baptême pour éviter l'espèce de tourments que souffrit le petit Dinocrate, avant qu'il n'en fût libéré par les prières de Perpétue.

Cette supposition s'accorderait très bien avec les tendances religieuses des Berbères, avec leur croyance à la magie, à l'astrologie, et au mauvais oeil. Le fait que les souffrances de Dinocrate constituent un reflet des legendes païenne

---

[66] AUG.: *De anima et eius orig.* I 10, 12; II 10, 14-12, 16; III 9, 12; IV 18, 27 *CSEL* 60, 312, 349-51, 369-70, 406-07.

[67] *Ibid.* I 10, 12 CSEL 60, 312.

[68] *Passio,* 2: "Adprehensi sunt adulescentes catechumeni, Revocatus et Felicitas con-serva eius, Saturninus et Secundulus. Inter hos et Vibia Perpetua..." (éd. Shewring, Londres 1931, p. 4).

[69] *Ibid.* 3: "Cum adhuc, inquit, cum prosecutoribus essemus... in ipso spatio pau-corum dierum baptizati sumus" (Shewring, pp. 4, 5).

[70] *Ibid.* 4: "Tunc dixit mihi frater meus: Domina soror, iam in magna dignatione es, tanta ut postules visionem"; *ibid.* 8 (quand Perpétue vit Dinocrate en vision): "Et cognovi me statim dignam esse, et pro eo petere debere" (Shewring, pp. 6, 9).

[71] AUG.: *De civ. Dei* XXI 18 CSEL 40 (2), 549-50.

sur les morts qui ont soif[72], et montre une idée traditionelle du destin de ceux qui sont morts avant terme, ne sert qu'à montrer l'élément indigène dans la théologie populaire africaine[73]. De cette croyance dans le sort misérable de ceux qui sont morts sans baptême, plus la doctrine du péché originel exprimée par saint Cyprien et ses collègues, pouvait développer la doctrine dite augustinienne de la damnation des enfants non-baptisés, qu'Augustin supposait être la doctrine de l'Église catholique. Mais à côté de cette doctrine, la foi populaire dans les intercessions des saints (foi que partage Augustin, dans le cas des chrétiens baptisés)[74] continuait.

Ses vues seraient-elles plus répandues dans l'ouest hors d'Afrique? C'est probable. Le premier à dénoncer le Pélagianisme en Afrique fut Paulin, diacre de Milan. Les adversaires de Pélage en Palestine c'étaient Orose, prêtre espagnol, saint Jérome, né en Dalmatie, Héros d'Arles et Lazare d'Aix, anciens évêques de Gaule. A Rome, dans la crise de 418, on trouve des anti-Pélagiens comme Marius Mercator et un certain Constance, qui fut attaqué par les Pélagiens. Donc, l'opposition à Pélage ne se bornait pas du tout à l'Afrique, et Augustin, dans le grand catalogue de citations patristiques qu'il cite contre Julien d'Eclane, y comprend les témoignages de Réticius d'Autun[75] et d'Olympius d'Espagne[76], avec celles de saint Hilaire, saint Ambroise, et les Pères grecs, pour démontrer l'antiquité de sa doctrine.

On doit se garder bâtir une argumentation trop lourde sur les citations courtes de Réticius et Olympius que cite Augustin, et de plus, il n'est pas évident en soi que les vues de ces deux Pères étaient typiques de leur régions, mais le langage de Réticius, avec ses références au *antiqui criminis pondus*, aux *prisca facinora* et au *veterem hominem cum ingenitis sceleribus* —références qu'Augustin ne manque pas de souligner— et celle d'Olympius, qui parle du *protoplasti mortifera transgressione vitium* semé en germe *ut peccatum cum homine nasceretur*, suggèrent que les tentatives que fit Augustin pour prouver que sa doctrine était celle des Pères n'étaient pas déraisonables.

Mais la doctrine africaine du péché originel, la doctrine énoncée par le concile de Carthage en 418 et défendue par Augustin, n'avait-elle pas quelque-chose de propre, quelque-chose de purement africaine? Dans un article très in-

---

[72] Cf. DÖLGER, F. J.: *Antike Parallelen zum leidenden Dinokrates*, en *Ant. u. Christ.* 2, 1930, cité par DODDS, E. R.: *Pagan and Christian in an Age of Anxiety*, Cambridge 1965, p. 52 *n*².

[73] Sur laquelle, cf. FREND, W. H. C.: *The Donatist Church*, Oxford 1952, ch. 8, "Factors relating to the conversion of North Africa to Christianity", pp. 94-111.

[74] AUG.: *De anima* IV 18, 27: "... porro autem in non vero corpore vera miseria fuit animae [Dinocratis], quae significabatur adumbrato corporis vulnere, de qua sororis sanctae orationibus merui liberari" CSEL 60, 407.

[75] C. Iul. I 3, 7 PL 44, 644. *Op. imp. c. Iul.* I 55 PL 45, 1078. *Voir* LABRIOLLE, P. de: *Hist. de la littérature latine chrétienne*, 3ᵉ éd., I. p. 343; GRIFFE, E.: *La Gaule chrétienne à l'époque romaine* I, 1947, p. 131.

[76] C. Iul. I 3, 8 PL 44, 644, 645. LABRIOLLE, P. de: *o. c.*, I. p. 449.

téressant[77], l'abbé Floëri essaye de démontrer que la doctrine qu'énonce le pape Zosime dans l'*Epistola Tractoria* n'est pas identique avec celle du deuxième canon de Carthage, et que, pendant que les Africains parlent du péché originel dans le sens d'*originalis reatus*, Zosime affirme tout simplement que l'enfant non-baptisé est esclave du péché, captif du péché, duquel il aurait contracté la mort spirituelle, mais sans qu'il soit nécessaire de parler d'un *peccatum*.

M. Floëri ne dit pas s'il regarde Augustin comme l'auteur de la doctrine africaine. Le titre de son article parle de la "doctrine augustinienne du péché originel", mais dans le texte il parle de la "doctrine africaine" et du "terme de péché, qu'employaient saint Augustin et le Concile de Carthage"[78], qui semble impliquer qu'il reconnaît l'existence d'une doctrine africaine traditionelle du péché originel, dont Augustin était le grand défenseur.

Cependant, ces considérations mises à part, rien n'est plus probable que Zosime aurait voulu éviter d'exprimer la doctrine du péché originel dans toute sa rigueur africaine, soit pour les considérations théologiques, soit pour les raisons plus personelles. Mais cela ne prouve pas de soi que la doctrine africaine avait quelque-chose de propre, et il semble plus prudent de croire, avec le P. Refoulé, que le *theologoumenon* de la damnation des enfants morts sans baptême se trouvait non seulement en Afrique, mais aussi en Italie —et peut-être en Gaule et en Espagne— avant même les débuts de la crise pélagienne en 411.

Cette théorie est appuyée par l'adhésion que les théologiens africains trouvaient dans l'Ouest au cours de la controverse pélagienne. Évidemment, le *theologoumenon* n'attirait pas tout le monde, même parmi eux qui ne sympathisaient pas avec les Pélagiens; mais il a dû recevoir une assex large mesure d'appui populaire, ce qui explique le triomphe final des vues africaines mieux que la force d'une seule personnalité, même celle d'Augustin.

Si notre interprétation est exacte, il ne faut pas regarder Augustin comme l'aggresseur dans la controverse pèlagienne, ni comme l'auteur de la doctrine du péché originel qui porte son nom. Qu'Augustin, par son intervention, ait changé le cours de la controverse, cela est clair; mais il n'entra pas dans la bataille de sa propre volonté mais avec répugnance, pour défendre la foi catholique, telle qu'il l'avait apprise, et qu'il jugeait en danger.

---

[77] FLOERI, F.: *Le pape Zosime et la doctrine augustinienne du péché originel*, en *Augustinus Magister* II. pp. 755-61.
[78] *Ibid.* pp. 755, 758.

IX

Libido and *Concupiscentia* in St. Augustine

We are warned by Augustine himself that there are certain topics, in a fallen world, upon which our discourse should be restrained by modesty, rather than assisted by eloquence[1], and I am well aware that the Augustinian doctrine of concupiscence has been a scandal to certain worthy persons in the past[2]. I do not desire to dwell on the scabrous; indeed, my concern is with a more general consideration of Augustine's teaching regarding lust than it usually receives. The subject, for obvious reasons, is apt to be discussed in its sexual connotation alone – a legacy, no doubt, from the last great struggle with Julian of Eclanum, who seems to have been well nigh obsessed with it[3]. Augustine was well aware of the sexual implications of the word lust. "Although there are many lusts yet, when the word 'lust' is spoken without any mention of the object, we commonly understand

---

[1] De Civitate Dei, XIV 26: *De rebus loquimur nunc pudendis et ideo, quamvis antequam earum puderet, quales esse potuissent coniciamus ut possemus, tamen necesse est, ut nostra disputatio magis frenetur ea, quae nos revocat, verecundia, quam eloquentia, quae nobis parum subpetit, adiuvetur.*

[2] E. g. the comment of Harnack that Augustine's remarks on marriage are 'höchst ekelhaft', Dogmengeschichte, Bd. III, 1890, 191, n. 3. The phrase was retained in the 3rd ed., III, 1897, 196, n. 8, and hence in the E. T., V, London, 1898, 211, n. 5. It disappears in the 4th ed., 1910, 210–211, n. 8. Harnack's comment is cited, with relish and an inadequate reference, by Thomas Allin, The Augustinian Revolution in Theology, London 1911, 142: "'Höchst ekelhaft' is the verdict of so staunch an ally as Harnack. 'Perfectly loathsome' indeed is the constant iteration of *membra genitalia, membrorum inobedientia, concubitus*, in his pages. It is the thought of an ex-profligate round whom, though risen, the grave clothes of his past are still clinging." Harnack and Allin are both, to my mind, unnecessarily squeamish.

[3] See Georges de Plinval, Pélage: ses écrits, sa vie, et sa réforme, Lausanne 1943, 360: "Les principes les plus élevés ne sont plus pour [Julien] qu'une matière de chicane. La seule question qu'il soit en mesure de traiter, non avec largeur de vues, mais avec abondance, est celle de la *libido*." This seems to me a thoroughly just verdict.

by it sexual desire"[1]. This declaration will be my starting point; and it will immediately be noticed that, in the passage quoted, Augustine employs the word *libido,* and not *concupiscentia.* One is tempted to ask whether this choice of a particular word has any significance, and to wonder whether there is a subtle difference between *libido* and *concupiscentia.* It is impossible, in the time at my disposal, to do more than to present my own view that, when used to describe sexual desire, (which I shall henceforth generally denominate concupiscence, to avoid confusion), the two words are virtually interchangeable[2]; but when any other lust is mentioned, *libido* is the one used, very occasionally supplemented by *cupiditas.*

I have said that I have not time to argue the case for the mutual interchangeability of *libido* and *concupiscentia,* when they mean concupiscence; but it is possible to demonstrate it by

---

[1] De Civ. Dei, XIV 16: *Cum igitur sint multarum libidines rerum, tamen cum libido dicitur neque cuius rei libido sit additur, non fere adsolet animo occurrere nisi illa, qua obscenae partes corporis excitantur.*

[2] Examples of their use together abound, and I will cite only three: (1) C. Duas Epist. Pelag., I 17, 34—35, where Augustine, discussing the condition of human sexuality before the Fall, offers his Pelagian adversaries the choice of four possibilities: that *libido* existed unrestrained; that it existed and had constantly to be restrained; that it was under the control of the will, (*aut tunc ad nutum voluntatis libido consurgeret, quando esse concubitum necessarium casta prudentia praesensisset*); or that it did not exist at all. He rejects the first two alternatives as unworthy, and assumes that the Pelagians will not accept the fourth on their own first principles. Of the third, he writes: *illud vobis saltem placebit, quod tertio loco posuimus, ut illa carnalis concupiscentia, cuius motus ad postremam, quae vos multum delectat, pervenit voluptatem, nunquam in paradiso, nisi cum ad gignendum esset necessaria, ad voluntatis nutum exsurgeret. Hanc si placet vobis in paradiso collocare, et per talem concupiscentiam carnis, quae nec praeveniret, nec tardaret, nec excederet imperium voluntatis, vobis videtur in illa felicitate filios potuisse generari, non repugnamus,* (ibid., 35). Here, in the same context, Augustine has replaced the word *libido* first by *carnalis concupiscentia* and, secondly, by the more common *concupiscentia carnis.* (2) Another example may be found in De Peccato Originali, XXXIV 39, where Augustine first speaks of marriage, which is itself good, as making a great good *etiam de libidinis malo,* and, a little later, (ibid., XXXVII 42), ennumerates the good of marriage — offspring, chastity, and the sacrament — and distinguishes it from the *carnalis concupiscentiae malum.* (3) Compare the references in De Nuptiis et Concupiscentia, I 16, 18 to the *pudenda carnis concupiscentia quae in paradiso nec ante peccatum fuit, nec post peccatum esse permissa est* with the statement in the Opus Imperfectum c. Iulianum, II 42, that both generation and birth might have taken place in Paradise *sine pudenda libidine . . . si nemo peccasset.*

a very cursory examination of the *De Nuptiis et Concupiscentia*,
Book I, where Augustine speaks of *libido*[1]; *concupiscentia*[2];
libido carnalis[3]; *carnalis concupiscentia*[4]; *carnis concupiscentia*[5];
and *pudenda carnis concupiscentia*[6], all to describe the state of
mind we call concupiscence. If it is asked why Augustine made
use of two different words to express the same emotion, one
obvious answer presents itself: that of literary convenience, by
which the monotony of the regular repetition of one of them is
reduced. This, however, is only part of the answer, for the words
themselves have an interest in the history of the Latin language.
Both of them appear in the Latin Bible, but only one of them,
libido, is classical, with a wide range of meaning; while *concupiscentia* is a Christian technical term, used exclusively by
Christian writers, and predominantly, though not exclusively,
in the sense of concupiscence. It is desirable to look at the history
of these two words a little more closely.

Libido, I have said, is a classical word, and common enough
in Latin literature. Basically, it seems to have a neutral sense of
desire; so we find in Lucretius, *De Rerum Natura*, the lines:

Quaeritur in primis quare, quod cuique libido
venerit, extemplo mens cogitet eius id ipsum —

(IV 779—80)

where *libido* means little more than "whim" or "fancy" — why is
it, Lucretius asks, that when anyone has the whim to think about
a certain thing, the mind immediately furnishes a mental image
of it? In a slightly more positive, but still primarily neutral
sense, I understand Sallust, *Bellum Jugurthinum*, 84,3: *Sed ea
res frustra sperata; tanta lubido cum Mario eundi plerosque
invaserat* — the senate hoped that the plebs would not want
to go campaigning with Marius, but this hope was disappointed,
because of the great desire which had taken hold of the com-
mons, filled with visions of loot and glory. Similarly, I think,
we may understand Livy, V 42: *non omnibus delendi urbem*

---

[1] De Nupt. et Concup., I 7, 8: *libidinis malum*; 8, 9; 15, 17; 21, 23;
24, 27.

[2] Ibid., 7, 8; 24, 27.

[3] Ibid., 5, 6.

[4] Ibid., 11, 12.

[5] Ibid., 17, 19.

[6] Ibid., 16, 18.

libido erat. This is the first sense of the word: "desire", without any strong suggestion that the object of the desire is good or evil.

Secondly, it can have an implication of concupiscence. So Livy, I 57: *Ibi Sex. Tarquinium mala libido Lucretiae per vim stuprandae capit.* The point here, of course, is that it is a *mala libido*, which implies that *libido*, in itself, is not necessarily evil, and so has to be qualified to fit these circumstances. More direct is Sallust, *Coniuratio Catilinae*, 28,4: *quibus lubido atque luxuria ex magnis rapinis nihil reliqui fecerant.* In this context, *libido* clearly has an unfavourable meaning: "ruined by dissolute and extravagant living" is the implication. Cicero, in the *Tusculanae Disputationes* 3, 2, 4: *qui pecuniae cupiditate, qui voluptatum libidine feruntur, quorumque ita perturbantur animi, ut non multum absint ab insania* is more general; *libido voluptatum* covers a wide range of dissolute desire. Indeed, none of these examples really approaches Augustine's habitual use of *libido* in the sense of *libido carnalis* and the best example I know, in his sense, is not the noun, but the adjective formed from it, in the poem which has been assigned to Petronius, Nero's arbiter of elegance. Certainly, one would like to think of the author of the *Satyricon* filling the rôle of Yeat's true love "down by the salley gardens", and bidding his beloved "take love easy":

> *Foeda est in coitu et brevis voluptas,*
> *et taedet Veneris statim peractae.*
> *Non ergo ut pecudes libidinosae*
> *caeci protinus irruamus illuc,*
> *nam languescit amor peritque flamma —*

which certainly fits Augustine's definition of *libido*, though the saint would hardly have approved the poet's remedy[1].

Next, there is a wider range of meaning, covering any evil desire; so Tacitus, *Annales*, 16,18: *Ergo crudelitatem principis, cui ceterae libidines cedebant, adgreditur.* Again, Cicero, *Tusculanae Disputationes*, 3, 5, 11: *Itaque nihil melius, quam quod est in consuetudine sermonis Latini, cum exisse ex potestate dicimus eos, qui ecfrenati feruntur aut libidine aut iracundia; quamquam ipsa iracundia libidinis est pars; sic enim definitur iracundia:*

---

[1] Which those interested will find in Baehrens, Poetae Latinae Minores, V 99, No. 101 and, with an English translation, in Helen Waddell, Medieval Latin Lyrics, London 1933, 14–15.

ulciscendi libido. This passage undoubtedly affected Augustine's thinking on the subject of *libido;* he has it in mind in the *De Civitate Dei,* XIV 15[1]; in Letter 138, II 9[2]; and in the *Confessions,* II 9,17[3]. Again, we may note Cicero, *Tusculanae Disputationes,* 4, 6, 11—12, where the Roman statesman discusses the four *perturbationes* by which, according to Zeno, the mind is troubled, and lists them as *libido; laetitia; metus;* and *aegritudo.* Augustine refers to this passage in the *Confessions,* X 14,22[4], and in the *De Civitate Dei,* XIV 8[5]. It is, however, significant that, in his list of the *perturbationes,* he substitutes for Cicero's *libido* the word *cupiditas*[6], which has, for him, a wider range of meaning, especially since Cicero himself describes *libido* as "cupiditas effrenata"[7].

Finally, there is the famous passage, cited by Augustine in the *De Civitate Dei,* III 14, and the inspiration of so much of his theme, Sallust, *Coniuratio Catilinae,* 2,2: *Post ea vero quam in*

---

[1] *Voluptatem vero praecedit adpetitus quidem, qui sentitur in carne quasi cupiditas eius, sicut fames et sitis et ea, quae in genitalibus usitatius libido nominatur, cum hoc sit generale vocabulum omnis cupiditatis. Nam et ipsam iram nihil aliud esse quam* ulciscendi libidinem *veteres definierunt; quamvis nonnumquam homo, ubi vindictae nullus est sensus, etiam rebus inanimis irascatur, et male scribentem stilum conlidat vel calamum frangat iratus. Verum et ista licet inrationabilior, tamen quaedam ulciscendi libido est, ut nescio qua, ut ita dixerim, quasi umbra retributionis, ut qui male faciunt, mala patiantur. Est igitur libido ulciscendi, qui ira dicitur; est libido habendi pecuniam, quae avaritia; est libido quomodocumque vincendi, quae pervicacia; est libido gloriandi, quae iactantia nuncupatur. Sunt multae variaeque libidines, quarum nonnullae habent etiam vocabula propria, quaedam vero non habent. Quis enim facile dixerit, quod vocetur libido dominandi, quam tamen plurimum valere in tyrannorum animis etiam civilia bella testantur.* Noted by Maurice Testard, Saint Augustin et Cicéron, II, Paris 1958, 62.

[2] *Quid est autem non reddere malum pro malo nisi abhorrere ab ulciscendi libidine, quod est accepta iniuria ignoscere malle quam persequi, et nihil nisi iniurias oblivisci?* Noted by Testard, op. cit., p. 108.

[3] *Nulla lucri mei, nulla ulciscendi libido.* Apparently not noticed by Testard.

[4] Noted by Testard, op. cit., II, p. 26.

[5] Noted by Testard, op. cit., II, p. 60.

[6] See Testard, op. cit., I, p. 269: '[Augustin] explique qu'il préfère *tristitia* pour son sens plus nettement spirituel, à *aegritudo* de Cicéron ou à *dolor* de Virgile, qui se disent plutôt du corps. [De Civ. Dei, XIV 7—8]. C'est sans doute une raison analogue qui le fait substituer *cupiditas,* d'une acceptance plus large, à *libido* dont il observe un peu plus loin le sense érotique très particulier'.

[7] Tusc. Disput., 4, 6, 12: *Quae autem a ratione aversa incitata est vehementius, ea libido est vel cupiditas effrenata, quae in omnibus stultis invenitur.* Noted by Testard, op. cit., I, 269, n. 5.

308

Asia Cyrus, in Graecia Lacedaemonii et Athenienses coepere urbis atque nationes subigere, lubidinem dominandi causam belli habere, maxumam gloriam in maxumo imperio putare.

From these passages, it is very plain that *libido*, in the sense of an evil desire, was common enough in classical Latin, but that it lacked the strongly sexual overtones of Augustine's *libido carnalis*. There is, however, another source of inspiration open to him: the Latin Bible, in which the word *libido*, although very much less frequent than *concupiscentia*, does occur, and invariably, so far as I am aware, in the sense of *libido carnalis*[1].

From the foregoing, it will be apparent that Augustine, when discussing lusts other than sexual, is almost certain to employ the standard word, *libido*; but that, at the same time, he was able to employ it as equivalent to *concupiscentia carnis*, because of its general literary history, and specifically biblical employment.

The case of *concupiscentia* is different. Here, we have a Christian technical word[2], with a very wide use in the Bible, generally, but not always, in a bad, and sexual connotation. I say generally because in one particular instance to which Augustine refers, it has a good sense. In the second book of the *De Nuptiis et Concupiscentia*, he defends himself against Julian of Eclanum, who had accused him of holding that, without the Fall, there would have been no *concupiscentia*, by saying: "I did not say: 'There would have been no *concupiscentia*' for there is a spiritual *concupiscentia* to which glory is due, by which Wisdom is desired, [he refers to Wisdom 6,21: *Concupiscentia itaque sapientiae deducit ad regnum perpetuum*]; but I said: '"There would have been no shameful *concupiscentia*'"[3]. Nevertheless, in practice, when Augustine speaks of *concupiscentia*, he means *concupiscentia pudenda*.

I now wish to turn to the operation of lust in the life of fallen humanity. As concupiscence, *libido carnalis* or *concupiscentia carnis*, it is the name given to the passionate, uncontrolled element in sexuality, which exists even in lawful wedlock where,

---

[1] The passages are: Judic. 19, 24; 20, 5; Tobias 3, 18; 6, 17. 22; Judith 10, 4; Ezech. 23, 9. 11. 20; Coloss. 3, 5.

[2] See Alexander Souter, A Glossary of Later Latin to 600 A. D., Oxford 1949, 69, s. v.: '(= ἐπιθυμία, ὄρεξις), desire, *generally* evil desire, (*not found outside Scripture and Christian writings*).'

[3] De Nupt. et Concup., II 30, 52: *Non dixi, "Nulla esset concupiscentia," quia est et glorianda concupiscentia spiritualis, qua concupiscitur sapientia: sed dixi, "Nulla esset pudenda concupiscentia".*

according to Augustine, it may be excused if it is directed to the
true end of marriage — the procreation of children[1]. Occasionally,
Augustine employs the word loosely, so that it amounts to little
more than the physical operation of the sexual organs[2]; but he
generally has in mind an element of desire which, by inducing
the highest of all physical pleasures, virtually overwhelms the
whole intellect[3]. This consideration led Agustine to declare that
the wise man would, if he might, beget children without this
emotion[4]. Such a distaste for sexual passion is not easily com-
prehensible to the modern reader, who may be led to believe that

---

[1] De Nupt. et Concup., I 15, 17: *Sed tamen aliud est, non concumbere nisi
sola voluntate generandi, quod non habet culpam; aliud carnis concumbendo
appetere voluptatem, sed non praeter coniugem, quod venialem habet culpam, etc.*

[2] E. g., Op. Imp. c. Iul., VI 22: *Concupiscentia porro carnis, per quam
iactus carnalium seminum provocatur, aut nulla in Adam fuit, aut in illo vitiata
est per peccatum. Aut enim sine illa poterant et genitalia congruenter moveri, et
coniugis gremio semen infundi, si tunc nulla fuit, aut ad nutum voluntatis etiam
ipsa servire, si fuit. Nunc autem si talis esset, nunquam caro contra spiritum
concupisceret. Aut ergo ipsa vitium est, si nulla fuit ante peccatum; aut ipsa sine
dubio est vitiata peccato; et ideo ex illa trahitur originale peccatum. De Civ. Dei,
XIV 16: Cum igitur sint multarum libidines rerum, tamen cum libido dicitur neque
cuius rei libido sit additur, non fere adsolet animo occurrere nisi illa, qua obscenae partes corporis excitantur.* This leads Michael Müller, Die Lehre des hl.
Augustins von der Paradiesesehe, Regensburg 1954, 29, to declare: 'Ganz deutlich kommt dies dadurch zum Ausdruck, daß Augustin selbst für den paradie-
sischen Zustand die "concupiscentia carnis" zugibt.' My own feeling is, however, that when Augustine talks about *concupiscentia carnis*, he always has in
mind, perhaps unconsciously, *concupiscentia carnis pudenda*, i. e. the physical
operation *plus* the element of lust due to the Fall. This explains Augustine's
point: *aut nulla in Adam fuit, aut in illo vitiata est per peccatum.* Augustine
certainly admitted the existence of a *motus genitalium* in Paradise; see C. d.
Epist. Pel., I 15, 31: *"Motum" inquit "genitalium, id est, ipsam virilitatem
sine qua non potest esse commixtio, a Deo dicimus institutam". Ad hoc responde-
mus, motum genitalium, et, ut verbo eius utar, virilitatem, sine qua non potest
esse commixtio, Deus sic instituit, ut nihil haberet pudendum.* In this sense,
I think Müller is right; but I am inclined to think that, in Op. Imp. c. Iul.,
VI 22, the *concupiscentia ... carnis, per quam iactus carnalium seminum provocatur* is the present day physiological phenomenon, in which *motus genitalium*
is accompanied by *libido carnalis.* This gives point to the next phrase: *aut
nulla in Adam fuit, aut in illo vitiata per peccatum.*

[3] De Civ. Dei, XIV 16: *Haec [libido] autem sibi non solum totum corpus
nec solum extrinsecus, verum etiam intrinsecus vindicat totumque commovet
hominem animi simul adfectu cum carnis adpetitu coniuncto adque permixto, ut
ea voluptas sequatur, qua maior in corporis voluptatibus nulla est: ita ut momento
ipso tempore, quo ad eius pervenitur extremum, paene omnis acies et quasi vigilia
cogitationis obruatur.*

[4] Ibid.

310

Augustine regarded sexual concupiscence, in itself, as a sin. A careful examination of his teaching, however, shows that this is not the case[1]. Concupiscence is not a sin; but it is a wound and a vice in human nature[2]; can be the occasion of sin, even in the baptised[3]; and is the means whereby Original Sin is transmitted. It is an infection which conveys an inherited legal liability. It is cleansed in baptism, but its effects are not removed, so that the children of baptised parents are themselves in need of the laver of regeneration[4]. Christ alone, Who was born of the Virgin Mary by the overshadowing of the Holy Spirit, is free from the fatal legacy, and could therefore be offered for the sins of others, for in that virginal conception and birth there was no place for concupiscence[5].

Carnal concupiscence dominated the debate between Augustine and Julian of Eclanum. It was the topic to which Julian returned again and again, in a fashion very tedious for the modern reader. Augustine, in his approach to the matter, had his thinking largely conditioned by his theological doctrine of the Fall. Because of his sin, Adam lost that control over his body which he had enjoyed in Paradise and, since all humanity participated, in some mysterious sense, in that primal sin, so all the weaknesses which that sin drew upon itself are passed on to succeeding generations. Our sexuality bears witness to our fallen condition; and Augustine thought that weakness was confirmed, in a remarkable

---

[1] See Alves Pereira, La doctrine du marriage selon saint Augustin, 2e éd., Paris 1930, 61: 'La concupiscence de la chair est donc un mal, mais elle n'est pas un péché. Saint Augustine distingue clairement entre un mal moral et un péché proprement dit. Tout péché est un mal moral, mais tout mal moral n'est pas un péché. La concupiscence est un defaut, un vice, une propension héréditaire au péché, sans être cependant un péché au sens rigoureux du mot.'

[2] C. d. Epist. Pel., I 13, 27; De Nupt. et Concup., I 23, 26.

[3] De Bono Coniugali, 6; De Nupt. et Concup., I 15, 17; C. Iul., V 3, 12.

[4] De Pecc. Orig., 39, 44. Augustine illustrates the fact that the children of baptised parents need the grace of baptism by the case of the cultivated olive, which produces the wild olive, C. d. Epist. Pel., I 6, 11; De Nupt. et Concup., I 19, 21; and by the fact the son of a circumcised father is born uncircumcised, C. Iul. VI 7, 20.

[5] Enchiridion, 13, 41: *Nulla igitur voluptate carnalis concupiscentiae seminatus sive conceptus, et ideo nullum peccatum originaliter trahens. Dei quoque gratia verbo patris unigenito, non gratia filio, sed natura, in unitate personae modo mirabili et ineffabili adiunctus atque concretus et ideo nullum peccatum et ipse committens, tamen propter similitudinem carnis peccati, in qua venerat dictus et ipse peccatum, sacrificendus ad diluenda peccata.* Cf. De Nupt. et Concup., I 12, 13; 35, 40.

way, by two observable phenomena: the physiological fact of the
disobedience of our members; and the widespread sense of
shame at nakedness, and the operations of sex[1]. Unfortunately,
as Professor Müller has pointed out[2], Augustine's physiological
knowledge, based upon the defective medical science of his day,
was inadequate, so that his belief that the disobedience of our
members is the penalty of the Fall, and was unknown in Paradise, is scientifically untenable, and therefore untenable by
Augustine's own principle that male and female were ordained
in the beginning as we see them today in the sexes[3]. On the
purely physiological level, the facts are more favourable to
Julian of Eclanum, though more by good luck than by any deep
or profound knowledge on his part.

This does not, of course, invalidate the whole of Augustine's
teaching on the matter of concupiscence. His understanding
of the deeper issues of sexuality was infinitely more profound
than that of the optimistic Julian, and it is difficult to see how
any observer, still clinging, however feebly, to traditional
Christian values, can fail to be persuaded, with Augustine, that
there is some deep disorder in the sexual instinct, as it exists
at present in the great majority of the human race.

Libido, in the sense of *concupiscentia carnis* is, however, only
one of the *libidines* by which our fallen will is assailed. Augustine
mentions a number of them in *De Civitate Dei*, XIV 15: *libido
ulciscendi*; *libido habendi pecuniam*; *libido vincendi*; *libido gloriandi*; and, outstandingly, the *libido dominandi*, the lust for
power, which forms the theme of so much of the *De Civitate Dei*.
The expression *libido dominandi* comes from the *Coniuratio
Catilinae* of Sallust, 2,2, and is quoted by Augustine in *De Civitate Dei*, III 14[4] where, indeed, it is the distinguishing mark of

---

[1] De Pecc. Mer. et Rem., I 16, 21; II 22, 36; De Nupt. et Concup., I 5–7,
6–8; 22, 24; C. d. Epist. Pel., I 16, 32; De Civ. Dei, XIV 15; Op. Imp. c. Iul.,
6, 22.

[2] Müller, Die Lehre des hl. Augustins von der Paradiesesehe, 24–25, citing
L. Ruland, Grenzfragen der Naturwissenschaften und Theologie, Munich
1930, 14–17. I have, unfortunately, been unable to consult a copy of Ruland's
book.

[3] De Civ. Dei, XIV 22.

[4] *Illo itaque vitio tantum scelus perpetratum est socialis belli atque cognati,
quod vitium Sallustius magnum transeunter adtingit. Cum enim laudans breviter
antiquiora commemorasset tempora, quando vita hominum sine cupiditate agita-
batur et sua cuique placebant: "Postea vero, inquit, quam in Asia Cyrus, in*

312

the *civitas terrena, quae cum dominari adpetit, etsi populi serviant, ipsa ei dominandi libido dominatur*[1]. As his work progresses, Augustine returns to this lust again and again[2]; it is, for him, the outstanding characteristic of earthly societies.

If we compare the two *libidines*, the *libido carnalis* and the *libido dominandi*, we see that they are, in Augustine's thought, closely linked. Both are a consequence of the Fall and, because of our seminal identity with Adam[3] — *Omnes enim fuimus in illo uno, quando omnes fuimus ille unus*[4] — we are all subject to them. The Fall was a failure in obedience on the part of a created being, which was utterly dependent upon its Creator for all its powers. Disobedience, therefore, drew upon itself, inevitably and most justly, a loss of control, shown both in the failure of fallen man to control his body and to resist sexual passion[5] and, at the same time, by a subjection to the lust to dominate others. Thus it was that, when Adam and Eve sinned, and became subject to the *libido carnalis*, the first fruit of their union was Cain, the fratricide, the founder of the first material image of the *Civitas Terrena*[6], whose citizens pursue their course in this world, dominated by the unnatural passion for rule, unnatural, because God created man, a rational creature, fashioned in His own image, to have dominion over the beasts, and not over his fellow men[7]. It was

---

Graecia Lacedaemonii et Athenienses coepere urbes atque nationes subigere, libidinem dominandi causam belli habere, maximam gloriam in maximo imperio putare" et cetera quae ipse instituerat dicere. Mihi huc usque satis sit eius verba posuisse. Libido ista dominandi magnis malis agitat et conterit humanum genus. Hac libidine Roma tunc victa Albam se vicisse triumphabat et sui sceleris laudem gloriam nominabat, quoniam laudatur, inquit scriptura nostra, peccator in desideriis animae suae et qui iniqua gerit benedicitur.

[1] De Civ. Dei, I, Praef.

[2] Ibid., XIV 28: *Illi in principibus eius vel in eis quas subiugat nationibus dominandi libido dominatur; in hac serviant invicem in caritate, et praepositi consulendo, et subditi obtemperando.* Ibid., XIX 14: *Sed in domo iusti viventis ex fide et adhuc ab illa caelesti civitate peregrinantis etiam qui imperant serviunt eis, quibus videntur imperare. Neque enim dominandi cupiditate imperant, sed officio consulendi, nec principandi superbia, sed providendi misericordia.* Ibid., XIX 15: *Et utique felicius servitur homini, quam libidini, cum saevissimo dominatu vastet corda mortalium, ut alias omittam, libido ipsa dominandi.*

[3] *In quo omnes peccaverunt*, C. d. Epist. Pel., IV 4, 7; C. Iul., I 5, 20, etc.

[4] De Civ. Dei, XIII 14.   [5] De Civ. Dei, XIV 15; Op. Imp. c. Iul., 6, 22.

[6] De Civ. Dei, XV 1: *Natus est igitur Cain ex illis duobus generis humani parentibus, pertinens ad hominum civitatem, posterior Abel, ad civitatem Dei. ... Scriptum est itaque de Cain, quod condiderit civitatem, Abel autem tanquam peregrinus non condidit.*   [7] Ibid., XIX 15.

therefore not inappropriate that the founder of Rome, the city destined to be the head of the *Civitas terrena* upon earth, should be another fratricide[1]. In a significant fashion, too, the twin *libidines* are brought together in the official worship of pagan Rome, with its immodest and shameful festivals[2]. The glories of conquest are thought to depend upon ritual obscenity, and Augustine draws particular attention to the spectacle of Cicero, *vir gravis et philosophaster*, who, as aedile designate, bore responsibility for the disgusting rites in honour of the goddess Flora[3].

The importance of these considerations lies in this: that there has been in the past a tendency, in practice at least, to study Augustine's teaching on sexual concupiscence in isolation from his doctrine of the lust for power. This can be explained in part from the historical circumstances of his writings; his works on *concupiscentia carnis* were addressed to Christian readers, and particularly directed against the Pelagians; those on the *libido dominandi* were primarily apologetic and were therefore, to a far greater degree, directed to a pagan audience. As a consequence, once the triumph of Christianity was assured, moral theologians turned to the anti-Pelagians writings for doctrine regarding the *libido carnalis*, while the *libido dominandi*, of interest largely to the statesman and political theorist, was very much left out of account where the individual Christian was concerned.

It is, however, apparent from the *De Civitate Dei* that Augustine did not envisage any division such as developed in later Christian thought, where preoccupation with sexual concupiscence assumed preponderant, and at times deplorable, proportions, and where the will to power and domination has been, if not exactly baptised, at least treated with the same sort of respectful consideration which is accorded in modern society to usury, and financial speculation.

But has Augustine's doctrine any relevance for the present generation? In one field at least he would seem to be surprisingly modern. We can hardly fail to observe that the two *libidines* with which he is principally concerned are precisely the two emotional energies which play a dominant rôle in modern psychiatric thought — the *libido* of Freud, derived in the first instance from

---

[1] Ibid., XV 5.
[2] Ibid., II, esp. 24–29.
[3] Ibid., II 27, citing Cicero, In Verrem, Actio sec., 5, 14, 36. Testard, op. cit., II, p. 43.

the sexual impulse, (Freud's choice of name is to be noted); and the drive to power of Alfred Adler, a former follower of Freud.* On a lower intellectual plane, we hardly need to be reminded of the manifestations of the *libido dominandi* in the world today; but it is illuminating to observe that, at a time when reticence about sexual matters in fiction is at a particularly low ebb, (at least in works written in the English language), there is a tendency in some of the least inhibited to make ambition, or even simple violence, the principal attraction, to which the erotic factor, though closely allied and gaudily depicted, is subordinated.

It will be observed how closely this confirms the Augustinian theological view of the impulses which spring from the *libido dominandi* and the *concupiscentia carnis*; for it is not to be supposed that the former affects human society as a whole, but spares the individual. Thus, the bishop of Hippo's teaching is strikingly relevant to our day and age. An opportunity exists for a more detailed study on these matters intended, not as an academic exercise, but as a practical investigation, in the light of the contemporary situation. Augustine, who anticipated in a remarkable way so much modern thought, is nowhere more relevant than in the field of psychology. Where he differs from many contemporany thinkers is, of course, in his treatment; both he and they agree on the need to restore the wounded human soul to wholeness[1], but for Augustine, such restoration can be affected only by the grace of God, a grace implanted by baptism, and acting upon the human soul so that, at the last, lust and concupiscence give way to a stronger influence: the indwelling charity in the hearts of the elect of God[2].

---

[1] De Trinitate, XV 28, 51: *Tu da quaerendi vires, qui invenire te fecisti, et magis magisque inveniendi te spem dedisti. Coram te est firmitas et infirmitas mea; illam serva, istam sana. Coram te est scientia et ignorantia mea; ubi mihi aperuisti, suscipe intrantem; ubi clausisti, aperi pulsanti. Meminerim tui, intelligam te, diligam te. Auge in me ista, donec me reformes ad integrum.*

[2] De Trin., XIV 17, 23; Enchir., 32, 121; De Nupt. et Concup., I 25, 28.

* I now understand that I did Adler an injustice; his drive is to achievement, which is not the same thing as power.

X

RUFINUS OF SYRIA AND AFRICAN PELAGIANISM

ONE VALUABLE result of recent research has been the demolition of what may be called the monolithic view of Pelagianism. We can no longer think of the Pelagians as constituting a party with a rigidly-defined doctrinal system but rather as a mixed group, united by certain theological principles which nevertheless left the individual free to develop his own opinions upon particular topics. Within the general framework of Pelagianism may be detected various shades of emphasis: the aristocratic ethos of Rome, vividly depicted by Mr. Brown in a recent article;[1] the exaggerated austerity shown by the writer called by Dr. Morris the "Sicilian Briton," with its requirement of absolute poverty and chastity as conditions for the Christian life and with a possible hint of a demand for social justice;[2] and, again, the personal attitude of Pelagius himself—a man admirably characterised by Dr. Evans as "fundamentally a Christian moralist."[3] Accordingly, it is misleading—except in general terms—to talk about the "Pelagian view" on any matter; rather, we must consider which particular Pelagian we have in mind—a task which is not always easy, in view of the disagreement among scholars as to the identity of the authors of many of our Pelagian tracts.[4]

In a similar fashion the interpretation of the rôle of St. Augustine in the Pelagian Controversy has of late undergone modification. He can no longer be regarded as a sort of self-appointed champion of orthodoxy who, under cover of zeal for the faith, contrived by strength of personality to force upon the Catholic Church a theology of his own invention. It is abundantly clear that at the beginning of the Pelagian Controversy Augus-

---

[1] P. Brown, 'Pelagius and his supporters: Aims and environment,' *Journal of Theological Studies*, New Series, 19 (1968) 93-114.

[2] J. Morris, 'Pelagian Literature,' JTS NS 16 (1965) 26-60; id. 'The Literary Evidence,' in *Christianity in Britain* 300-700, ed. M. W. Barbley & R.P.C. Hanson (Leicester University Press, 1968) 55-73; but against this, see W. Liebeschutz, "Did the Pelagian movement have social aims?" *Historia* 12 (1963) 227-41; id. "Pelagian evidence on the last period of Roman Britain," *Latomus* 26 (1966) 436-47.

[3] R. F. Evans, *Pelagius: Inquiries and Reappraisals* (New York, 1968) 42.

[4] For my purposes I assume that the six tracts published by Caspari are the work of one author and that the *De Vita Christiana, De Virginitate, Ad Celantiam,* and *De Lege* are the work of Pelagius, as proposed by Evans, *Four Letters of Pelagius* (New York, 1968); but my argument does not turn upon these particular identifications.

tine was reluctant to assail Pelagius personally,[5] and the unyielding rigour with which he maintained his position against Julian of Eclanum in the closing years of his life is not paralleled in the doubts and hesitations which he revealed, in confidence, to Jerome in 415, when the controversy was still young.

The battle over Pelagianism, until its final condemnation by Pope Zosimus in 418, was fought in three different areas: at Rome, where the movement first began, and where the disturbances which it provoked eventually secured its suppression by an alarmed imperial government; in Palestine, where Jerome had been engaging Pelagius even before the arrival of Orosius in 415; and finally in Africa, where the heresy was first denounced and where it found its most implacable opponents in the Catholic bishops: hard and confident, singularly free from any doubts about the rightness of their position, and past-masters of the art—learned in the hard school of the struggle with Donatism—of presenting their case in the most effective way at the imperial court at Ravenna.[6]

The character of the first attack on Pelagianism in Africa is worth considering, since it throws some light upon the parties involved. In the first place, the Pelagian who provoked the African onslaught was not Pelagius himself but his ally, Caelestius. Secondly, it is to be observed that the charges brought against Caelestius were primarily concerned with the question of infant baptism and not with the major issues of grace and predestination with which the Pelagian Controversy is traditionally associated.[7]

This fact is of interest when one considers the situation in Africa at the time, that is to say, in the aftermath of the Donatist Controversy. Augustine saw Pelagius, fleetingly and without any exchange of words, at the Conference of Carthage in June 411. Shortly afterwards there came the first intimation of Pelagianism on African soil, in an overheard remark made by certain persons of no great standing, that children were to be baptized, not to obtain remission of sins but sanctification in Christ—a view which Augustine regarded as novel, but did not then consider neces-

---

[5] See G. Bonner, 'Les origines africaines de la doctrine augustinienne sur la chute et le péché originel,' *Augustinus* (Madrid, 1967) 107; Evans, *Pelagius*, 70.

[6] Techniques included bribery according to Julian of Eclanum, *Op. Imp.* 1.42 (PL 45. 1065. 52-1066. 3). Augustine replied that Julian was either a liar or a fool.

[7] The charges brought against Caelestius were: that Adam was created mortal and would have died whether he sinned or not; that Adam's sin injured himself and not the human race; that new-born infants are in the same state as Adam was before the Fall; that all humanity does not die through Adam's death or sin nor rise through Christ's resurrection; that the Law admits men to heaven as well as the Gospel; and that before the coming of Christ there had been sinless men. See Marius Mercator, *Commonitorium super nomine Caelestii*, 1.1. (PL 48. 68-69).

sary to refute.[8] Now this view, that infants should be baptized for sanctification and not for remission of sins, is a commonplace in Pelagian thought, and was maintained by Caelestius (with a suitable genuflection to the credal formula *in remissionem peccatorum*) in the statement of faith which he presented to Zosimus in 417.[9] For our immediate purpose, its significance lies in the fact that it represents precisely the feature in Pelagian doctrine which would impress an African familiar with the sort of discussions which the Donatist Controversy had generated. The theology of baptism had inevitably loomed large in the debates between Donatist and Catholic; but the baptism which the disputants had in mind was that of adults, and the Donatist bishop Petilian of Constantine accordingly made an issue of Augustine's omission of the words *sancte* and *sciens* when quoting his definition of a valid baptism: "What we look for is the conscience of the giver, giving in *holiness*, to cleanse that of the recipient. For he who *knowingly* receives faith from the faithless receives not faith but guilt."[10] For the Donatists the typical baptizand was the adult convert, coming to receive the sacrament in the Church of the Saints—the normal situation in the pre-Constantinian epoch—and the theology of infant baptism accordingly played little part in their doctrinal system.

Oddly enough, considering the importance of the question of infant baptism in the Pelagian Controversy, it appears that Pelagius himself had little interest in the subject.[11] Pelagius addressed his message to adult believers whom he urged to live Christian lives; accordingly "his reflection upon the sacrament of Christian initiation is built on the model of adult baptism and makes scarce sense if baptism is administered to infants."[12] Thus the issues raised at Carthage by the introduction of Pelagianism were at best incidental to the thought of the heresiarch himself. The significance of this will become clear hereafter.

---

[8] *De Pecc. Mer. et Rem.* 3.6.12 (ed. Urba & Zycha, CSEL 60. 139. 10-16).

[9] *Apud* Aug., *De Pecc. Orig.* 5.6-6.6: 'In libello autem, quem Romae edidit, qui gestis ibi ecclesiasticis allegatus est, ita de hac re loquitur, ut hoc se credere ostendat, unde hic dubitare se dixerat. nam verba eius ista sunt: "infantes autem", inquit, "debere baptizari in remissionem peccatorum secundum regulam universalis ecclesiae et secundum evangelii sententiam confitemur, quia dominus statuit regnum caelorum nonnisi baptizatis posse conferri. . . . in remissionem autem peccatorum baptizandos infantes non idcirco diximus, ut peccatum ex traduce firmare videamur, quod longe a catholico sensu alienum est, quia peccatum non cum homine nascitur, quod postmodum exercetur ab homine, quia non naturae delictum, sed voluntatis esse monstratur."' (ed. Urba & Zycha, CSEL 42. 169-23-170.1,13-18).

[10] *C. Litt. Pet.* 2.3.6; 4.8; 3.20.23: 'Conscientia namque *sancte* dantis attenditur, quae abluat accipientis nam qui fidem *sciens* a perfido sumpserit, non fidem percipit, sed reatum.' (ed. M. Petschenig, CSEL 52. 25.5-11; 179.23-180.16).

[11] See the judgment of P. Brown, *Augustine of Hippo: A Biography* (London, 1967) 352: "The Pelagian . . . was contemptuous of babies."

[12] Evans, *Pelagius*, 118.

For the moment it is to be remarked that, despite their very different parentage, Donatism and Pelagianism had much in common in their respective theologies. Both laid stress on personal holiness, Donatism in terms of Christian initiation, Pelagianism in terms of a post-baptismal life lived under the Law of Christ. "Righteousness . . . is nothing else than not to sin; but not to sin is to observe the precepts of the Law."[13] Both Donatism and Pelagianism are, in fact, survivals from the thought-world of the early Church, in which the converted Christian broke with his previous life, abandoned his secular interests, and thereafter lived a life that was new in a psychological as well as in a theological sense. Both movements accordingly assumed—Donatism explicitly, Pelagianism implicitly—that the Church of Christ must always be a holy remnant in a pagan world, in marked contrast to the Augustinian doctrine of the *corpus permixtum*.

In this context it is worth considering whether the accusation brought against Pelagius at the Synod of Diospolis that he had taught that the Church below is without spot or wrinkle may not have been something more than a mere controversial indictment designed to associate him with the Donatists—a possibility which Augustine himself seems to have recognized.[14] The passage in question certainly appears in the writings of Pelagius—it occurs in the *De Virginitate* and can be paralleled in other works.[15] Did Pelagius' accusers, when they formulated this charge, have any information that Pelagianism found support among former Donatists and Donatist sympathisers? The question cannot be answered in our present state of knowledge; but Caelestius certainly enjoyed considerable success in his propaganda activities at Carthage before his condemnation,[16] and his adherents subsequently displayed a tenacity worthy of the Donatists, and did not hesitate to bring charges of innovation and heresy against their Catholic opponents.[17] The possibility

---

[13] Pel., *De Virg.*, 5: 'Iustitia ergo non est aliud quam non peccare; non peccare autem legis praecepta servare." (PL 30, 171 B).

[14] *De Gest. Pel.* 12.27 (p. 80 Urba & Zycha).

[15] Pel., *De Virg.* 10: 'Quamquam enim nulli Christianorum peccare liceat, et omnes quicumque spiritalis lavacri sanctificatione purgantur, immaculatam decurrere conveniat vitam, ut Ecclesiae, quae *sine macula, sine rugis*, sine aliquo eiusmodi esse describitur, possint visceribus intimari . . .' (PL 30. 176 C). Cf. *Exp. in Eph.* 5. 27 (ed. Souter, p. 378. PL Suppl. 1.1304); *De Lege* 1 (PL 30. 109 C).

[16] *De Gest Pel.* 35.62: 'Ista haeresis cum plurimos decepisset et fratres, quos non deceperat, contubaret, Caelestius quidam talia sentiens ad iudicium Carthaginensis ecclesiae perductus episcoporum sententia condemnatus est.' (116. 18-21 Urba & Zycha).

[17] Aug., *Serm.* 294. 21. 20; 'Impetremus ergo, si possumus, a fratribus nostris, ne nos insuper appellent haereticos, quod eos talia disputantes nos appellare possimus forsitan, si velimus, nec tamen appellamus.' (PL 38. 1348. 17-20).

of an alliance between certain elements in Donatism and African Pelagianism is at least a reasonable hypothesis.

However, the gravamen of the charge brought against Caelestius was not Donatism but the denial of the transmission of Original Sin. This is not surprising; I have suggested elsewhere that the so-called Augustinian doctrine of Original Sin is really an African doctrine which Augustine accepted as catholic teaching and defended but did not originate.[18] The interesting thing about Caelestius' answer to the charge is that he did not deny the accusation but claimed that there was no defined doctrine on the matter. "I have told you that as regards the transmission of sin I have heard various people within the Catholic Church deny it and others assert it. It therefore follows that the affair is a matter of opinion, not of heresy. I have always said that infants need baptism and ought to be baptized. What more does my accuser want from me?"[19] The Carthaginian tribunal was unimpressed and excommunicated Caelestius; but the latter continued to hold his own view, and unhesitatingly declared it in his appeal to Zosimus in 417.[20]

Despite Caelestius' confident assertion that he had heard various people within the Catholic Church deny the transmission of Original Sin, repeated demands from his prosecutor, Paulinus of Milan, produced only one name: "The holy priest Rufinus, who resided at Rome with the holy Pammachius." It seems clear that this Rufinus is to be identified with Rufinus the Syrian who, according to Marius Mercator, first sowed the seeds of Pelagianism at Rome in the pontificate of Anastasius (399-402) and corrupted Pelagius who thereafter became the principal disseminator of the heresy.[21] As it happens, one work of Rufinus has survived—the *Liber de Fide*, now preserved in a sixth-century manuscript at Leningrad. This was first published by Sirmond in 1650 and reprinted by Garnier in his edition of Marius Mercator's works in 1673 (PL 48. 451-488) with a valuable commentary which still repays study. A critical text and English translation by Dr. M. W. Miller appeared in 1964[22] and will be used in the present article.

---

[18] Bonner, *art. cit. supra* n[5].
[19] *De Pecc. Orig.* 4.3. (169. 11-15 Urba & Zycha).
[20] See above n[9].
[21] Mar. Merc., *Lib. Subn. in verb. Iul. Praef.* 2: 'Hanc ineptam et non minus inimicam rectae fidei quaestionem, sub sanctae recordationis Anastasio Romanae Ecclesiae summo pontifice, Rufinus quidam natione Syrus Romam primus invexit, et ut erat argutus, se quidem ab eius invidia muniens, et per se proferre non ausus, Pelagius gente Brittanum monachum tunc decepit eumque ad praedictam apprime imbuit atque instituit impiam vanitatem.' (PL 48. 111. 5-13).
[22] *Rufini Presbyteri Liber de Fide: A Critical Text and Translation with Introduction and Commentary* by Sister Mary William Miller (The Catholic University of America Patristic Studies Vol. 96) (Washington D. C., 1964).

The *Liber de Fide* was the subject of an important study by Professor Altaner in 1950.[23] In this essay, Altaner argued convincingly for accepting Garnier's identification of Rufinus of Syria with the monk of that name sent by Jerome to Rome in 399. Against Garnier however, Altaner held that the *De Fide* was originally written in Latin and not translated from the Greek and his argument—which is accepted by Dr. Miller—is of importance in any attempt to date the work. Garnier had considered that it was written in Greek in the east and translated into Latin in Italy before 410. Altaner considered that such early dating was impossible, on the ground both that Augustine would have been quick to detect and refute any early manifestation of Pelagianism and also because the Pelagian doctrine of cc. 29-42 is (in his opinion) too well-developed and organized for an early treatise. Furthermore, arguing from the belief that Augustine was the first theologian to hold the *theologoumenon* of the damnation of unbaptized infants, Altaner regarded the *De Fide* as an answer to the earliest anti-Pelagian writings of Augustine, notably the *De Peccatorum Meritis* written in 412. Accordingly he maintained that the *De Fide* can hardly be earlier than 413. Its *terminus ad quem* is indicated by the absence of any reference to Nestorianism. Therefore, according to Altaner, the *De Fide* must have been written at some time between 413 and 428,[24] and these arguments are accepted by Dr. Miller in her edition.[25]

However, since Père Refoulé, following a suggestion of Père de Blic,[26] has established an impressive case for regarding the *De Fide* as the Pelagian work refuted by Augustine in the *De Peccatorum Meritis et Remissione*,[27] it is clear that Altaner's argument fails and the *De Fide* must be earlier than 412. Furthermore, certain considerations not only strengthen Refoulé's case, but also suggest a date of composition considerably earlier than 412.

In the first place if we suppose, as Altaner did, that the *Liber de Fide* was composed as an answer to the *De Peccatorum Meritis*, it must be regarded as a singularly badly prepared one. The greater part of the

---

[23] B. Altaner, 'Der *Liber de Fide* ein Werk des Pelagianers Rufinus des "Syrers,"' *Theologische Quartalschrift* 130 (1950) 432-49; reprinted in *Kleine Patristische Schriften*, hrsg. von G. Glockmann (Texte und Untersuchungen zur Gesch. d. altchristlichen Literatur Bd 83), Berlin 1967, 467-82.

[24] *Ibid.*, pp. 426-28.

[25] Miller, *op. cit.* pp. 8-10.

[26] J. de Blic, 'Le péché originel selon saint Augustin,' *Recherches de Sciences religieuse* 16 (1927) 518-19.

[27] F. Refoulé, 'Datation du premier concile de Carthage contre les Pélagiens et du *Libellus Fidei* de Rufin,' *Revue des études augustiniennes* 9 (1963) 41-49.

work is devoted to a denunciation of the classical trinitarian heresies of the East—Arianism, Eunomianism, and Sabellianism; a defence of the perpetual virginity of Mary (c. 43) and of the doctrine of the resurrection of the body (c. 51). In a work of sixty-one chapters only cc. 29-41 and 48 can be regarded as indubitably Pelagian, and not all the doctrine there expressed can be called unorthodox. Accordingly, if the *De Fide* were primarily intended as a refutation of Augustine, one can only say that the author was remarkably slow in coming to the point.

One cannot, of course, altogether exclude the possibility that the *De Fide* displays an extreme subtlety, leading the unwary reader through pages of orthodox belief in order to confront him, all unprepared, with heretical doctrine. Such at least was the opinion of the writer who added the famous gloss on f. 1ʳ of the Leningrad manuscript, probably in the seventh century: "Hic liber qui attitulatur Rufini non te seducat, O pie lector, quia Pelagianus est et blasphemiis Pelagianorum plenus. Simulans enim contra Arianos disputationem, venena suae hereseos inseruit."[28] However, commonsense and the principles of pamphleteering alike suggest that this is a singularly inept way of refuting an adversary or making propaganda. Rufinus' technique—if technique it is—is better suited to a time when disputed principles are still an open question than to the period when battle has been joined.

Furthermore the Traducianists—whom Rufinus certainly dislikes and condemns—are not so much wicked and heretical as stupid. They are mad (c.28: *dementia capti;* c.39: *insaniunt*) it is true; their ignorance of Divine Scripture—an ignorance which Rufinus is remarkably free in imputing to anyone with whom he disagrees—leads them "to burst out into an impious and unreasonable judgment about Christ, asserting that He destines unbaptized children to the punishment of everlasting fire;"[29] but Rufinus is more impressed by their folly than by their wickedness. The villain of his denunciation is Origen, who is never mentioned without some pejorative epithet or phrase. *Impie Origenes ac nefarie fatus est*[30]—*nefarius Origenes*[31]—*nefariam Origenis haeresim*[32]—*impius Origenes*[33]—such is Rufinus' opinion of the great Alexandrian theologian. Twice Rufinus washes his hands of the wretched creature—*Sed Origenes nunc eiusque socii dimittantur*[34]—but subsequently he returns

---

[28] Miller, *op. cit. p.* 36 nᵗ; PL Suppl. 1. 1099.
[29] *De Fide* 41 (117. 5-9 Miller).
[30] *Ibid.* 17 (72.34 Miller).
[31] *Ibid.* 21 (80.19 Miller).
[32] *Ibid.* 22 (82. 17-18 Miller).
[33] *Ibid.* 26 (88.11 Miller).
[34] *Ibid.* 22, 27 (82. 31-32, 90. 10-11 Miller).

to the attack.[35] There can be no question that his book is intended, among other things, as an attack upon Origen and his supporters. Compared with Origen the Traducianists, although wrong to the point of wickedness, are secondary opponents.

These facts may provide a clue to the date of the *Liber de Fide*. If we accept the view that the work was originally written by Rufinus the Syrian in Latin, we have to decide at what point between his arrival in Rome in 399 and the writing of Augustine's *De Peccatorum Meritis* in 412 an attack on Origen would have been most appropriate. The obvious date is the pontificate of Anastasius, whom we know to have responded enthusiastically to the advances of Theophilus of Alexandria, when the latter embarked on his anti-Origenistic crusade.[36] In these circumstances it would not be surprising if Rufinus of Syria, soon after his arrival in Rome *en route* for Milan in 399, carrying literary material provided by Jerome for his denunciation of Rufinus of Aquileia's translation of the *Peri Archon,* should have decided to make his own contribution to the attack on Origen's teaching. This would confirm Marius Mercator's statement that Rufinus introduced Pelagianism at Rome in the pontificate of Anastasius.

Moreover, Rufinus' refutation of traducianism in the *De Fide* may explain a passage in the Apology which his namesake of Aquileia addressed to Pope Anastasius in the second half of 400,[37] as a preliminary to the longer reply to Jerome in the following year. In his apology Rufinus assures Anastasius of his belief in the catholic doctrines of the Trinity, the Incarnation, the resurrection of the body and the everlasting punishment of the damned. With regard to Origen he declares that he is simply a translator, not an advocate or defender. He also says that he understands that questions have been raised regarding the origins of the human soul. On this matter he has read various theories: that it is transmitted by human generation—a view held by Latin authors like Tertullian and Lactantius and perhaps some others; that it is created by God for each individual; and again that after being created by God the already-existing soul is sent by His judgment to be born in a particular body—the view held by Origen and some Greek writers. So far as he himself is concerned, Ru-

---

[35] *Ibid.* 36: '. . . sicut impius Origenes exposuit' (108. 9-10 Miller).
[36] See F. Cavallera, *Saint Jérome: sa vie et son oeuvre,* 1. 1. (Louvain/Paris, 1922) 255-64.
[37] For date, see Cavallera, *op. cit.* p. 260 n³.

finus declares that he has no fixed opinion, holding only to the tradition of the Church that God is the maker alike of souls and bodies.[38]

It would be convenient to regard this passage as being inspired by Rufinus of Syria's denunciation of those holding the Origenistic doctrine of the precreation of souls or traducianism[39] but the temptation must be resisted. We can only say that Rufinus of Aquileia's words indicate that discussion about the origin of the human soul had recently arisen at Rome and that Rufinus himself believed that none of the various theories proposed—creationism, traducianism, or precreationism—represented declared catholic doctrine. "It is a matter of opinion not of heresy," as Caelestius was to declare at a later date. Rufinus the Syrian, on the other hand, rejected alike any doctrine of precreation or traducianism. "The holy priest Rufinus who resided at Rome with the holy Pammachius—I heard him say that there is no transmission of sin."[40]

From this it would appear that there is a line of descent from the writings of Rufinus of Syria at Rome in about 400 A.D. to the propositions of which Caelestius was accused at Carthage in the winter of 411/412. If this is true, then Rufinus fully deserves the style of founder of Pelagianism implied by the words of Marius Mercator. However, it is important to be clear about what is meant by this title. In the first place, Rufinus' influence on Pelagianism was upon the doctrines of Adam's sin and the fate of unbaptized infants rather than on the larger issues of grace and predestination which Augustine debated with Pelagius, Julian, and the

---

[38] Rufin., *Apol. ad Anas.* 6: 'Audio et de anima quaestiones esse commotas. De qua re utrum recipi debeat quaeremonia aut abici vos probate. Si autem et de me quid sentiam quaeritur, fateor me de hac quaestione apud quamplurimos tractatorum diversa legisse. Legi quosdam dicentes quod pariter cum corpore per humani seminis traducem etiam anima defundatur, et hoc quibus poterant adsertionibus confirmabant. Quod puto inter Latinos Tertullianum sensisse vel Lactantium, fortassis et alios nonnullos. Alii adserunt quod formatis in utero corporibus Deus cotidie faciat animas et infundat. Alii factas iam olim, id est, tunc cum omnia Deus creavit ex nihilo, nunc eas iudicio suo dispenset nasci in corpore. Hoc sentit et Origenes et nonnulli alii Graecorum. Ego vero cum haec singula legerim, Deo teste dico quia usque ad praesens certi et definiti aliquid de hac quaestione non teneo, sed Deo relinquo scire quid sit in vero et si cui ipse revelare dignabitur. Ego tamen haec singula et legisse me non nego, et adhuc ignorare confiteor, praeter hoc quod manifeste tradit ecclesia, Deum esse et animarum et corporum conditorem.' (ed. Simonetti, CC 20. 27. 11-19).

[39] *De Fide* 27, 28: 'Sicut ergo qui ita credunt impie credere comprobantur [animam partem Dei esse], sic etiam illi qui animas dicunt ante corpora factas fuisse multum a pietate distare inveniuntur. Unde impius Origenes, Gentilium captus errore et ab eo nolens penitur abscedere, novarum etiam studens auctor esse sectarum, coniecturis illorum alio modo translatis, edocuit de quibus in praesenti disputandum esse non arbitror, ne nos multum verborum mittamus in silvam. . . . Quia igitur nonnulli sunt qui, dementia capti, dicunt quod ex una anima primi hominis Adam anima Evae mulieris assumpta sit; nonnulli etiam, quod ex solo Adam cum seminis iactu in omnes qui ex eo nati fuerunt animae transmissae sint; et alii, quod ex Eva sola magis animae fuere translatae et sic a parentibus ad eorum liberos deductae sint, respondendum est his hoc modo . . .' (88. 8-16; 90. 12-19 Miller).

[40] *De Pecc. Orig.* 3. 3. (168. 13-15 Urba & Zycha).

alarmed ascetics of Southern Gaul. Secondly, while it is apparent that these particular doctrines of Rufinus can fairly be described as Pelagian, it is by no means certain that they were his main theological interest. His motive in writing the *De Fide* cannot now be established. We know that there was a second book, of which two excerpts were incorporated by the sixth-century writer John the Deacon in his *Expositio in Heptateuchum*,[41] but neither of these throws any light on Pelagianism. It therefore remains an open question whether Rufinus was the conscious founder of Pelagianism or whether he merely held certain views which later were adopted by Pelagian theologians without necessarily regarding them as the basis of his religious belief. His inactivity during the Pelagian Controversy might be thought to favour the second alternative, if it were not for the fact that we do not know the date of Rufinus' death, and he may well have been dead before the Controversy started.

Furthermore, Rufinus' views were not taken over by more famous Pelagians without modification. The first charge brought against Caelestius at Carthage, that Adam was created mortal and would have died whether he sinned or not, is not the doctrine of Rufinus. According to him, "Adam and Eve were created immortal according to the soul but mortal according to the body; nevertheless they would not have tasted death, as blessed Enoch merited, if only they had been willing to obey God's command."[42] This view, if we except the reference to Enoch "meriting" translation, is substantially that of Augustine in the *De Peccatorum Meritis*: "Although Adam was dust according to the body and had an animal body yet, if he had not sinned, he would have passed into the incorruption promised to the faithful and to the saints without any punishment of death."[43] Indeed, Rufinus' picture of the condition of Adam and Eve in Paradise is curiously like that of Augustine in his later works, for Adam and Eve, according to Rufinus, if they had obeyed God's command would, after the procreation of children, have been made immortal by the fruit of the tree of life.[44] Similarly, according to Augustine writing in 421, if

---

[41] Paris, B.N. MS. lat. 12,309, ff. 73ᵛ, 94ʳ (printed by Miller, p. 48 n[102]).

[42] *De Fide* 29: 'Illos igitur primos homines, Adam dico et Evam, licet immortales secundum animam creatos esse dixerim, mortales vero secundum corpus; numquam tamen mortem gustassent, siquidem mandatum Dei servare voluissent, sicut beatus Henoch meruit.' (94. 6-10 Miller).

[43] *De Pecc. Mer. et Rem.* 1.2.2.: 'Quamvis enim secundum corpus terra esset et corpus in quo creatus est animale gestaret, tamen, si non pecasset, in corpus fuerat spiritale mutandus et in illam incorruptionem quae fidelibus et sanctis promittitur, sine mortis supplicio transiturus.' (4. 7-11 Urba & Zycha).

[44] *De Fide* 30: 'Sic igitur possumus dicere etiam de Adam simul et Eva quod si praeceptum Dei mandatumque servassent, etiam post liberorum procreationem, gustato ligno vitae, immortales iugitur permanissent, non egentes in posterum victus et incrementi vel nuptiarum.' (96. 7-12 Miller).

Adam had persevered he would in due time after the birth of children and without any interposition of death have been brought to a better state.[45] Again, Rufinus' description of the immediate consequences of the Fall, in which the perception by Adam and Eve of their own nakedness is understood in a sexual connotation,[46] is exactly that of Augustine,[47] though without Augustine's preoccupation with the psychology of concupisence which occupies so much space in the Fourteenth Book of the *De Civitate Dei*.

It is clear then that the views attacked in the first charge against Caelestius in 411/412, namely that Adam was created mortal and would have died, whether or not he sinned, is not that of Rufinus nor, for that matter, of Pelagius.[48] Of the other five theses, Rufinus would certainly have agreed with the second, that the sin of Adam injured himself and not the human race;[49] with the third, that infants today are born in the same state in which Adam was before the Fall;[50] and with the sixth, that even before the coming of Christ there had been sinless men.[51] With regard to the fourth, that the whole of mankind neither dies in Adam's death or sin nor rises through Christ's resurrection, he would certainly have accepted the first part, but would possibly have been reluctant to dissociate any created being from the benefit of Christ's resurrection completely.[52] With regard to the fifth, that the Law admits to the kingdom

---

[45] *Enchir.* 28.104: 'Quapropter etiam primum hominem deus in ea salute, in qua conditus est, custodire voluisset eumque opportuno tempore post genitos filios sine interpositione mortis ad meliora perducere' (PL 40. 231. 18-22).

[46] *De Fide* 31: 'Dicit enim Moyses: *Erant autem ambo nudi, tam Adam quam uxor eius, et non erubescebant.* Non Moyses hoc dixit, quasi illi, incontinentiae caecitate decepti, pudorem spernerent nuditatis, sed ostendit eos, tamquam infantes, necdum cupiditatem coeundi habere. Unde post praevaricationem, nuditate perspecta, non totius dico corporis, sed illius partis, quam etiam Cham, Noe dormiente, viderat, tunc demum, creandorum liberorum cupiditatem adepti et intellegentes nuditatem suam, ficorum foliis verenda texerunt.' (98.27-36 Miller).

[47] e.g. *De Pecc.Mer. et Rem.* 1. 16.21: "Tunc. ille extitit bestialis motus pudendus hominibus, quem in sua erubuit nuditate' (21.2-4 Urba & Zycha).

[48] *Exp. in Rom.* 5. 12 (ed. Souter p. 45. PL Suppl. 1. 1136); *De Virg.* 6. (PL 30. 172 B).

[49] *De Fide* 39: 'Post haec igitur Dei testimonia, insaniunt qui, per unum hominem Adam, omnem orbem terrarum iniquitatis flagitiorumque condemnant.' (112. 6-8 Miller).

[50] *Ibid.* 38: 'Quod autem liberi non pro parentibus puniantur neque parentes pro liberis, aperte rursus edocuit Deus cum ad Moysem prophetam diceret: *Non morientur patres pro filiis, neque filii pro parentibus, unusquisque in peccato suo morietur.*' (110. 16-20 Miller).

[51] *Ibid.* 39: 'Neque enim meminit usquam divina Scriptura quasi ipsi [Adam et Eva] secundo peccaverint, sicuti de Cain, quod secundo peccavit narrare non distulit, quippe cum etiam de Abel, quod a peccatis fuerit alienus, aperte docuerit. Quid vero etiam de Henoch atque Elia dicent, quod, cum bene placuissent Deo, *translati sunt ut mortem penitus non viderent*, non ab Adam praevaricatione prohibiti permanere immortales, cum per eosdem clare docuerit unigenitus Deus ante carnalem adventum suum spem ipsam resurrectionis.' (112.23-32 Miller).

[52] *Ibid.* 49: 'Nam propterea etiam virtutes caelestes per solam fidem creantur in Christo, quia et istas omnes in semetipso renovavit.' (126. 9-11 Miller).

of heaven no less than the Gospel, he might likewise have hesitated, for his treatise makes clear his recognition of the saving work of Christ, which he sees operating retrospectively in the case of the saints of the Old Testament,[53] although his doctrine of grace—such as it was—was certainly inadequate by Augustine's standards.

Rufinus may therefore be regarded as being in large measure the inspirer, whether consciously or not, of African Pelagianism. The word African is used advisedly, since the issue of infant baptism had a particular importance in Africa, partly no doubt because the theology of baptism, as has already been suggested, was already a topic of interest because of the Donatist Controversy, and partly because of the African interest in the doctrine of Original Sin and its consequences. The first hint of Pelagianism at Carthage was the remark overheard by Augustine that what infants gained from baptism was not remission of sins but sanctification in Christ. This is precisely the view of Rufinus: "Infants receive baptism not because of sins, but in order that, possessing spiritual procreation, they may be, as it were, partakers of His heavenly kingdom."[54] "Infants who are not in sin also merit the grace of baptism in order that, begotten in Christ by a new generation, they may also become co-heirs of His kingdom, in accordance with blessed Paul: *If then any man is in Christ, he is a new creature.*"[55] Here we have the famous doctrine of the baptism of infants in order that they may be made members of the kingdom of heaven. Moreover Rufinus claims dominical authority when he declares that infants are "strangers to all sin;"[56] denies as an "impious and unreasonable judgment about Christ" the belief "that He destines unbaptized children to the punishment of everlasting fire, which in the Scriptures is usually called gehenna;"[57] and employs the argu-

---

[53] *Ibid.* 39, where Rufinus quotes the Petrine account of Christ preaching to the spirits in prison (1 Pet. 3. 19-21).

[54] *Ibid.* 40: 'Baptisma igitur infantes non propter peccata percipiunt sed ut, spiritalem procreationem habentes, quasi per baptisma in Christo creentur et ipsius regni caelestis participes fiant.' (114. 23-27 Miller). Cited by Augustine, *De Pecc. Mer. et Rem.* 1.18.23 (22. 18-23 Urba & Zycha).

[55] *Ibid.* 48: 'Infantes, qui in peccatis non sunt, merentur etiam baptismatis gratiam ut, in Christo nova generatione creati, etiam, regni eius coheredes efficiantur, secundum beatum Paulum: *Si qua in Christo nova creatura.*' (126. 4-8 Miller).

[56] *Ibid.* 41: 'Pariter etiam Dominus noster Iesus Christus de parvulis docet, quod ab omni peccato sint alieni, cum dicit: *Amen dico vobis, nisi conversi fueritis et efficiamini sicut parvuli, non intrabitis in regnum caelorum.*' (116. 27-31 Miller).

[57] *Ibid.*: 'Quia igitur quidam Scripturarum inscientia divinarum in nefariam et iniustam de Christo vocem audent erumpere, asserantes eum pueros minime baptizatos aeterni ignis poenae deputare, qui assolet in Scripturas gehenna nominari . . .' (116. 5-8 Miller). Cf. Aug., *Serm.* 293.9: 'Hic aliquis occurrit, et dicit mihi: Quomodo *omnes*? Qui ergo in *gehennam* mittendi sunt, qui cum diabolo damnabuntur, qui aeternibus ignibus torquebuntur?' (PL 38. 1333. 35-38).

ment—subsequently to be widely used in Pelagian circles—that if infants
are baptized on account of Adam's sin, those born of Christian parents
ought not to be baptized.[58] In short, Rufinus provides a manual of Pelagian teaching, not of the metaphysical issues of grace and predestination, but of the hardly less important topics of Orginial Sin and infant
baptism.

Should we regard Rufinus' denunciation of traducianism as being in
any way directed against Augustine, now that Altaner's theory that the
De Fide was an answer to the *theologoumenon* of the damnation of unbaptized infants as expounded in the *De Peccatorum Meritis* and Sermon
294 is no longer tenable? It is possible that Rufinus had read at least
two of Augustine's earlier writings. First, the *De Libero Arbitrio*, in the
third book of which Augustine referred to the four theories about the
origin of the human soul, with the comment that to the best of his knowledge no definitive opinion had been expressed on the matter by Catholic
writers.[59] The *De Libero Arbitrio* was finally completed in 395 and one
could imagine Rufinus being spurred by this passage to expound his own
view of creationism, and denounce precreationism and traducianism. Furthermore Rufinus raises as an objection to traducianism the fact that newly-
baptized infants are permitted to taste death[60]—a fact which had troubled
Augustine.[61] It is interesting to note that both these passages from the *De
Liberio Arbitrio* were quoted by Augustine in his letter to Jerome of 415
on the origin of the soul, with the remark that the work was being widely
read.[62]

There was, however, another work of Augustine which could have
been known to Rufinus: the *De Diversis Quaestionibus* addressed to Sim-

---

[58] *Ibid.* 40: 'Et siquidem propter peccatum Adam baptizantur infantes, qui ex parentibus
Christianis nati sunt baptizari minime debebant, et quasi sancti perinde haberentur, quia de
parentibus sunt fidelibus procreati.' (114. 14-17 Miller). Cf. Aug., *De Pecc. Mer. et Rem.*
2. 25. 41. (112.11-113.10 Urba & Zycha).

[59] *De Lib. Arb.* 3.21.59: 'Harum autem quatuor de anima sententiarum, utrum de pro-
pagine veniant an in singulis quibusque nascentibus novae fiant an in corpora nascentium
iam alicubi existentes vel mittantur divinitus vel sua sponte labantur, nullam temere adfirmare
oportebit. Aut enim nondum ista quaestio a divinorum librorum catholicis tractatoribus pro
merito suae obscuritatis et perplexitatis evoluta atque illustrata est, aut si iam factum est nondum in manus nostras huiusce litterae pervenerunt.' (ed. Green, CSEL 74. 138. 8-16). Cf. the
views of Rufinus in 400, cited above n[38].

[60] *De Fide* 40: 'Sin vero, ut ipsi asserunt, propter peccatum Adam moriuntur infantes,
dicant nobis cur statim batizati mortem gustare permittuntur . . .' (111. 9-11 Miller).

[61] *De Lib. Arb.* 3. 23.67: 'Quo loco etiam illud perscrutari homines solent, sacramentum
baptismi Christi quid parvulis prosit, cum eo accepto plerumque moruntur priusquem ex eo
quicquam cognoscere potuerint. Qua in re satis pie recteque creditur prodesse parvulo eorum
fidem a quibus consecrandus offertur.' (145. 5-10 Green).

[62] Aug., *Ep.* 166. 3.7; 7.18. (ed. Goldbacher, CSEL 44. 555, 556, 571, 572).

X

plicianus of Milan in 397. Here is expressed, in language which anticipates that of the later anti-Pelagian treatises, the Augustinian doctrine of the Fall in all its rigour.

> Now all men are a lump of sin since, as the Apostle says, *in Adam all die,* and to Adam the entire human race traces the origin of its sin against God. Sinful humanity must pay a debt of punishment to the supreme divine justice. Whether that debt is exacted or remitted there is no unrighteousness. . . . So the Apostle represses the impudent questioner: *O man, who art thou that repliest against God?*[63]

The election of Jacob and the rejection of Esau without any antecedent merit or offence is discussed at length, leading once more to that familiar quotation: *O man, who art thou that repliest against God?*[64] The sinister expression *originalis reatus* makes its appearance.[65] In short, if the view that unbaptized infants are eternally lost is not explicitly stated, it is most certainly implied.

One detail may support the view that Rufinus had read the *De Diversis Quaestionibus.* In this work Augustine refers to the case of the centurion Cornelius to show that faith must precede good works but is itself insufficient to secure entry into the kingdom of heaven without the sacrament of baptism.[66] Rufinus also refers to Cornelius and his treatment is subtly different. He agrees that he needed the indispensable baptism of water to share in the resurrection of Christ; but he neverthe-

---

[63] *De Div. Quaest. ad Simpl.* 1.q.2.16: 'Sunt igitur omnes homines (quandoquidem, ut Apostolus ait, *in Adam omnes moriuntur,* a quo in universum genus humanum origo ducitur offensionis Dei) una quaedam massa peccati, supplicium debens divinae summaeque iustitiae, quod sive exigatur, sive donetur, nulla est iniquitas. A quibus exigendum, et quibus donandum sit, superbe iudicant debitores: quemadmodum conducti ad illam vineam iniuste indignati sunt, cum tantumdem aliis donaretur, quantum illis redderetur. Itaque huius impudentiam quaestionis ita retundit Apostolus: *O homo, tu quis es, qui respondeas Deo?*' (PL 40. 121. 3-15).

[64] *Ibid.* 7-16. It is worth noting that Rufinus' only reference to Esau and Jacob is as a proof of the sinlessness of newly-born infants. *De Fide* 41: 'Et iterum de Esau et Iacob docet, sic dicens: *Cum necdum nati essent nec aliquid fecissent boni vel mali*' (118.6-8 Miller).

[65] *Ibid.* 20: 'In omnibus est etiam spiritus vitalis terrena membra vivificans, omnisque natura hominis dominatu animae et famulatu corporis conditione mirabili temperata: sed concupiscentia carnalis de peccati poena iam regnans, universum genus humanum tanquam totam et unam conspersionem originali reatu in omnia permanente confuderat.' (PL 40. 126. 2-8).

[66] *Ibid.* 2: 'Non enim catechumeni non credant, aut vero Cornelius non credebat Deo, cum eleemosynis et orationibus dignum se praeberet cui angelus mitteretur; sed nullo modo ista operaretur, nisi ante credidisset; nullo modo autem credidisset, nisi vel secretis per visa mentis aut spiritus, vel manifestioribus per sensus corporis admonitionibus vocaretur. Sed in quibusdam tanta est gratia fidei, quanta non sufficit ad obtinendum regnum caelorum; sicut in catechumenis, sicut in ipso Cornelio antequam Sacramentorum participatione incorporaretur Ecclesiae.' (PL 40. 111.49- 112.6). Significantly, Augustine returns to the case of Cornelius in 401, in one of his rare references to infant baptism in his anti-Donatist writings. *De Baptismo* 4.24.31 (ed. Petschenig, CSEL 51.259).

less holds that even before his water-baptism Cornelius had, like the Apostles, received the baptism of the Spirit and was therefore free from sin.[67] This he regards as confirming his thesis that infants need baptism, not for the remission of sins but in order that they may inherit the kingdom of heaven. His reasoning leads to the same practical conclusion as Augustine's; but the premisses are utterly different.

The above parallel cannot be regarded as proof that Rufinus had read the *De Diversis Quaestionibus;* but the possibility exists and Augustine, when reading the *De Fide,* can hardly have failed to remark the bitter criticism which it develops of his basic assumptions. *Insaniunt qui, per unum hominem Adam, omnem orbem terrarum . . . condemnant.* The remark must have stung.

Can we detect any particular way in which the *Liber de Fide* may have affected Augustine's thought during the Pelagian Controversy? It is possible that its influence may be discerned in the anguished letter sent to Jerome by the hand of Orosius in the spring of 415; for here Augustine sees, with agonized clarity, the two problems of the divine love, raised by belief in the damnation of the unbaptized, and of the divine justice, raised by any non-traducian theory of the origin of the human soul. 'So many thousands of souls which, when infants die, depart from their bodies without the remission of the Christian sacrament—by what equity are they damned, if the newly created individual souls without any preceding sin but only by the will of the Creator cleave to the individuals being born?'[68]—what is this question but the obvious reaction to Rufinus' confident assertion: 'Children, therefore . . . being wholly innocent and utterly inexperienced in wickedness, and ignorant also of the difference between good and evil, are not at all subjected to the punishment of everlasting fire.'[69] Augustine, as E.R. Fairweather has rightly observed, was no *tortor infantium;*[70] he believed in the justice of God no less than did

[67] *De Fide* 40: '. . . . Cornelius, qui testimonio Dei iustitia nitebatur, quique baptisma Spiritus sicut et apostoli perceperat, et Sancti Spiritus particeps erat, quo in se habitante peccatum penitus habere non poterat necessario tamen etiam illo baptismate quod per aquam traditur dignus habitus est ut, secundum beatum Paulum, *complantatus propter mortem similitudinis Christi, etiam eius resurrectionis coheres existeret.*' (114.30-115.4 Miller).

[68] Aug., *Ep.* 166. 4.10. (560.15-561.4 Goldbacher).

[69] *De Fide* 41: 'Pueri igitur, sicut ipsa divina Scriptura perdocuit, quasi penitus innoxii neque malitiam prorsus experti, boni etiam vel mali discretionem ignorantes, ignis aeterni poenae minime mancipantur, quippe cum ignis aeternum supplicium impiis ac peccatoribus praeparatum sit. Sed et isti quidem cum sua imperitia dimittantur.' (118. 8-14 Miller).

[70] E. R. Fairweather, 'St. Augustine's interpretation of infant baptism,' *Augustinus Magister* (Paris, 1954) 2. p. 899.

Julian of Eclanum;[71] but his sense of the necessity for salvation by in-corporation in the Body of Christ through the sacrament of baptism over-came all notions of divine equity and drove him at the last, to declare that no theory of the origin of the human soul could be accepted which appeared to cast doubt upon the practice of the universal Church of bap-tizing infants *in remissionem peccatorum*.[72] For with all due respect, I can-not accept Mr. Brown's description of Augustine's sermons on infant bap-tism as "demagoguery."[73] Rather, I would see them as a passionate defence of Augustine's belief that in Christ alone is our hope of salvation.

> All who are reborn do indeed ascend to heaven; and of the rest never a one. And all who are reborn ascend to heaven by the grace of God; and *no one has ascended into heaven but He who descended from heaven, the Son of Man who is in heaven*. And why? Because all who are reborn are made His members, and Christ alone who was born of Mary is one Christ, and with His Body the one Christ is the head. Therefore it was His will to say: *No one has ascended but He who descended*. No one has therefore as-cended except Christ. If you wish to ascend, be in the Body of Christ, if you wish to ascend, be a member of Christ.[74]

These words might have come from one of Augustine's sermons against the Donatists. In fact they are taken from the great sermon against Pelagian-ism which he preached in the Basilica Maiorum at Carthage on 27 June 413. Against the Pelagian no less than against the Donatist Augus-tine maintains that only in the Body of Christ is there hope of salva-tion. This is why he cannot envisage any middle place between heaven and hell for unbaptized infants such as he supposed—probably errone-ously—the Pelagians to teach.[75]

Now it is clear that Augustine would find—or think that he had found—this notion of a middle place implied in the *De Fide* with its as-sertion that infants, although without sin, must be baptized to have a place in the kingdom of heaven and this, combined with the denial of any trans-mission of Original Sin, would make Rufinus' treatise in Augustine's eyes

---

[71] See Brown, *Augustine of Hippo*, 392 f.

[72] *C. duas Epp. Pel.* 3.10.26: 'Sed hoc dico tam manifestum esse secundum scripturas sanctas originale peccatum atque hoc dimitti lavacro regenerationis in parvulis tanta fidei catholicae antiquitate atque auctoritate firmatum, tam clara ecclesiae celebritate notissimum, ut quidquid de animae origine cuiuslibet inquisitione vel adfirmatione disseritur, si contra hoc sit, verum esse non possit.' (519. 6-11 Urba & Zycha).

[73] Brown, *art. cit. supra* n¹ p. 110.

[74] Aug., *Serm.* 294.10.10 (PL 38. 1341).

[75] See F. Refoulé, 'La distinction "Royaume de Dieu—Vie éternelle" est-elle pélagienne?' *Recherches de science religieuse* 51 (1963) 247-54.

very much the source-book of the opinions which the disciples of Caelestius were spreading in Africa when Augustine first read the *De Fide*,
apparently in 412. One may therefore regard it as one of the principal
works against which Augustine's anti-Pelagian sermons were directed.
Rufinus of Syria may accordingly be given a place, not merely as a founder
of Pelagianism but as the Pelagian theologian who first attracted Augustine's attention and determined, to no small degree, his decision—painful
though it was and a source of disquiet as late as 415—to lay aside all scru-
ples regarding the justice of the damnation of unbaptized infants and to
trust solely in the wisdom of God and the grace of Christ, which alone
brings salvation, and is conferred on the recipient in the sacrament of
baptism which is, in turn, efficacious only in the Body of Christ, which is
the Catholic Church.

Durham University
England

XI

AUGUSTINE AND MODERN RESEARCH
ON PELAGIANISM

Author's note

This lecture was delivered on Palm Sunday, March 22, 1970. The delay in its appearance in print in an enlarged version is a matter of regret for me, but has been due to a number of factors, both personal and professional. I hope that the delay has at least enabled me to develop the original into an organized whole, and to present a sketch of the early history of Pelagianism which will be of interest both to the general reader and to the Augustinian specialist.

I cannot conclude this note without some expression of gratitude to Rev. Robert P. Russell, O.S.A. and to his colleagues of the Augustinian Institute for all the kindness and hospitality lavished upon my wife and myself during our stay at Villanova, which provided a delightful foretaste of what we were to enjoy throughout our visit to the United States in March and April 1970. The welcome given by Americans to the foreign visitor is proverbial; but in our case we can only express our feelings by borrowing the words of the Queen of Sheba: "Behold, the half of it was not told me."

University of Durham,   G. B.
Feast of the Annunciation 1972.

AUGUSTINE AND PELAGIANISM IN THE LIGHT OF MODERN RESEARCH

The word Pelagianism is commonly employed in two different ways. It is used by dogmatic theologians to describe the heresy which dispenses with any need for Divine Grace and denies any transmission of Original Sin. Whether any individual theologian ever maintained precisely such a doctrine is of little importance in this branch of theology, which is philosophical rather than historical and concerned with ideas rather than with personalities.[1] In a similar fashion the term Augustinianism is often used to describe a type of predestinarian theology which, although it hardly does justice to the richness and subtle nuances of Augustine's thought,[2] nevertheless serves as a useful shorthand, provided only that it be not taken too literally. No harm is done by employing such generalisations, so long as their limitations are recognized.

The second use of Pelagianism, and the one with which we are here concerned, is to describe an ascetic movement within the Christian Church during the late Fourth and early Fifth centuries, a movement composed of disparate elements which came, in the course of time, to be associated under the name of the British theologian and exegete Pelagius, though his claim to be the dominating spirit of the movement is, at best, debatable. A considerable mythology, not to say demonology, has attached itself to Pelagianism—

1

   . . . the proudest heresy of all
That lifts to heaven a self-asserting face,
In tone severe and grave denies the Fall,
   Disowns the need of Grace
—but it is not the purpose of this enquiry to add
to that mythology. The merits and deficiencies
of the thought of Pelagius and his friends will be
left to the judgement of others. Here, we are concerned only to supply an account and an interpretation of Pelagianism and of Augustine's dealings
with it in the light of modern research, to be an historian rather than a judge. Condemnation and
approbation are, for our purposes, irrelevant.

I

We have reached a particularly interesting point
in our understanding of the Pelagian Controversy
and of Augustine's rôle therein. Thanks to the work
of many scholars in recent years it now seems possible to describe the origins and development of
the movement in a way that does justice to the parties involved, without extenuation but also without
malice; and while it would be presumptuous at
this stage to claim to offer a definitive picture,
an outline may nevertheless be sketched which is
a good deal clearer than was the case even a decade
ago in the hope that, ten years hence, there will
have been a further advance in our knowledge and
understanding.

One warning is, however, necessary. Greater
knowledge and greater understanding do not, in

2

the field of historical research—and still more in the field of research into the history of doctrine—necessarily lead to simplification, but rather to an increased appreciation of the complexity of situations and issues, and this is particularly true of the Pelagian Controversy. In the first place, we have to consider a series of events which took place in a number of geographically widely-separated areas, notably Italy, Africa and Palestine. Secondly, in seeking the origins of Pelagianism—and the name alone is a question-begging one, since it ascribes to Pelagius an importance in the movement which he may well not deserve—the historian must be prepared to consider incidents and disputes which may, at first sight, appear to have little relevance to the heresy which is traditionally held to deny the need for Grace. Finally, one should avoid any facile use of the style "Pelagians" as a blanket-term to cover a number of highly individual personalities. Pelagius; Caelestius; the anonymous Sicilian writer whom Dr. Morris has christened the Sicilian Briton; and Julian of Eclanum—none of these holds views exactly like the others. And, on the other side, it is well to remember that Augustine, despite his intellectual eminence, was not the first or the only opponent of Pelagianism. Not the least of the contributions which Dr. Robert Evans has made to Pelagian studies is his emphasis on the importance of St. Jerome as an actor in the Pelagian affair.[3] In a similar fashion Père Hamman has made clear the decisive character of the intervention of Paul Orosius at Jerusalem in 415 for the development of the controversy,[4] while Dr. Paredi has drawn attention to the part played in the whole affair by Paulinus of Milan.[5] Thus an attempt to sketch Pelagianism in the light of modern research cannot, even in outline, be a simple one; but it may be suggested, paradoxically, that from a demonstration of its complexity will result a certain increase of clarity.

II

What, however, are we to understand by modern research? Few words have a more constantly changing signification than "modern" and, in the present instance, a case could be made for including under this heading the great savants of the Seventeenth century like Jacques Sirmond, James Ussher, Pasquier Quesnel, Jean Garnier, Enrico Noris, Le Nain de Tillemont, and their Eighteenth century successors, the brothers Ballerini. Of the importance of the contribution of these scholars to the understanding of Pelagianism there can be no question; but to give an account of their work is beyond the scope of the present study. It must suffice to say, for the sake of an example, that one text vital for our understanding of the movement— namely the *Liber de Fide* of Rufinus the Syrian— was discovered and published by Sirmond as long ago as 1650 and that its significance was appreciated by Garnier, who printed it with learned annotations in the appendix to his edition of Marius Mercator in 1673.[6]

4

For our purposes, however, the starting-point
for the modern interpretation of Pelagianism may
be deemed to be the publication of a critical edition
of a number of Pelagian treatises by the Norwegian
scholar, C. P. Caspari, in 1890.[7] The importance
of Caspari's work lay in the fact that it showed
precisely how far Pelagianism was removed from
being the rationalistic, humanitarian movement
which it is so often deemed to be. In the fierce
denial of the propriety of Christians possessing
riches, in the exaltation of virginity over marriage,
and in the terrible picture of the Last Judgement
in the *Epistola de malis doctoribus*, there was revealed the grim, fanatical streak, so easily overlooked in the popular picture of the Pelagian movement. Indeed, it seemed that a society run on Pelagian lines, far from being easy -going and tolerant,
would have much in common with the bracing moral
climate of Geneva under the rule of John Calvin.

The author of the treatises published by Caspari
is unknown. Apart from Georges de Plinval, few
contemporary scholars would assign them to Pelagius himself; but the name of the author is lacking.
He writes from Sicily, and his equation of *in Francia
et in Saxonia* with *in omni barbaria* and a reference
to a long and dangerous sea-voyage have persuaded
Dr. Morris that he was a native of Britain.[8] I see
no justification for such an assumption. A voyage
from Gaul to Sicily may as well be called long and
dangerous as a voyage from Britain to Gaul. That
the theological views of the anonymous Pelagian
writer were more extreme than those of Pelagius

5

is clear. It would be convenient to identify him with Caelestius, the ablest man of action among the Pelagians; but this cannot be done with any certainty. It therefore seems best to refer to the author of Caspari's treatises as the Sicilian Anonymous, and avoid any guess as to his place of origin.

Caspari's publication of 1890 was matched in importance by the appearance, in the period 1922-1931, of Souter's edition of Pelagius' commentary on the Pauline Epistles,[9] written at Rome in the years before his views became the subject of debate and therefore of great importance as evidence for his thought before any question of unorthodoxy had been raised. The recovery of this commentary has been largely due to the labours of two men: Heinrich Zimmer and Alexander Souter. It is not here possible to recapitulate the steps by which Pelagius' work was identified in the period between the publication of a version of his commentary ascribed to Jerome by Erasmus in 1516 and the appearance of Souter's edition of the text in 1926. It can only be said, briefly, that the decisive work, begun by Zimmer in his book *Pelagius in Irland*[10] published in 1901, was taken up and completed by Souter, who fully and generously acknowledged the debt which he owed to Zimmer's researches. One may fairly say that the modern revaluation of Pelagius has been due in large measure to the availability of Souter's edition, and the historian must acknowledge his debt to the textual critic for providing the text upon which historical judgements must be based.

Besides Pelagius' commentary and the treatises edited by Caspari, a number of other Pelagian documents have come to light in recent times. These include a group of fragments on trinitarian and christological themes collected by Martini in 1938[11] and a treatise *De Induratione Cordis Pharaonis*, discovered by Dom Morin (who, needless to say, interested himself in the Pelagian dossier as in so many other branches of patristic and medieval textual study) and published by him in Georges de Plinval's *Essai sur le style et la langue de Pélage* in 1947.[12] A commentary on Job ascribed to Julian of Eclanum has been known since 1897.[13] Thus, a very considerable quantity of Pelagian literature is available for study, estimated by Dr. Morris as amounting to rather more than a thousand columns of Migne.[14] Much of it has in the past been assigned to orthodox writers like Augustine and Jerome, and the ascription to any particular Pelagian author is controversial. It will here be assumed (following Dr. Evans) that Pelagius is the author of the Pauline Commentaries; the *Epistola ad Demetriaden*; the *Libellus Fidei* presented to Pope Zosimus; the treatises *De Vita Christiana; De Virginitate; Ad Celantiam*; and *De Lege*; the excerpts on the Trinity and the Incarnation; and three works surviving only in fragments: the *De Natura*; the *De Libero Arbitrio*; and the *Liber Eclogarum* (also called the *Liber Capitulorum* and the *Liber Testimoniorum*).[15] To the Sicilian Anonymous will be assigned two letters: *Honorificientiae tuae* and *Humanae referunt litterae* and four

treatises: *De Divitiis; De Malis Doctoribus* (called
by Dr Morris *De Operibus); De Possibilitate non
Peccandi*; and *De Castitate.*[16] Finally to this group
of Pelagian writings must be added a single, seminal
work: the *Liber de Fide* of Rufinus the Syrian, said
by Marius Mercator to have been the original inspirer of Pelagian theology[17] and destined to exercise a great influence on the course of the Pelagian
Controversy through the activities of Pelagius'
friend and disciple, Caelestius.

It will be seen from the foregoing that we are
well provided with source material. We must now
briefly consider the historical investigations which
have determined the state of our present knowledge
of Pelagianism. Here the point of departure must
be the biography of Pelagius by Georges de Plinval,
published in 1943, a work which has been fairly
described as "fundamental but far from definitive."[18]
Its importance lies in the fact that it seeks to understand Pelagius, not as the heresiarch of later ages
but as a theologian of the Fifth century, to see
him as a man not as a monster. The same may
be said of Torgny Bohlin's study of 1957, *Die
Theologie des Pelagius und ihre Genesis.*[19] Dr. Bohlin
was able to make use of Souter's edition of Pelagius'
Pauline commentaries (a work composed before the
crisis of 415-418 and therefore better evidence for
his views than the writings which appeared when
his theology was already under fire) to attempt
to establish what Pelagius was actually trying to
do. Finally to these studies should be added the
work of Robert F. Evans, *Pelagius. Inquiries and*

Reappraisals. It is the merit of this admirable book to have demonstrated the significance of the Jovinianist and Origenist controversies of the Fourth century in determining the course of the Pelagian Controversy in the Fifth and to have emphasised the rôle of Jerome, so often neglected as an opponent of Pelagius. Furthermore, in a balanced though confessedly tentative appreciation of the theology of Pelagius, Dr. Evans uttered a warning against any over-hasty rehabilitation, resulting from a recoil from the apparent injustices of the past.[20]

Besides these longer studies there is a great quantity of material embodied in articles in learned journals, which can here be mentioned only in a selective and cursory fashion. First, one must record the important article by Berthold Altaner on Rufinus the Syrian, which appeared in 1950[21] and which has been followed by articles by Professor Marrou[22] and the present writer[23] in 1968 and 1970 respectively. The result of this investigation has been an increased appreciation of the importance of this enigmatic figure in determining the development of Pelagianism, an importance which had been appreciated by the scholars of the Seventeenth century but comparatively neglected in more recent times. Another line of approach is that put forward by Dr. J. N. L. Myres in an article in the *Journal of Roman Studies* in 1960,[24] which sought to establish a relationship between the repudiation of direct Roman rule by the *civitates* of Britain in 410 and the apparent strength of Pelagianism in Britain

twenty years after that date, as reported in the
Life of St. Germanus. Dr. Myres connected these
two phenomena by suggesting that Pelagianism was
not simply a religious movement, but also a movement of social protest against the injustice and
corruption of the contemporary Roman Empire.
Myres' theory has been adopted and developed by
Dr. J. R. Morris in two learned and forceful articles
published in 1965 and 1968.[25] Powerful arguments
against it have, however, been urged by Dr. W.
Liebeschuetz;[26] and subsequent investigations by
Dr. A. Cameron[27] and Dr. Evans[28] seem to have invalidated still further the Myres-Morris thesis which,
for the purposes of this essay, will be disregarded.
It is perhaps worth observing that it has always
appealed to historians of Roman Britain rather than
to church historians who approached Pelagianism as
a Christian movement of the Mediterranean region.

Finally must be mentioned two articles by Mr
Peter Brown published in *The Journal of Theological
Studies* in 1968 and 1970.[29] In these is brilliantly
depicted the ethos of Roman Pelagianism, the area
in which the movement arose and where it was
finally condemned in 418. Perhaps the outstanding
contribution of Mr Brown to Pelagian studies has
been his demonstration that the soul of Pelagianism
is not to be sought in theological propositions but
in a particular outlook, a desire to be a true Christian
in the superficially-Christianized society of the Fifth-
century Roman Empire. This demonstration has,
to a very great degree, determined the approach of
the present investigation.

10

The above list of studies is, admittedly and inevitably, selective and is largely confined to the contribution of scholars writing in English. Yet it may not unreasonably be claimed that a reading of the works described will give a very fair picture of the present state of knowledge regarding Pelagianism and of the great controversy which it provoked, in which Augustine was to be so deeply and so personally involved during the last fifteen years of his life.

III

Our first task in clearing the ground for discussion is to consider when and where Pelagianism arose and what constituted its dominant characteristic. Here it may unhesitatingly be affirmed that tradition has been correct in assigning the immediate origins of Pelagianism to Rome during the years when Pelagius was a leading personality there, namely from about 390 to 409. I would not, however, consider that tradition has been justified in regarding the dominant characteristic of Roman Pelagianism as the theological doctrine commonly associated with the name of its reputed founder. Rather I would maintain that what characterises Roman Pelagianism in its formative years is its combination of asceticism and moralism. Mr. Peter Brown, an authority on these matters, has described the ascetic discipline and aims of Pelagianism as "the least original aspect of the movement,"[30] and this judgement is incontrovertible; but it is precisely

11

the ascetic discipline and aims of Pelagianism which
provide the common element which links such different thinkers as Pelagius, Caelestius and the
Sicilian Anonymous; and if we are to discover the
ordinary Pelagian—a personage hardly less elusive
than the ordinary man, but no less important in
determining the general development of events—
we shall probably not go far wrong if we look for
him in the ascetic group of the Christian Roman
aristocracy of the late Fourth and early Fifth
centuries, exemplified by such persons as the Virgin
Demetrias; her mother, Juliana; her grandmother,
Proba; and the devout married couple Pinianus
and Melania the younger, friends alike of Pelagius
and Augustine. The eventual theological commit-
ment of these persons is, for our purposes, irrelevant
—Juliana took care to dissociate herself from
Pelagius once the question of heresy was raised,[31]
just as those "two noble youths Timasius and
James" had done at a somewhat earlier date.[32]
Pinianus and Melania interceded for him in 417
but remained themselves firmly orthodox.[33] What
is significant is their earlier attachment to the notion
of Christian perfection. Melania the younger, with
her fervent devotion to the ideal of marital continence, her fixed policy of liquidating her vast estates
to give to the poor, and her assiduous study of the
Scriptures (with the *Lives of the Saints* thrown in
by way of light reading),[34] might well be the incarnation of the ideal of life proposed by the Sicilian
Pelagian writer in the letter *Humanae referunt litterae* and in the treatises *De Divitiis* and *De Casti-*

12

tate— all of which, indeed, might have been appro-
priately addressed to Melania's husband Pinianus
who did not, at first, altogether share his wife's
uncompromising self-abnegation.[35]

The ethos of Pelagianism is, then, an aristocratic
asceticism, with the hauteur and exclusiveness which
goes with it. Here, too, Pelagianism is derivative.
The noble ladies who clustered around Pelagius
in the 390's were not essentially different in outlook
from those who had admired Jerome in the early
380's, in the golden days of Pope Damasus, and
Jerome's angry denunciations of Pelagius as a
ladies' man, uttered in about 394 in the aftermath
of the affair of Jovinian,[36] were hardly reasonable
coming as they did from a divine who, despite a
recorded preference for avoiding the gaze of ladies
of rank,[37] never managed in practice to escape from
the society of devout duchesses. In fact, Pelagius
had done no more than take over the part which
Jerome had had to relinquish when he left Rome
for Palestine in 385 and was doing it, apparently,
without exciting the violent opposition which
Jerome had encountered, largely through his own
lack of tact. This, no doubt, constituted the real
head and fount of Pelagius' offence in Jerome's
eyes: he was succeeding where a better man had
failed.[38]

Roman Pelagianism was a lay movement. It
had, it is true, clerical supporters like the presbyter
Sixtus, later destined to be bishop of Rome; but
its real strength was to be found among the laity.
Augustine recognised this as early as 416:

13

After the promulgation of the older heresies there has lately been introduced, not by bishops or presbyters, or indeed by any persons of the clerical estate, but by certain men who have affected the monastic life, a heresy which disputatiously resists, under colour of defending our free will, that grace of God which we have through our Lord Jesus Christ, and endeavours to overthrow the foundation of the Christian faith of which it is written: *Since by one man came death, by one man came also the resurrection of the dead; for as in Adam all die, even so in Christ shall all be made alive.*[39]

Pelagianism was, in fact, the Roman counterpart of similar ascetic movements throughout the Roman Empire—Priscillianism in Spain would be a comparable example. Augustine speaks of men who "affected the monastic life" (*a quibusdam veluti monachis*). The Pelagians did not build monasteries. Rather, they sought to make the Christian Church one great monastery. "The stream of perfectionism which, in a Jerome, a Paulinus, an Augustine, had flowered in a concentrated jet, will be widened, by Pelagius and his followers, into a flood, into whose icy puritanism they would immerse the whole Christian community."[40]

It was this ascetic and moralistic basis which both constituted the strength of Pelagianism at Rome and which also ensured that the movement would eventually fall apart, as it did once Pelagius and his allies were condemned. All the activity of the indefatigable Caelestius, all the repetitious writing of the equally indefatigable Julian, could not conceal the fact that specifically Pelagian theology as such meant very little to the rank and file of the movement. The ascetic life could be lived within the framework of Augustinian theology; the theological issues of Grace, Free Will and Original Sin were not, for most people, sufficiently important to justify leaving the communion of the Catholic Church.

IV

The strength and motivating force of Roman Pelagianism in the heyday of its success—that is from about 390 to 409—was the ideal of ascetic renunciation of which Pelagius was a persuasive, though not an extreme, advocate—when the controversy over Jovinian broke out in 392 he was as much opposed to Jerome's violent attack on marriage as he was to Jovinian's view that no differences of merit attach to the states of virginity, widowhood or marriage.[41] Pelagius' specific contribution to the theology of Pelagianism will be discussed later. For the present it will be useful to consider the development of Augustine's own theology during the period when Pelagianism was making progress at Rome.

For Augustine the last ten years of the Fourth century witness the transformation of the Christian convert living a collegiate life at Thagaste, still full of enthusiasm for the intellectual Platonizing Christianity which he had learned at Milan, to the

15

priest and bishop of Hippo, the student of the Bible, and especially of St Paul. In 396 or 397 there occurred a major development in his thought. One fruit of this was the *Confessions;* and it was a quotation from the Tenth Book of the *Confessions:* "Give what Thou commandest and command what Thou wilt!" which alarmed and distressed Pelagius at some time during the first decade of the Fifth century.[42] Nevertheless there is, for our purposes, a still more significant work of Augustine: the treatise written in 396 or 397 in answer to certain questions of scriptural exegesis sent to him by Simplicianus, once Augustine's spiritual counsellor just before his conversion and now Ambrose's successor (or destined successor) as bishop of Milan. The *De Diversis Quaestionibus ad Simplicianum* is, as Augustine himself recognised, a work of major importance both for his own religious development and for his subsequent part in the Pelagian Controversy.[43] From his own account it would seem that it was while Augustine was actually working on this treatise that he suddenly came to understand the message of St Paul expressed in the words: *What have you that you did not receive? If then you received it, why do you boast as if it were not a gift?*[44] It was in the light of this sudden perception that Augustine developed his exegesis of the ninth chapter of the Epistle to the Romans producing a doctrine, as he afterwards realised, which could with complete propriety have been issued in the course of the Pelagian Controversy. All the familiar features of Augustinianism appear: the

massa peccati, the *tradux peccati et poena mortalitatis,* the familiar texts: *O man, who art thou that
repliest against God?* and *Inscrutable are His judgements and His ways past finding out!*

Now all men are a mass of sin since, as the
Apostle says, *In Adam all die,* and to Adam the
entire human race traces the origin of its sin
against God. Sinful humanity must pay a debt
of punishment to the supreme divine justice.
Whether that debt is exacted or remitted there is
no unrighteousness. . . . So the Apostle represses
the impudent questioner. *O man, who art thou
that repliest against God?* A man so speaks back
to God when he is displeased that God finds fault
with sinners, as if God compelled any man to sin
when He simply does not bestow His justifying
mercy on some sinners, and for that reason is
said to harden some sinners, not because He
drives them to sin but because He does not have
mercy upon them. He decides who are not to
be offered mercy by a standard of equity which
is most secret and far removed from human powers
of understanding. *Inscrutable are His judgements
and His way past finding out.* . . . Then of all
[mankind] was formed one mass coming from
inherited sin and the penalty of mortality, though
God formed and created what was good. In all
there is form and the fitting together of the body
in such concord of the members that the Apostle
can use it as an illustration of how charity is
obtained. In all the spirit of life vivifies the
earthly members and man's whole nature is won-

17

derfully attuned as the soul rules and the body obeys. But carnal concupiscence now reigns as a result of the penalty of sin, and has thrown the whole human race into confusion, making of it one lump in which the original guilt remains throughout.[45]

Thus, long before the Pelagian Controversy began, Augustine had developed his own characteristically "Augustinian" doctrine. All that is lacking in the *De Diversis Quaestionibus* is the specific declaration of the doctrine of the damnation of unbaptised infants; and this doctrine, if not exactly expressed, is unquestionably implied.

It is likely—though we have no positive information on the matter—that the treatise addressed to Simplicianus would be well received at Milan, where its general theological tendency would be observed to be in harmony with the doctrinal legacy of Ambrose. This is not to suggest that Augustine derived his doctrine from Ambrose, since apart from a reference in the *De Natura et Gratia* in 415,[46] provoked by Pelagius, it is not until the *De Gratia Christi et de Peccato Originali* of 418 that we find in Augustine's writings any appeal to Ambrosian authority—a fact which suggests that it was only in the fires of controversy that Augustine turned to Ambrose for support.[47] Yet it is possible, not only that Augustine's work was well received at Milan but also that it influenced the course of the future Pelagian Controversy in an unexpected way.

V

Augustine wrote his treatise for Simplicianus in 396 or 397. Some two years later, in 399, there arrived in Italy that mysterious and somewhat sinister figure Rufinus the Syrian who, according to Marius Mercator, first sowed the seeds of Pelagianism at Rome and employed Pelagius as his agent in propagating the virus of heresy. The identity and influence of this Rufinus have been much discussed since Jacques Sirmond first published the *Liber de Fide* in 1650 from two manuscripts at Corbie, of which one—a Sixth-century uncial, written in Italy in a centre of high calligraphic standards—is now in the Public Library at Leningrad (MS. Q. v. l. 6)[48] while the other has disappeared. A colophon on f. 61ʳ of the Leningrad manuscript assigns the work to *Rufinus presbyter provinciae Palestinae*.[49] The Pelagian character of the work was apparent at a very early date. A gloss on f. 1ʳ, perhaps to be assigned to the Sixth century, warns the reader against its blasphemies, and suggests that it should be replaced in any future copy by Augustine's *De Vera Religione*, which is of about the same length. A further gloss of the Eighth century asserts that the author is not Rufinus but Pelagius.[50]

There is, however, no reason to assign the *Liber de Fide* to Pelagius or to any author other than Rufinus the Palestinian presbyter. The problem is to see if he can be identified. Most scholars today would regard him as being identical with the Rufinus the Syrian mentioned by Marius Mercator, and to be the priest Rufinus who resided at Rome with Jerome's friend Pammachius and to whose authority Caelestius appealed at his trial at Carthage in 411.[51] A further problem, however, arises. Is this Rufinus identical with the priest of that name sent by Jerome from Bethlehem to Milan in 399 to give assistance in a legal action concerning a certain Claudius, who was on trial on a capital charge? The majority of those who have recently discussed the problem accept such an identification. A notable exception is Professor Marrou who argues that, in the first place, Jerome's messenger would not have had time in a short stay at Rome *en route* for Milan to found a philosophical school; secondly, that he would have had to dissemble his Pelagian views while at Jerome's monastery; and, finally, that if Jerome's monk had indeed been the inspirer of Pelagianism, Jerome's enemies would hardly have failed to draw attention to the fact.[52]

Of these objections two do not seem to be very serious. The first sees Pelagianism primarily in terms of a theological movement. If, however, our present interpretation of Pelagianism is accepted— namely, that it was an ascetic movement with which certain theological opinions became associated—then Rufinus may be regarded as the founder, not in the sense of providing an ideology to draw men together but as the inspirer of certain views which were destined to procure subsequent notoriety and condemnation. The contribution of Rufinus to Pelagianism was his denial of any transmission of Original Sin, and his views on this matter could have been briefly expressed during his passage through Rome and afterwards popularised in the *Liber de Fide*. One does not have to assume that he was the author of the theories regarding Grace and Free Will later developed by Pelagius. Again, while one may well believe that any expression of nascent Pelagianism at Bethlehem would have produced a violent reaction from Jerome, there is no need to assume that the denial of traducianism would necessarily have been a constant topic of discussion in the Bethlehem community in the last decade of the Fourth century. One may reasonably suppose that Rufinus' anti-traducian views were developed after his departure from Jerome's monastery by the discussions on the origin of the human soul to which the Origenist Controversy gave rise. The third objection, namely that Jerome's enemies would hardly have overlooked the erroneous views of his protégé, is more serious. We must, however, take into account the assertion by Marius Mercator that Rufinus disseminated his heresy during the pontificate of Anastasius with discretion, employing Pelagius as his mouthpiece.[53] It was not until 411 that the storm finally broke, and then in Africa, far from Rome. The statement of Innocent I in January 417 that he had no knowledge as to whether there were any Pelagians at Rome suggests that their theological opinions had either been concealed or urged with some reserve.[54] By this time Rufinus may well have been dead—a possibility which is the more likely in view of his complete inactivity during the course of the Controversy.

21

Indeed, the supposition is confirmed by the words of Caelestius at his trial at Carthage in 411: "The holy priest Rufinus who resided at Rome with the holy Pammachius,"[55] for here, as Professor Marrou points out, the word "holy" is equivalent to "of good memory." Both Rufinus and Pammachius were already dead.[56]

It seems, then, that Professor Marrou's objections are not overwhelming and we shall, for our purposes, assume the identity of Rufinus, the inspirer of Pelagianism, with the priest of that name from Jerome's monastery as a working hypothesis, and he will be regarded as the author of the *Liber de Fide*.

Berthold Altaner, in an important article which appeared in 1950, argued that the *Liber de Fide* was written as an answer to Augustine's first anti-Pelagian work, the *De Peccatorum Meritis et Remissione*, and could therefore not have been composed before 413.[57] However, Père Refoulé,[58] following a suggestion by Père de Blic,[59] has established beyond reasonable doubt that Augustine knew and quoted Rufinus' work in the *De Peccatorum Meritis*, from which it follows that the *Liber de Fide* must have been composed before 412. But how long before? An examination of the text of the *De Fide* suggests that the author's animus is directed even more against Origen than against those who believe in any transmission of Original Sin and this, as I have argued elsewhere,[60] suggests a date of composition within the period 399-402, that is to say during the pontificate of Anastasius, who condemned Origenism at the instigation of Theophilus of Alexandria in 400. Such a date would agree very well with the circumstances of Rufinus' mission. He arrived in Rome when the scandal caused by his namesake, Rufinus of Aquileia's, translation of Origen's *De Principiis* was at its height, bearing letters for Pammachius and for Rufinus himself, and would appear to have joined with Pammachius in suppressing the letter to Rufinus.[61] As the attack on Rufinus of Aquileia developed it would not be surprising if Rufinus of Syria had entered the fray and added his own contribution, the *Liber de Fide*.

But why include a denunciation of traducianism with the attack on Origen ? As a general explanation it may be said that once Origen's theory of the pre-existence of souls before they come into bodies has been rejected, some consideration of alternative theories becomes necessary, and of these the only two acceptable to most orthodox thinkers of the Patristic Age were traducianism and creationism. Jerome recognised this in his attack on John of Jerusalem of 397 in which, significantly, he recorded his distaste for traducianism—a distaste which persisted so that, at the end of his life, he still preferred creationism.[62] Thus, the attack on traducianism by Rufinus in 399 did not constitute a complete break with the tendency of Jerome's opinions. More specifically, it is possible that Rufinus encountered traducianism in rigorous form at Milan, when he went there in connexion with the case of Claudius, disliked it and, since the *De Fide* is cast in the form of a confession of faith in which all heresies are

23

duly noted and denounced, included it in his list
of errors. It is conceivable, though unprovable,
that he actually encountered and read Augustine's
Quaestiones ad Simplicianum or, as Professor Marrou
suggests, the *Confessions*, with its emphasis on the
woes of infancy and the pathetic condition of the
sons of Adam. Not, indeed, that it would have
been necessary for Rufinus to have gone to Milan
to encounter traducianism, for this doctrine is specifically mentioned by Rufinus of Aquileia in the
Apology which he addressed to Pope Anastasius
in the second half of 400 as being commonly held
by Latin theologians like Tertullian and Lactantius. [63] Rufinus of Aquileia declared that he had
no personal theory of the origin of the human soul
but regarded the matter as open[64]—an attitude
which Caelestius tried to maintain at Carthage
eleven years later in the face of the accusations of
Paulinus of Milan. "As regards the transmission
of sin I have heard various people within the Catholic Church deny it and others assert it. It may
therefore fairly be regarded as a matter of opinion,
not of heresy."[65] Unhappily for Caelestius his African
judges took a different view.

It was not, however, to the authority of Rufinus
of Aquileia but to that of Rufinus the Syrian that
Caelestius appealed in 411 and it is necessary to
consider the latter's influence on the Pelagian movement as a whole. Two facts must be observed.
First, although Rufinus is described by Marius
Mercator as the founder of Pelagianism, he is appealed to by Caelestius alone in the course of the

controversy. (It has already been remarked that he was probably dead when it broke out). Secondly, although Marius Mercator calls Caelestius the disciple of *Pelagius*, and not Rufinus, it would seem that it was Caelestius, and not Pelagius, who was impressed by the Rufinian denial of the transmission of Original Sin; for in the *Liber de Fide*, apart from a passing reference to the grace of baptism without any particular theological significance,[66] the word *gratia* is not mentioned, and we have therefore no justification for regarding Rufinus as the inspirer of the ideas which Pelagius was later to develop in the *De Natura* and the *De Libero Arbitrio*. Certain of Rufinus' notions—for example, his belief that Adam and Eve never sinned again after the Fall and his assertion that there were sinless men among the saints of the Old Testament[67]—can be paralleled in the writings of Pelagius;[68] but Rufinus' particular theme: that infants are free from sin and are baptised to be made inheritors of the Kingdom of Heaven,[69] is one which appealed to Caelestius rather than Pelagius, being maintained by him in the statement of faith which he presented to Zosimus at Rome in 417,[70] although he then represented himself, with an unwonted modesty, as a humble petitioner submitting his faith to the judgement of the Apostolic See.[71]

Two points may be noticed about Rufinus the Syrian, small in themselves but together throwing light upon his background. First, his nationality. Marius Mercator described him as being *natione Syrus*,[72] and if he were indeed a Syrian by birth

25

one would expect the *Liber de Fide* to have been originally composed in Greek, as both Sirmond and Jean Garnier believed. However Altaner, following the Maurists, has advanced cogent philological reasons for supposing that the work was originally written in Latin,[73] which further led him to argue that Rufinus was, in fact, a Latin who had spent a sufficiently long time in Jerome's cloister at Bethlehem to acquire a good knowledge of Greek and who was called a Syrian by Marius Mercator only in the vague sense of one coming from Syria.

I would, however, question whether it is necessary to force Marius Mercator's evidence in this way, even if one accepts (as I do) that the *De Fide* was originally written in Latin. In the first place, examples can be found in the later Roman Empire of Greek-speaking orientals who chose to write in the Latin tongue—the historian Ammianus Marcellinus and the poet Claudian come readily to mind. In the case of Rufinus, however, there is a second consideration, if we accept the view that he was the priest sent by Jerome to Italy to help in the case of Claudius, arraigned on a capital charge, for this would suggest some knowledge of law on his part and one of the centres for the study of Roman Law in the East was the city of Beirut in Syria, where teaching was given exclusively in Latin until the beginning of the ninth decade of the Fourth century.[74] It would therefore be possible for a Greek-speaking Syrian to acquire a command of Latin in the course of his legal studies.

26

To suggest that Rufinus the Syrian learned Latin at Beirut while studying law and subsequently perfected his command of the language theologically while associated with Jerome at Bethlehem is at best only an hypothesis; but it is an hypothesis which enables us to dispense with the necessity to explain away our authorities as we otherwise have to do. It also reconciles the apparently contradictory statements of Mercator that Rufinus was originally a Syrian (*quondam natione Syrus*) and of the colophon of the *Liber de Fide* that he was a priest of the province of Palestine. Furthermore, if correct, it also sheds light on another assertion of Marius Mercator, namely, that the doctrine that Adam and Eve were created mortal and did not injure their posterity by their sin, was first evolved among certain Syrians, and especially in Cilicia by Theodore of Mopsuestia.[75] Now the relation of Theodore of Mopsuestia to Pelagianism has been much discussed by scholars who come to very different conclusions. On the one hand, Robert Devresse can declare that "the Pelagian doctrine of Theodore is a myth,"[76] while on the other Julius Gross is equally emphatic: "The proposition according to which Adam was created mortal is authentic teaching of Theodore, although he certainly did not always employ it consistently."[77] Günter Koch, in his study of the attainment of salvation in the theology of Theodore, recognises that there are in fact two different strands in his thought: a traditionally orthodox view of the Fall and of its consequences; and another, in which the present mutability of the human condition is

27

contrasted with the unchangeable character of creation made new in Christ.[78] In other words, the exclusive approaches of Devresse and Gross cannot be justified from the texts of Theodore themselves. However, for our purposes, the tradition that Theodore taught that man was created mortal and was punished for his sin by death, and not by a loss of immortality leading to death, is apparently true of one aspect of his thought. Indeed, Koch considers that the doctrine of the notorious fragments preserved by Marius Mercator from Theodore's work directed against Jerome, *Against those who say that men sin by nature and not by will*, represents an authentic, though extreme, expression of one particular side of his doctrine, though he has reservations about the authenticity of the fragments themselves.[79]

It is not possible to pursue the question of Theodore of Mopsuestia's possible influence on Pelagianism any further here, although it may be noted that the subject demands further consideration by Augustinian scholars. What seems clear is that there may be a link between Theodore's teaching and that of Rufinus of Syria on the matter of Adam's mortality and—more unexpectedly—that there exists a similarity between Rufinus' doctrine and that of Augustine; for Rufinus, no less than the bishop of Hippo, holds that Adam in Paradise, though created mortal, had a conditional immortality:

> Adam and Eve were created immortal according to the soul but mortal according to the body; nevertheless they would never have tasted death,

28

as blessed Enoch merited, if only they had been willing to obey God's command.[80]

This is Rufinus' view; but it is also Theodore's[81] and, more surprisingly, it is also Augustine's: Adam was created with an animal body but, if he had persevered, it would eventually have been changed into a spiritual body.[82] Thus both Rufinus and Augustine—and, incidentally, Pelagius himself[83]— are in agreement against the view with which Caelestius was charged at Carthage in 411: that Adam was not only created mortal but would have died whether he sinned or not. More surprisingly still, perhaps, this doctrine of the conditional immortality of Adam, common to both Rufinus and Augustine, is also accepted by the Pelagian theologian who is normally regarded as an archrationalist; for Julian of Eclanum could argue that the institution of marriage proved that men were destined to die precisely as Rufinus had done, while accepting Rufinus' qualification that, despite this fact, "if Adam and Eve had obeyed God's command they would certainly never have tasted death."[84] Indeed, on this matter there is a remarkable degree of agreement between Augustine and Julian: they differ, essentially, in their understanding of the end of marriage. For Julian, its purposes are fundamentally biological: to perpetuate the race. For Augustine, its end is primarily spiritual: to complete the number of the elect in the Kingdom of God. The gulf between the two controversialists is established not by facts but by orientation of mind and this, in the last resort, is what separates Augustine from Pelagianism.

29

We have no evidence of the degree to which Rufinus of Syria influenced Pelagius and Caelestius except on the specific issue of the denial of traducianism and the doctrine of infant baptism, not for the remission of sins but for incorporation into the Kingdom of Heaven. Even here, one may guess, it was Caelestius rather than Pelagius whom he influenced. Pelagius recorded arguments against traducianism in his commentary on Romans and did so, as Augustine noted, [85] in a somewhat ambiguous manner without committing himself. No doubt this was in large measure due to the discretion and regard for his personal safety which subsequently characterised Pelagius at the Synod of Diospolis— he would rather disown a friend than expose himself to danger; but it may also spring from the fact that Pelagius was not theologically very interested in babies.[86] It was the Christian life of adults and the rôle of baptism in that life which interested him. Here, paradoxically, the Pelagian view was fully in accord with the principle of classical humanism which held that "the whole aim of . . . education was the formation of adults, not the development of the child."[87] This fact may be significant; for it was in the faults of childhood that Augustine was to find evidence for the doctrine of Original Sin.[88] By concentrating on adult psychology the Pelagians were able to avoid consideration of the theological issues raised by infant baptism. Indeed, one may wonder whether the question of infant baptism would ever have played the part which it did in the Pelagian Controversy if historical accident had not

30

brought Caelestius to Africa, where the theology of infant baptism had an interest which it did not arouse elsewhere.[89]

VI

We have, then, two elements which determined the character of Roman Pelagianism: (i) the ascetic impulse, which it shared with other Christian movements, but which had a peculiar intensity in the life of the Christian Roman aristocracy at the end of the Fourth century; and (ii) the theological views of Rufinus the Syrian, which were destined to have profound consequences in the future. It is to be observed that both these elements look back to an earlier period in Church history; the ascetic to the birth of monasticism at Rome and the Roman sojourn of Jerome; and the Rufinian to the Origenist crisis of the days of Anastasius. Any future historian of the Pelagian Controversy will have to give more attention to these antecedent elements than has been customary in the past, if he is to do justice to his theme. But having said this we are left with the question: what was the specific rôle of Pelagius himself in the movement which has taken his name?

This question is difficult to answer, if only because Pelagius remains, after all our seeking, a somewhat shadowy figure. We do not know the date of his birth or when and where he died.[90] Our information about his personal appearance comes from his enemies and does not pretend to be objective.[91] Nor is our ignorance in any way enlightened by the

31

survival of pure fantasies about his background.
One can still find theological students repeating the
long-exploded fable that he was of Irish origin and
that his name represents a hellenization of Muirchu[92] or that he was a Welshman named Morgan—
a remarkable piece of false philology since, as
Hugh Williams pointed out as long ago as 1912,
Pelagius' British contemporaries would simply have
borrowed the Latin name which might, through
constant use, have become Pelag or Peleg but
certainly not Morgan.[93]

The fact is that what little we know about Pelagius
comes either from the pens of his enemies or from
the incidental evidence of his own writings, and it
is easy to do him an injustice, by considering him
simply in terms of the opinions for which he was
condemned rather than as an independent thinker.
However, enough of his work remains to enable us
to maintain with some confidence that he did not
think and write merely to justify Pelagianism but
was a theologian in his own right, interested in
scriptural exegesis and trinitarian theology, a
Christian thinker who wished, first and foremost,
"to be an orthodox theologian of the Catholic
Church and to be known as such."[94] Dr. Evans
has provided us with an outline, which he makes
clear is not intended to be a final one, of the theology
of Pelagius; and it is to be hoped that some time in
the future he or some other scholar will give us a
full exposition of the theological system of Pelagius.
Here, however, we are concerned with a more
limited theme, as a guide to our historical under-

standing, and it is with this in mind that we must try to answer the question: what was the contribution of Pelagius to Pelagianism?

It has been observed that a particular feature of Pelagius' thought is its anti-Manichaean tendency.[95] One reason for this is an obvious one: the Manichaean population of Rome was a considerable one, as Augustine discovered when he arrived there in 383,[96] and the Manichees seem to have had a tendency to make converts from among the intellectuals.[97] There is, however, a deeper possible reason: the necessity of defending Christian asceticism at Rome from the charge of Manichaeism to which it was so easily exposed and to which Jerome bears witness in the famous letter to Eustochium written in 384: "when they see a woman with a pale and sad face they call her a wretched solitary and a Manichee."[98] Mere abuse of the ascetic by the self-indulgent? Perhaps; but what did the Manichees say about themselves?

I have rejected silver and gold, I carry no copper coin in my purse being content with my daily bread and taking no thought for the morrow whence my belly shall be filled or my body clothed, and you ask me whether I accept the Gospel! You see in me Christ's beatitudes which make the Gospel and you ask whether I accept it! You see a man poor and mild, a peaceful man of pure heart, mourning, hungering and thirsting, persecuted for righteousness' sake, and you doubt whether I accept the Gospel![99]

33

Thus Faustus the Manichee. Two years after
Jerome's letter to Eustochium the execution of
Priscillian and his companions at Trier in 386
provided a demonstration of the very real danger
to which Christian ascetics might be exposed when
they aroused the enmity of worldly churchmen;
and the Priscillianist movement had many features
in common with Pelagianism.[100] In the light of
such considerations one can understand Pelagius'
reactions to Jerome's intervention in the affair of
Jovinian; for Jerome went too far in his attack
on marriage and appeared in his writings to justify
all the accusations which their critics brought
against the ascetics.[101] Pelagius himself insisted
that the pursuit of asceticism must imply no
disparagement of matrimony. "The rule of apostolic
doctrine neither equates the works of marriage with
continence with Jovinian, nor condemns wedlock
with Mani."[102] Not all Pelagians share their leader's
moderation. The Sicilian Anonymous, a man after
Jerome's own heart, proposed the life of poverty
and continence with an enthusiasm which would
have gladdened the heart of any Manichaean
Elect;[103] but this was not the attitude of Pelagius.

I would therefore suggest that the contribution
of Pelagius to Pelagianism was to provide a theological basis to defend Christian asceticism against
any charge of Manichaeism and to justify the
assurance that a virtuous life is possible for the
Christian if he will only try. Such a theological
justification was desirable on grounds of expediency,
in view of the hostility to asceticism shown in cer-

34

tain quarters, and of practical psychology for, as
the author of the Pelagian tract *On the possibility
of not sinning* pointed out, if a man is told that he
does not need to sin he will be encouraged to make
every effort and will, at the very least, avoid some
sins which he would otherwise have committed.[104]
In supplying this justification of asceticism Pelagius
would find the Rufinian denial of traducianism a
useful weapon; but he was himself more concerned
to discuss the possibility of human sinfulness in
terms of the natural potentialities of man's God-
given nature considered in the abstract than to
consider the modifications produced in that nature
by the actual circumstances of human life after
the Fall. Hence it came about that Pelagius'
theology "found its centre of gravity in the problem
of man," formulated "in such a way as to make the
Christian doctrine of man clearly distinguishable
from Manichaean notions of man and so ... to
combat whatever influences and traces of Manichaeism [were] to be found within the Church."[105]

VII

The operations against Rome by Alaric the Goth
which culminated in the sack of 410 proved crucial
for Pelagianism in two ways. First, they broke
up the Pelagian group at Rome and drove many
of its adherents, including the leaders, overseas,
with the result that Italy ceased to be the intellectual centre of the movement.[106] Secondly, they
brought Pelagian ideas and ideals into contact

35

with other Christian traditions, and so provoked
discussion and denunciation which might never
have occurred if Pelagianism had remained concentrated at Rome.

In this respect Caelestius' decision to remain in
Africa when Pelagius left Carthage for Palestine
is crucial, for it meant that the Rufinian element
in Pelagianism, of which Caelestius was the principal exponent, came into contact with a society in
which the theology of baptism was at that moment
a major talking-point on account of the Donatist
Controversy.[107] Historically speaking, Pelagius and
Caelestius could not have arrived in Africa at a more
portentous time than on the eve of the Conference
of Carthage of 411 between the Catholics and the
Donatists. Indeed, the possibility that Caelestius
found support in Africa from among former Donatists and Donatist sympathisers is worth condiser-
ation. The ecclesiology of Donatism and Pelagianism had remarkable affinities. Both contended
for a pure Church, the one by external separation,
the other by an internal migration. The attempts
made by Pelagius' accusers in Palestine to associate
his views with Donatism may have been something
more than a mere technique of controversy.[108]

Caelestius appears to have had considerable success in propagating his doctrines in Africa before
his condemnation by a local Carthaginian synod in
the autumn or early winter of 411,[109] and it must
be emphasised that these views were concerned
with anti-traducianism rather than with any denial
of Grace or assertion of Free Will. The first reference

to Pelagian doctrine in Africa available to us is Augustine's account of hearing certain persons declare that what children gained from baptism was sanctification, not remission of sins—a commonplace of Pelagian theology.[110] The charges brought against Caelestius at his trial—that Adam was created mortal and would have died whether he sinned or not; that Adam's sin injured himself and not the human race; that new-born infants are in the same state as was Adam before the Fall; that all humanity does not die through Adam's death or sin, nor rise through Christ's resurrection; that the Law admits men to heaven as well as the Gospel ; and that even before the coming of Christ there were sinless men[111]—are a development of Rufinus of Syria's attack on traducianism. A development, it must be emphasised; for the views ascribed to Caelestius went further than did those of Rufinus. The first, that Adam would have died whether he sinned or not, is not the doctrine of Rufinus or Pelagius, but was developed by the more radical strain in Pelagianism represented by Caelestius.[112]

Thus it happened that the more radical development of the Rufinian strain in Pelagianism came to be propagated in precisely that area where it would attract most attention. Furthermore, it was at Carthage, in the person of the Deacon Paulinus, that Caelestius encountered the Ambrosian tradition of Milan. The combination at the synod of Carthage of Paulinus of Milan as accuser and Aurelius of Carthage as judge symbolizes the united opposition of other Christian traditions to Roman

37

Pelagianism. "I say," declared Aurelius, "that although Adam as established in Paradise is said to
have been originally created undying (*inextermina-
bilis*) he was afterwards made corruptible through
disobeying the commandment. Do you say this,
brother Paulinus?"[113] Paulinus agreed; and by his
agreement Caelestius was exposed to the direct
question: "What is the state of unbaptized infants
today? Is it that of Adam before the Fall or does
it carry with it the guilt of the Fall resulting from
the Original Sin from which it is born?"[114]—to
which he could reply only that there was no one
opinion among Catholics and that he personally
had always maintained the need for infant baptism.[115] This might have saved him at Rome; at
Carthage it procured his excommunication. Pelagianism had not only sustained its first check; it
had incurred it from the most dangerous possible
opponents.

However, the excommunication of Caelestius by
a Carthaginian council did not, in itself, imply any
judgement on Pelagius in Palestine; nor did it auto-
matically associate Augustine, a bishop of Numidia,
with any campaign against him. Indeed, the part
played by Augustine in the Pelagian Controversy
up to the year 416 is marked by a curious reserve.
He defended the traditional African doctrine of infant baptism for the remission of sins by writing
the *De Peccatorum Meritis et Remissione* and by
preaching. In the *De Spiritu et Littera* in 412 he
answered in passing certain doctrines which he had
read in Pelagius' commentary on Romans, though

without any mention of Pelagius by name.[116] In
413, with what appears in retrospect as a curious
lack of caution, he sent Pelagius the famous letter[117]
which, by saying nothing in particular but saying it
very well, subsequently provided that accommo-
dating theologian with a testimonial which he was
to employ—not perhaps unreasonably in the circumstances—at the Synod of Diospolis. Even in 415,
when he had read Pelagius' work *De Natura* and
first discovered—or so he afterwards said—its
pernicious tendency, Augustine still replied in a
mild tone, omitting any mention of Pelagius' name
and suggesting that the faults of the *De Natura*
arose from the author's zeal for moral rectitude.[118]

This reserve towards Pelagius did not arise from
the fact that, up to 415, Augustine was not much
concerned with Pelagianism; for in fact he was.
In 414 he received a letter from Hilary of Syracuse
reporting the propaganda activity of the Pelagian
party in Sicily and had replied to it at length in a
letter amounting to a short treatise.[119] Among the
assertions reported by Hilary was the doctrine that
a rich man can only be saved if he renounces all
his wealth[120]—a doctrine of the Sicilian Anonymous,[121] going beyond what Pelagius asserted. Thus
by 414 Augustine had become acquainted with
Pelagianism in its most extreme form; and it is to
be noted that his reaction to this challenge is not
simply a moderate and reasoned defence of the
propriety of a Christian possessing riches, based on
the principle of I Timothy 6:17: *As to the rich of
this world, charge them not to be haughty, nor to set*

their hopes on uncertain riches but on God who richly furnishes us with everything to enjoy, but also a plea for the ordinary Christian, not an enthusiast or an ascetic after the Pelagian fashion, but anxious to live the Christian life according to his own limited capacities. Augustine opposed Pelagian rigorism which, if it had had its way, would have transformed the whole Christian Church into a vast monastery, from the experience of a Christian pastor who was aware of the limitations of the ordinary man, and he deplored the Pelagian practice, while extolling standards which Augustine accepted as constituting the higher way, of depreciating the more limited capabilities of the majority of Christians. Here he was in a strong position since, as he pointed out, he had himself fulfilled the dominical injunction to sell all that he had and to follow Christ.[122] Yet the tone of his argument suggests that it was Pelagian arrogance, rather than their doctrine, which perturbed him. Pelagians were still at this time brethren to be reasoned with and, if possible, retained in the fellowship of the Church rather than heretics to be denounced.[123]

Augustine's initial caution in dealing with Pelagius himself is easily explained. In the first place, he had to take into account Pelagius' reputation for sanctity which could not be lightly ignored. Again there were, one may suppose, the constraints imposed by friendship. Augustine and Pelagius had in common friends like Paulinus of Nola and Pinianus and Melania, and nothing would be gained by gratuitously assailing a man who enjoyed the esteem of such excellent and influential Christians. Finally we may note quite simply the sheer pressure of Augustine's other preoccupations. In the very letter to his friend Evodius, written at the end of 415, in which Augustine announces that he has written "a great book against the heresy of Pelagius" —namely, the *De Natura et Gratia*—he also states that he has recently added two books to the *De Civitate Dei*, delivered three sermons on the Psalms; sent a letter to Jerome on the origin of the soul and another on the Epistle of James (both topics raised by considerations advanced by Pelagian propaganda), and composed a treatise for Orosius against the Origenists and the Priscillianists.[124] If to all this literary activity we add Augustine's continued preoccupation with the liquidation of Donatism and the demands of his episcopal duties, his disinclination for a direct, personal confrontation with Pelagius is understandable.

What changed Augustine's attitude towards Pelagius? Dr. Evans has argued persuasively in favour of regarding this as being due to reading the *De Natura*, sent to him by Timasius and James, not only on the grounds that Augustine repeatedly says that it was this book which opened his eyes to the menace of Pelagian teaching to Christian orthodoxy, but also because of another consideration, which may well have weighed more heavily: Pelagius was now quoting by name a considerable number of Catholic authors in support of his views, and the last-named of these was Augustine himself.[125]

41

VIII

The alarm which this discovery would undoubtedly have occasioned in Augustine's mind could only
have been enhanced by the events of the year 416.
To understand this we must consider the course of
events in Palestine, where Pelagius had been living
since his departure from Africa in 411. Here he
had found a warm welcome from Bishop John of
Jerusalem and renewed acquaintance with an old
enemy in the person of Jerome. Dr. Evans, to whom
we are indebted for an admirable revaluation of
Jerome's part in the Pelagian Controversy, has
argued that Jerome's distraction from his commentary on Jeremiah, which he began to write about
414, may have been due to past charges of excessive
reliance on Origen and of unreasonable depreciation
of marriage being now revived by Pelagius.[126] One
may accept this suggestion with one qualification.
It is difficult to imagine Jerome being at any time
the wholly innocent victim of unprovoked aggres-
sion.

In 415 there arrived in Bethlehem the Spanish
priest Orosius, who had come to Africa to seek
Augustine's help against heresy in his native Spain
and had been sent on to Palestine (in his own words)
to learn the fear of God from Jerome and (more
prosaically) to act as a suitable bearer of two letters
from Augustine.[127] On the assumption that Rufinus
the Syrian was indeed a monk of Jerome's cloister
J. A. Davids has suggested that Orosius may well
have been asked to warn Jerome about the pernici-

ous character of his views.[128] There is, however, a
third possible reason for the mission of Orosius to
Bethlehem. His fellow-countryman Avitus of Braga
says that he was sent to Palestine "by the African
bishops,"[129] from which Davids suggests that Orosius
was specially deputed by the body of the African
episcopate to make common cause with Jerome
against Pelagian doctrines. This would help to
explain why Jerome's letter to Ctesiphon, written
before Orosius' arrival in Bethlehem, makes no
reference to the question of infant baptism, which is
in fact only mentioned at the end of the third book
of his *Dialogue against the Pelagians*.[130] Until Orosius came to Palestine, Jerome was unaware of the
Rufinian element in Pelagianism.

Orosius, on his arrival in Palestine in the summer
of 415, found Jerome already engaged in controversy
with Pelagius, thus continuing the debate which
had begun as early as 394 over the affair of Jovinian.
Pelagius was established at Jerusalem, in high favour with Bishop John and enjoying the support
and admiration—it may be supposed—of many of
the Roman refugees who had flocked to Palestine
after the sack of Rome of 410. The alliance between
John of Jerusalem and Pelagius is easily explained.
Pelagius' reputation for sanctity apart, he and John
shared a common, and understandable, antipathy.
John had fallen out with Jerome at the time of
Theophilus of Alexandria's crusade against Origenism, and the two men had never been reconciled.
Jerome for his part thought he recognized in Pelagius' teaching the doctrine of *apatheia* and accord-

ingly labelled him as an Origenist—an accusation
which has, in the past, earned him a rather patronis-
ing rebuke from historians,[131] but one which was,
from Jerome's point of view as Dr. Evans has pointed
out,[132] not entirely without justification. And
behind this immediate disagreement was the bitter
memory of Jerome's incautious tirade against
Jovinian, which had so embarrassed his friends and
which had provoked Pelagius to intervene in defence
of a balanced theology of asceticism.

The diocesan synod assembled by Bishop John
at Jerusalem on 30 July 415 is a decisive event in
the history of the Pelagian Controversy. Without
it, it is conceivable that Pelagius' book *De Natura*,
written in answer to Jerome and criticized by
Augustine in the *De Natura et Gratia*, might eventually have procured his condemnation without the
intervention of Orosius; but the conduct of the
latter at the Jerusalem synod made it inevitable.
Our knowledge of the proceedings of that synod
comes from the pen of Orosius, who writes with a
sense of burning resentment; but from his biased
account it is possible to form some picture of what
happened. Orosius had, apparently, been invited
to supply the clergy present at the synod with
information about the background to the dispute
between Jerome and Pelagius. He came equipped
with a copy of Augustine's letter to Hilary of Syracuse which he read to the synod. From the outset
he displayed a violent hostility to Pelagius and a
studied insolence to Bishop John which can only
have damaged his cause. Despite invitations from

John to assume the official rôle of prosecutor he refused, maintaining that the decisions of an African council and the opinions of leading Latin theologians constituted in themselves an effective condemnation which only required endorsement by the Eastern clergy—an endorsement which Orosius assumed to be absolutely obligatory on their part.[133]

Orosius' behaviour marks a new stage in the Pelagian Controversy, so far as Pelagius himself was concerned. Augustine, in the *De Natura et Gratia*, had answered Pelagius without naming him; Jerome, in the *Dialogus adversus Pelagianos* which appeared shortly after the synod of Jerusalem, employed fictional names; but Orosius brought the whole affair into the open. Pelagianism, he subsequently declared in his *Apology*, was contrary to the tradition of the Church, as witnessed by the writings of Cyprian, Hilary and Ambrose, besides of course those of Orosius' heroes, Augustine and Jerome;[134] it revived the heresies of Origen, Priscillian and Jovinian.[135] At the Synod of Jerusalem the names of Pelagius and Caelestius were linked together by Orosius as joint sowers of heresy in Africa, and the extreme teachings of the Sicilian Pelagians, which Pelagius had never countenanced, were laid at his door.[136] After the intervention of Orosius the disparate elements in Pelagianism were lumped together in such a way that they were never again untangled in the course of the controversy. Furthermore, Orosius assumed that the condemnation of Caelestius by an African tribunal necessarily implied the condemnation of Pelagius—a *non sequi-*

45

tur which John of Jerusalem was not slow to point out.[137] Indeed, it is difficult to imagine a worse advocate of African theology before an Eastern synod.

It was, however, the sequel to the Synod of Jerusalem which proved decisive. When he saw that the synod was not prepared to condemn Pelagius, Orosius realised that he had, at all costs, to avoid any decision which would appear to call in question the judgement of the Carthaginian council which condemned Caelestius. Accordingly he endeavoured to persuade the synod that the whole matter was a Latin affair, best understood by Latins and therefore to be referred to Innocent of Rome for his adjudication. According to his own account he succeeded, and seemed to have saved the situation; but when he presented himself at Jerusalem for the Feast of the Dedication on 12 September 415 Bishop John denounced him publicly as one who held that a man could not be free from sin even with God's help.[138] This accusation represented an alarming change of fortune; in the eyes of a Greek like John of Jerusalem it appeared that the theology defended by Orosius—a theology avowedly based upon the teaching of Jerome and Augustine—amounted to the doctrine that fallen human nature is so corrupted by sin as to be incapable of sinlessness even with the aid of Divine Grace. This would be, in itself, disturbing enough for Augustine, when he came to hear of it; but the exoneration of Pelagius by the Synod of Diospolis in December brought the whole of African teaching

on Grace and Original Sin under judgement. Pelagius had, as it happened, only secured his acquittal
by disowning Caelestius,[139] but the Africans did not
know this. What they did know was the letter of
Pelagius which came into Augustine's hands: "By
the sentence of fourteen bishops our statement was
received with approbation in which we affirmed
that a man is able to live without sin and easily
keep the commandments of God if he pleases."[140]
As early as 413 the Pelagians in Africa had asserted
that they had the churches of the East on their
side,[141] and it was to meet this claim that Augustine
appealed to the authority of St Cyprian, a common
hero of East and West, in the famous sermon
preached in the Basilica Maiorum at Carthage on
27 June.[142] Now, in 416, it appeared that the claim
of the Pelagians might be justified. Caelestius had
been ordained priest at Ephesus;[143] Pelagius had
been acquitted at Diospolis of a dossier of charges
drawn up by the two exiled Gallic bishops, Heros
of Arles and Lazarus of Aix-en-Provence. Heros
and Lazarus had been the victims of politics;
but in the eyes of the Africans they were theologically thoroughly respectable, and Heros had been
a disciple of St Martin of Tours.[144] It seemed that
the East had decisively rejected the doctrine of
the West. African orthodoxy—and to the African
bishops this was equivalent to Catholic orthodoxy—
was in danger.

There was, however, for the Africans in 416 another cause for alarm, even more disturbing than
a possible breach with the East. At the Synod of

Jerusalem Bishop John had apparently agreed that the case of Pelagius and Caelestius should be referred to Rome.[145] If Caelestius were to make such an appeal, endorsed as it would be by the acquittal of Pelagius at Diospolis and the consideration that the Church of Ephesus had seen fit to ordain Caelestius himself to the priesthood, and if the Carthaginian decision of 411 were to be set aside, then a crisis might well develop in the relations between Africa and the Apostolic See such as had been unknown since the dispute between Cyprian and Stephen in the Third century. Pelagius had friends at Rome; the priest Sixtus (destined to be a future pope) was reported to be one of them. It was therefore imperative that Innocent of Rome should be persuaded to condemn the doctrines associated with the names of Pelagius and Caelestius. Speedy action was essential; and to it were added all the resources of African epistular diplomacy. The decisions of the councils of Carthage and Milevis were communicated to Rome and Innocent was implored to "add the authority of the Apostolic See to the statutes of African littleness."[146] The period of waiting while Innocent, with an agonizing deliberation, made up his mind must have been a torment for the African bishops.

For Augustine it must have been especially painful. His views, together with those of Jerome, had been invoked by Orosius as the authority for the condemnation of Pelagianism—and the Eastern bishops had ignored them. "It was," says Mr. Brown, "a crushing defeat for the 'experts.'"[147] It was something more: a terrible blow to Augustine's theory of the *Catholica*, which he had maintained against the Donatists: one Church, one faith. He had told Cresconius to look for the true faith in the churches which had received the Pauline Epistles, and now Caelestius had been ordained at Ephesus;[148] he had referred him to the Church of Jerusalem, of which the first bishop had been St James,[149] and in that church Pelagius had escaped condemnation, even though Bishop John had claimed to represent Augustine's person. The events in the East struck at the whole notion of Catholic unity which dominates Augustine's ecclesiology. Accordingly, the endorsement by Innocent of the decisions of the Councils of Carthage and Milevis became essential, in Augustine's eyes, not merely to vindicate African theology, but to establish it as the doctrine of the universal Church.

In the event Innocent gave the required support to the decisions of the African councils. Considering, however, the circumstances in which it was procured, in the absence of both the accused, it may be felt that Innocent's successor, Zosimus, his fussy authoritarianism notwithstanding, deserves more sympathy than he commonly receives from historians of all shades of opinion for his willingness to reopen the case and to hear the appeals of the two men whom his predecessor had condemned unheard.[150] But the Africans were not to be moved. Nothing could be more damaging from their point of view than to have their publicly-proclaimed decisions set aside; and they had an unanswerable

argument: *causa finita est.*[151] To what degree they
used other, less reputable, methods to win over the
imperial court at Ravenna we cannot say; at a
later date Julian of Eclanum was to speak of the
offerings of the poor and the legacies of rich women
being used to corrupt the civil authorities.[152] It
can only be observed that the African bishops had,
in the course of the Donatist Controversy, become
masters of the art of dealing with the secular arm
and that art, in the later Roman Empire, commonly
involved the judicious bestowal of tokens of esteem
and affection. But quite apart from any African
manipulation, the outbreak of violence at Rome
between the Pelagian party and its Catholic opponents, with inevitable reminiscences of the attack
on Jerome's monastery at Bethlehem in 416, would
in any case have spurred the government to act.[153]
The language of the imperial rescript condemning
Pelagianism makes plain the official point of view:
". . . a rumour has lately reached the ears of Our
Gentleness that within Our most holy City of Rome
and elsewhere the pestiferous venom has so established itself in the minds of certain persons that the
path of right belief has been broken up, schools
of opinion rent into factions, and occasion for
hostile dissension introduced."[154] Pelagius and
Caelestius were denounced in language which suggests that they were as much regarded as disturbers
of the peace as religious innovators: "This subtle
heresy considers it a particular mark of low breeding
to agree with other people and the palm of outstanding good sense to destroy what is generally ap-

proved."[155] With surprising perception the imperial chancery had taken the measure of Pelagianism and high-lighted its fundamental flaw: the self-confident superiority, derived from the aristocratic milieu in which it first grew and flourished and carried over into the Christian life.

On 1 May 418, the day following the promulgation of the imperial rescript, a general council of the African Church assembled at Carthage and there passed the famous series of nine canons against Pelagianism, of which the first two effectively comprehended the Rufinian teaching condemned in the person of Caelestius in 411 while the remainder dealt with the views attributed to Pelagius either at the Synod of Diospolis or expressed in the literature which the debate had engendered.[156] So was erected by conciliar decree that monument to African doctrine which was destined to remain a permanent force in Latin theology. It is, however, to be observed that when Pope Zosimus—whether impelled by pressure of circumstances or deciding in his own good time is hard to say—came finally to condemn Pelagius and Caelestius, he did not employ the language of the Council of Carthage but, like his predecessor Innocent, declared that by baptism infants are delivered from the death brought about by Adam's sin, without any reference to the hereditary guilt of sin which figures so prominently in African theology.[157] Rome was not prepared to give an unqualified endorsement to the full rigour of African doctrine; and Zosimus may well have felt that African controversial techniques were no

recommendation of their opinions. Had they not
led his predecessor, Innocent, to believe that the
Pelagians denied any need for baptism—*Illud vero,
quod eos [Pelagianos] vestra fraternitas asserit praedicare, parvulos aeternae vitae praemiis etiam sine
baptismatis gratia posse donari, perfatuum est?*[158]—
an assertion which would have been rejected by
any serious Pelagian.[159] Indeed, Roman reserve
about African theology continued long after the
Pelagian issue was decided. Pope Celestine might
vindicate Augustine's orthodoxy in the face of
Semi-Pelagian criticism; but he went no further.
He neither approved Augustinianism nor anathe-
matised Semi-Pelagianism.[160]

IX

In 418 Jerome sent a short letter of congratulation
to Augustine, couched in the most laudatory terms.
"At all times," he wrote, discreetly disregarding
certain inconvenient facts of the history of their
acquaintance,

I have esteemed Your Blessedness with becoming
reverence and honour and have loved the Lord
and Saviour dwelling in you. But now we add, if
possible, something to that which has already
reached a climax, and we heap up what was
already full, so that we do not suffer a single hour
to pass without the mention of your name because
you have, with the ardour of unshaken faith,
stood your ground against opposing storms and
preferred, so far as was in your power, to be

delivered from Sodom, though you should come
forth alone, rather than linger behind with those
who are doomed to perish.

Augustine was further informed that he was "famous
throughout the world," revered by Catholics and
hated by heretics[161]—precisely like Jerome himself.
It was the supreme accolade, the final recognition
of one master by another.

This early testimony to Augustine's part in the
Pelagian Controversy anticipates the verdict of
posterity; and in one sense it is, of course, correct.
No other individual can claim such preëminence in
the struggle against Pelagius and his supporters.
Yet the popular picture of the Pelagian Controversy, with Augustine standing, as it were, in the
centre of events, dominating the African bishops
and imposing his personal theology upon them, is
unconvincing both in terms of the temperament of
Augustine's colleagues—ever an independent-mind-
ed body of men—and the evidence of Augustine's
own writings; for these display, besides the confident
front which the saint maintained in controversy,
another side, more personal and more touching,
revealed in a famous letter to Jerome in 415. The
origin of the human soul, which is the theme of this
letter, had exercised Augustine's mind from the
time of his conversion, being discussed by him as
early as the *De Libero Arbitrio*, to which he specifically refers in this letter. By 415, however, the subject was no longer one of merely abstract theological
interest; for on it now turned the whole question
of divine justice, once the theologoumenon of the

damnation of unbaptised infants was accepted.
Augustine saw the problem with a painful clarity.
"I ask you," he wrote to Jerome,

where can the soul, even of an infant snatched
away by death, have contracted the guilt which,
unless the Grace of Christ has come to the rescue
by that sacrament of baptism which is administer
ed even to infants, involves it in condemnation?
. . . Teach me, I beg you, what I may teach to
others. . . . Where therefore is the justice of the
condemnation of so many thousands of souls
which, in the deaths of infant children, leave
this world without the benefit of the Christian
sacrament if, being newly created, they have—
not through any preceding sin of their own but
by the will of the Creator—become united to the
individual bodies which they were created to
animate and upon which they were bestowed by
Him who certainly knew that every one of them
was destined, not through any fault of its own,
to leave the body without receiving the baptism
of Christ?[162]

Jerome had no answer to the problem which had
been given a special prominence during the Origenistic Controversy and Augustine fell back upon
acceptance of African tradition, which he believed to
be the mind of the Catholic Church, preferring
rather to place his confidence in the hidden justice
of God than to admit the possibility of any salvation
other than that bestowed in the sacrament of baptism, in which we die and rise again with Christ.[163]
Four years after the despatch of this letter to

Jerome, Vincentius Victor was to inform the world
of his own well-assured views on the origin of the
human soul and Augustine was moved to express
the wish that the young man could come to Hippo
and talk with him—a discussion would be so much
more valuable than a written treatise.[164] One can
imagine that Augustine would have had many things
to say to his self-confident youthful critic, things
which could not easily be committed to paper.

There is, however, another piece of evidence,
hardly less revealing, contained in the *De Gestis
Pelagii*, written in 417 after Augustine had received
a copy of the minutes of the Synod of Diospolis
and felt himself able definitively to refute the
Pelagian account of the proceedings. When, in the
course of his narration, Augustine comes to deal
with his own relations with Pelagius, he adopts a
curiously apologetic air, explaining that he had,
at first, heard Pelagius' name uttered with com-
mendation and respect and became convinced of
his heretical tendencies only when he read the *De
Natura*.[165] He reproduces the fulsome letter of
thanks which he had received from Timasius and
James for his refutation of Pelagius[166] and also
quotes, and explains at some length, the highly
complimentary letter which he himself sent to
Pelagius in 413.[167]

Why does Augustine take so much trouble to
explain and defend his relations with Pelagius?
To us, it may seem inconceivable that anyone could
for a moment have regarded Augustine as having
been unduly lenient in his treatment of the British

theologian; but reflection suggests that in African circles at least things may have seemed rather different in the early months of 416, when reports of the events in Palestine began to arrive in the West. Had not Augustine spoken of Pelagius with respect in the *De Peccatorum Meritis et Remissione*? Had he not provided him with the letter which helped to establish his good faith in the eyes of the Synod of Diospolis? Again, in replying to the *De Natura*, a work in which Pelagius had cited Augustine among others in support of his own views, had he not omitted any mention of Pelagius' name and even suggested that the heretic had been led into error by misapplied zeal for the faith? Yet again, in the aftermath of the Synod of Diospolis, when the hortatory work ascribed to Pelagius and addressed to a certain widow was produced, had not Augustine been prepared to doubt its authorship on the ground that a similar misattribution had once occurred to himself?[168] In these circumstances one can well imagine that there could have been criticism of Augustine by colleagues who were not overawed by his intellectual eminence and who were determined that African theological integrity should be vindicated. If to criticism at home for lack of zeal against Pelagius were added anxiety at the Palestinian accusation directed against his disciple Orosius, of teaching that men cannot avoid sin even with the Grace of God—an inference from his teaching which Augustine had tried to forestall when he wrote the *De Spiritu et Littera* for the benefit of the puzzled Marcellinus[169]—one can understand why

Augustine emerges, from 416 onwards, as the leader of African opposition to Pelagianism in any and every form. Mr. Brown has observed that Augustine "lived to see the fundamentals of his life's work challenged in his old age."[170] It is possible that the challenge may have been more direct, and personally more damaging, than Mr. Brown implies, and that in 416 it appeared to Augustine that his very reputation as a theologian was at stake.

It is in the light of such a situation that we can understand the increasing use of the appeal to antiquity in Augustine's later anti-Pelagian writings. In the *De Peccatorum Meritis et Remissione* in 411-412 he can cite only Cyprian and Jerome in support of his teaching;[171] in the *De Gratia Christi et de Peccato Originali* of 418 he cites Ambrose several times; in the six books of the *Contra Iulianum*, published in 421-422, Ambrose is quoted more than thirty times and to his testimony is added that of authors like Reticius of Autun, Olympius of Spain and Hilary of Poitiers.[172] *Securus iudicat orbis terrarum;* the principle which Augustine had asserted against the Donatists had now to be maintained against the Pelagians. Augustine had no desire to be anything other than a doctor of the Catholic Church.

Yet, on the interpretation of the evidence which is here proposed, it would seem that Augustine's dominating rôle in the struggle with Pelagianism was thrust upon him rather than sought out. In 415 he found himself cited as an authority for the views which Pelagius was propounding in the *De Natura;* in 416 the reports of the synods of Jerusa-

lem and Diospolis seemed to suggest that his
theological views had been rejected by Greek theologians. For a time his very reputation as a Catholic
theologian must have seemed to hang in the balance
and, what was worse, the principles upon which he
had founded his life as a Christian pastor appeared
to be questioned. Perhaps the unyielding rigour
which Augustine displayed in the later days of the
Pelagian Controversy, which so distressed the
Christian ascetics of Gaul, is to be understood as
the reaction of an aging man who had seen his
fundamental beliefs challenged and then vindicated.
It has been said that "nearly all that Augustine
wrote after his seventieth year is the work of a
man whose energy has burned itself out, whose
love has grown cold."[173] This verdict, by one of
the most learned and sympathetic interpreters of
Augustine's thought, will find an echo in the hearts
of many of those who have studied works like the
De Dono Perseverantiae and the *Opus Imperfectum
contra Iulianum* and presumably underlies Mr.
Brown's reference to the "cold competence of an
old, tired man, who knew only too well how to
set about the harsh business of ecclesiastical controversy."[174] No doubt age played its part in determining the tone of Augustine's later writings; but
one cannot exlude the long-term effect of a deep
psychological shock. In the first major engagement
of the Pelagian Controversy the first principles of
Augustine's Christian life were questioned and then
vindicated by the verdict of Church and Emperor;
but the strain had its effect. Thereafter, Augustine

could not afford to make any concessions or offer
any terms other than those of unconditional sur-
render without prejudicing in his own eyes that
understanding of the Christian faith which came
to him in 396 when replying to the questions of
Simplicianus of Milan. This explanation would account both for the harshness which he showed at
the last to Pelagius, whose zeal for faith and morals
would otherwise have found an echo in Augustine's
own heart, and for his resolute refusal to compromise
with the Massilian divines, whom he nevertheless
regarded as brethren and not as heretics.[175] Augustine's conviction of the rightness of his own
position was absolute; but it was a conviction which
had been hardened in the fires of controversy which
left no place for toleration or compromise.

Historical proof of a psychological explanation
of this character is in the very nature of things impossible; but such an explanation agrees very well
with that sense of "love grown cold" which characterises the last writings of the great saint and Christian teacher in whose honour the Augustine Lectures
are instituted.[176]

NOTES

1. For specimens of the "theological" view of Pelagianism, see R. F. Evans, *Pelagius. Inquiries and reappraisals* (New York / London 1968), 1-2, 66-67. J. R. Lucas, "Pelagius and St. Augustine," *JTS* NS xxii (1971), 73-85 understands Pelagianism in the theological sense.

2. See the comment of John Burnaby, *Amore Dei. A study of the Religion of St. Augustine* (London 1938), 231: "The system which generally goes by the name of Augustinianism is in great part a cruel travesty of Augustine's deepest and most vital thought."

3. Evans, *Pelagius*, 6 ff.

4. A. Hamman, "Orosius de Braga et le pélagianisme," *Bracara Augusta* xxi (1968), 1-12.

5. Angelo Paredi, "Paulinus of Milan," *Sacris Eruditi* xiv (1963), 206-30.

6. Reprinted in Migne, *PL* xlviii, 449-88.

7. C. P. Caspari, *Briefe, Abhandlungen und Predigen aus den zwei letzten Jahrhunderten des Kirchlichen Altertums und dem Anfang des Mittelalters* (Christiana 1890).

8. John Morris, "Pelagian Literature," *JTS* NS (1965), 37, 40: "He was a Briton who wrote in Sicily, and is therefore most fitly described as the 'Sicilian Briton.'"

9. Alexander Souter, *Pelagius's Expostions of thirteen Epistles of St. Paul* [Texts and Studies Vol. IX] (Cambridge 1922-1931);

but see C. Charlier, "Cassiodore, Pélage et les origines de la vulgate paulinienne," *Studiorum Paolinorum Congressus Internationalis Catholicus 1961* (Rome 1963), 1-10 cited by Evans, *Pelagius*, 139 n^{93}.

10. Heinrich Zimmer, *Pelagius in Irland* (Berlin 1901).

11. P. C. Martini in *Antonianum* xiii (1938), 319-34 (on which see Evans, *Pelagius*, 158 n^6); reprinted in Migne, *PL Supplementum* i (cited here as *PLS*).

12. *Liber de Induratione cordis Pharaonis*, ed. G. Moris in G. de Plinval, *Essai sur le style et la langue de Pélage* (Fribourg-en-Suisse 1947), 137-203; reprinted in *PLS*.

13. Ed. A. Amelli, *Spicilegium Casinense* III, 1 (1897); reprinted in *PLS*.

14. Morris, art. cit. [n^8], p. 27.

15. See R. F. Evans, *Four letters of Pelagius* (New York /London 1968), 34-35.

16. Printed by Caspari, op. cit. [n^7]; reprinted *PLS* i.

17. Mar. Merc., *Lib. Subnot. in Verba Iul.*, 2: "hanc ineptam et non minus inimicam rectae fidei quaestionem sub sanctae recordationis Anastasio Romanae ecclesiae summo pontifice Rufinus quondam natione Syrus Romam primus invexit et, ut erat argutus, se quidem ab eius invidia muniens, per se proferre non ausus, Pelagium gente Brittanum monachum tunc decepit eumque ad praedictam adprime imbuit atque instituit impiam vanitatem" (*ACO* I, v, 5. 36-40).

18. Peter Brown, "Pelagius and his supporters. Aims and environment," *JTS* NS xix (1968), 94 n^2.

19. Torgny Bohlin, *Die Theologie des Pelagius und ihre Genesis* (Uppsala/Wiesbaden 1957).

20. Evans, op. cit. [n^1].

21. Berthold Altaner, "Der *Liber de Fide* ein Werk des Pelagianers Rufinus des 'Syrers,'" *Theologische Quartalschrift* cxxx (1950), 432-49, reprinted in *Kleine Patristische Schriften* [Texte und Untersuchungen zur Geschichte des altchristlichen Literatur Bd 83] (Berlin 1967), 467-82.

22. H. I. Marrou, "Les attaches orientales du Pélagianisme," *Académie des inscriptions et belles-lettres : Comptes rendus des séances de l'année 1968 juillet-octobre* (Paris 1968), 459-72.

23. G. Bonner, "Rufinus of Syria and African Pelagianism," *Augustinian Studies* i (1970), 31-47.

24. J. N. L. Myres, "Pelagius and the end of Roman rule in Britain," *JRS* 1 (1960), 21-36.

25. John Morris, "Pelagian Literature," *JTS* NS xvi (1965), 26-60; "The Literary Evidence," in *Christianity in Britain 300-700*, edd. M. W. Barley & R. P. C. Hanson (Leicester University Press 1968), 55-73.

26. W. Liebeschuetz, "Did the Pelagian movement have social aims?" *Historia* xii (1963), 227-41; "Pelagian evidence on the last period of Roman Britain," *Latomus* xxvi (1967), 436-47.

27. A. Cameron. "Celestial consulates. A note on the Pelagian letter *Humanae referunt*," *JTS* NS xix (1968), 213-15.

28. See Evans, *Pelagius*, 90-121 for an exposition which makes clear how little social considerations determined his thought.

29. P. Brown, "Pelagius and his supporters. Aims and environment," *JTS* NS xix (1968), 93-114; "The Roman patrons of Pelagius," *JTS* NS xxi (1970), 56-72.

30. Brown, "Pelagius and his supporters," 104-05 n[7].

31. See Aug., *Ep.* 188, i, 3 (*CSEL* lvii, 121. 3-8).

32. Brown, *Augustine of Hippo* (London 1967), 359 speaks of Timasius and James as having "betrayed" the *De Natura* of Pelagius to Augustine; but it is surely fairer to see them as two former enthusiasts who later came to wonder where precisely their teacher's theology was leading them. Their action is proof, if any were needed, that the heretical strain in Pelagius' thought was not, in the first place, a discovery of Augustine's.

33. Aug., *De Grat. Christ. et de Pecc. Orig.*, I, ii, 2 (*CSEL* xlii, 125. 13-20).

34. *Vie de Sainte Mélanie*, 23 (*Sources Chrétiennes* xc, 174).

35. Ibid., 3, 8. See the comments of the editor, D. Gorce, pp. 37 ff., 111-12.

36. Hieron., *Ep.* 50, 5: "Inter mulierculas sciolus sibi et eloquens videbatur" (*CSEL* liv, 393. 23-394. 1). The identification of the unnamed monk of this letter with Pelagius, first proposed by Plinval, *Pélage*, 47-55, seems today to be generally accepted. See Evans, *Pelagius*, 31-37.

37. Hieron., *Ep.* 127, 7: "Denique, cum et me Roman cum sanctis pontificibus Paulino et Epiphanio ecclesiastica traxisset necessitas ... et verecunde nobiliarum feminarum oculos declinarem ..." (*CSEL* lvi, 150. 22-23, 25).

38. Note the bitterness of Jerome's complaint against Pelagius, *Ep.* 50, 2: "Inventus est homo absque praeceptore perfectus, πνευματόφορος καὶ θεοδίδακτος, qui eloquentia Tullium, argumentis Aristotelem, prudentia Platonem, eruditione Aristarchum, multitudine librorum χαλκέντερον Didymum, scientia scripturarum omnes sui temporis vincat tractatores" (*CSEL* liv, 389. 11-15).

39. Aug., *De Gest. Pel.*, xxxv, 61: "post veteres haereses [inlata est] etiam modo haeresis non ab episcopis seu presbyteris vel quibusque clericis, sed a quibusdam veluti monachis, quae contra dei gratiam, quae nobis est *per Iesum Christum dominum nostrum*, tamquam defendendo liberum arbitrium disputaret et conaretur evertere christianae fidei firmamentum, de quo scriptum est: *per unum hominem mors et per unum hominem resurrectio mortuorum; sicut enim in Adam omnes moriuntur, sic et in Christo omnes vivificabuntur*" (*CSEL* xlii, 115. 23-116. 9).

40. Brown, "Pelagius and his supporters," 103.

41. See Evans, *Pelagius*, 26-42.

42. Aug., *De Dono Persever.*, xx, 52 (*PL* xlv, 1026).

43. Aug., *Retract.*, II, 1 [27] (*CSEL* xxxvi, 131-32); *De Praedest. Sanct.*, iv, 8 (quoting *Retract.*, II, 1 [27]) (*PL* xliv, 965-66); *De Dono Persever.*, xx, 52, xxi, 55: " ... Quod autem dicunt: 'non opus fuisse huiusmodi disputationis incerto minus intelligentium tot corda turbari, quoniam non minus utiliter sine hac definitione praedestinationis per tot annos defensa est catholica fides, tum contra alios, tum maxime contra Pelagianos, tot catholicorum et aliorum et nostris praecedentibus libris,' multum miror eos dicere; nec attendere, ut de aliis hic taceam, ipsos libros nostros et antequam Pelagiani apparere coepissent, conscriptos et editos, et videre quam multis eorum locis futuram nescientes Pelagianum haeresim caedebamus, praedicando gratiam qua nos Deus liberat a malis erroribus et moribus nostris, non praecedentibus bonis meritis nostris, faciens hoc secundum gratuitam misericordiam suam. Quod plenius sapere coepi in ea disputatione quam scripsi

ad beatae memoriae Simplicianum episcopum Mediolanensis
Ecclesiae, in mei episcopatus exordio, quando et initium fidei
donum Dei esse cognovi et asserui. . . . videant, inquam, utrum
in primi libri posterioribus partibus, eorum duorum quos mei
episcopatus initio, antequam Pelagiana haeresis appareret, ad
Simplicianum Mediolanensem episcopum scripsi, remanserit aliquid
quo vocatur in dubium, gratiam Dei non secundum merita nostra
dari; et utrum ibi non satis egerim, etiam initium fidei esse donum
Dei; et utrum ex iis quae ibi dicta sunt, non consequenter eluceat,
etsi non sit expressum, etiam usque in finem perseverantiam non
nisi ab eo donari, qui nos praedestinavit in suum regnum et gloriam" (*PL* xliv, 1025-26, 1027).

44. *Retract.*, II, 1 [27]: "In cuius quaestionis solutione laboratum
est quidem pro libero arbitrio voluntatis humanae; sed vicit dei
gratia, nec nisi ad illud potuit perveniri, ut liquidissima veritate
dixisse intellegatur apostolus: *quis enim te discernit? quid autem
habes quod non accepisti? si autem accepisti, quid gloriaris, quasi
non acceperis?*" (*CSEL* xxxvi, 132. 6-12).

45. *De Div. Quaest. ad Simpl.*, I. q. 2, 16, 22: "Sunt igitur omnes
homines (quandoquidem, ut Apostolus ait, *In Adam omnes moriuntur*, a quo in universum genus humanum origo ducitur offensionis
Dei) una quaedam massa peccati, supplicium debens divinae summaeque iustitiae, quod sive exigatur, sive donetur, nulla est iniquitas. . . . Itaque huius impudentiam quaestionis ita retundit
Apostolus: *O homo, tu quis es qui respondeas Deo.* Sic enim respondet
Dei, cum ei displicet quod de peccatoribus conqueritur Deus,
quasi quemquam Deus peccare cogat, si tantummodo quibusdam
peccantibus misericordiam iustificationis suae non largiatur, et
ob hoc dicatur obdurare peccantes quosdam, quia non eorum miseretur, non quia impellit ut peccent. Eorum autem non miseretur,
quibus misericordiam non esse praebendam aequitate occultissima
et ab humanis sensibus remotissima iudicat. *Inscrutabilia* enim
sunt iudicia eius, et investigabiles viae ipsius. . . . Tunc facta est
una massa omnium, veniens de traduce peccati et de poena mortalitatis, quamvis Deo formante et creante quae bona sunt. In omnibus est enim species et compago corporis in tanta membrorum
concordia, ut inde Apostolus ad charitatem obtinendam similitudinem duceret. In omnibus est etiam spiritus vitalis terrena mem-

bra vivificans, omnisque natura hominis dominatu animae et famulatu corporis conditione mirabili temperata: sed concupiscentia carnalis de peccati poena iam regnans, universum genus humanum tanquam totam et unam conspersionem originali reatu in omnia permanente confuderat" (*PL* xl, 121, 125-126). Tr. J. H. Burleigh, *Augustine : Earlier Writings* [Library of Christian Classics Vol. VI] (London 1953), 398, 403-04.

46. *De Nat. et Grat.*, lxiii, 74, 75 (*CSEL* lx, 289.9 - 291.8)

47. *De Grat. Christ. et de Pecc. Orig.*, I, xliv, 48; II, xli, 47. See A. Paredi, "Paulinus of Milan," *Sacris erudiri* xiv (1963), 212-13.

48. Ed. by Sister Mary William Miller, *Rufini Presbyteri Liber de Fide* [The Catholic University of America Patristic Studies Vol. XCVI] (Washington, D. C. 1964). For a description, see E. A. Lowe, *Codices Latini Antiquiores* (Oxford 1966), Vol. XI, p. 10 No 1614; Miller, op. cit., pp. 30-31, 46-47.

49. Leningrad MS. Q.v.I.6, f. 61ʳ: "Explicit Rufini presbyteri provinciae Palaestinae *Liber de Fide*, translatus de Graeco in Latinum sermonem" (Miller 36 n^2).

50. Ibid., f. 1ʳ: "Hic liber qui attitulatur Rufini non te seducat, O pie lector, quia Pelagianus est et blasphemiis Pelagianorum plenus. Simulans enim contra Arrianos disputationem venena suae hereseos inseruit. Unde horter caritatem tuam ut hanc blasphemiam de vestro codice abscidatis et pro ea librum Sancti Augustini *De Vera Religione* describite ut quantitatem codicis reparetis" (Miller 36 n^4); f. 61ʳ: "Huc usque blasphemiae Pelagii heretici contra fidem catholicam quas sub nomine Rufini catholici falso titolo indidit" (Miller 36 n^6).

51. *De Grat. Christ. et de Pecc. Orig.*, II, iii, 3: "Caelestius dixit: 'sanctus presbyter Rufinus Romae qui mansit cum sancto Pammachio; ego audivi illum dicentem, quia tradux peccati non sit'" (*CSEL* xlii, 168. 12-14).

52. Marrou, art. cit. [n^{22}], pp. 464-65.

53. See above, n^{17}.

54. Innocent *apud* Aug., *Ep.* 183, 2: "nam si Pelagius, quocumque restitit loco, eorum animos, qui facile vel simpliciter crederent disputanti, hac adfirmatione decepit, seu hic illi in urbe sunt, quod nescientes nec manifestare possumus nec negare . . ." (*CSEL* xliv, 726. 2-6); *Coll. Avell.*, 41 (*CSEL* xxxv (1), 93. 16-19).

55. See above, n^{51}.

56. Marrou, art. cit. [n^{22}], p. 461: ". . .ici et la *sanctus* n'a bien entendu que la valeur très générale de "vénéré,", "de saine mémoire" —s'agissant de défunts: Pammachiue est mort à cette date, Rufinus aussi."

57. See above, n^{21}.

58. F. Refoulé, "Datation du premier concile de Carthage contre les Pélagiens et du *Libellus fidei* de Rufin," *Revue des Études Augustiniennes* lx (1963), 44-49.

59. J. de Blic, "Le péché originel selon saint Augustin," *Recherches de Science Religieuse* xvi (1927), 518-19.

60. G. Bonner, art. cit. [n^{23}], pp. 37, 38.

61. F. Cavallera, *Saint Jérome, sa vie et son œuvre*, i (Louvain 1922), t. 1, pp. 250 n^1, 254; t. 2, pp. 37, 38.

62. Hieron., *C. Ioan. Hierosol.*, 22: ". . . Cain et Abel, primi ex primis hominibus, unde habuere animas? Omne deinceps humanum genus, quibus animarum censetur exordiis? Utrum ex traduce, iuxta bruta animalia: ut quomodo corpus ex corpore, sic anima generetur ex anima? an rationabiles creaturae desiderio corporum paulatim ad terram delapsae, novissime etiam humanis illigatae corporibus sint? An certe (quod ecclesiasticum est secundum eloquia Salvatoris) *Pater meus usque modo operatur, et ego operor* . . . quotidie Deus fabricatur animas" (*PL* xxiii, 389 A B); *C. Rufinum Apol.*, ii, 4: ". . . anima ista, quam suscepit Iesus, eratne antequam nasceretur ex Maria? an in origine virginali, quae de Spiritu sancto nascebatur, cum corpore simul creata est, vel iam in utero corpore figurato, statim facta et missa est de coelo? E tribus unum quid sentias, scire desidero. Si fuit antequam nasceretur ex Maria, necdum ergo erat anima Iesu et agebat aliquid, ac propter merita virtutum postea facta est anima eius. Si cepit ex traduce, humanarum igitur animarum, quas aeternas fatemur, et brutorum animantium, quae cum corpore dissolvuntur, una conditio est. Sin autem figurato corpore statim creatur et mittitur, fatere simpliciter, et nos scrupulo libera" (*PL* xxiii, 446 D 447 A; *Ep.* 126 [*inter* Aug. 165], 1: ". . . an certe ex traduce, ut Tertullianus, Apollinaris et maxima pars occidentalium autumat, ut, quomodo corpus ex corpore, sic anima nascatur ex anima et simili cum brutis animantibus condicione subsistat" (*CSEL*

66

lvi, 143. 13-16). This last letter was written in 412/3 and represented Jerome's final position (as Augustine recognized, *Ep.* 190, vi, 20: "... significavit ... se potius fieri quam propagari animas credere" [*CSEL* lvii, 156. 2-3]).

63. Rufinus, *Apol. ad Anas.*, 6: "Audio et de anima quaestiones esse commotas. De qua re utrum recipi debeat quaeremonia aut abici vos probate. Si autem et de me quid sentiam quaeritur, fateor me de hac quaestione apud quamplurimos tractatorum diversa legisse. Legi quosdam dicentes quod pariter cum corpore per humani seminis traducem etiam anima defundatur, et hos quibus poterant adsertionibus confirmabant. Quod puto inter Latinos Tertullianum sensisse vel Lactantium, fortassis et alios nonnullos" (*CC* xx, 27. 1-8). Jerome specially remarked upon this passage and quoted it, *C. Rufin. Apol.* ii, 8 (*PL* xxiii, 449 D - 450 B), though he had doubts about the reference to Lactantius (ibid., ii, 10, col. 452 B) which became an outright and characteristic denial, iii, 30: "... licet de Lactantio apertissime mentiaris" (*PL* xxiii, 501 B).

64. Ibid.: "Ego tamen haec singula et legisse me non nego, et adhuc ignorare confiteor, praeter hoc quod manifeste tradit ecclesia, Deum esse et animarum et corporum conditorem" (*CC* xx, 27. 16-19).

65. Caelestius *apud* Aug., *De Grat. Christ. et de Pecc. Orig.*, II, iv, 3 (*CSEL* xlii, 169. 11-13).

66. Rufinus, *De Fide*, 48: "Unde infantes, qui in peccatis non sunt, merentur etiam baptismatis gratiam ut, in Christo nova generatione creati, etiam regni eius coheredes efficiantur" (Miller 126. 4-7).

67. Ibid., 39: "Neque enim meminit usquam divina Scriptura quasi ipsi secundo peccaverint, sicuti de Cain, quod secundo peccavit narrare non distulit, quippe etiam de Abel, quod a peccatis fuerit alienus, aperte docuerit. Quid vero de Henoch atque Elia dicunt, quod, cum bene placuissent Deo, *translati sunt ut mortem penitus non viderent*, non ab Adam praevaricatione prohibiti permanere immortales, cum per eosdem clare docuerit unigenitus Deus ante carnalem adventum suum spem ipsam resurrectionis? Quid etiam de Noe dicent, quem Deus iustum esse testatur?" (Miller 112. 23-33).

68. Pel., *De Natura apud* Aug., *De Nat. et Grat.*, xxi, 23, xxxvi, 42: "Quaeritur etiam parvulis tantus medicus opitulator et ipse [Pelagius] dicit: *Quid quaeritis? sani sunt propter quos medicum quaeritis. nec ipse primus homo ideo morte damnatus est; nam postea non peccavit.* . . . . Deinde commemorat eos, 'qui non modo non pecasse, verum etiam iuste vixisse referuntus: Abel, Enoch, Melchisedech, Abraham, Isaac, Iacob, Ioseph, Iesu Nave, Finees, Samuhel, Nathan, Helias, Heliseus, Micheas, Danihel, Ananias, Azarias, Misael, Ezechiel, Mardocheus, Simeon, Ioseph, cui desponsata erat virgo Maria, Ioannes.' . . . *certe*, inquit, *primo in tempore Adam et Eva, ex quibus Cain et Abel nati sunt, quattuor tantum homines fuisse referuntur. peccavit Eva—scriptura hoc prodidit— Adam quoque deliquet—eadem scriptura non tacuit—sed et Cain pecasse ipsa aeque scriptura testata est, quorum non modo peccata, verum etiam peccatorum indicat qualitatem. quodsi et Abel peccasset, hoc sine dubio scriptura dixisset; sed non dixit: ergo nec ille peccavit, quin etiam iustum ostendit*" (*CSEL* lx, 248. 25-28, 263. 15-20, 265. 12-19); cf. *De Gest. Pel.*, x, 22: "suspectum enim me facit etiam illud, quod cum in eodem libro, cui respondi, apertissime dixerit 'Abel iustum numquam omnino peccasse,' modo ait: 'non autem diximus quod inveniatur aliquis ab infantia usque ad senectam qui numquam peccaverit, sed quoniam a peccatis conversus proprio labore et dei gratia possit esse sine peccato'" (*CSEL* xlii, 75. 24-76. 3); *De Libero Arbitrio, apud* Aug., *De Grat. Christ. et de Pecc. Orig.*, II, xiii, 14: "omne bonum ac malum, quo vel laudabiles vel vituperabiles sumus, non nobiscum oritur, sed agitur in nobis; capaces enim utriusque rei, non pleni nascimur et ut sine virtute ita ut sine vitio procreamur atque ante actionem propriae voluntatis id solum in homine est, quod deus condidit" (*CSEL* xlii, 175. 22-27). See Plinval, *Pélage*, 297-300 and Evans, *Pelagius*, 104.

69. Rufinus, *De Fide*, 40: "Baptisma igitur infantes non propter peccata percipiunt, sed ut, spiritalem procreationem habentes, quasi per baptisma in Christo creentur et ipsius regni caelestis participes fiant" (Miller 114. 23-27).

70. Caelestius *apud* Aug., *De Grat. Christ. et de Pecc. Orig.*, II, v, 5: "In libello autem, quem Romae edidit, qui gestis ibi ecclesiasticis allegatus est, ita de hac re loquitur, ut hoc se credere ostendat,

unde hic dubitare se dixerat. nam verba eius ista sunt: 'infantes autem,' inquit, 'debere baptizari in remissionem peccatorum secundum regulam universalis ecclesiae et secundum evangelii sententiam confitemur, quia dominus statuit regnum caelorum nonnisi baptizatis posse conferri. quod quia vires naturae non habent, conferri necessarium est per gratiae libertatem'" (*CSEL* xlii, 169. 23-170. 3).

71. Ibid., vi, 7: ". . . quia superius in eodem libello suo [Caelestius] de huius modi quaestionibus locuturus ante praedixerat: 'si forte ut hominibus quispiam ignorantiae error obrepsit, vestra sententia corrigatur'" (*CSEL* xlii, 171. 2-5).

72. See above, n^{17}.

73. Altaner, art. cit. [n^{21}], pp. 440-45 (*KpS* 475-78).

74. H. I. Marrou, *A History of Education in Antiquity*, ET by G. Lamb (New York: Mentor Books 1964), 390.

75. Mar. Merc., *Lib. Subnot. in Verba Iul.*, 1: "Quaestio contra catholicam fidem apud nonnullos Syrorum et maxime in Cilicia a Theodoro quondam episcopo oppidi Mampsisteni [*leg.* Mopsuesteni] iamdudum nota, nunc usque penes paucos eorum admodum roditur nec ea palam profertur, sed ab ipsis qui de ea fornicantur, velut catholicis intra ecclesias interim retinetur, progenitores videlicet humani generis Ada, et Evam mortales a deo creatos nec quemquam posterorum sua praevaricatione transgressi laesisse, sed sibi tantum nocuisse; se mandati reos apud deum fecisse, alterum penitus nullum" (*ACO* I, v, 5.30-36).

76. Robert Devresse, *Essai sur Théodore de Mopsueste* (Studi e testi 141) (Rome 1948), 164.

77. Julius Gross, "Theodor von Mopsuestia ein Gegner der Erbsündenlehre," *Zeitschrift für Kirchengeschichte* lxv (1954), 8.

78. Günter Koch, *Die Heilsverwirklichung bei Theodor von Mopsuestia* (Münchener theologische Studien 2: Systematische Abt., Bd 31) (Munich 1965), 58-75 and note his conclusion (p. 71): "Wie aber lassen sich beide Konzeptionen vereinbaren? Einerseits 'Gedanken nahe denen Augustins,' anderseits eine 'pelagianisierende Lehre,' wie es Amann nennt? Unseres Erachtens ist eine volle Harmonisierung nicht möglich, beide Konzeptionen sind als bestehend anzuerkennen."

79. Ibid., pp. 59 n^{92}, 70.

80. Rufinus, *De Fide*, 29: "Illos igitur primos homines, Adam dico et Evam, licet immortales secundum animam creatos esse dixerim, mortales vero secundum corpus; numquam tamen mortem gustassent, siquidem mandatum Dei servare voluissent, sicut beatus Henoch meruit" (Miller 94. 6-10).

81. Theod. Mopsuest., *In Ioh.* xvii, 11: "Postquam creatus est primus homo a Deo, reus factus est mortis propter peccatum cum omnibus qui ex eo nati sunt; quippe qui ex parte quadam naturali primorum hominum receperunt exsistentium suam. Quia ita etiam gignere possunt homines, propterea merito participationem naturalem cum eis receperunt. Et quia communem habent naturam, ita etiam mortem naturae impositam, contraxerunt" (ed. Vosté, *CSCO, Script. Syr.* Ser. IV, tom. 3, 224. 12-18).

82. Aug., *De Pecc. Mer. et Rem.*, I, ii, 2: "quamvis enim secundum corpus terra esset et corpus in quo creatus animale gestaret, tamen, si non pecasset, in corpus fuerat spiritale mutandus et in illam incorruptionem quae fidelibus et sanctis promittitur, sine mortis supplicio transiturus" (*CSEL* lx, 4. 7-11).

83. Pel., *Exp.* 45. 12: "quo modo, cum non esset peccatum, per Adam advenit, ita etiam, cum paene aput nullum iustitia remansisset, per Christum est revocata; et quo modo per illius peccatum mors intravit, ita et per huius iustitiam vita est reparata" (*PLS* i, 1136. 20-25).

84. Iul. *apud* Aug., *Op. Imp. c. Iul.*, vi, 30: "Haud sane impugnavero eos qui autumant Adam, si dicto audiens exstitisset, ad immortalitatem potuisse pro remuneratione transferri. Enoch quippe et Eliam translatos legimus, ne viderunt mortem. Verum aliud sunt instituta naturae, aliud praemia obedientiae. Non est enim tanti unius meritum, ut universa quae naturaliter sunt instituta perturbet. Exercuisset se igitur in reliquiis innata mortalitas, etiamsi primus ille in aeternitatem a diuturnitate migrasset. Non inficiabili coniectura, sed certo res tenetur exemplo: siquidem Enoch filii, immortalitate parentis non potuerunt asseri a conditione moriendi. . . . Rem in absoluto positam Christi quoque confirmavit auctoritas. Nam cum ei Sadducaei questionem exemplo septinubae mulieris intulissent, rogantes, si corporum excitatio crederetur, a quo marito esset potissimum vindicanda, respondit: *Erratis, nescientes Scripturas, neque Dei virtutem; in resurrectione*

70

enim neque nubent, neque uxores accipient; neque enim morientur.
Conscius operis sui, propter quid coniugia instituisset expressit,
videlicet ut damna mortis fetura suppleret; statim autem cessatum
iri munificam fecunditatem, cum mors avara cessaverit. Si ergo,
Christo teste qui condidit, fertilitas ob hoc creata est, ut cum fra-
gilitate confligeret, et haec conditio nuptiarum ante peccatum or-
dinata est; apparet quoque mortalitatem non ad praevaricationem
spectare, sed ad naturam ad quam spectare leguntur et nuptiae.
Illa ergo lex quae promulgata est, id est, *Quacumque die ex inter-
dicto ederis, morte morieris*: poenalis mors intelligitur, non corporalis;
peccatis, non seminibus imminans; quam non incurrit nisi prae-
varicatio, non evadit nisi emendatio" (*PL* xlv, 1579, 1580); cf.
Ruf., *De Fide*, 29: "Rursus autem, si Adam et Eva immortales
essent secundum carnem creati, numquam audissent a Deo: *Cres-
cite et multiplicamini et implete terram*; nam qui manducare et
bibere et coire et crescere et terram implere iussi sunt, hi penitus
immortales esse non poterant, sicut etiam Dominus noster Iesus
Christus, docens Sadducaeos, dicebat: *Filii saeculi huius nubunt
et traduntur ad nuptias; illi vero qui digni habebuntur saeculo
illo et resurrectione ex mortuis, neque nubunt, neque ducunt uxores,
neque enim ultra mori poterunt, aequales enim angelis sunt*" (Miller
94. 21-31).

85. Pel., *Exp.* 46, 47. 15: "hi autem qui contra traducem peccati
sunt, ita illam impugnare nituntur: 'si Adae,' inquiunt, 'peccatum
etiam non peccantibus nocuit, ergo et Christi iustitia etiam non
credentibus prodest; quia similiter, immo et magis dicit per unum
salvari quam per unum ante perirant.' deinde aiunt: 'si baptis-
mum mundat antiquum illut delictum, qui de duobus baptizatis
nati fuerint debent hoc carere peccato: non enim potuerunt ad
filios transmittere quod ipsi minime habuerunt. illut quoque
accidit quia, si anima non est ex traduce, sed sola caro, ipsa tantum
habet traducem peccati et ipsa sola poenam meretur.' iniustum
esse dicentes, ut hodie nata anima, non ex massa Adae, tam antiquum peccatum portet alienum. dicant etiam nulla ratione con-
cedi, ut deus, qui propria homini peccata remittit imputet aliena"
(*PLS* 1137. 17-37). Cf. Ruf., *De Fide*, 40: "Et siquidem propter
peccatum Adam baptizantur infantes, qui ex parentibus christianis
nati sunt baptizari minime debebant, et quasi sancti perinde haber-

entur, quia de parentibus sunt fidelibus procreati" (Miller 114. 13-
17); and see the comment of Aug., *De Pecc. Mer. et Rem.*, III, iii,
6: "Videsne, obsecro, quemadmodum hoc totum Pelagius non ex
sua, sed ex aliorum persona indiderit scriptis suis. usque adeo
sciens nescio quam esse novitatem, quae contra antiquam et
ecclesiae insitam opinionem nunc coeperit" (*CSEL* lx. 132. 15-18).

86. Cf. P. Brown, *Augustine of Hippo. A Biography* (London
1967), 352: "The Pelagian . . . was contemptuous of babies" and
Evans, *Pelagius*, 118: "[Pelagius's] reflection upon the sacrament
of Christian initiation is built on the model of adult baptism and
makes scarce sense if baptism is administered to infants."

87. Marrou, op. cit. [n74], p. 297. Pierre Riché, *Éducation et
culture dans l'Occident barbare 6e-8e siècle* (Paris 1962), 48-49
notes that Christianity, by following the teaching of Christ, might
have transformed the spirit of ancient education, but failed to do
so.

88. Aug., *Conf.*, I, vii, 11 (*CSEL* xxxiii, 9. 1-10. 11).

89. See the remarks of E. TeSelle, *Augustine the Theologian*
(London 1970), 260-62.

90. For a discussion of his origins, see Plinval, *Pélage*, 47-71.

91. See Evans, *Pelagius*, 34, 35.

92. So J. B. Bury, *The Life of St Patrick* (London 1905), 43:
"His name represents, doubtless, some Irish sea-name such as
Muirchu, 'hound of the sea.'" On this, see Plinval, *Pélage*, 58, 59.

93. H. Williams, *Christianity in Early Britain* (Oxford 1912),
200, 201 and *nn*.

94. Evans, *Pelagius*, 92.

95. Bohlin, *Die Theologie des Pelagius*, 10-15.

96. Aug., *Conf.*, V, x, 19: "plures enim eos Roma occultabat"
(*CSEL* xxxiii, 106. 14-15).

97. See Brown, *Augustine of Hippo*, 54.

98. Hieron., *Ep.* 22, 13: "et quam viderint tristem atque pallen-
tem, miseram et monacham et Manichaeam vocant, et consequenter;
tali enim proposito ieiunium heresis est" (*CSEL* liv, 161. 4-6).

99. Aug., *C. Faustum*, V, 1 (*CSEL* xxv (1), 271. 15-24). F. C.
Burkitt long ago drew attention to the superficial resemblance
between the Manichaean Elect and the Christian monk. "But
there was a difference between the inner attitude of the Manichee

ascetic and the orthodox Christian monk. The latter, whether hermit or coenobite, had retired from the world with a conscious-ness of sin and a sense of personal unworthiness. It is not for no-thing that 'mourner' is one of the Syriac technical terms for a Christian monk. The Manichee Elect does not appear to have been a 'mourner.' He was indeed fenced about with tabus—'touch not, taste not, handle not'—but by virtue of his profession he was already Righteous, and he was called *Zaddīḳā*, i.e. 'the righteous,' by his co-religionists" (*The Religion of the Manichees* (Cambridge 1925), 46).

100. Both Priscillianism and Pelagianism sought to impose the standards of the cloister on the individual Christian. Both had a rich and aristocratic element—Sulpicius Severus calls Priscillian *familia nobilis, praedives opibus* (*Chron.*, II, 46 [*CSEL* i, 99. 21-22] while the Gallic orator Pacatus Drepanius waxes indignant at the fate of his disciple Euchrotia, *clari vatis matrona* ("obiecie-batur enim atque etiam probabatur mulieri viduae nimia religio et diligentius culta divinitas" *XII Panegyrici Latini*, ed. Baehrens, 297. 14-16). Both were essentially lay movements which attracted some clerics. To both might be applied Professor Christopher Brooke's comment on the heresies of the early Middle Ages: "It is indeed a striking and puzzling fact that orthodox popular preach-ers tended to become monks, abandon the world, and retreat behind the walls of monasteries; those who adhered to the apostolic life tended to become heretics" (*Medieval Church and Society* (London 1971), 148). This judgement might well be investigated with regard to the Christian world of the fourth and fifth centuries.

101. Evans, *Pelagius*, 30.

102. Pel., *Ep. ad Celantiam*, 28: "apostolicae doctrinae regula nec cum Ioviniano aequat continentiae opera nuptiarum nec cum Manicheo coniugia condemnat" (inter Hieronymi *Ep.* 148 [*CSEL* lvi, 352. 23-25]).

103. See the *De Divitiis* (*PLS* i, 1380-1418) and the *Epistola de Castitate* (ibid., cols 1464-1505).

104. *De Poss. non Peccandi*, 3: ". . . At vero, si audiat, posse se non peccare, necesse est, ut, quod possibile cognoverit, nitatur implere; et cum implere contendit, etsi non ex omni, ex maxima tamen parte perficiet. Is etiam, si aliquo fuerit delicto fragilitatis

causa praeventus humanae, certe aut rarius peccabit aut levius" (*PLS* i, 1460. 31-38).

105. Evans, *Pelagius*, 92.

106. Brown, "Pelagius and his supporters," 100.

107. Bonner, art. cit. [n23], pp. 32, 33.

108 Ibid., pp. 34, 35.

109. Aug., *Ep.* 157, iii, 22: "Multa de his quaestionibus in aliis nostris opusculis et ecclesiasticis sermonibus diximus, quoniam fuerunt etiam apud nos quidam, qui, ubicumque poterant, haec sui erroris nova semina spargerent, quorum nonnullos per ministerium nostrum fratrumque nostorum misericordia domini ab illa peste sanavit. nec tamen hic deesse aliquos arbitror maxime apud Carthaginem sed iam occulte mussitant timentes ecclesiae fundatissimam fidem" [written in 414] (*CSEL* xliv, 470. 27-471. 7); ibid., *De Gest. Pel.*, xxxv, 62: "Ista haeresis cum plurimos decepisset et fratres, quos non deceperat, conturbaret, Caelestius quidam talia sentiens ad iudicium Carthaginensis ecclesiae perductus episcoporum sententia condemnatus est (*CSEL* xlii, 116. 18-21). For the date of this synod, see Refoullé, art. cit. [n58], pp. 47-49.

110. Aug., *De Pecc. Mer. et Rem.*, III, vi, 12 (*CSEL* lx, 139. 10-16).

111. Mar. Merc., *Commonitorium super nomine Caelestii*, 1 (*ACO* I, v, 66. 9-16); *Lib. Subnot. in Verb. Iul.*, 2 (ibid., p. 6. 14-24); Aug., *De Gest. Pel.*, xxxv, 65 (*CSEL* xlii, 120. 4-13).

112. See Bonner, art. cit. [n23], p. 41.

113. Aug., *De Grat. Christ. et de Pecc. Orig.*, II, iv, 30 (*CSEL* xlii, 169. 3-6).

114. Ibid. (*CSEL* xlii, 169. 6-9).

115. Ibid.: "Caelestius dicit: 'iam de traduce peccati dixi, quia intra catholicam constitutos plures audivi destruere necnon et alios astruere, licet quaestionis res sit ista, non haeresis. infantes semper dixi egere baptismo ac debere baptizari. quid quaerit aliud?'" (*CSEL* xlii, 169. 11-15).

116. Evans, *Pelagius*, 74-75.

117. Aug., *Ep.* 146 (*CSEL* xliv, 273. 20-274. 9).

118. Aug., *De Nat. et Grat.*, i, 1: "Librum quem misistis, carissimi filii Timasi et Iacobe, intermissis paululum, quae in manibus erant, cursim quidem, sed non mediocri intentione perlegi et vidi

hominem zelo ardentissimo accensum adversus eos, qui cum in peccatis humanam voluntatem debeant accusare, naturam potius accusantes hominum per illam se excusare conantur" (*CSEL* lx, 233. 1-6).

119. Aug., *Ep.* 157 (*CSEL* xliv, 449. 10-488. 10).

120. *Apud* Aug., *Ep.* 156: ". . . quidam Christiani apud Syracusas. . . [dicunt] divitem manentem in divitiis suis regnum dei non posse ingredi" (*CSEL* xliv, 448. 12, 15-16).

121. *De Divitiis*, 18: "Non frustra ergo Dominus eam rem ubique paene arguit atque condemnat, cuius cupiditatem omnium scelerum seminarium noverat. Nec inmerito divitibus per difficillimi exempli conparationem regni caelestis quodammodo aditum clausit, quos malorum omnium causa inlaqueatos videbat. *Facilius*, inquit, *camelus per foramen acus transibit, quam dives in regnum caelorum.* Quid de tam evidenti loco diutius aliquid disputare necesse est, nisi tantum divites admonere, ut tunc demum sciant, se caelestis gloriae possessores fore, cum aut tam magnum acum repererint, per cuius foramen camelo sit transire possibile, aut tam modicum camelum, cui etiam acus angustissimus aditus penetrabilis sit. Quod si hoc penitus inpossibile est, quomodo illud, quod adhuc inpossibilius definitur, inplebitur, nisi forte, bene dispensatis opibus suis, dives sufficiens aut pauper ingredi contendat, quo opulens intrare non poterat" (*PLS* i, 1407. 41-1408. 5).

122. Aug., *Ep.* 157. iv, 39: "Ego, qui haec scribo, perfectionem, de qua dominus locutus est, quando ait diviti adulescenti: *Vade, vende omnia quae habes, et da pauperibus et habebis thesaurum in caelo et veni, sequere me,* vehementer adamavi et non meis viribus sed gratia ipsius adiuvante sic feci. Neque enim, quia dives non fui, ideo minus mihi inputabitur; nam neque ipsi apostoli, qui priores hoc fecerunt, divites fuerunt. sed totum mundum dimittit, qui et illud, quod habet et quod optabat habere, dimittit. quantum autem in hac perfectionis via profecerim, magis quidem novi ego quam quisquam alius homo, sed magis deus quam ego. et ad hoc propositum, quantis possum viribus, alios exhortor et in nomine domini habeo consortes, quibus hoc per meum ministerium persuasum est sic tamen, ut praecipue sana doctrina teneatur nec eos, qui ista non faciunt, vana contumacia iudicemus dicentes eis nihil prodesse, quod pudice quamvis coniugaliter vivunt,

75

quod domos suas et familias Christiane regunt, quod operibus misericordiae sibi thesaurizant in posterum, ne ista disputando non scripturarum tractatores sed earum accusatores inveniamur. quod ideo commemoravi, quoniam isti, quando talia dicere prohibentur ab eis, qui hoc domini consilium non ceperunt, respondent eos ideo talia disputari nolle, quoniam vitiis suis favent et dominica praecepta implere detrectant, quasi non, ut de his taceam, qui licet infirmiores religiose tamen utuntur divitiis, etiam ipsi cupidi et avari male his utentes et in terreno thesauro cor luteum configentes, quia et ipsos necesse est usque ad finem portet ecclesia sicut illa retia usque ad litus pisces malos, tolerabiliores in ea sunt quam isti, qui talia sermocinando et disseminando ita se videri magnos volunt, quia divitias suas vel quantulacumque patrimonia ex praecepto domini vendiderunt, ut eius haereditatem, quae usque ad fines terrae dilatatur atque diffunditur, hac doctrina non sana perturbere atque evertere moliantur" (*CSEL* xliv, 485. 15-486. 22).

123. Ibid., iii, 22: ". . . nos tamen malumus eos in ecclesiae compage sanari, quam ex illius corpore velut insanabilia membra resecari" (*CSEL* xliv, 472. 2, 3).

124. Ibid., *Ep.* 169, iv, 13: ". . . scripsi etiam grandem quemdam librum adversus Pelagii haeresim cogentibus nonnullis fratribus, quibus contra gratiam Christi opinionem perniciosam ille persuaserat" (*CSEL* xliv, 621. 20-23).

125. Ibid., *De Nat. et Grat.*, lxvii, 80, 81 (*CSEL* lx, 293. 19-296. 29).

126. Evans, *Pelagius*, 6-25.

127. Orosius, *Apol.*, 3: "latebam. . . in Bethlehem, traditus a patre Augustino, ut timorem Domini discerem sedens ad pedes Hieronymi" (*CSEL* v, 606. 19-21). Cf. Aug., *Ep.* 169, iv, 13 (*CSEL* xliv, 620. 26-621. 16).

128. J. A. Davids, *De Orosio et sancto Augustino Priscillianistarum adversariis commentatio historica et philologica* (The Hague 1930), 23.

129. Avitus, *Epist. ad Palchonium*: ". . . Sed quoniam misericors Deus, meo voto vestro que merito provocante, dignatus est indulgentiae suae gratiam, primum ut dilectissimus filius et compresbyter meus Orosius usque ad has partes ab Africanis episcopis mitteretur . . ." (*PL* xli, 805-806). See Davids, op. cit., pp. 23-24.

130. Hieron., *Dialogus adv. Pelagianos*, III, 17-19, esp. 19: "Scripsit dudum vir sanctus et eloquens episcopus Augustinus ad Marcellinum . . . duos libros de infantibus baptizandis contra haeresim vestram, per quam vultis asserere, baptizari infantes non in remissionem peccatorum, sed in regnum coelorum, iuxta illud quod scriptum est in Evangelio: *Nisi qui renatus fuerit ex aqua et Spiritu sancto, non potest intrare in regnum coelorum.* Tertium quoque ad eundem Marcellinum contra eos qui dicunt idem quod vos, posse hominem sine peccato esse, si velit, absque Dei gratia. Et quartum nuper ad Hilarium contra doctrinam tuam, multa perversa fingentem. Alios quoque specialiter tuo nomini cudere dicitur, qui necdum in nostras venere manus" (*PL* xxiii, 616 C-617 A).

131. Plinval, *Pélage*, 273; echoed by John Ferguson, *Pelagius. A Historical and Theological Study* (Cambridge 1956), 77ff.

132. Evans, *Pelagius*, 21, 56.

133. Orosius, *Apologeticus*, 5: "Porro autem episcopus Iohannes nihil horum audiens a nobis exigere conabatur, ut accusatores nos ipso iudice fateremur. responsum saepissime est ab universis: ' nos accusatores huius non sumus, sed quid fratres tui, patres nostri, senserint et decreverint super hac haeresi, quam nunc laicus praedicat, intimamus, ne Ecclesiam, tuam praesertim ad cuius sinum convolavimus, te ignorante conturbet.' at ille cum saepe nos docendi simulatione in aliquam professionis speciem temptaret inducere . . . responsum per me est: ' nos filii Ecclesiae catholicae sumus; non exigas a nobis, pater, ut doctores super doctores esse audeamus aut iudices super iudices. patres, quos universa per Orbem Ecclesia probat, quorum communioni vos adhaerere gaudetis, damnabilia haec esse dogmata decreverunt: illis probantibus nos oboedire dignum est, cur interroges filios quid sentiant, cum patres audias quid decernant?'" (*CSEL* v, 609. 3-11, 17-23).

134. Ibid., 1: "patres enim et qui iam quieverunt martyres et confessores, Cyprianus, Hilarius et Ambrosius, et quibus etiam nunc permanere adhuc in carne necessarium est, qui sunt columnae et firmamenta Ecclesiae catholicae, Aurelius Augustinus et Hieronymus, multa iam adversus hanc nefariam haeresim absque designatione nominum haereticorum scriptis probatissimis ediderunt" (*CSEL* v, 604. 7-13).

77

135. Ibid.: "quanquam et haec venenatissimorum dogmatum abominatio habet etiam nunc viventes mortuos mortuosque viventes. nam Origenes et Priscillianus et Iovianianus, olim apud se mortui, in his vivunt, et non solum vivunt verum etiam loquuntur" (*CSEL* v, 604. 13-17).

136. Ibid., 3, 4: "ilico a pusillitate mea postulastis universa, ut si quid super hac haeresi, quam Pelagius et Caelestius seminarunt in Africa gestum esse cognoscerem, fideliter ac simpliciter indicarem. exposui coronae vestrae breviter ut potui, Caelestium iam ad honorem presbyterii subrepentem apud Carthaginem plurimis episcopis iudicantibus proditum auditum convictum confessum detestatumque ab Ecclesiae ex Africa profugisse; contra librum vero Pelagii beatum Augustinum discipulis ipsius Pelagii prodentibus ac petentibus plenissime respondere, extare etiam in manibus meis epistulam supra memorati episcopi, quam nuper ad Siciliam ordinasset, in qua multas quaestiones haereticorum retudit: quam etiam ibidem ut legerem praecepistis et legi. . . . tunc idem episcopus nobis omnibus ait: 'haec, quae leguntur, in alios dicta sunt, dicta autem de Pelagio suggerendum putatis; si in ipsum ergo Pelagium quid dicatis, expromite" (*CSEL* v, 606. 23-607. 11, 608. 5-8).

137. Ibid., 4: ". . . episcopus Iohannes ilico eum, hominem videlicet laicum in consessu presbyterorum, reum haereseos manifestae in medio catholicorum sedere praecepit et deinde ait: 'Augustinus ego sum,' ut scilicet persona quasi praesentis assumpta liberius ex auctoritate eius qui laedebatur ignosceret et dolentium animos temperaret" (*CSEL* v, 607. 22-608. 4).

138. Ibid., 7 (*CSEL* v, 611. 9-18).

139. Aug., *De Gest. Pel.*, xiv, 30; xix, 43; xxxiii, 58 (*CSEL* xlii, 83. 24-84. 26; 98. 18-99. 3; 112.22-114.14).

140. Ibid. xxx, 54: "quattuordecim episcoporum sententia definitio nostra comprobata est, qua diximus posse hominem sine peccato esse et dei mandata facile custodire, si velit" (*CSEL* xlii, 107. 6-8).

141. Ibid., xi, 25: "haec sunt, quae nonnullis fratribus quidam talia sentientes ita persuadere conabantur, ut de orientalibus comminarentur ecclesiis quod, nisi qui haec tenerent, earum possent iudicio condemnari" (*CSEL* xlii, 79. 6-9).

142. Aug., *Serm.* 294. See G. Bonner, *St Augustine of Hippo. Life and Controversies* (London 1963), 323.

143. Council of Milevis *apud* Aug., *Ep.* 176, 4: "... Caelestius ... ad presbyterium in Asia dicitur pervenisse" (*CSEL* xliv, 667. 6-7); Mar. Merc., *Common. super nomine Caelestii*, 2: "Ephesum Asiae urbem contendit ibique ausus est per obreptionem locum presbyterii petere" (*ACO* i, v, 66. 23-24).

144. Prosper, *Chronicon* ad ann. 412: "heros, vir sanctus et beati Martini discipulus ..." (*MGH, Auct. ant.*, xi, 466) See E. Griffe, *La Gaule Chrétienne à l'Époque romaine* II, i (Paris/Toulouse 1957), 190-205; O. Chadwick, *John Cassian*, 2nd ed. (Cambridge 1968), 35 n^4.

145. Orosius, *Apol.*, 6: "multisque aliis actitatis Iohannes episcopus novissimam sententiam protulit, confirmans tandem postulationem intentionemque nostram, ut ad beatum Innocentium, papam Romanum, fratres et epistulae mitterentur" (*CSEL* v, 610. 20-611. 2).

146. Council of Carthage *apud* Aug., *Ep*, 175, 2: "... ut statutis nostrae mediocritatis etiam apostolicae sedis adhibeatur auctoritas" (*CSEL* xliv, 655. 5-6).

147. Brown, *Augustine of Hippo*, 357.

148. Aug., *C. Cresc.*, II, xxxvii, 46: "vos itaque secundum vestrum errorem vel potius furorem accusare cogimini non solum Caecilianum et ordinatores eius, verum etiam illas ecclesias, quas in scripturis apostolicis et canonicis pariter legimus, non solum Romanorum, quo ex Africa ordinare paucis vestris soletis episcopum, verum etiam Corinthiorum, Galatarum, Ephesionum, Thessalonicensium, Colossensium, Philippensium, ad quas apertissime scribit apostolus Paulus" (*CSEL* lii, 406. 19-26).

149. Ibid.: "Hierosolymitanam, quam primus apostolus Iacobus episcopatu suo rexit" (*CSEL* lii, 406. 26-407. 1).

150. It must, however, be admitted that the sincerity of Zosimus' action is somewhat compromised by the violent hostility which he displayed towards Heros and Lazarus, arising—at least in part— from his own close relationship with Patroclus, Heros" supplanter as bishop of Arles and the favourite of the Patrician Constantius, Gall Placidia's husband and the dominating personality at the imperial court, whose favour may have been responsible for Zosimus'

election. See L. Duchesne, *Early History of the Christian Church*, ET Vol. III (London 1924), 159-62.

151. Plinval, *Pélage*, 311-12 has discussed the meaning of this celebrated phrase; see also Bonner, op. cit. [n142], p. 343 n1.

152. Aug., *Op. Imp. c. Iul.*, iii, 35 (*PL* xlv, 1262).

153. Prosper, *Chronicon* ad ann. 418 (*MGH, Auct. ant.* xi, 468). See Bonner, op. cit. [n142], p. 344.

154. "Si quidem aures mansuetudinis nostrae recens fama perstrinxerit, inter sacratissimam urben nostram aliaque loca, ita pestiferum virus quorumdam inolevisse pectoribus, ut interrupto directae credulitatis tramite, scissis in partes studiis asserendi, materia impacatae dissensionis inducta sit" (*PL* xlviii, 383 A, 384 A.)

155. ". . . insignem notam plebeiae aestimat vilitatis sentire cum cunctis, ac prudentiae singularis palmam communiter approbata destruere . . ." (*PL* xlviii, 381 A).

156. See G. Bonner, "Les origines africaines de la doctrine augustinienne sur la chute et le péché originel," *Augustinus* (1967), 102-03.

157. See F. Floëri, "Le Pape Zosime et la doctrine augustinienne du péché originel," *Augustinus Magister* (Paris 1954), ii. pp. 755-61.

158. *Apud* Aug., *Ep.* 182, 5 (*CSEL* xliv, 720. 6-8).

159. Caelestius *apud* Aug., *De Grat. Christ. et de Pecc. Orig.*, II, v, 5: "infantes autem debere baptizari in remissionem peccatorum secundum regulam universalis ecclesiae et secundum evangelii sententiam confitemur, quia dominus statuit regnum caelorum nonnisi baptizatis posse conferri" (*CSEL* xlii, 169. 26-170. 1). See F. Refoulé, "La distinction 'Royaume de Dieu-Vie éternelle' est-elle pélagienne?" *Recherches de Science Religieuse* li (1963), 247-54.

160. Celestine, *Ep.* 21 (*PL* 1, 528C-530B). See Chadwick, op. cit. [n144], pp. 131-32.

161. Hieron. *apud* Aug., *Ep.* 195 (*CSEL* lvii, 214. 10-216. 2).

162. Aug., *Ep.* 166, iii, 6; iv, 10 (*CSEL* xliv, 554. 9-11, 559. 7, 15-561. 6).

163. E. R. Fairweather, "St. Augustine's interpretation of infant baptism," *Augustinus Magister* (Paris 1954), ii. p. 899.

164. Aug., *De Nat. et Orig. Animae*, III, xiv, 21: "utinam tua scripta tecum legere possem et conloquendo potius quam scribendo quae sint emendanda monstrarem! facilius hoc negotium perage retur nostra inter nos sermocinatione quam litteris; quae si scribenda esset, multis voluminibus indigeret" (*CSEL* lx, 377. 6-10).

165. Aug., *De Gest. Pel.*, xxiii, 47: "Cum vero mihi etiam liber ille datus esset a servis dei, bonis et honestis viris Timasio et Iacobo, ubi apertissime Pelagius obiectam sibi a se ipso tamquam ab adversario, unde iam grandi invidia laborabat, de dei gratia quaestionem non aliter sibi solvere visus est, nisi ut naturam cum libero arbitrio conditam dei diceret gratiam, aliquando idque tenuiter nec aperte ei coniugens vel legis adiutorium vel remissionem etiam peccatorum: tum vero sine ulla dubitatione mihi claruit, quam esset christianae saluti venenum illius perversitatis inimicum. nec sic tamen operi meo, quo eundem librum refelli, Pelagii nomen inserui, facilius me existimans profuturum, si servata amicitia adhuc eius verecundiae parcerem, cuius litteris iam parcere non deberem" (*CSEL* xlii, 101. 3-15).

166. Ibid., xxiv, 48 (*CSEL* xlii, 102. 7-103. 3).

167. Ibid., xxvii, 52-xxviii, 53 (*CSEL* xlii, 105. 17-106. 24).

168. Ibid., vi, 19 (*CSEL* xlii, 71. 19-72. 15).

169. Aug., *De Spir. et Lit.*, i, 1: ". . . rescripsisti te moveri eo, quod in posteriore duorum libro fieri posse dixi, ut sit homo sine peccato, si voluntas eius non desit ope divina adiuvante, sed tamen praeter unum, in quo omnes vivificabuntur, neminem fuisse vel fore, in quo hic vivente esset ista perfectio. absurdum enim tibi videtur dici aliquid fieri posse, cuius desit exemplum . . ." (*CSEL* lx, 155. 5-10).

170. Brown, *Augustine of Hippo*, 353.

171. See P. Batiffol, *Le catholicisme de Saint Augustin*, 5th ed. (Paris 1930), ii. pp. 480-82; A. Paredi, "Paulinus of Milan," *Sacris erudiri* xiv (1963), 212-13.

172. Aug., *C. Iul.*, I, iii, 7-9 (*PL* xliv, 644, 645). See Bonner, art. cit. [n[156]], p. 115.

173. Burnaby, op. cit. [n[2]], p. 231.

174. Brown, *Augustine of Hippo*, 384.

175. Aug., *De Praedestinatione Sanctorum*, i, 2 (*PL* xlv, 961).

176. One must, however, notice a characteristic of Augustine
the controversialist to which I have drawn attention elsewhere
(art. cit. [n156], p. 103): in all his great controversies—against the
Manichees and the Donatists—he begins in a friendly spirit,
inviting his opponents to reasoned discussion. His outlook hardens
throughout the controversy and ends on a note of bitterness. This
is a not uncommon development in controversialists, and Augustine
did not rise above it; though it is worth remembering that in his
debates he never descends to what N. H. Baynes has called "ecclesiastical Billingsgate"—the vituperation which disfigures the
writings of some other Fathers of the Church.

XII

Some remarks on Letters 4* and 6*

In his study of the influence of Augustine on the Greek Church during the Patristic period and early Middle Ages, Berthold Altaner came to the conclusion that although a number of Augustine's writings reached the East during his lifetime, the only work which was very probably, though not absolutely certainly, translated into Greek was the *De Gestis Pelagii*, which Altaner identified among the books read by the Patriarch Photius of Constantinople in the ninth century[1]. Since Photius was ignorant of Latin he must have read Augustine in translation. It has always been a puzzle, to the present writer at least, why the *De Gestis Pelagii*, a treatise of considerable historical importance but hardly one of the most brilliant productions of Augustine's pen, should have been chosen for translation into Greek. The new Augustinian letters provide material for resolving the problem.

Letter 4* is addressed to a bishop named Cyril, who may with reasonable certainty be identified with Cyril of Alexandria. In it Augustine refers to a certain Justus who, residing in the East and apparently at Alexandria, had acquired a copy of *De Gestis Pelagii*. This work had given offence to two

---

1. Berthold ALTANER, ' Augustinus in der griechische Kirche bis auf Photius, ' *Kleine patristische Schriften* (TU bd 83) (Berlin 1967), 73ff. Altaner laid stress on the words of Photius : Οὕτως Αὐγουστῖνος ἐν τοῖς πρὸς Αὐρέλιον τὸν Καρταγένης πάππαν διέξεισιν (*Bibl.* Cod. 54, ed. R. Henry, Tom. I [Paris 1959], p. 44) and on various details which, in his opinion, could only have come from the *De Gestis Pelagii* : ' Besonders deutlich tritt seine Abhängigkeit von der Darstellung Augustins hervor, wenn er berichtet, Pelagius sei teils deshalb freigesprochen worden, weil er gewisse ihm von den Anklägern vorgeworfenen Sätze ableugnete oder sie ausdrücklich verurteilte, teils weil er andere von ihm verfochtene Gedanken als unverfänglich hinstellte und behauptete, seine Gegner hätten sie missverstanden. Der Bericht des Photius lässt klar erkennen, dass er nicht aus den Akten der Synode von Diospolis, sondern aus der obergenannten Schrift Augustins geschöpft hat ' (p. 75).

Clearly, the words of Photius do not directly indicate the *De Gestis Pelagii*. Henry, in his translation, renders them : ' C'est ainsi qu'Augustin rapporte le fait dans ses lettres à Aurèle, patriarche de Carthage ' — a version which misrepresents Photius' word πάππαν, which could be derived directly from Augustine's phrase ' sancte papa Aureli ' (*gest., Praef.*) ; but at the very least, as Altaner argues, they are persuasive evidence for identification.

unnamed Latins (*Latini sunt enim utrique et de occidentali ecclesia*) by the passage in which Augustine disputes the statement made by Pelagius that at the Last Judgement no mercy will be shown to sinners, who will be burned in everlasting fires[2]. The two critics disputed the genuineness of the passage, and even accused Justus of having forged it himself. To vindicate his reputation Justus had come to Hippo and collated his text with the author's copy in order to establish that the disputed passage was indeed original. Reassured on this point, he prepared to return to Alexandria, bearing a letter to Cyril which conveyed Augustine's greetings and warned his colleague against Justus' critics who, as Latins, might otherwise have been able to lurk undetected in the East, under cover of the general ignorance of their language, and continue to maintain false doctrine.

This episode, trivial in itself, provides fresh material for our understanding of the role of Cyril in the Pelagian Controversy. In the past it has been customary to regard him as being sympathetic, if not to Pelagianism, at least to individual Pelagians, including Pelagius himself[3], on the strength of a letter in the *Collectio Avellana*, addressed to him, apparently in 418, by a bishop named Eusebius, who is otherwise unknown.* Eusebius expresses dismay that Cyril, with rather uncharacteristic mildness, has not seen fit to excommunicate Pelagian sympathisers, following the condemnation of their leader by Pope Innocent in 417[4]. Given the evidence of this letter, Cyril's later hostility towards Pelagianism at the time of the Council of Ephesus could only be explained as part of his campaign against Nestorius, and not inspired by genuine conviction. It now looks as if Cyril's part in the Pelagian Controversy was rather more consistent. From *Letter* 4* it appears that it was Cyril who furnished Augustine with a copy of the minutes of the Synod of Diospolis[5], and not John of Jerusalem, as might have been supposed from Augustine's letter to John of 416, which specifically asks for them. From the opening words of this letter it is clear that Augustine had expected a letter from John in answer to one of his own and was disappointed (to use no stronger word) at his colleague's lapse from ecclesiastical protocol[6]. No doubt John's sympathy with Pelagius and his indignation with Orosius, Augustine's indiscreet admirer, would explain his failure to reply. By the summer of 417 at the latest, however, a copy of the minutes of the Synod of Diospolis was in Augustine's possession[7]. As

* This bishop is apparently Eusebius of Cremona.

---

2. *gest.* 3, 9.

3. e.g. G. de PLINVAL, *Pélage. Ses écrits, sa vie et sa réforme* (Lausanne 1943), 329.

4. *Collect. Avell.*, 49. *CSEL* XXXV, 113-5.

5. *Ep.* 4*, 2, 1 : ' Recolit quantum arbitror sinceritas tua misisse te nobis gesta ecclesiastica habita in provincia Palestina, ubi Pelagius putatus catholicus absolutus est. ' *CSEL* LXXXVIII, 26. 12-14.

6. *Ep.* 179, 1 : ' ... Quod tuae sanctitatis scripta non merui, nihil audeo suscensere : melius enim perlatorem credo defuisse, quam me suspicor a tua veneratione contemptum, domine beatissime et merito venerabilis frater. ' *CSEL* XLIV, 691, 15-18.

7. ALTANER, art. cit., p. 64 ; O. Perler, *Les voyages de saint Augustin* (Paris 1669), 465,

Altaner pointed out, it is surprising that neither in the *De Gestis Pelagii* itself nor in the *Retractationes* does Augustine reveal how these minutes came into his possession[8]. *Letter* 4* reveals that it was through the good offices of Cyril.

However, our evidence about Augustine's dealings with Cyril goes beyond this, since the very fact that in *Letter* 4* Augustine refers to the receipt of the minutes of the Synod of Diospolis from Cyril implies an earlier letter requesting them. There is, indeed, a reference to a letter from Augustine to Cyril in a remark by Julian of Eclanum in Book VIII of his work addressed to Florus, quoted by Augustine in the *Opus Imperfectum*. In this passage Julian speaks of a letter sent by Augustine to Alexandria, which boasted of Jerome's dialectical triumph over Pelagius in his *Dialogue against the Pelagians*, written in 415[9]. It was against Jerome's work that Pelagius directed his own *De Libero Arbitrio*, apparently composed in 416. Altaner has suggested that the appearance of Pelagius' treatise would have constituted a motive for Augustine to write to Cyril, alerting him to the dangers of Pelagian theology and commending the criticisms of Jerome[10]. It would not be unreasonable — though wholly undemonstrable — to suppose that the same letter could have included a request for the minutes of the proceedings at Diospolis, which would have been communicated to Cyril as a matter of routine courtesy.

At all events, Cyril duly obliged his colleague and Augustine was able to write the *De Gestis Pelagii*. A copy of this came into the hands of Justus, under what circumstances Augustine does not say. What seems to be clear is that the two Latins who impugned its reliability were either disciples of Pelagius or, at the very least, influenced by the anti-Origenistic sentiments which were characteristic of Pelagian moral rigorism. Significantly, the passage they questioned was the one in which Augustine denied the proposition that at the Judgement all sinners would be condemned to eternal fire — a denial of which was of the utmost importance to Augustine, in view of his belief that perfect sinlessness is not possible in this life, and that so long as they are in the body the saints of God will have to pray for their trespasses to be forgiven. It was this attack upon the reliability of his text which brought Justus to Hippo, in order to verify it at the fountain-head, and his visit furnished Augustine with the opportunity to write to Cyril, commending Justus to his care, and warning him against Justus' detractors.

What is the date of this letter ? Clearly, it must be some time after the publication of *De Gestis Pelagii* to allow for Justus being able to obtain a

---

assigns the composition of *gest.* to the spring of 417, which implies that the minutes arrived before the end of 416.

8. ALTANER, p. 64 n[2].

9. *op. imp.* IV, 88 : ' IVL. De quo opere tu in illa epistola quam Alexandriam destinasti, ita gloriaris, ut dicas Pelagium, Scripturarum ab eo oppressum molibus, arbitrium liberum vindicare non posse '. PL XIV, 1389.

10. ALTANER, pp. 64-5.

copy and, after criticism in the East, to bring it to Hippo. On the other hand, there is no particular reason to suppose that any great time had elapsed since publication and it therefore seems reasonable to assign the letter either to the later part of 417 or to the early months of 418. My own preference would be for the later date, to allow for copying and diffusion outside Africa.

There is no direct statement in Augustine's letter that he either had sent or was sending Cyril a copy of *De Gestis Pelagii*. Indeed, since that work was based upon a copy of the minutes of the Synod of Diospolis which Cyril had himself supplied, Augustine might have felt that his own exposition would have been redundant. On the other hand, he was exceedingly anxious to vindicate his own position against Pelagius, and we may well suppose that he would have ensured that as many persons were acquainted with the facts regarding Pelagius' acquittal as possible. Furthermore, the fact that he commended Justus to Cyril's protection and mentioned the *De Gestis Pelagii* in his letter could well have aroused Cyril's interest ; and we know from the later history of Cyril's career that an efficient translation service was available at Alexandria. It would not be difficult to imagine that Cyril would have been sufficiently interested by Augustine's letter to arrange to have the *De Gestis* translated into Greek and so provide a version which could have been available to Photius four centuries later. Such a suggestion can only be an hypothesis ; but it makes sense and fits the facts of the situation. Thus *Letter* 4* provides an important link in the chain of evidence which explains why of all the many writings of Augustine the *De Gestis Pelagii* was probably the only one available in Greek translation until the work of Maximus Planudes in the late thirteenth century.

But this, of course, is far from being the only, or even the main, interest of the evidence of this letter for understanding the Pelagian Controversy. Rather, it is important as showing the degree to which Augustine interested himself in the day-to-day details of the struggle. I have elsewhere[11] tried to emphasise the effect upon Augustine of Pelagius' account of the decision of the Synod of Diospolis, which seemed to endorse his teaching that men can be sinless and easily keep the commandments of God if they so will[12]. This appeared to cast doubt, not only on Augustine's personal theology, but upon his whole understanding of the catholicity of the Church : the faith is one, and it cannot be that there will be any divergence, whether in East or West. One can readily understand the haste and the concern with which Augustine set about writing to the East in 416, to John of Jerusalem expressing his surprise that no account of the Palestinian proceedings had been sent to him, and to Cyril, asking if he could provide the copy which John

---

11. *Augustine and Modern Research on Pelagianism* (Augustine Lecture for 1970) (Villanova, Pa. 1972).

12. *gest.* 30, 54.

had failed to supply. For Augustine the debate with Pelagius became a personal matter in the course of the year 416, and he spared no effort to bring it to a victorious conclusion.

This personal involvement is further revealed by *Letter 6**, addressed to Atticus of Constantinople, in which Augustine is concerned with that prevailing issue during the later stages of the Pelagian debate, the charge that his views on the relation of concupiscence to Original Sin were those of a Manichee. Such a charge was an obvious one, given Augustine's doctrine of Original Sin, which could easily be represented as teaching that human sexuality was something intrinsically evil. A defence of the dignity of Christian marriage against his Pelagian critics was therefore essential for Augustine, and nowhere more than in the Christian East, where the idea of sexually-transmitted original guilt was repugnant to the mind of many Greek theologians, who equated it with Encratism and Manichaeism. Pier Franco Beatrice has drawn attention to the rôle of Julian of Eclanum in the Pelagian Controversy as the spokesman of the aristocratic and humanistic mentality of much Greek orthodox opinion[13], while Peter Brown[14] has pointed out that the Roman circles in which Pelagianism arose and developed had a particular interest in Constantinople, as a consequence of their enthusiastic support of the cause of John Chrysostom, whose sermons on St Paul were translated into Latin by a Pelagian deacon, Anianus of Celeda, and cited as evidence against ' the Traducians[15] '. In such circumstances, there would be nothing surprising in Augustine sending Atticus a statement of his teaching on carnal concupiscence and its relation to the good of marriage as an antidote to local Pelagian propaganda.

But what is the date ? At the beginning of the letter Augustine speaks of the bearer, the presbyter Innocent, who apparently had recently come from Constantinople, though without bringing a letter from Atticus, a letter which Augustine had apparently expected, because he had heard a rumour that Augustine was dead[16]. This rumour Innocent was able to contradict, having information from others who had more recently seen Augustine ; but Atticus remained doubtful and declined to compose a personal letter, so that Augustine had to make do, as he says, with one addressed to his *unianimus frater*[17] who, in this context, may most persuasively be identified with Aure-

---

13. *Tradux Peccati : Alle fonte della dottrina agostiniana del peccato originale* (Studia Patristica Mediolanensia 8) (Milan 1978), 256.

14. *The Patrons of Pelagius, Religion and Society in the Age of Saint Augustine* (London 1972), 214-5.

15. *PG* 1, 471.

16. *Ep.* 6*, 1, 2 : ' nam cum aliud fama iactasset, sicut mihi supradictus frater rettulit, tamquam de homine credidisti ; quid enim tam credibile est quam cum dicitur mortuus esse mortalis, quod procul dubio cuilibet in carne viventi quandoque venturum est ? sed cum ab aliis recentioribus nuntiis me vivere audisset atque indicasset dilectioni tuae, plurimum te fuisse gratulatum et deo gratias egisse narravit, licet vobis adhuc esset incertum. ' *CSEL* LXXXVIII, 32. 9-16.

17. Ibid., 2. 1.

lius of Carthage, though the term might well have been applied to Alypius of Thagaste, devoted friend, tireless ecclesiastical diplomat, and fervent anti-Pelagian. Now the presbyter Innocent may well be indentical with the bearer of the letter from Jerome to Augustine and Alypius (*Ep.* 202) which Goldbacher assigned to a date between late summer and the beginning of November 419[18], since it was during this period that Innocent was in the East, where he had been sent by the African Council which met at Carthage on 25 May 419, to bring back an authentic copy of the Nicene canons, for use in their dispute with Rome over the case of the presbyter Apiarius. These canons were at hand for the Africans to despatch to Rome on 6 November. Thus, Innocent would have been available for Augustine to employ as a letter-carrier to the East in the late spring of 419 ; and since *Letter* 6* seems to treat of the topics discussed by Augustine in Book I of *De Nuptiis et Concupiscentia*, written in the winter of 418-419 — the first occasion on which Augustine specifically discussed the question of the relation between Original Sin and concupiscence — it would seem reasonable to assign *Letter* 6* to 419.

Dr Divjak mentions, but rejects, this dating[19]. His reason is that Innocent could hardly have taken this particular letter on his journey because of the reference to Augustine's death : if Innocent had been at Constantinople in the early months of 419, before the Council of Carthage of that year, he would not have needed reports from more recent messengers to assure him that Augustine was still alive, since he would have comme directly from Carthage. Divjak does not believe — though without giving any reasons — that *Letter* 6* can be later than 419, so he proposes to assign it to 416 or early 417.

The difficulty about this dating comes from evidence which Divjak has himself provided : the resemblance between the theme of *Letter* 6* and that of the *De Nuptiis et Concupiscentia*. Berthold Altaner long since remarked that the composition of *De Nuptiis et Concupiscentia* inaugurated a new phase in the theological debate between Augustine and the Pelagians[20], now led by Julian of Eclanum, and *Letter* 6* seems to belong to this later phase. Furthermore, Augustine had good reason for writing to Atticus on this issue after the condemnation of Pelagius, since Constantinople seems to have been something of a center of Pelagian activity in the East. Caelestius visited it, apparently in the spring of 417, only to be expelled by Atticus[21] (he was to try his luck again, with Nestorius, in 429). It was the Pelagian bishop Florus who, at Constantinople, found the copy of Mani's

---

18. *CSEL* LVIII, 52.

19. *CSEL* LXXXVIII, pp. LVI-LVII.

20. ALTANER, *Altlateinische Übersetzungen von Chrysostomusschriften, KPS,* 420. M.-F. BERROUARD, *Les lettres 6* et 19* de saint Augustin, Revue des Études Augustiniennes* XXVII (1981), 270, observes that the ideas, developed in *nupt. et conc.* I, are foreshadowed in *gr. et pecc. or.* of mid-418.

21. Marius MERCATOR, *Comm. super nom. Caelestii,* 2, 3. *PL* XLVIII, 70A-75A.

Letter to Menoch which, duly despatched to Julian, provided him, as he thought, with decisive evidence that Traducianism and Manichaeism taught the same doctrines[22]. Again, Prosper of Aquitaine, in verses which unhappily are as rhetorical as they are imprecise, speaks of the care exercised by the good bishop Atticus in the city of Constantinople, when he eloquently confounded the legates of the heretics with ancient doctrine. However much their evil hearts tried to cloak their true purpose with legal subterfuge, they suffered the ignominy of silent rejection[23]. Augustine, in *Letter 6**, appears to give confirmation to this picture by congratulating Atticus on the pastoral care which he had shown *ut et corrigeretur quorundam Pelagianorum perversitas et calliditas caveatur*[24].

There is, however, another reference to Atticus' pastoral zeal which may provide a clue for dating this letter. Pope Celestine, writing to Nestorius in 428, provides a more forceful picture : *Atticus ... eos ita persecutus est ut iis ne standi quidem illic copia praestaretur*[25]. This suggests rigorous action, such as is hardly likely to have been taken on any scale before the promulgation of Honorius' rescript of 30 April 418, condemning Pelagius and Caelestius or — and perhaps more probably — the edict of 9 June 419, which threatened penal sanctions against anyone failing to take action against the Pelagians, and instructed Aurelius of Carthage to inform his colleagues of the need for action[26]. Given Julian of Eclanum's contacts in the East it would not be surprising to find a Pelagian group at Constantinople against which Atticus might have taken action in accordance with the edict of 419. Conceivably the letter to the *unianimus frater* mentioned

---

22. *c. Iul. imp.* III, 166, 187 : ' IVL. sed quia post editionem illorum [*sc.* ad Turbantium librorum], oratu tuo, beatissime pater Flore, apud Constantinopolim Manichaei epistola inventa est, atque ad has directa partes, opera est aliqua eius inserere, ut intelligant omnes, unde haec pro traduce argumenta descendant... AVG. Finisti tandem, quae de Manichaei epistola, quam tui collegae Flori orationibus adiutus te invenisse laetaris, contra nos putasti esse dicenda.' *PL* XLV, 1316, 1327.

23. PROSPER, *Carmen de Ingratis*, 61-66 :

quid loquar et curam magna quam gessit in urbe
Constantinopoli docto bonus ore sacerdos
Atticus antiqua legatos haereticorum
confutando fide ? de qua tunc impia corda,
quamvis se obducto tegerent velamine forma
iudicii et tacitae tulerint tormenta repulsae.

(ed. Huegelmeyer, p. 46)

24. *Ep.* 6, 2, 1 *CSEL* LXXXVIII, 32. 23-24.

25. CELESTINE, *Ep.* 13, 1, 8 : ' Atticus... eos ita persecutus est pro rege communi ut iis ne standi quidem illic copia praestaretur... Cur tamen ea quae in hos tunc sunt acta quaeruntur, cum certum sit illinc ad nos a catholico tunc antistite Attico gesta directa ? ' *PL* l, 469B, 481A.

26. Inter AUG., *Ep.* 201, 1, 2 : ' ... decrevimus, ut, si quis eos in quacumque provinciarum parte latitare non nesciens aut propellere aut prodere distulisset, praescriptae poenae velut particeps subiaceret... religio itaque tua competentibus scriptis universos faciet admoneri scituros definitione sanctimonii tui hanc sibi definitionem esse praescriptam... ' *CSEL* LVII, 297. 2-5, 11-12 - 298. 1.

by Augustine was an account of his actions, undertaken in response to a letter of Aurelius, written in obedience to the imperial directive.

It is possible, however, that Augustine's reference to the correction of Pelagian perversity and defence against Pelagian guile concerns, or at least includes, Caelestius' attempt to ingratiate himself with Atticus immediately before his appeal to Pope Zosimus in 417. Our authority here is Marius Mercator. Unfortunately he is chronologically imprecise, but he states that Caelestius, after living for some years at Ephesus after his condemnation at Carthage in 411, visited Constantinople, was there detected by Atticus and, having been duly expelled from the city, hastened to Zosimus at Rome. From this information Jean Garnier deduced — surely correctly — that Caelestius' trial before Atticus must have occured in the early months of Zosimus's pontificate, and probably in April or May 417[27].

A further detail supplied by Marius Mercator may be relevant here. He states that after the condemnation of Caelestius, Atticus sent letters to the bishops of Asia and to those of Thessalonica and Carthage. If the *unianimus frater* of Augustine's letter is indeed Aurelius, it could be that the letter which he received is that recorded by Mercator as having been sent to the Bishop of Carthage. But this would not, in itself, impose a date of 417 on *Letter 6**. Indeed, given the cautious and diplomatic nature of Atticus[28], he might very well have delayed writing until it was clear that Caelestius was on the losing side. This possibility would seem to be confirmed by the otherwise curious omission on Augustine's part to make any reference to Atticus' rejection of Caelestius in his anti-Pelagian polemic during the years immediately following 417. It seems strange that he should have neglected such an obvious testimony to African orthodoxy, which had unmasked and condemned the heretic as early as 411.

I would therefore maintain that *Letter 6** is not likely to be earlier than 419. How can such a view be related to the comings and goings of its bearer, the presbyter Innocent ?

It seems reasonable, though unprovable, to identify Innocent with the individual sent to Alexandria in the late spring of 419 to obtain an authentic copy of the canons of Nicaea and to assume, with Goldbacher, that in the course of his visit to the East he visited Jerome at Bethlehem and brought back Letter 202. Divjak, in accepting this identification, argues that it excludes the possibility of a date of 419 for *Letter 6**, since Innocent must have been in the East during the second half of that year, and if he visited Constantinople in the early months (a risky undertaking, since the period 11 November-12 March was the ' closed season ' for sea-travel)[29], he would

---

27. *PL* XLVIII, 74B.

28. See the comment by M. Th. DISDIER in *DHGE* Tom. 5, art. *Atticus*, col. 162 : ' Le malheur voulut que cet homme, taillé pour la diplomatie, s'engageât dans l'état ecclésiastique. '

29. PERLER, *Les voyages* ..., 68-9.

hardly have required reassurance from more recent travellers to persuade Atticus that Augustine was still alive.   This argument, however, overlooks the fact that Innocent had visited the East in 418, as is made clear by Jerome's letter to Augustine and Alypius : ' Sanctus Innocentius presbyter, qui huius sermonis est portitor, anno praeterito, quasi nequaquam Africam reversurus, mea ad dignationem vestram scripta non sumpsit[30] '.   Now the date of Letter 202 is established by Jerome's reference to the still recent death of Eustochium, which occurred in the winter of 418-419.   We have therefore proof, not only that Innocent was at Bethlehem in 418, but that he was unable to carry Jerome's letters *quasi nequaquam Africam reversurus*.   This could have been because he was going on to Constantinople.   He would not, in that case, have arrived there fresh from Africa and would have needed the information of later messengers to refute the rumour of Augustine's death.   He could then have collected the letter to the *unianimus frater* for transmission to Africa.

There is, however, one great difficulty about this reconstruction, a difficulty so great as virtually to rule it out of court.   Why should Augustine in 419 entrust a letter for Atticus to Innocent, who was going to Alexandria, when there was already a messenger detailed for Constantinople in the person of the subdeacon Marcellus[31] ?   One can understand Innocent extending his journey beyond Alexandria to include a visit to the great recluse of Bethlehem ; but to go on to Constantinople, when a messenger had already been sent there, seems utterly pointless.

It appears, therefore, that we are constrained to accept a date for *Letter* 6* of 420 or even later.   Indeed, the only absolute limit is the death of Atticus on 8 October 425.   However, my own preference would be for an earlier rather than a later date, on the assumption that Augustine would have been anxious to refute the Pelagian accusation of teaching Manichaean doctrine as quickly as possible.   For that reason I should date *Letter* 6* to the period when Julian of Eclanum's work addressed to Turbantius demanded a reply, possibly at the time when Augustine was engaged upon the second book of *De Nuptiis et Concupiscentia*, which Professer Perler would assign to the winter of 420-421[32].   This is the view of Père Marie-François Berrouard in an article which recently appeared in the *Revue des Études Augustiniennes*, with which I find myself in complete agreement[33].   Dr Berrouard suggests that Augustine's letter was written at the time when

---

30. HIERON., *Ep.* 143 inter Aug., *Ep.* 202, 1. *CSEL* LVII, 299. 7-9. See F. CAVALLERA, *Saint Jérome : sa vie et son œuvre* (Louvain 1922), I. pp. 61-2 ; II. pp. 337-8 (where the reference is wrongly given as *Ep.* 142).

31. See *Ecclesiae Occidentalis Monumenta Iuris Antiquissima*, ed. C. H. Turner (Oxford 1899-1939), I. p. 612 lines 6-9 : ' ... per filium nostrum Marcellum subdiaconum vestrum scripta vestrae Dilectionis cum omni gratulatione suscepi '.

32. PERLER, op. cit., pp. 316 ff., 469.

33. See above, n. 20, I am most grateful to Fr. Berrouard for having made a copy of his article available before the conference, and for his subsequent comments.

164

Julian, forced to leave Italy and take refuge in the East, was endeavouring to secure the support of the oriental episcopate. If Julian had, by this time, found shelter with Theodore of Mopsuestia in Cilicia, Augustine might well have thought it imperative to anticipate any propaganda which he might make in the Eastern capital by sending a letter to Atticus clarifying his own teaching on marriage.

Letters 4* and 6* are the most illuminating among the newly-published Augustinian letters relating to the Pelagian Controversy. This is not to overlook *Letter* 19*, which provides fresh evidence of the role of St Jerome as an anti-Pelagian polemicist at the critical phase of the struggle with Pelagius ; the *aperçu* on local episcopal understanding of the theology of infant baptism afforded by *Letter* 5* ; and the exposition of Augustine's own theology of Original Guilt and the need for baptism provided by *Letter* 2* to Firmus. Perhaps fortunately, these new letters do not impose any need for a radical revision of our understanding of the Pelagian Controversy ; but they do provide clarification of the course of the affair and provide some valuable new evidence for the historian. We have reason to be grateful to Dr Divjak for making them available.

RETRACTATIO

In this paper I suggested that it seems reasonable to assign *Letter* 4* to the later part of 417 or to the early months of 418, with my own preference for the later date, to allow for the time required for copying and diffusion outside Africa.

In conversation afterwards, Père M.-F. Berrouard, O.P., drew my attention to the use of the adjective *Pelagianus* on three occasions in this letter (p. 28, lines 2, 19, 26), which suggests a later date in the controversy, when the Pelagian party of opposition had emerged. This argument seems to me persuasive, especially because it allows further time for the multiplication and diffusion of copies of the *De Gestis Pelagii* in an age which relied on book-copying by hand for the multiplication of texts. I would therefore, on these grounds, accept a somewhat later date, perhaps about 420-421, when Augustine was composing the *Contra Duas Epistolas Pelagianorum*, as preferable to my original suggestion.

INDEX